Hands Up Education is a not-for-profit organization and international community of practice, creating and sharing high-quality teaching resources. The core focus of our work is on Latin and Classics for a modern curriculum.

All income generated by SUBURANI will be invested in supporting Classics teaching in schools around the world.

SUBURANI

Published by Hands Up Education Community Interest Company.

First published in 2020.

All papers used in this book have been sourced from sustainable forests.

British Library Cataloguing in Publication Data.
A catalogue record for this book is available from the British Library.

ISBN 978-1-912870-01-1

Copyright © 2020 by Hands Up Education Community Interest Company.

All rights reserved. No part of this publication may be reproduced or transmitted in any form or by any means, electronic or mechanical, including photocopying, recording, or any information storage or retrieval system, without prior permission in writing from the publishers.

Printed in the United Kingdom.

Hands Up Education Community Interest Company 133-134 Bradley Road, Little Thurlow, Haverhill, CB9 7HZ, United Kingdom.
www.hands-up-education.org, contact@hands-up-education.org

Contents

Maps	2
Chapter 1: Subūra	7
Chapter 2: Rōma	23
Chapter 3: lūdī	39
Chapter 4: deī	55
Chapter 5: aqua	71
Chapter 6: servitium	87
Chapter 7: Londīnium	103
Chapter 8: Britannia	119
Chapter 9: rebelliō	135
Chapter 10: Aquae Sūlis	151
Chapter 11: mare	167
Chapter 12: incendium	183
Chapter 13: Arelātē	199
Chapter 14: artifex	215
Chapter 15: vīlla	231
Chapter 16: nūptiae	247
Reference	265
Vocabulary for learning	266
Grammar	270
English to Latin dictionary	280
Latin to English dictionary	282
Ancient authors	297
Timeline	300

The Roman Empire
AD 64

According to legend, Rome was founded as a small village in 753 BC. By AD 64, when our stories begin, Rome had grown into a huge city, and its armies had conquered a vast empire. Rome controlled lands in areas we now think of as North Africa, the Middle East, Asia, and Europe.

Population

Approximately one million people lived in Rome itself, but between 50 and 100 million people lived in the empire it governed. Some of those people lived in cities, but most lived in small towns, villages, and on farms.

Provinces

The Romans organized their empire into provinces, each under the control of a governor. The shape and size of a province was influenced by natural features (such as mountain ranges or large rivers) and by the location of local peoples and cultures.

Mare Internum

Rome's empire centred around the Internal Sea (*Mare Internum*), which we now call the Mediterranean Sea (the sea in the middle of the land). As it was often quicker to travel by sea than by land, the Mare Internum helped to link together the various peoples and goods of the Empire.

Roads and rivers

To help people, goods, and armies move around the Empire more easily, the Romans built a network of over 50,000 miles of roads. Major rivers, such as the Rhône and the Rhine, also played an important part in the movement of goods.

Information

The Romans built a system of staging posts, where riders with government messages could change horses and rest overnight if necessary. In normal situations it was more important that a message arrived safely than that it arrived quickly, and messengers usually travelled about 30 miles in a day. However, if a message was urgent riders could cover over 100 miles in a single day.

Maps

AMPHITHEATRE OF NERO
BATHS OF NERO
FIELD OF MARS
PANTHEON
TEMPLE OF ISIS AND SERAPIS
BATHS OF AGRIPPA
SAEPTA JULIA
THEATRE OF POMPEY
BRIDGE OF AGRIPPA
BRIDGE OF AURELIUS
CIRCUS FLAMINIUS
THEATRE OF BALBUS
THEATRE OF MARCELLUS
TEMPLE OF JUPITER OPTIMUS MAXIMUS
CAPITOLINE HILL
RIVER TIBER
TIBER ISLAND
TEMPLE OF ASCLEPIUS
BRIDGE OF AEMILIUS
FORUM BOARIUM
AVENTINE HILL

0   1/4   1/2   3/4   1 MILE
Scale (approximate)

Maps

ROME
AD 64

- ARCH OF CLAUDIUS
- AQUA VIRGO
- QUIRINAL HILL
- VIA FLAMINIA
- VIMINAL HILL
- FORUM OF AUGUSTUS
- FORUM OF CAESAR
- ROMAN FORUM
- SUBURA
- GREAT DRAIN
- SACRED WAY
- ESQUILINE HILL
- DOMUS TRANSITORIA
- PALATINE HILL
- AQUA CLAUDIA
- IMPERIAL PALACES
- CIRCUS MAXIMUS

Chapter 1: Subūra

Sabīna

1   ego sum Sabīna.

ego in Subūrā habitō. ego sum in īnsulā.

hōra prīma est.

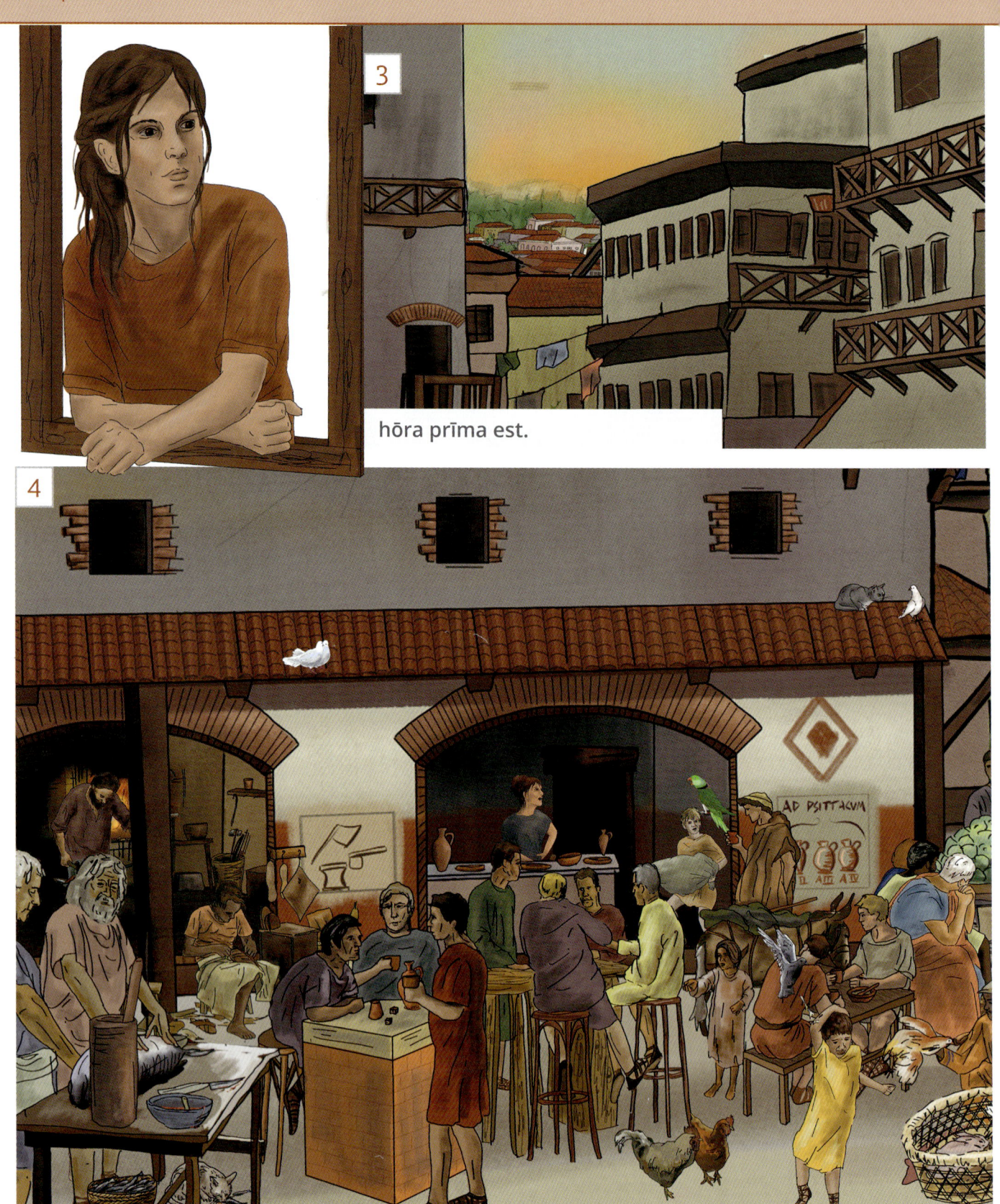

Subūra nōn est quiēta.   Subūra est clāmōsa.

5 popīna est in Subūrā.

6 Rūfīna est in popīnā. Rūfīna in popīnā labōrat.

7 pater meus est Faustus.

8 Rūfīna, ubi es tū? tū dormīs?

FAVSTVS EST FVR

pater in īnsulā labōrat. pater est … negōtiātor.

9 salvē, frāter! ego nōn dormiō. hōra prīma est. ego sum in popīnā.

Rūfīna est amita mea.

10
tū labōrās?
11
vah!
ego semper labōrō!
12
ubi est fīlia mea?
13
14
Sabīna,
ubi es tū?
15
tū es in īnsulā?
16
salvē, amita!
ego sum in īnsulā.
tū legis,
Sabīna?
17
minimē,
ego nōn legō!
18
tū in īnsulā labōrās?

Chapter 1: Subūra

19 certē ego labōrō.

ego sum in cellā.

20 ego in cellā legō. ego nōn labōrō.

21 hercle!

amita intrat! pater intrat!

22 Sabīna legit!

23 tū es mendāx! tū es mendāx!

certē Sabīna est mendāx!

īnsula est clāmōsa. Subūra nōn est quiēta.

The Subura

Sabina and her family are living in the Subura, a densely populated district near the centre of Rome, in AD 64. Here huge numbers of people lived packed together in multistorey apartment buildings, and the population density was probably greater than that of modern London or New York. As well as being a residential area, the Subura was a centre of trade and manufacturing. Its narrow, crooked streets were notorious for noise, bustle, and dirt.

At night the streets were unlit, and violence and crime were common. Many of the streets had no pavements and were too narrow for traffic. In order to reduce congestion in the wider streets, wheeled traffic (with the exception of carts carrying building material) was banned in the city for most of the daylight hours.

tū errās clāmōsā in Subūrā.
You wander about in the rowdy Subura.

The poet Martial wrote this to his friend. Martial came from Spain to live in Rome in AD 64.

Few blocks of flats from ancient times survive in Rome. This image shows a road in Ostia, the harbour town near Rome.

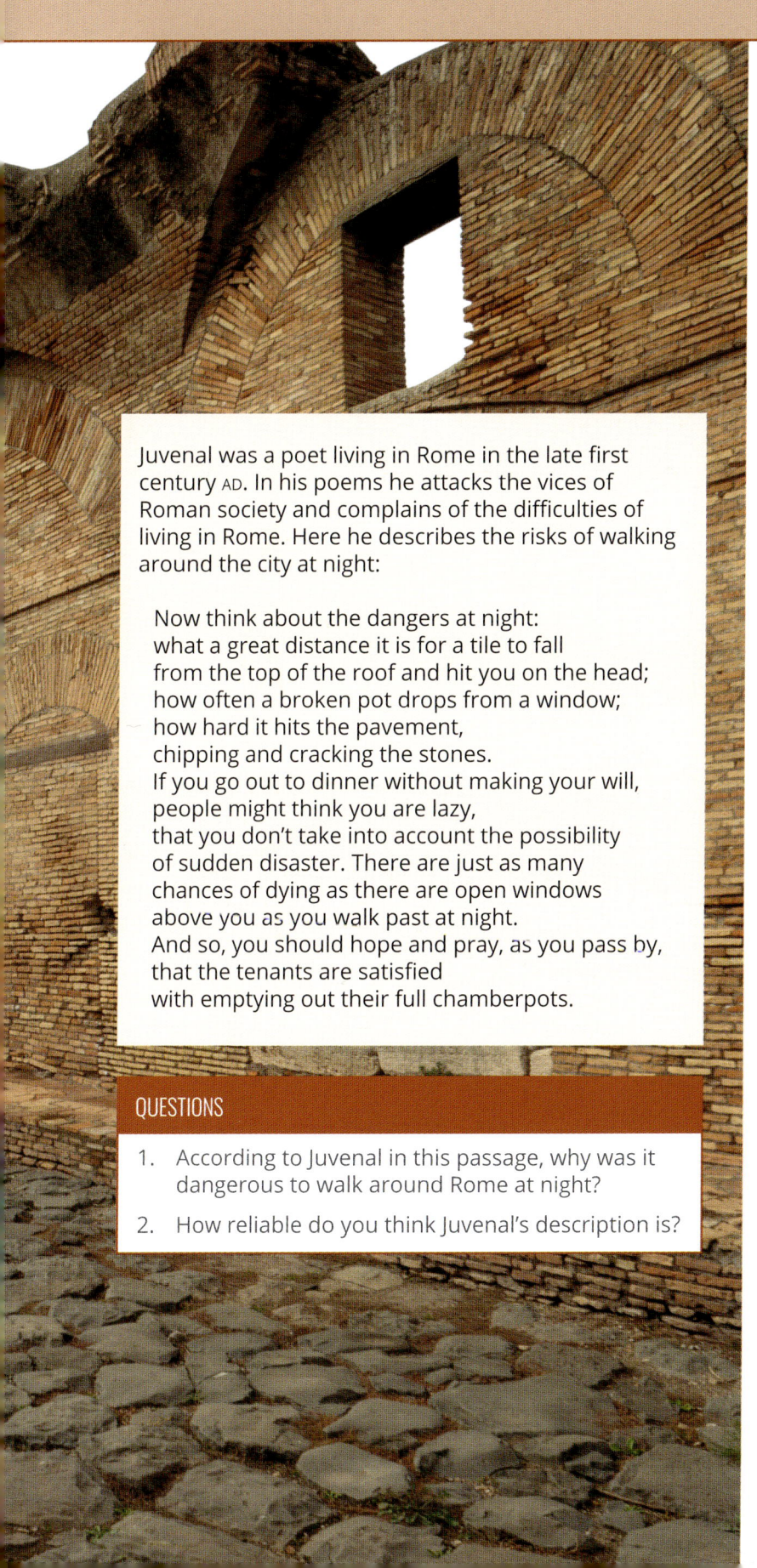

Juvenal was a poet living in Rome in the late first century AD. In his poems he attacks the vices of Roman society and complains of the difficulties of living in Rome. Here he describes the risks of walking around the city at night:

> Now think about the dangers at night:
> what a great distance it is for a tile to fall
> from the top of the roof and hit you on the head;
> how often a broken pot drops from a window;
> how hard it hits the pavement,
> chipping and cracking the stones.
> If you go out to dinner without making your will,
> people might think you are lazy,
> that you don't take into account the possibility
> of sudden disaster. There are just as many
> chances of dying as there are open windows
> above you as you walk past at night.
> And so, you should hope and pray, as you pass by,
> that the tenants are satisfied
> with emptying out their full chamberpots.

A busy street in modern Naples (above), and a street with apartment buildings from Ostia (below).

How similar do you think a street in the Subūra might have been to these two?

QUESTIONS

1. According to Juvenal in this passage, why was it dangerous to walk around Rome at night?
2. How reliable do you think Juvenal's description is?

LANGUAGE NOTE 1: WHO'S DOING WHAT?

1. Look at these sentences:

   ego semper labōr**ō**.   ego in Subūrā habit**ō**.
   tū in īnsulā labōrā**s**?   tū in popīnā dormī**s**.
   amita in popīnā labōra**t**.   Sabīna in īnsulā legi**t**.

2. In Latin, the **ending** of the verb tells us who is carrying out the action.

   -**ō**   e.g. **ego labōrō**   *I work, I am working*
   -**s**   e.g. **tū dormīs**   *you sleep, you are sleeping*
   -**t**   e.g. **pater intrat**   *the father enters, the father is entering*

3. The verb in the following sentences follows a slightly different pattern:

   ego **sum** Sabīna.   *I am Sabina.*
   tū **es** mendāx.   *You are a liar.*
   Subūra **est** clāmōsa.   *The Subura is rowdy.*

4. Note that **est** can mean *is*, *it is*, or *there is*:

   hōra prīma **est**.   *It is the first hour.*
   popīna **est** in Subūrā. *There is a bar in the Subura.*

LANGUAGE PRACTICE

1. Translate these sentences:

   a. ego in īnsulā habitō.
   b. tū in popīnā labōrās.
   c. Sabīna intrat.
   d. ego in cellā legō.
   e. tū nōn dormīs.
   f. ego labōrō.

2. Translate these sentences:

   a. ego sum in īnsulā.
   b. negōtiātor in Subūrā est.
   c. tū es in popīnā.
   d. Subūra nōn est quiēta.

This image shows a 30 m high firewall built from nearly indestructible volcanic rock. The wall separated the Forum of Augustus, of which the remains can be seen in the foreground, from the Subura. The wall ensured fires couldn't spread to the Forum from the apartment blocks of the Subura, and also created a physical barrier between the grand, marble Forum and the cramped and dirty Subura behind it.

The population of the city of Rome

> Come, look at this mass of people, for whom the roofs of the vast city of Rome can barely provide shelter. The majority of them are away from their homeland. They have flocked here from their rural towns and cities, from all over the world. Some were brought here by ambition, others by the need to run for office, or as an ambassador, or to enjoy the luxuries of city life, a good education, or the public games. Others have come because of a friendship, or on business, for which there are great opportunities here. If you ask them all, 'Where are you from?', you'll find that the majority of them have left their homes to come to this greatest and most beautiful city, though it wasn't their home city.
>
> *Seneca, Letter to his mother Helvia.*

In AD 64 about one million people lived in the city of Rome, making it the largest city in the western world until London in 1801. All these people lived in a relatively small city. The fact that a large part of the city was taken up by temples, palaces, fora, theatres, circuses, and the great town residences of the rich and powerful, meant that the majority of the population lived in densely populated areas. Probably the most famous of these neighbourhoods was the Subura.

Coming to Rome

Rome attracted people both from nearby regions in Italy and from the farthest reaches of the Empire. Wealthy people might have come to Rome to undertake a career in politics, ordinary people might have been attracted by the employment opportunities in the large city, and the very poor might have arrived in the hope of receiving the free grain dole that the emperor gave out. The largest group by far, however, were enslaved people. They came to Rome against their will and most of them were then sold at the many slave markets in the city.

A multicultural city?

It is hard to work out what percentage of Rome's population had migrated to the city, rather than being born there. Estimates of the total number of immigrants vary from 6% to 30%, so possibly as much as a third of the city's inhabitants were not from Rome originally. And a much larger percentage of the population would have had parents or grandparents who weren't from Rome.

Although many people moved to Rome from elsewhere, it is hard to know how multicultural the city would have felt to a modern observer. A wide variety of cultural and religious practices from across the Empire flourished among the immigrants living in the city, and Romans of all backgrounds embraced their new traditions and religions. Judging from the records that survive, it seems that people did not often state where they came from. This suggests, perhaps, that it was not considered particularly important to them. The extent to which immigrants and their descendants felt like outsiders, or slotted seamlessly into a multicultural melting pot of peoples, is nearly impossible to know.

QUESTIONS

1. What opinion do you think Seneca has of the newcomers to the city?
2. Compare the makeup and density of Rome's population to that of your own town.

Seneca, a well-known Roman intellectual, was tutor and adviser to the young Emperor Nero during the early part of his reign.

Lūcīlius

hōra octāva est. Subūra nōn est quiēta. Subūra est clāmōsa. Faustus est in īnsulā. fīlia est in popīnā. Sabīna in popīnā labōrat. servus est in viā. servus prō lectīcā ambulat. iuvenis est in lectīcā. iuvenis est Lūcīlius. mendīcus est in viā. mendīcus est Mānius.

Mānius	salvē! ego sum mendīcus!	5
servus	tū nōbīs obstās!	

Sabīna ē popīnā exit.

Sabīna　　Mānius est senex!

Lūcīlius ē lectīcā exit. hercle! tēgula cadit.

Sabīna　　cavē!　　　　　　　　　　　　　　　　10

tēgula in viā cadit. Lūcīlius est perterritus.

Sabīna　　Subūra est perīculōsa! certē tū in Subūrā nōn habitās.

Lūcīlius ērubēscit. Sabīna rīdet. Mānius nōn rīdet.

Vocabulary:

- **octāva** *eighth*
- **servus** *slave, enslaved person (male)*
- **in viā** *in the road*
- **prō lectīcā** *in front of the/a litter*
- **ambulat** *walks*
- **iuvenis** *young person*
- **mendīcus** *beggar*
- **nōbīs obstās** *you are in our way*
- **ē popīnā exit** *comes out of the bar*
- **senex** *old person*
- **tēgula cadit** *a roof tile falls, is falling*
- **cavē** *look out!*
- **perterritus** *terrified*
- **perīculōsa** *dangerous*
- **ērubēscit** *blushes*
- **rīdet** *laughs*

Replica Roman roof tiles.

Women at work

Some women, like Rufina, worked outside the home. It is difficult to know how many women did work, and how much of the work in Rome was done by women (whether enslaved or free). This is because there is relatively little evidence for women working. This may just be because of a bias in the way Romans represented working women, though it might also suggest that it was less common for a woman to have a job.

The lack of evidence might be explained by the fact that many women must have been occupied with having and raising children and domestic work, such as making clothes. Many probably helped in their family business, but this could go unrecorded in our evidence. However, we do also know about women in specialist occupations, such as textile-workers, doctors, and artisans, as well as about women doing jobs usually associated with men (fish sellers, innkeepers, barbers). Additionally, there were women working as performers, dancers, and sex workers.

HOC
(This [cup is mine].)

NON
MIA EST
(No! It's mine!)

QVI VOLT
SVMAT.
OCEANE
VENI BIBE
(Whoever wants it, take it! Oceanus, come and drink!)

Drawing of a wall painting from a **popīna** *in Pompeii, in Italy.*

QUESTION

What do you think the role of the woman is? Is she a serving woman, a customer, the owner, or someone else entirely?

Living in an insula

> The Latin word for a block of flats is *īnsula*, which literally means 'island'. The apartment blocks probably got this name because the separate buildings surrounded on all sides by streets resembled islands surrounded by sea.

Like the vast majority of Rome's population, Sabina's family lived in a rented flat in a multistorey block. Only the very wealthy owned their own house. Sabina's father was the landlord of an insula. Faustus didn't own the building; the owner would be a rich man who had bought the insula as an investment. The landlord was responsible for managing the property and collecting rent from the other tenants. Rents in Rome were extremely high, so evictions for non-payment must have been commonplace.

High rent wasn't the only problem tenants faced. Many of the blocks were flimsily built, with foundations which were not strong enough to support the structure. As a result, these ramshackle buildings often collapsed or caught fire.

Rich and poor lived in the same building. Unlike modern high-rise blocks where the penthouse is often the most desirable apartment, in a Roman insula the best accommodation was on the ground and first floors, while the poorest tenants had rooms on the upper floors and in the attics. The risks from fire and collapse were greater on the upper floors. Moreover, there was no running water on the upper floors, so the tenants at the top had to collect water from the public fountains and carry it up several flights of stairs. The rooms at the top were dark and, in winter, they could have been very cold. The windows did not have glass, so the only protection from the wind and rain was wooden shutters or curtains. Some tenants owned a portable heater (*foculus*), which would have heated the room by burning wood or charcoal, creating a very smoky atmosphere.

The ground floor of an insula was often divided into shops and workshops, which had openings facing onto the street. These units sometimes had a backroom or a mezzanine floor where the shopkeeper or craftsman and his family lived – very cramped quarters for a family. (A mezzanine is a half-floor, between the ground floor and the first storey, which was accessed by a ladder.) There were all kinds of shops and workshops in the Subura – bakers, barbers, cobblers, and many others – and lots of places selling food and drink either to eat

The inhabitants of the insula would have used oil lamps to light their rooms. They usually burned olive oil, as it was widely available.

This ceramic oil lamp is decorated with a charioteer driving a two-horse chariot.

Sanitation was poor. Although some ground-floor and possibly first-floor apartments had lavatories, for the most part people used chamber pots, urinated in the street, or went to one of the public lavatories. There were giant clay pots in the street for collecting urine and emptying chamber pots, and other waste went into the sewer.

Above: inside of the remains of an insula in Rome, built just a short distance from the temples of the Capitoline Hill.

There was often no running water in the insula, so people would have to collect water from public fountains (like this one from Pompeii, in Italy).

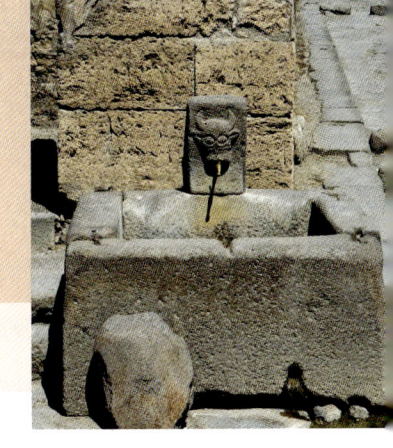

in or to take away. Many flats had very limited cooking facilities, perhaps an open fire, or none at all, so if people wanted cooked food they had to eat out. Many people would have survived on a diet of bread, cheese, and fruit.

For most of its inhabitants, life in Rome was dangerous, unpredictable, and, compared with what we are used to, unsanitary. As accommodation was so cramped and cooking facilities limited, most people would have spent a lot of time outside, so public spaces and amenities were very important.

LANGUAGE NOTE 2: READING LATIN

1. Look at these sentences:

   ego in Subūrā habitō.
   I live in the Subura.

   Sabīna in popīnā labōrat.
   Sabina is working in the bar.

   The Latin sentences tell us **who** is carrying out the action, then **where**, then **what** they're doing. The English sentences tell us **who** is carrying out the action, then **what** they're doing, then **where**.

2. Look at these sentences:

   Sabīna est in cellā.
   Sabina is in the room.

   ego sum in Subūrā.
   I am in the Subura.

   In these Latin sentences, the order of the words in the Latin and the English is the same.

3. When you are reading Latin, try to read it from left to right and get used to the order in which the information comes.

4. If you are translating into English from Latin, you will need to make your English sound natural.

LANGUAGE PRACTICE

3. Complete the sentences with a correct choice from the box, then translate your sentences.

   | ego | tū | ambulat | habitō | iuvenis | dormīs |

   a. .... in lectīcā dormit.
   b. .... labōrās, soror?
   c. ego in Subūrā ....
   d. .... nōn sum in cellā.
   e. Sabīna in viā ....
   f. tū in īnsulā ....

*Sign advertising wines for sale at a popina in Herculaneum, in Italy. The popina is called **ad cucumās** (at the cooking pots).*

*Four different wines are sold, at 4, 3, 4, and 2 **assēs** (pence) per **sextārius** (about half a litre).*

nox

nox est. Sabīna in cellā est. Subūra nōn est quiēta. Sabīna nōn dormit.

turba in popīnā est. Rūfīna in popīnā labōrat. Faustus in popīnā bibit. fūr quoque in popīnā est. fūr est pauper.

Faustus	Rūfīna! ubi es tū, soror?
Rūfīna	quid est, frāter?
Faustus	fūr est in popīnā!
Rūfīna	quid? fūr est in popīnā? ubi est fūr?
Faustus	tū es fūr! vīnum est nimium cārum!
Rūfīna	tū es asinus, frāter. vīnum nōn est nimium cārum. tū nimium bibis!

Faustus ērubēscit. turba rīdet. fūr quoque rīdet. popīna est clāmōsa. turba nōn est cauta. fūr nōn est pauper.

nox *night*

turba *crowd*
bibit *drinks, is drinking*
fūr *thief*
quoque *also*
pauper *poor*
soror *sister*
quid est? *what is it?*

vīnum *wine*
nimium *too (much)*
cārum *expensive*
asinus *fool, donkey*

cauta *careful, cautious*

Left: a popina in Pompeii, with vats sunk into the bar.

Right: a wall painting from Pompeii, showing people playing dice in a popina.

*Sabina's aunt runs a popina, a bar which sold drinks and food for people to take away, eat on the street, or consume inside. Romans drank wine, which they mixed with water. In a popina the wine was stored in jars (**amphorae**), and then transferred to jugs for serving. Hot food was cooked on a stove and probably served from the pan.*

Rome in AD 64

Beginnings

The origins of Rome are shrouded in mystery. The original settlement expanded from a secure hilltop location, gradually absorbing its neighbours until it dominated the whole Italian peninsula.

The descendants of those early settlers wanted to create a date for the foundation of their city. Using calculations based on the four-year cycle of the ancient Olympic Games, the Romans chose the year 753 BC for the beginning of Rome. They even selected a date: to this day modern Romans celebrate their city's birthday on 21 April. By the time Emperor Augustus established one-man rule in 27 BC, more than 700 years later, Rome was the centre of a vast empire (see the map on pages 2–3).

Nero

In AD 54 the teenage Nero became the fifth emperor. The title of emperor always passed down through the male line, because women could not hold political office in Rome. However, some female members of the imperial household, including Nero's mother Agrippina, exercised considerable power.

By the time our story begins, Nero has been emperor for ten years. The early part of his reign was relatively stable. The young emperor was under Agrippina's control and supervised by two advisers: the philosopher and intellectual Seneca (see page 15) and a military commander called Burrus. Violent uprisings at opposite ends of the Empire were successfully put down, and in Rome Nero behaved as a generous and benevolent ruler.

Nero was also a great supporter of the arts. Unusually for an emperor, he took part in plays himself, and he gave poetry and musical performances. He was also a fan of sports, and on occasion drove chariots in races (where his competitors let him win).

However, there was another side to Nero's character, and he did not cope well with the power available to an emperor. His behaviour became more erratic and cruel, and on his orders increasing numbers of people (usually those who displeased him or he felt were a threat) were exiled or killed. Just five years into his reign, he even had his mother killed, possibly because she disapproved of an affair he was having, or because he resented her attempts to control him. Perhaps it was a combination of the two. From that point on, he set few boundaries on his own behaviour.

Nevertheless, Nero's support for arts and sports made him popular with much of the population of the Empire, particularly the poor, who benefited most from the spending on entertainment. Others felt that it was not appropriate for an emperor to act in plays or take part in chariot races. Some wealthier Romans resented his legal and tax reforms which benefited the common people.

Most of our information about Nero comes from Roman historians, who themselves belonged to the wealthy upper classes and were hostile to Nero. However, like us, Romans were a broad mix of people, with a range of views and interests. In AD 64 different individuals would have had varying opinions about their city and their emperor.

*Gold coin with the head of Nero, from AD 66. It is printed with the words IMP NERO CAESAR AVGVSTVS. IMP is an abbreviation of **imperātor**, which means 'emperor'.*

> The abbreviation AD stands for **Annō Dominī** (meaning 'in the year of our Lord'). We use it to indicate a year after the traditional date of the birth of Jesus Christ. A year BC is 'before Christ'. AD is not the only Latin abbreviation that we still use in English. Can you think of any others?

---

753 BC — Traditional foundation of the city of Rome.

27 BC — Augustus becomes sole ruler of the Roman Empire.

AD 54 — Nero becomes emperor at the age of 16.

AD 64 — The year our story begins. How old is Rome?

Chapter 2: Rōma

Via Flāminia

1

2 equus in viā prōcēdit.   Giscō equum dūcit.

3 turba est in viā.   Giscō turbam vituperat.

4

st! Giscō! fīlius dormit.

Catia fīlium tenet.

5 canis est Celer.
Celer in sepulcrō stat.

6

Giscō Celerem vocat.

7

pauper est in sepulcrō. canis pauperem videt.

8

bau! au!

pauper canem vituperat.

9 vah!
Celer est amīcus!
tū amīcum habēs!

10 īnfāns nōn dormit.
Giscō īnfantem tenet.

11 ecce! arcus est in viā!
arcus est magnificus!

12 Catia arcum videt.
imperātor quoque est magnificus.
tū imperātōrem vidēs?

13 īnfāns est laetus.

14 imperātor est ... Claudius.
Giscō Catiam ānxiē spectat.

15 Catia nōn est laeta.
Catia est Britannica.

16 salvē! ego sum Currāx.
tū cellam quaeris?
certē ego cellam quaerō.
servus Giscōnem salūtat. Giscō servum salūtat.

dominus meus īnsulam in Subūrā habet.
īnsula est optima.
dominus est Faustus.

First impressions

As Gisco and Catia approached Rome along the Via Flaminia, they passed the Field of Mars (*Campus Martius*), named after the god of war because it was originally where soldiers did military training. Later it was used as a recreational space, but over the years temples, monuments commemorating Roman victories, and other grand buildings were constructed there.

On the Field of Mars, Catia and Gisco would have seen monuments and gardens. One of the most impressive was the Altar of Peace (*Āra Pācis*), which had been built by the first emperor, Augustus. Next to this was a huge obelisk from Egypt, which acted as a sundial. Its shadow fell across the centre of the marble altar on Augustus' birthday.

They then passed through the Arch of Claudius which was built into the Aqua Virgo, one of the aqueducts which brought water into the city. In this area were the city's largest public bathing complexes. One of these, the Baths of Nero, had been completed only two years before, in AD 62, and surpassed all others in size and grandeur. There were also theatres, temples, and Nero's wooden amphitheatre.

As they got closer, the Temple of Jupiter Optimus Maximus (Jupiter the Best and Greatest) on the Capitoline Hill would have loomed above them. Coming round the side of the Capitoline Hill, they would enter the heart of the city, the Roman Forum.

> **QUESTION**
>
> What impression would walking into Rome along the Via Flaminia have made on visitors and newcomers?

The obelisk now stands in the Piazza di Montecitorio in Rome.

The Arch of Claudius was built to celebrate Emperor Claudius' conquest of Britain in AD 43. The arch has not survived, but we can get an idea of what it looked like from this coin.

A Roman road (the Via Appia) lined with tombs, as it is now. Roman tombs were placed beside the roads outside the city boundary to separate the dead from the living.

The Ara Pacis was decorated with reliefs of processions, the imperial family, Roman gods, and important scenes from Rome's legendary beginnings.

A Roman aqueduct. This one is in Segovia, in Spain.

The growth of Rome

By the time of our story, Rome was a large, bustling city and the centre of a huge empire. It began as a tiny village on the River Tiber, and over centuries it grew into a mass of winding alleys punctuated with grand open spaces.

Location, location, location

The site of the earliest settlement is often said to have been the Palatine Hill, which provided a good defensive position. As Rome grew, it expanded into the surrounding hills. Famously, Rome was built on seven hills (in fact there are more): the Palatine, Capitoline, Esquiline, Aventine, Quirinal, Viminal, and Caelian. According to legend, the Palatine Hill was the home of Rome's founder, Romulus. It later became the place where the emperors' palaces were built. About 15 miles downriver was Rome's harbour, Ostia. From there, ships brought goods upriver to the docks in Rome near Tiber Island.

Water and waste

The Great Drain (*Cloāca Maxima*) was constructed in about 600 BC to drain the marshy land that lay between the hills of Rome. It was originally an open-air canal, but the Romans later covered it over and constructed a sewage system to remove waste from the city into the Tiber. Aqueducts supplied the city with fresh water from springs in the surrounding countryside. This abundance of water was a key factor in maintaining the growing population of Rome, and soon came to symbolize power and wealth.

All roads lead to Rome?

By the first century AD Rome was at the centre of a huge empire. A network of roads linked Rome to the cities of the Empire. Although large quantities of food and building materials were imported by sea, they were also transported via the well-maintained roads leading into Rome. These roads also enabled traders and labourers to come into the city each day from the surrounding countryside.

The Via Flaminia, one of the roads out of Rome to the north, was a route that was often taken to and from northern Gaul (France) and Britannia (Britain). The Via Appia went south to Brundisium on the south-east coast of Italy. From here travellers could sail on to Greece and the East. The Via Aurelia left Rome to the west, crossing the Tiber at the Aemilian bridge and following the coast through north-west Italy and into southern Gaul.

A model of the earliest settlement on the Palatine Hill.

> In my opinion, the three most impressive achievements which best display the greatness of Rome's Empire are the aqueducts, paved roads, and sewers.
>
> Dionysius of Halicarnassus

The main routes in and out of Rome.

Forum Boārium

clāmor est in popīnā. Rūfīna ē popīnā exit. Rūfīna Sabīnam vocat.

Rūfīna   Sabīna! psittacus nōn adest!

Sabīna Quārtillam vocat. Quārtilla est ancilla. Sabīna cum Quārtillā psittacum quaerit.

Sabīna cum Quārtillā ad Forum Boārium venit. mercātor est in forō. mercātor cibum habet. mercātor cibum vēndit. 5

mercātor   ego multum cibum habeō! cibus meus est optimus!

mercātōrem intentē spectat Quārtilla. mercātor psittacum habet.

Quārtilla   salvē, mercātor! tū psittacum habēs. tū psittacum vēndis?
mercātor   minimē, ego cibum vēndō. psittacus est meus. 10
psittacus   tū es mendāx! tū es mendāx!
Sabīna   certē tū es mendāx! tū es fūr!

Sabīna psittacum vocat. psittacus ad Sabīnam volitat. Quārtilla rīdet. Sabīna psittacum tenet et ē forō currit.

Forum Boārium *Forum Boārium (cattle market)*
clāmor *noise, shouting*
psittacus *parrot*
adest *is here*
ancilla *slave, enslaved person (female)*
cum *with*
ad *to*
venit *comes*
mercātor *merchant*
cibum *food*
vēndit *sells*
multum *much, a lot of*
intentē *carefully*

volitat *flies*
et *and*
currit *runs*

The Cloaca Maxima ran under the city from the north-east, through the Roman Forum, and into the River Tiber at the Forum Boārium. It drained excess water and removed waste and sewage. Other smaller sewers were connected to the Cloaca Maxima, serving public toilets, baths, and public buildings. Romans believed that the goddess Cloacina looked after the sewer.

What was a forum?

At the centre of most Roman towns there was a forum, a rectangular open space surrounded by buildings and colonnades (covered walkways), similar to a square or piazza in a modern city. Originally a forum was a marketplace, with stalls selling food, clothes, pots and pans, jewellery, and all the other things people needed.

Owing to the size of the city, Rome had many fora spread across its different neighbourhoods. People from all classes of society gathered in the fora to shop, conduct business such as banking, socialize, or visit temples and public buildings. Some fora were used mostly for public business and ceremonies. In these, lawyers argued cases in the law courts, candidates up for election made speeches, religious processions and ceremonies took place, and the emperor made appearances.

Rome also had fora which specialized in the sale of certain foods such as fish, pork, herbs and vegetables, and wine. One such market was the *Forum Boārium*, close to the docks at Tiber Island. Originally the cattle market (the Latin word for 'cow' is *bōs*), it grew into an important commercial centre. It was also a religious centre, home to several temples.

As the population of the city grew, more fora were constructed, and several of these were built by emperors and powerful men. The general Julius Caesar built a new forum attached to the Roman Forum, and Emperor Augustus built another forum next to this a few decades later. The emperors Vespasian, Nerva, and Trajan built a further three new fora, creating a network of linked imperial fora in the heart of Rome. These fora, with their grand temples, monuments, and public buildings, were constructed at the emperor's expense. They showed off to all who visited them the wealth, power, and generosity of the emperor.

QUESTIONS

1. What buildings and activities can you spot in this image?
2. Compare market squares in towns today with the fora in Rome. To what extent do you think they fulfil the same functions?

Market square in the town of Mantua, Italy.

LANGUAGE NOTE 1: NOMINATIVE AND ACCUSATIVE CASES

1. Look at the following sentences:

    Catia fīlium tenet. Giscō **Catiam** spectat.
    Catia is holding her son. Gisco looks at Catia.

    equus in viā prōcēdit. Giscō **equum** dūcit.
    The horse walks along the road. Gisco leads the horse.

    canis in sepulcrō stat. Giscō **canem** vocat.
    The dog is standing on the tomb. Gisco calls his dog.

2. In Latin, the endings of **nouns** change as their role in the sentence changes. If they are carrying out the action they have one ending, and if they are receiving the action of the verb they have a different ending. We call these different forms of nouns 'cases'.

3. When a noun is carrying out the action, we say it is in the **nominative case**.

Rūfīna Sabīnam vocat.	*Rufina calls Sabina.*
Lūcīlius ērubēscit.	*Lucilius is blushing.*
mercātor cibum vēndit.	*The merchant is selling food.*

4. When a noun is receiving the action of the verb, we say it is in the **accusative case**.

Giscō **cellam** quaerit.	*Gisco is looking for a room.*
ego **cibum** vēndo.	*I'm selling food.*
Sabīna **clāmōrem** audit.	*Sabina hears a noise.*

In Latin, the order of information is usually, but not always, nominative accusative verb:

Catia fīlium tenet.
tū mendīcum vidēs.
Giscō canem vocat.
mercātōrem spectat Quārtilla.

In the last example, how can you tell that it's Quartilla who is watching the merchant, rather than the merchant watching Quartilla? Why might the writer have changed the usual order of information?

Forum Rōmānum

Faustus cum servō Forum Rōmānum intrat. servus est Lūcriō. Forum Rōmānum est clāmōsum.

cūria est in Forō Rōmānō. prō cūriā Lūcriō senātōrem videt. magnum servum habet senātor.

Lūcriō   ecce! senātor adest. tū magnam pecūniam dēbēs ... 5
Faustus   hercle!

Faustus cum Lūcriōne ad basilicam festīnat. sed senātor Faustum prō basilicā videt. senātor cum magnō servō ad basilicam ambulat.

senātor   salvē, negōtiātor! tū pecūniam meam habēs?
Faustus   salvē, senātor! ego pēnsiōnem nōn habeō, sed ... 10
senātor   quid tū dīcis?
Lūcriō   Faustus pecūniam semper trādit. Faustus nōn est fūr.

senātor signum dat. magnus servus Lūcriōnem verberat. Lūcriō cadit.

Faustus   pecūniam nōn habeō!
senātor   tū pecūniam nōn habēs, sed fīliam habēs. ego 15
           ancillam quaerō. cavē, negōtiātor. urbs est perīculōsa.

senātor ē forō exit. Faustus perterritus est.

Rōmānum *Roman*

cūria *Senate House*
senātōrem *senator (wealthy politician)*
magnum *big, large*
pecūniam *money, sum of money*
dēbēs *owe*
basilicam *hall*
festīnat *hurries*
sed *but*
pēnsiōnem *rent (payable by Faustus to the owner of the insula)*
dīcis *say*
trādit *hands over*
signum dat *gives a signal*
verberat *beats, hits*

urbs *city*

Photograph taken in the Roman Forum, showing the floor and column bases of the Basilica Aemilia in the foreground, and the side of the Senate House behind it. The Basilica Aemilia was a large hall where bankers and merchants conducted business.

The Forum Romanum

The Roman Forum (*Forum Rōmānum*) was an open square surrounded by magnificent buildings. It was the political, religious, and commercial centre of Rome and the whole Empire. People of all classes, both inhabitants of the city and visitors, came to the Forum to socialize, engage in public and private business, worship, listen to speeches, watch processions, and just to gaze in amazement at the splendour of the public buildings. Rome was a city of contrasts, and one of the biggest contrasts was between the grandeur of its public spaces and the poverty of the streets and buildings where the majority of people lived and worked.

A **basilica** was a large public hall. There were two stretching along the sides of the Forum Romanum. Their colonnaded fronts provided shade for people to walk and socialize. The Basilica Julia (*below*) housed the law courts. The Basilica Aemilia was a place for bankers and merchants to conduct business. The entire building was faced with marble and the front was decorated with sculptures; a frieze showed scenes from early Roman legend and history, including the abandonment of Romulus and Remus.

Concordia was the goddess who symbolized unity among the different classes of the Roman people. Her temple was a lavishly decorated marble building, and some of it still survives.

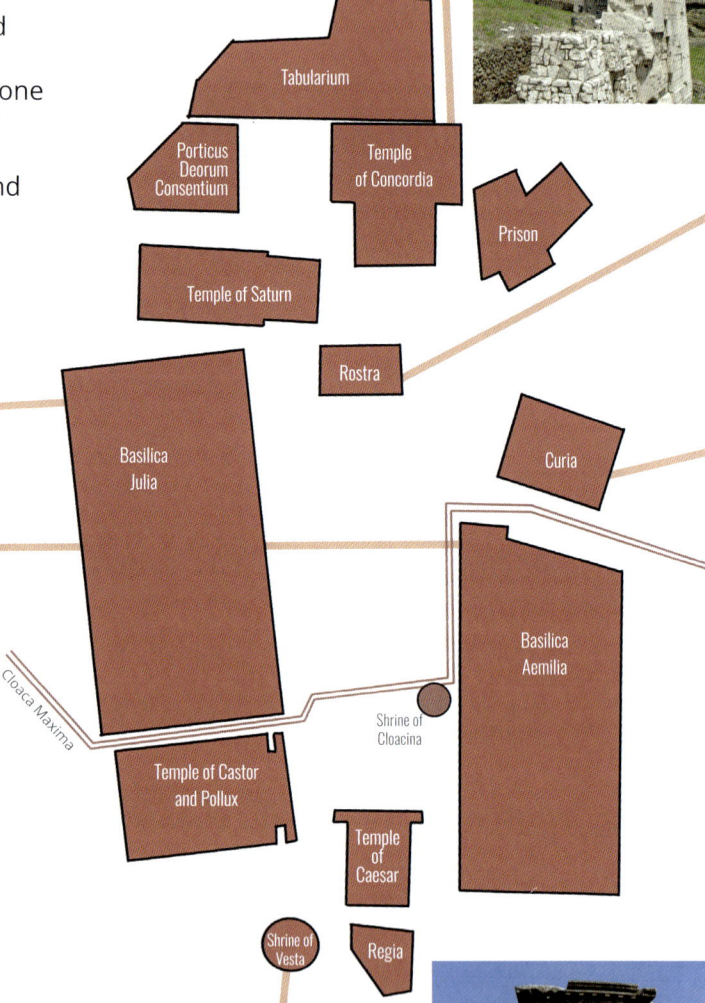

Vesta was the goddess of the hearth and of fire. Roman temples were usually rectangular, but the shrine of Vesta was a small circular building. Inside the shrine was the sacred fire, which symbolized the survival and prosperity of Rome and was never allowed to go out.

Chapter 2: Rōma

The Golden Milestone (*mīliārium aureum*) was a tall column in the Forum Romanum which marked the starting point of the network of roads which radiated from Rome to all parts of Italy and the Empire. The distances to the cities of the Empire were inscribed on it in gilded bronze letters. It was erected by Emperor Augustus as a symbol that Rome was the centre of the Empire. Its location in the Forum is not known.

I'll show you where you'll easily find every sort of man, ... whether it's a wicked man or a virtuous one that you seek, honest or dishonest. If you want to find a perjurer, go to the **Curia**, for a liar and a boaster, go to the **Shrine of Cloacina**. At the old shops are those who lend or borrow money, and behind the **Temple of Castor and Pollux** are those you trust at your peril.

This extract from a comedy by Plautus gives an impression of the variety of people in the Forum Romanum.

The **Rostra** was a high stone platform. The emperor and his family stood on the Rostra to show themselves to the people and to make speeches.

The **Curia** was the Senate House, where the emperor and Senate met to discuss affairs of government. The building which now stands in the Forum Romanum (*below*) is a later restoration.

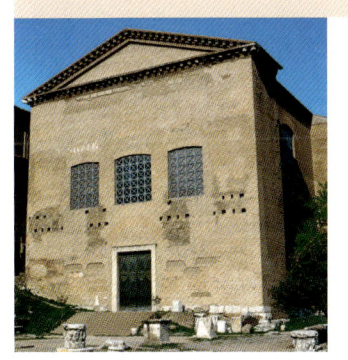

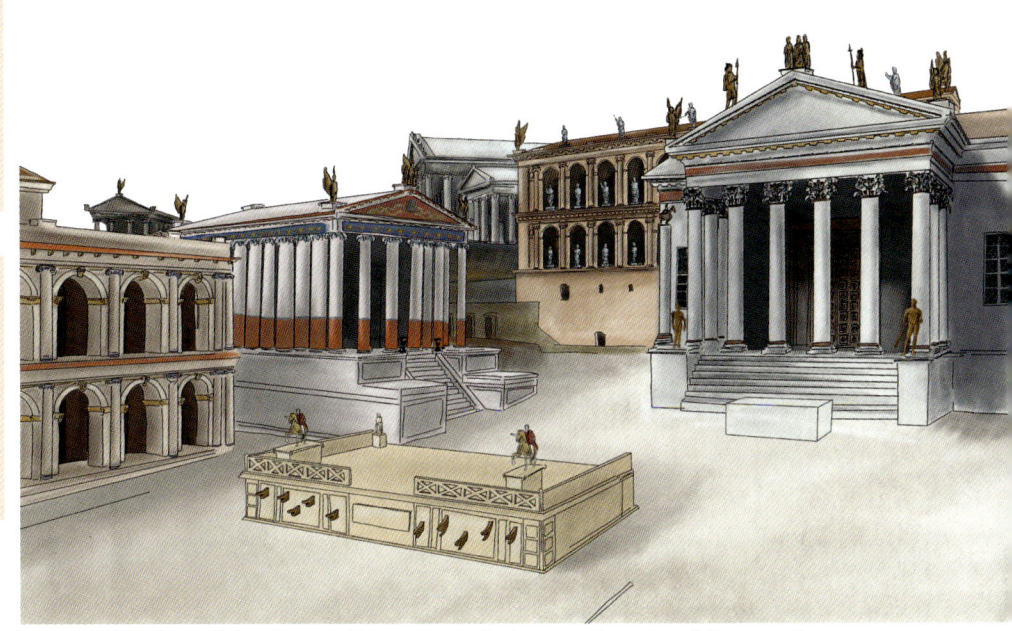

A reconstruction of the Forum Romanum, facing the Temple of Concordia with the Capitoline behind.

The Forum Romanum today, facing the remains of the Temple of Concordia.

LANGUAGE NOTE 2: DECLENSIONS

1. Some Latin nouns end **-a** in the nominative and **-am** in the accusative case:

   | Nominative: | **Rūfīna** | **hōra** | **turba** | **īnsula** |
   | Accusative: | **Rūfīnam** | **hōram** | **turbam** | **īnsulam** |

   These are known as **first declension** nouns.

2. Some Latin nouns end **-us** in the nominative and **-um** in the accusative case:

   | Nominative: | **Faustus** | **amīcus** | **cibus** | **servus** |
   | Accusative: | **Faustum** | **amīcum** | **cibum** | **servum** |

   This group of nouns is known as the **second declension**.

3. Other Latin nouns, which have a variety of endings in the nominative case and end **-em** in the accusative case, are **third declension**:

   | Nominative: | **Giscō** | **īnfāns** | **canis** | **imperātor** |
   | Accusative: | **Giscōnem** | **īnfantem** | **canem** | **imperātōrem** |

LANGUAGE PRACTICE

1. Copy each sentence below, completing the ending of the noun. Then translate each sentence. Use the language note above for help with the noun endings.

   a. Giscō can... videt.

   b. Rūfīn... amīcum vocat.

   c. mercātor cib... vēndit.

   d. amīc... Faustum salūtat.

   e. ego īnsul... spectō.

   f. tū īnfan... tenēs.

cella

Currāx per urbem festīnat. servus Giscōnem et Catiam ad Subūram dūcit. servum Rūfīna videt.

Rūfīna   salvē, Currāx!
Currāx   veterānus cellam quaerit, domina. veterānus est Giscō. Giscō uxōrem et fīlium habet. et canis est Celer.

fīlium tenet Catia. marītus Celerem mulcet. Rūfīna Giscōnem et uxōrem salūtat. Rūfīna īnfantem laudat, sed canem ānxiē spectat. Rūfīna vīnum et multum cibum portat. Catia cibum cōnsūmit.

Catia   cibus est optimus, Rūfīna!

Currāx Giscōnem ad cellam dūcit. Currāx cellam laudat.

Currāx   cella est quiētissima. cella aspectum optimum habet. cella est …
Giscō   parva et obscūra!

subitō cadit tēgula et columba per rīmam volitat. Celer lātrat. magnus mūs per iānuam currit.

Giscō   mūs in cellā habitat. cella nōn est optima, sed tū es negōtiātor optimus, Currāx!

per *through*

domina *mistress*
veterānus *veteran, retired soldier*
uxōrem *wife*
marītus *husband*
mulcet *strokes*
laudat *praises*
portat *carries, brings*
cōnsūmit *eats*

aspectum *view*

parva *small*
obscūra *dark*
subitō *suddenly*
columba *dove*
rīmam *hole, crack*
lātrat *barks*
mūs *rat*
iānuam *door*

A cup showing a hunting dog.

LANGUAGE NOTE 3: GENDER OF NOUNS

1. All Latin nouns have a gender. They are masculine, feminine, or neuter.

2. Almost all **first declension** nouns are **feminine**, e.g. **īnsula** (*apartment block*) and **turba** (*crowd*).

3. Most **second declension** nouns are **masculine**, e.g. **cibus** (*food*) and **equus** (*horse*).

   Some second declension nouns end **-um** in both the nominative and the accusative cases, e.g. **vīnum** (*wine*) and **forum** (*marketplace*). These nouns are **neuter** and we will study them further in Chapter 4.

4. Some **third declension** nouns are **masculine**, some are **feminine**, and some are **neuter**. For example, **clāmor** (*noise*) is masculine, **nox** (*night*) is feminine, and **caput** (*head*) is neuter.

5. When you look up a noun in the dictionary, its gender is indicated by *m.*, *f.*, or *n.*

LANGUAGE PRACTICE

2. Using the dictionary on pages 283–296, write down the declension and gender of each noun.

   For example: **amita,** 1st declension, feminine.

   - **a.** psittacus
   - **b.** soror
   - **c.** cloāca
   - **d.** mercātor
   - **e.** sepulcrum
   - **f.** hōra

3. Select the correct form of the noun to complete each sentence, then translate.
   a. ego .... videō. (equus, equum)
   b. .... canem vocat. (servus, servum)
   c. tū .... habēs? (pecūnia, pecūniam)
   d. .... in popīnā sedet. (senex, senem)
   e. .... Faustus audit. (clāmor, clāmōrem)

4. Select the correct form of the verb to complete each sentence, then translate.
   a. ego cibum .... (habet, habeō, habēs)
   b. Mānius in viā .... (sedēs, sedeō, sedet)
   c. tū in popīnā .... (labōrat, labōrās, labōrō)
   d. ego in Subūrā .... (habitō, habitat, habitās)
   e. Faustus īnsulam .... (intrō, intrās, intrat)

*Fragments from the **Fōrma Urbis Rōmae**, the map of the city of Rome.*

The Forma Urbis Romae was an enormous map, measuring about 18 x 13 m and created around AD 211. Inscribed on stone was the plan of every architectural feature in the ancient city, from large public monuments to small shops. Only 10–15% of the original stone map survives, broken into 1,186 pieces.

Romulus and Remus

The story goes that, long before Rome existed, refugees from the Trojan War founded a hilltop town in Italy, which they called Alba Longa. Hundreds of years later the leader of the town, Numitor, was driven out by his brother. Numitor's only child, Rhea Silvia, was forced to become a priestess and forbidden to have any children, so that Numitor would have no more descendants.

However, Rhea Silvia was visited by the god Mars (or so the story goes) and later gave birth to twin sons, Romulus and Remus. They were sent to be drowned, 12 miles away in the River Tiber. What then happened to those boys is the story of the foundation of Rome.

- Read or listen to the myth of Romulus and Remus – there are many versions!

Altar to Mars and Venus.

The Wolf

Look at Source 1. What aspects of the myth can you see on the altar? The Romans celebrated the idea that Romulus and Remus were suckled by a wolf, in a cave now known as the Lupercal (in Latin, *lupa* means wolf). If you were writing a foundation story about a civilization, why might you have the founders suckled by a wolf, and in a cave? Later, the twins were brought up in the fields by a shepherd. How might that part of the story help poorer Romans relate to them? The shepherd's name, by the way, was Faustulus, 'Little Faustus'.

> **SOURCE 2** Remus jumped over Romulus' new walls, mocking his brother. Romulus, in anger, killed his brother and added: 'The same fate awaits anyone else who crosses my walls.'
> *Livy*

Fratricide

Read Source 2. Romulus killed his brother, an act known as fratricide. Do you think it is a problem that Rome's founder committed fratricide? Livy was writing at the time when Rome had recently endured many years of civil war (where Romans fought and killed other Romans), and already had a vast empire. How does Romulus' murder of his brother fit into that context? What message do Romulus' words send out to other nations?

Ancestors

The twins' mother, Rhea Silvia, was descended from Aeneas, a Trojan prince who was himself the son of Venus, goddess of love. Their father was Mars, god of war. Why might the Romans want to create the idea that they were descended from these two deities? What characteristics would you expect from people who were the children of Venus and Mars?

> **SOURCE 3** All myths and legends have an element of truth.
> *Alfonsina Russo, Italian archaeologist.*

Myth, legend, or history?

Look at Source 3. The story of Romulus and Remus is a myth. It isn't true, but some people feel that parts of it may be. Archaeological evidence shows that there was a settlement on the Palatine Hill at the time of the mythological foundation of Rome (753 BC). Which aspects of the myth do you think may be based on fact? Which are fiction? Is it easy to tell? What is the difference between myth, legend, and history?

RESEARCH

Find out more about:

- Other foundation myths for Rome. Why might there be more than one story?
- The Trojans and the Trojan War. How does the story of Rome connect with the story of Troy?
- Foundation myths of other cultures. What do they say about how they see themselves?

Chapter 3: lūdī
Circus Maximus

1. Sabīna per urbem festīnat.
2. puella Sabīnam salūtat. puella est Iūlia.
3. puellae ad Circum festīnant.
4. maxima turba est in Circō.

5. amīcus Sabīnam salūtat.
6. amīcī Iūliam salūtant.
7. iuvenis vīnum bibit. fūr labōrat.
8. iuvenēs vīnum bibunt. fūrēs labōrant.
9. subitō senātor plaudit.
10. senātōrēs plaudunt. imperātor adest.

11 Nerō sedet. senātōrēs quoque sedent.

12 magnus clāmor est in Circō. quadrīga Circum intrat.

13 quadrīgae Circum intrant.

14 Sabīna Lūcīlium videt.   Lūcīlius rīdet.

15 Sabīna patrem et amīcum videt.
Faustus et amīcus spōnsiōnem faciunt.

16 fīlia est ānxia.

17 quid tū facis?

mātrōna clāmat.

18 īnfēlīx!

mātrōnae clāmant.

19 prasinus vincit. Lūcīlius est laetus.

20 mē miserum!

Faustus et amīcus nōn sunt laetī.

LANGUAGE NOTE 1: NOMINATIVE PLURAL AND PLURAL VERBS

1. Look at the following pairs of sentences:

   puella ad Circum festīnat.
   The girl hurries to the Circus.

   puellae ad Circum festīnant.
   The girls hurry to the Circus.

   amīcus Sabīnam salūtat.
   A friend greets Sabina.

   amīcī Iūliam salūtant.
   The friends greet Julia.

   fūr labōrat.
   A thief is working.

   fūrēs labōrant.
   The thieves are working.

2. In Latin, the endings of both the nominative noun and the verb indicate whether one person or more than one person is carrying out an action.

3. If one person is doing something, Latin uses the nominative singular (**puella, amīcus, fūr**). If more than one person is doing something, Latin uses the nominative plural (**puellae, amīcī, fūrēs**).

   Compare the nominative singular and plural forms of each declension:

SINGULAR	1st decl.	2nd decl.	3rd decl.
nominative	**puella**	**amīcus**	**fūr**

PLURAL			
nominative	**puellae**	**amīcī**	**fūrēs**

4. Notice that the **-nt** ending of the verb also indicates that more than one person is carrying out the action:

puellae festīnant.	*The girls are hurrying.*
iuvenēs clāmant.	*The young people are shouting.*
frātrēs bibunt.	*The brothers are drinking.*

5. Note the use of **sunt** in the following sentences:

   | **amīcī nōn sunt laetī.** | *The friends are not happy.* |
   | **senēs sunt in popīnā.** | *The old men are in the bar.* |

Public festivals

Romans did not have days off work each week, as we do now. But throughout the year they celebrated a number of religious festivals, and these days were public holidays: the *diēs fēstī* (festival days). On festival days all business was suspended and even some slaves were allowed time off. Anyone caught conducting public business could be fined. The number of festival days increased over time, and under Nero people probably had more than eighty days off a year.

The celebrations included religious rites such as processions, prayers, and offerings to the gods. Often there were also public entertainments called *lūdī* (games). Most ludi were held annually, but some were held every four years, and the *lūdī saeculārēs* were meant to be held every 100 years (although the Romans appeared to have lost count quite often). Two types of entertainment associated with festivals were chariot-racing and theatrical performances.

Free to attend

The ludi were free to attend for all spectators, and were mostly paid for by the state. Money came from taxes, or sometimes fines from lawbreakers. However, the games were also referred to as *mūnera*, literally 'gifts', as they were often paid for by wealthy citizens and the emperor as gifts to the people of the city. New festivals were added frequently. In AD 59, when Nero first shaved his beard, he celebrated his passage into adulthood with a new festival, the Juvenalia. This festival was then repeated annually.

A festival for everything

Festivals were held in honour of a wide range of gods and occasions, and each had its own rituals and traditions.

Florales April–May	• *In honour of the goddess Flora, celebrating the fertility of spring.* • *In AD 68 the emperor presented a tightrope-walking elephant at the games.*
Apollinares July	• *In honour of Apollo.* • *First celebrated to secure the aid of the god Apollo in the war against Hannibal.*
ludi Romani September	• *In honour of Jupiter.* • *The chief festival and one of the oldest.* • *The first festival to include drama.*
Plebeii November	• *Instituted to celebrate and entertain the common people of Rome (the plebeians).* • *Mainly featuring chariot races, it also included a cavalry parade.*

RESEARCH

Find out about the entertainments and traditions associated with one festival. Choose either a festival from the table above, or one of the following: Augustales, Victoriae Caesaris, Ceriales, Saeculares, Taurii.

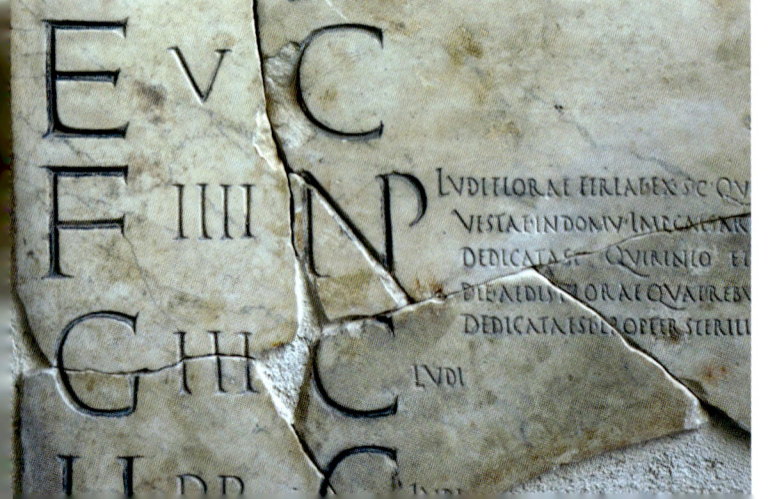

*We have several surviving examples of Roman calendars, called **fāstī**, on which the year's business days, political events, and festival days were shown. Some festival days were on the same date each year, others were held on different dates, while some were one-off events.*

This fragment of a calendar is inscribed on stone. The left-hand letters and numbers indicate the date. The letters NP in the second row indicate the day was a public holiday and its note explains that the Ludi Florae, the games of Flora, were held.

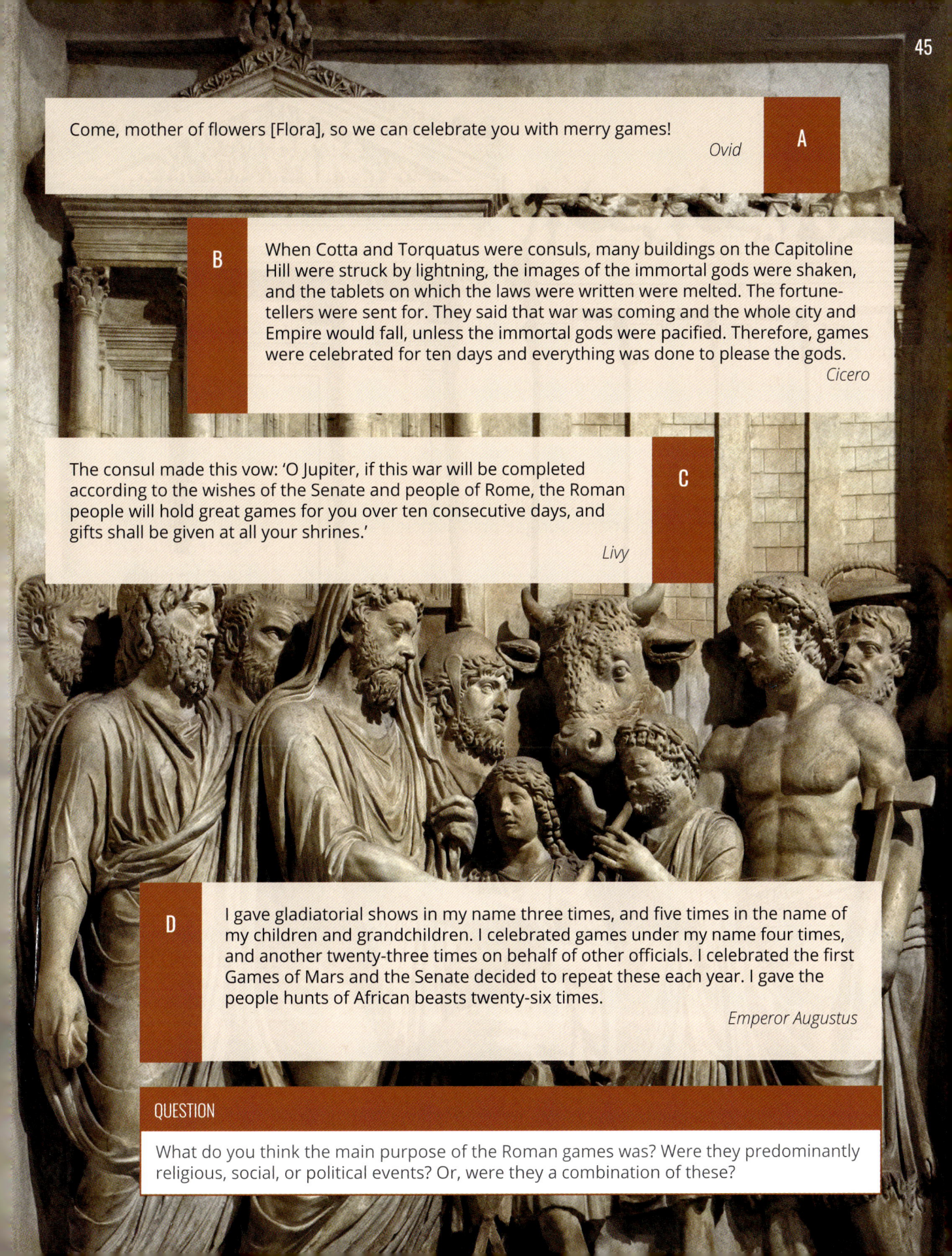

A — Come, mother of flowers [Flora], so we can celebrate you with merry games!
Ovid

B — When Cotta and Torquatus were consuls, many buildings on the Capitoline Hill were struck by lightning, the images of the immortal gods were shaken, and the tablets on which the laws were written were melted. The fortune-tellers were sent for. They said that war was coming and the whole city and Empire would fall, unless the immortal gods were pacified. Therefore, games were celebrated for ten days and everything was done to please the gods.
Cicero

C — The consul made this vow: 'O Jupiter, if this war will be completed according to the wishes of the Senate and people of Rome, the Roman people will hold great games for you over ten consecutive days, and gifts shall be given at all your shrines.'
Livy

D — I gave gladiatorial shows in my name three times, and five times in the name of my children and grandchildren. I celebrated games under my name four times, and another twenty-three times on behalf of other officials. I celebrated the first Games of Mars and the Senate decided to repeat these each year. I gave the people hunts of African beasts twenty-six times.
Emperor Augustus

QUESTION

What do you think the main purpose of the Roman games was? Were they predominantly religious, social, or political events? Or, were they a combination of these?

palma

Faustus est in Circō. Giscō quoque est spectātor in Circō. veterānus Faustum salūtat. turba clāmōsa est.

Giscō	tū pecūniam āmittis?	
Faustus	vah! ego spōnsiōnēs faciō et ego magnam pecūniam āmittō.	
Giscō	īnfēlīx es.	5
Faustus	certē, īnfēlīx sum. albus nōn vincit.	
Giscō	russeus quoque est īnfēlīx. aurīga est mortuus.	
Faustus	lūdī sunt perīculōsī!	

cursus secundus est. quattuor quadrīgae Circum intrant. spectātōrēs quadrīgās vident et maximē clāmant. aurīgae puellās dēlectant. puellae aurīgās laetē spectant.

Faustus	spōnsiōnem facis?	
Giscō	ita vērō. albus est optimus.	
Faustus	quid dīcis?	
Giscō	equī sunt magnificī.	15

Faustus spōnsiōnem iterum facit. spectātōrēs tacent. mappa cadit. aurīgae equōs agitant.

Faustus	vah! albus est nimium lentus.	
Giscō	mēta est. albus trēs equōs maximē agitat, sed ūnum equum retinet.	20
Faustus	hercle! est naufragium! trēs quadrīgae sunt in naufragiō!	
Giscō	albus vincit!	

albus palmam tollit. spectātōrēs magnam clāmōrem tollunt. Faustus tacet. negōtiātor veterānum laetē spectat.

---

palma *palm; victory*

spectātor *spectator*

āmittō *I lose*

albus *white; white team*
russeus *red; red team*
aurīga *charioteer*
mortuus *dead*
lūdī *games, races*
cursus *race*
secundus *second*
quattuor *four*
maximē *very much, a lot*
dēlectō *I please, delight*
laetē *happily, gladly*
ita vērō *yes, absolutely*

iterum *again*
taceō *I am silent, I am quiet*
mappa *cloth, flag*
agitō *I drive, drive on*
lentus *slow*
mēta *turning post*
trēs *three*
ūnus *one*
retineō *I hold back, restrain*
naufragium *crash, wreck*
tollō *I raise, hold up*

LANGUAGE PRACTICE

1. Complete each sentence using the correct form of the nominative noun, then translate.
   a. quattuor .... in Circō sedent. (senātor, senātōrēs)
   b. .... pecūniam habent. (mātrōna, mātrōnae)
   c. .... vīnum bibit. (senex, senēs)
   d. .... per urbem ānxiē ambulant. (ancilla, ancillae)
   e. .... in viā lātrat. (canis, canēs)
   f. .... cibum in forō quaerunt. (puella, puellae)

2. Complete each sentence using the correct form of the verb, then translate.
   a. puellae quadrīgam in Circō .... (spectat, spectant)
   b. Currāx canem in viā .... (audit, audiunt)
   c. dominus meus cellam .... (habet, habent)
   d. in forō .... multī mercātōrēs. (est, sunt)
   e. fīlia Lūcriōnem in īnsulā .... (videt, vident)
   f. frātrēs vīnum in popīnā .... (bibit, bibunt)

Mosaic from Lugdunum (Lyon in modern France), showing a chariot race in a circus. Eight quadrigae are competing, two from each team. The central barrier is a **eurīpus** (channel filled with water), divided into two parts.

Chariot-racing

Chariot-racing was the most popular form of public entertainment in ancient Rome, and attracted huge crowds. Races were held in a circus, an oval-shaped open-air stadium, like a modern athletics track. The Circus Maximus was the largest man-made structure in the Roman Empire and could hold 150,000 spectators.

> One of the finest and most wonderful structures in Rome.
>
> *Dionysius of Halicarnassus*

> The vast facade of the Circus rivals the beauty of the temples. It is a suitable place for a nation which has conquered the world, a sight worth seeing for its own sake as well as for the spectacles presented there … The emperor, as a spectator, shares the public seats as much as he does the spectacle. In this way, Trajan, your subjects can look on you in their turn; they will be able to see not just the imperial box, but the emperor himself, seated amongst his people.
>
> *Pliny*

In this extract from a speech, Pliny praises Emperor Trajan for adding more seats to the Circus Maximus.

QUESTIONS

1. Why do you think Trajan and other emperors provided buildings like the Circus Maximus?
2. Why was it important for the emperor to attend the chariot races?

Box for presiding magistrate

The presiding magistrate sat in a box above the starting gates. He dropped a white cloth (*mappa*) onto the track as a sign that the race was about to start. This was probably followed by a trumpet signal.

carcerēs

At one end of the track were twelve **carcerēs** (starting gates), the stalls where the chariots and horses lined up before the race. Each carcer had a gate. At the start of the race, an attendant pulled a lever which activated a spring mechanism. This pulled out the latches of each gate so that they flew open, all at the same time. Near the carceres were temples, a reminder of the religious associations of the sport.

eurīpus

The area within the centre of the track, called the **eurīpus** (channel), acted as a crash barrier. This is also sometimes known as the *spīna*. It was decorated with statues of the gods; there was also an obelisk, which had been brought from Egypt by Emperor Augustus. At one end were seven wooden eggs and seven bronze dolphins. These were moved to show the spectators which of the seven laps was now in progress.

shops

On the outside of the Circus there was a colonnade with shops and bars.

pulvinar

The emperor had his own box, the *pulvinar*, on the Palatine side of the Circus Maximus. At the end of the procession which preceded the start of the day's events, the images of the gods were taken to the pulvinar, and from there they presided over the games, along with the emperor. This was an opportunity for the emperor to show himself to his subjects and to display his generosity in hosting the games and providing the amenities. In return, people had the opportunity to ask the emperor for favours.

Altar of Consus

Near the *mētae* was an underground altar of the god Consus. This was uncovered only on the days of his festival, the Consualia. Consus was a god of fertility and of horses.

mētae

At either end of the track there were three tall, conical pillars made of gilded bronze. These were the turning posts. The charioteers drove as close as possible to the *mētae* to take the corner and reduce the distance covered, but this was a dangerous tactic. Crashes often occurred at the metae. A crash was called a *naufragium* (shipwreck).

cavea

The spectators were accommodated in three tiers facing each other. The first tier was stone, the second wood. The third tier was probably standing room only. There was a wall separating the track from the front row to protect spectators.

A day at the Circus

The day began with a procession through the streets of Rome. Leading the procession were statues of the gods. Next came magistrates, young noblemen, charioteers, dancers, musicians, incense burners, and temple attendants. After entering the Circus Maximus, the procession circled the track and the statues of the gods were taken to the pulvinar.

When the signal was given, the horses and chariots burst out of the starting gates. Up to twelve chariots, each usually with a team of four horses, driven by a charioteer, charged down the lanes in parallel, going anticlockwise round the track. At a certain marker, they were allowed to cross lanes.

The charioteer would now try to drive his horses as close as possible to the euripus, to shorten his path. Then, at the metae he had to slow down the horses to negotiate the bend.

The charioteer wrapped the reins tightly around his body and used his weight to help him steer. If the chariot crashed, he would be dragged along by the horses and risked death or serious injury, so he carried a knife tucked into his belt to cut himself free from the reins. After seven laps, the trumpet sounded to announce that the winner had crossed the finishing line. He then went up to the judges' box to receive his prize – a palm branch, a wreath, and money – before doing a victory lap.

post lūdōs

spectātōrēs per urbem discēdunt. tōta urbs est clāmōsa. omnēs
viae sunt plēnae. multī spectātōrēs in viā ambulant. lectīcae lentē
prōcēdunt. mendīcī senātōrēs salūtant. servī mendīcōs et spectātōrēs
vituperant. omnēs tabernae sunt plēnae. mercātōrēs mātrōnās
salūtant. mātrōnae mercātōrēs audiunt et tabernās intrant. 5

omnēs popīnae sunt plēnae. amīcī popīnās intrant. ancillae vīnum
portant. amīcī bibunt. fūrēs labōrant. sed Rūfīna et Quārtilla sunt
ānxiae. lūdī Rūfīnam et Quārtillam nōn dēlectant. duo aurīgae ad
popīnam ambulant.

Rūfīna　　mē miseram! 10

aurīgae popīnam intrant.

aurīga　　ohē, popīnāria! ancilla tua est pulchra!
prīmus

aurīga secundus ancillam capit. aurīgae maximē rīdent.

aurīga　　ecce, popīnāria! ego ancillam tuam habeō!
secundus

Catia aurīgam secundum audit. Catia ex īnsulā currit. Catia 15
gladium tenet.

Catia　　quid dīcis?

aurīgae gladium vident. aurīgae sunt perterritī et
ē popīnā currunt. Quārtilla et Rūfīna attonitae sunt.

Catia　　vah! in Britanniā multae fēminae gladiōs habent. 20

---

post *after*

discēdō *I leave, depart*
tōtus *whole*
omnis *all, every*
plēnus *full*
lentē *slowly*
taberna *shop, inn*
audiō *I hear, listen*

duo *two*

ohē! *hey!*
popīnāria *barkeeper*
tuus *your*
pulcher *beautiful, handsome*
capiō *I take, grab*

ex *out of*
gladius *sword*

attonitus *astonished, shocked*
Britannia *Britannia, Britain*
fēmina *woman*

LANGUAGE NOTE 2: ACCUSATIVE PLURAL

1. Compare the accusative singular forms of the first, second, and third declensions:

   veterānus cellam quaerit.
   The veteran is looking for a room.

   ego cibum vēndō.
   I'm selling food.

   tū imperātōrem vidēs?
   Do you see the emperor?

2. In this chapter we have met examples of the accusative plural:

   amīcī popīnās intrant.
   Friends are entering bars.

   in Britanniā multae fēminae gladiōs habent.
   In Britain many women have swords.

   mendīcī senātōrēs salūtant.
   The beggars are greeting the senators.

3. Compare the forms you have now met of the three declensions:

SINGULAR	1st decl.	2nd decl.	3rd decl.
nominative	puella	amīcus	fūr
accusative	puellam	amīcum	fūrem

PLURAL			
nominative	puellae	amīcī	fūrēs
accusative	puellās	amīcōs	fūrēs

4. You may have noticed that, in the third declension, the **-ēs** ending is used for both the nominative and the accusative plural. Look at the following sentence:

   mercātōrēs canēs spectant.

   How do we know whether the merchants are watching the dogs, or the dogs are watching the merchants? Unless there's a strong reason to think otherwise, assume the nominative is first. So this sentence means *The merchants are watching the dogs.*

Charioteers

This mosaic shows four charioteers, one from each of the four teams or factions (*factiōnēs*). They wear tunics in the colour of the team they represent, just like a modern football strip or a jockey's shirt. Their chests are bound with leather straps for protection and they wear helmets, possibly of leather, in their team colours. Each charioteer is holding a whip. Four teams of charioteers competed regularly in Rome: green, blue, red, and white. Each team had its fans. The green team was the most popular with the common people. Juvenal says that some people even clothed their children in green shirts.

Status and fame

Most charioteers were slaves or former slaves. Although they belonged to the lowest class of Roman society, they could win fame and fortune if they were lucky and skilful enough to survive – they were the pop stars and celebrities of their day. A charioteer who started out as a slave could even win enough money to buy his freedom.

> **QUESTION**
>
> Study these sources. What can we learn from them about charioteers and their place in Roman society?

Source 1

From Suetonius' biography of Emperor Caligula:

> He was so devoted and dedicated to the Green team that he often dined in the stable and stayed there. At a party he gave a charioteer called Eutychus a gift of two million sesterces.

Source 2

Pliny the Elder recorded a story he had read about in the 'Daily Records':

> At the funeral of Felix, the charioteer of the Reds, one of his supporters threw himself on the pyre.

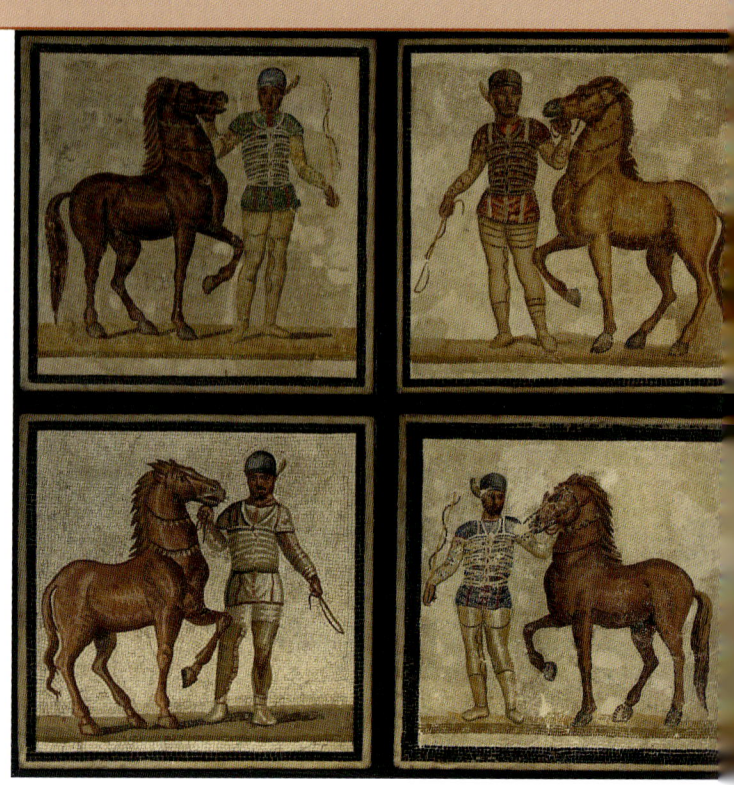

Source 3

An inscription from the tomb of a charioteer called Polynices:

> M. Aurelius Polynices, a home-born slave, lived 29 years, 9 months, and 5 days. He won 739 races, receiving the palm of victory. Of these victories, 655 came with the Red team, 55 with the Green, 12 with the Blue, and 17 with the White. He won 40,000 sesterces 3 times, he won 30,000 sesterces 26 times, and 11 times he won a race with no prize. He raced in an eight-horse chariot 8 times, in a ten-horse chariot 9 times, and in a six-horse chariot 3 times.

Source 4

Martial wrote this poem about the charioteer Scorpus, who had died. Scorpus is speaking:

> **ego sum Scorpus, clāmōsī glōria Circī**
>
> I am Scorpus, the glory of the noisy Circus, your much-applauded, short-lived darling, Rome. Envious Fate snatched me away when I was not yet twenty-seven years old. She counted my victories and thought I was an old man.

LANGUAGE PRACTICE

3. Add the missing endings to the nouns to match the English translations.

   a. Giscō fūr… in īnsulā videt.
   Gisco sees a thief in the apartment block.

   b. Currāx mendīc… in viā audit.
   Currax hears the beggars in the street.

   c. ego mātrōn… prō templō salūtō.
   I greet the ladies in front of the temple.

   d. tū cib… in popīnā habēs?
   Do you have food in the bar?

   e. Rūfīn… Cati… et fīli… salūtat.
   Rufina greets Catia and her son.

   f. sen… serv… et mercātōr… in Circō spectant.
   The old men watch the slaves and the merchants in the Circus.

A terracotta plaque showing a four-horse chariot approaching the metae (the turning posts). The charioteer is wearing leggings, a cap, and a short tunic, with leather straps wrapped round his body for protection. The reins are tied tightly round his waist. A fallen charioteer can be seen at the base of the meta.

Three phases of ruling

The Romans claimed that a Trojan prince, Aeneas, left Troy and settled in Italy. There, his son created a new town, Alba Longa, which his descendants ruled for hundreds of years. One of the kings of Alba Longa had a grandson called Romulus.

Monarchy (753–509 BC)

Romulus founded Rome and was its first king. Six kings succeeded him, until the monarchy came to an end with Tarquinius Superbus (Tarquin the Proud). The seven kings of Rome were Romulus, Numa Pompilius, Tullus Hostilius, Ancus Marcius, Tarquin the Elder, Servius Tullius, and Tarquin the Proud.

The birthplaces of the kings reflect the development of Rome: as the Romans brought nearby Sabine women to be their wives, the early kings alternated between true Romans (Romulus and Tullus Hostilius) and Sabines (Numa Pompilius and Ancus Marcius). Finally, Tarquin the Elder came from Etruria, north of Rome, reflecting Etruscan influence in Rome.

Republic (509–31 BC)

Angry at the behaviour of Tarquin the Elder's son, Tarquin the Proud, a group of wealthy Romans, led by Marcus Junius Brutus, overthrew the monarchy and created a new political system that they called *Rēs Pūblica*, which means 'that which the people control': hence our modern name for it, the Roman Republic. In the new system Rome was governed by both a Senate and the People of Rome.

The Senate was composed of senior, wealthy Roman men, many of whom had been politicians, and they took the political decisions in Rome. The People, in fact, meant only Roman-born male citizens – not women, slaves, or non-citizens.

The People voted for or against laws proposed by the Senate, and each year they elected politicians to run the day-to-day life of the city. The two chief magistrates were the consuls. The politicians belonged to the aristocracy. To prevent the return of one-man rule, the politicians were elected to work in pairs or groups, and there were strict rules to avoid individuals being regularly re-elected to public office.

The system clearly gave more power to the aristocracy than to everyone else, but for centuries it created a very stable form of government. Under the Republic, Rome gradually developed a huge empire.

Empire (31 BC–AD 476)

During the first century BC a weakness in the Republic became apparent. The huge size of the Empire required large armies commanded by powerful generals, and those generals started to want more power. A series of bitter civil wars among its generals plunged Rome into crisis.

The civil wars ended only when one general, Octavian (later called Augustus), was victorious. He changed the Republican system back into rule by one man, becoming Rome's first emperor. As the Romans traditionally did not approve of rule by a single individual, Augustus maintained all the institutions of the Republic (the Senate, the politicians, and the elections). However, he kept for himself the most important positions of power: he was Commander in Chief of the army (*imperātor*), Chief Priest (*pontifex maximus*), and had continuous consular power (chief magistrate for life), among other things. By the time he died, the Romans had become used to this new form of government, and they continued to be ruled by emperors until the collapse of the Empire in the fifth century AD.

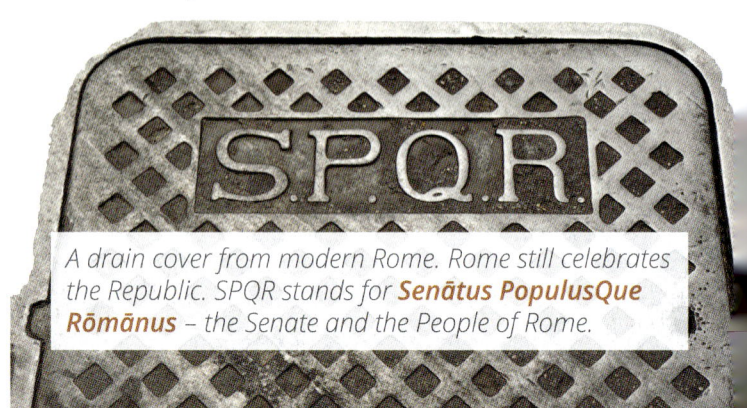

*A drain cover from modern Rome. Rome still celebrates the Republic. SPQR stands for **Senātus PopulusQue Rōmānus** – the Senate and the People of Rome.*

Chapter 4: deī

> The number of divine beings living in the city can be thought of as larger than that of humans.
>
> *Pliny the Elder*

saxum

Mānius īnsulam intrat. Christiānī sunt in īnsulā. Christiānī mendīcum accipiunt. mendīcus Rūfīnam et Quārtillam videt. domina et ancilla Christum adōrant.

subitō saxum per fenestram volitat. Quārtilla saxum tollit.

Quārtilla   est verbum in saxō! 5

Rūfīna verbum legit: 'cavē!'

Mānius   magnum perīculum est, Rūfīna!
Rūfīna   multa perīcula sunt in Subūrā, sed perīcula nōn timeō. Christus est rēx.
Mānius   quid? rēgem nōn habent Rōmānī! 10
Rūfīna   ego Christum sōlum adōrō. Christus caelum regit. rēgnum exspectō. rēgnum advenit.
Mānius   sed deōs Rōmānōs nōn adōrās. perterrita nōn es?
Rūfīna   ego perterrita nōn sum, quod praemium meum est in caelō. Christus multa gaudia nūntiat. gaudium meum est plēnum. 15

subitō fax per fenestram volitat. mendīcus est perterritus.

Mānius   ei! incendium advenit!
Quārtilla   saxa et incendia nōn timeō. Christus est saxum meum. 20

ancilla facem exstinguit. omnēs Christiānī ancillam laudant.

---

saxum *rock, stone*
Christiānus *Christian*
accipiō *I accept, take in, receive*
Christus *Christ*
adōrō *I worship*
fenestra *window*
verbum *word*

perīculum *danger*
timeō *I fear*
rēx *king*
sōlus *only, alone*
caelum *sky, heaven*
regō *I rule*
rēgnum *kingdom*
exspectō *I wait for, expect*
adveniō *I arrive*
deus *god*
quod *because*
praemium *reward*
gaudium *joy, pleasure*
nūntiō *I announce*
fax *torch*
ei! *ai!*
incendium *fire*

exstinguō *I put out*

Christianity

Rufina and Quartilla were Christians. Christianity was a new religion which had originated in the Roman province of Judaea. The earliest followers of Jesus Christ were Jews, but soon Christianity attracted non-Jewish believers and spread outside Judaea. Some of the first Christians, such as Peter and Paul, were in Rome during the reign of Nero, preaching and converting others to Christianity. Their message was that anyone who worshipped Jesus Christ and led a good life would be rewarded with a blessed afterlife. For this reason Christianity appealed to the poor and slaves.

Christians believed that there was only one god: Christianity was a monotheistic religion. Because they did not acknowledge any other gods, Christians refused to participate in the public worship of the Roman state gods. This might explain why the Romans were less tolerant of Christianity, though they generally accepted other religions and embraced new practices.

> the Christians ... a group of individuals given over to a new and harmful set of superstitions.
> *Suetonius*

This Christian funerary monument from AD 313 is decorated with portraits of the early Christians Peter and Paul, who lived in the first century AD.

> The common people called them Christians, and they were hated for their vices. Christus, who gave them their name, had been executed in the reign of Emperor Tiberius, on the order of the procurator Pontius Pilate. The deadly superstition had been suppressed for a while, but was starting to break out again, not only in Judaea, where the evil had originated, but even in Rome itself, to where everything in the world that is foul and shameful flows and becomes popular.
> *Tacitus*

Minucius, a Christian living in the third century AD, lists some of the worst accusations against the Christians (he later refutes all the charges):

> The Christians attract women (since women are weak and gullible) and ignorant men, the dregs of society. They despise the temples and reject the gods, they mock our ceremonies, pity our priests. Why do they make such an effort to hide what they worship? Why do they never speak in public? Why do they never assemble freely, unless they are secretly worshipping something which is either illegal or shameful? They can neither show nor see that god of theirs. Yet they believe that he is present everywhere, and that he looks closely into everyone's character, everyone's actions, their words, even their hidden thoughts.
> *Minucius*

LANGUAGE NOTE 1: 2ND DECLENSION NEUTER NOUNS

1. Most second declension nouns, such as **lūdus** (*game*) and **mendīcus** (*beggar*), are masculine. You have already met their nominative and accusative endings in Chapters 2 and 3.

2. Some second declension nouns, such as **perīculum** (*danger*) and **vīnum** (*wine*), are neuter. Their endings are different from those of the masculine nouns. Study the following sentences:

    vīnum est cārum.
    The wine is expensive.

    Faustus vīnum bibit.
    Faustus is drinking wine.

    In the singular, both the nominative case and the accusative case end **-um**.

    multa perīcula sunt in Subūrā.
    There are many dangers in the Subura.

    ego perīcula nōn timeō.
    I don't fear the dangers.

    In the plural, both the nominative case and the accusative case end **-a**.

3. Compare the endings of masculine and neuter nouns in the second declension:

SINGULAR	game (m.)	beggar (m.)	danger (n.)	wine (n.)
nominative	lūd**us**	mendīc**us**	perīcul**um**	vīn**um**
accusative	lūd**um**	mendīc**um**	perīcul**um**	vīn**um**

PLURAL				
nominative	lūd**ī**	mendīc**ī**	perīcul**a**	vīn**a**
accusative	lūd**ōs**	mendīc**ōs**	perīcul**a**	vīn**a**

Vesta

The goddess Vesta had a shrine in the heart of the city, in the Forum Romanum, where the fire of Vesta was kept burning at all times. If it was ever allowed to go out, it would jeopardize the safety of the entire state. The Romans held a festival in honour of Vesta every June: the Vestalia.

The Vestal Virgins, the priestesses who looked after the fire, were thought to be essential to the prosperity and security of the city. When she became a priestess, a Vestal Virgin took a vow of chastity for thirty years. The Vestals lived in the House of the Vestals, at the foot of the Palatine Hill, and held a special position in Roman society: they were given a place of honour at public games, were considered incorruptible and therefore did not have to take an oath to give evidence in court, and their person was sacrosanct, meaning that anyone who injured them would be condemned to death. However, if a Vestal ever neglected her duty she was beaten, and if she was caught breaking her vow of chastity, she would be punished by being buried alive.

State religion

The Roman state religion was a complex system of religious observances that affected all aspects of public and private life in Rome. At the heart of Roman religion was the need to keep *pāx deōrum*, 'peace with the gods'. This was done by worshipping the many gods that looked after Rome with sacrifices, festivals, rituals at temples, and processions. The most important ceremonies were held publicly, and a large portion of the population would attend. If people did not take part in sufficient numbers, the deity might be offended, and this would disrupt the pax deorum.

The Romans honoured many gods; this kind of religion is called polytheistic. The main gods the Romans worshipped corresponded roughly to the Greek Olympian gods, a group of twelve gods whose statues stood in the Forum Romanum. Their temples survive all over the Empire.

SOURCE 1

Firstly, when determining the nature of the gods, the question presents itself whether they exist or not. 'It's difficult to deny.' Well, I think it is difficult to deny, when speaking publicly, but in a conversation with friends, it would be easy. I myself, as a priest, believe that the ceremonies and public rites should be observed most piously. I should like to be persuaded that the gods exist not only as a matter of opinion, but also as a proven truth.

Cicero

1. What are the reasons for worshipping the gods according to this list? Do people worship gods only in order to get something from them?

SOURCE 2

There are different forms of address to the gods, one form for making requests, another form for averting evil, and another for securing help.[1] We see how our highest officials[2] use certain words for their prayers. So that not a single word should be omitted or said at the wrong time, it is the duty of one person to precede the official by reading the words before him from a written copy[3] and of another person to keep watch on every word, and of a third to see that silence is not broken, which would be a bad omen. Meanwhile a musician plays the flute to prevent anything else being heard.[4] Indeed, there are memorable instances recorded of cases where either the sacrifice has been interrupted and ruined, or a mistake has been made in reading out the prayer.[5]

Pliny the Elder

2. The highest officials (politicians and the emperor) were in charge of the prayers.

3. A priest would read the prayers from a book phrase by phrase, and the official would repeat them.

4. Many prayers would be spoken as part of public ceremonies, so there could be plenty of potential interruptions and noises.

5. If a ritual was performed in any way incorrectly, the officials would start all over again from the beginning.

SOURCE 3

This statue shows Emperor Augustus in his ceremonial robes as the Chief Priest (*pontifex maximus*). From Augustus' time onwards, the emperor took on the role of Pontifex Maximus, putting him in charge of all religious worship in the Empire.

QUESTIONS

1. Why did the Romans participate in the state religion?
2. The Romans did not separate religion from politics. What do you think are the consequences of having no separation between religion and politics?

Vestālia

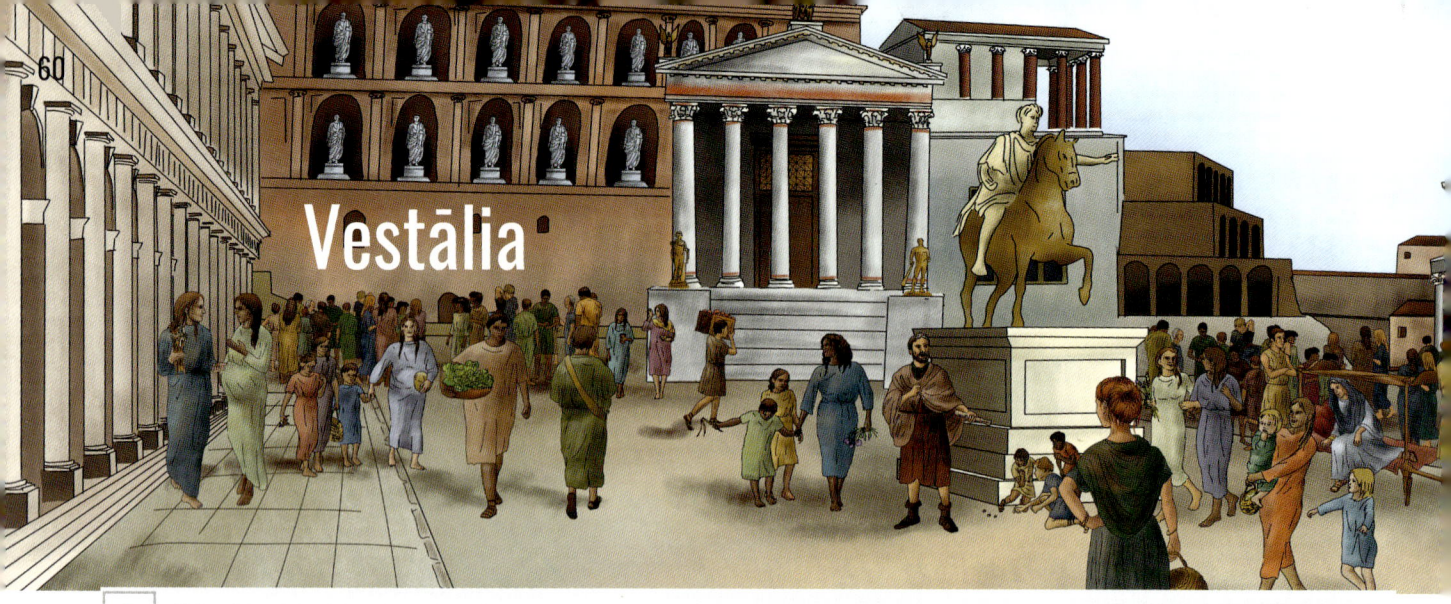

1 diēs fēstus est. Forum Rōmānum est clāmōsum. mātrōnae Rōmānae Vestālia celebrant.

2 tībīcinēs per forum prōcēdunt.

3 tībīcinēs vestīmenta pulchra gerunt. cūr vōs vestīmenta sordida geritis?

nōs vestīmenta sordida gerimus, quod nōs Vestālia celebrāmus. dea Vesta familiās cūrat.

4

5 multa templa sunt in forō.
ūnum templum est rotundum.

6 mātrōnae templum intrant.
virginēs Vestālēs ignem sacrum cūrant.

Chapter 4: deī

7 nōs sumus in Forō Rōmānō.
nōs ad templum prōcēdimus.

8 nōs dōnum portāmus.
omnēs mātrōnae dōna portant.

9 vōs estis in forō.
vōs ad templum venītis?

certē, nōs ad templum venīmus, Cornēlia!
nōs Vestālia spectāmus.

10 ecce! asinī sunt in viā!
vōs asinōs pulchrōs vidētis?

11 stercus quoque est in viā!
cavē stercus, Cornēlia!

LANGUAGE NOTE 2: 'WE' AND 'YOU'

1. Look at these sentences:

   nōs ad templum prōcēdimus. **nōs dōnum portāmus.**
   We are heading to the temple. *We are carrying a gift.*

   vōs vestīmenta sordida geritis. **vōs ad templum venītis?**
   You are wearing dirty clothes. *Are you coming to the temple?*

2. The -**mus** ending of the verb indicates **we** are carrying out the action, and the -**tis** ending shows **you** (plural) are carrying out the action.

3. You have now met the following endings of the verb:

-**ō**	e.g. **labōrō**	*I work, am working*
-**s**	e.g. **vidēs**	*you (singular) see, are seeing*
-**t**	e.g. **dormit**	*he/she/it sleeps, is sleeping*
-**mus**	e.g. **spectāmus**	*we watch, are watching*
-**tis**	e.g. **venītis**	*you (plural) come, are coming*
-**nt**	e.g. **portant**	*they carry, are carrying*

   For example, the endings of the verb **vocō** (*I call*) change as follows:

vocō	*I call, am calling*
vocās	*you (singular) call, are calling*
vocat	*he/she/it calls, is calling*
vocāmus	*we call, are calling*
vocātis	*you (plural) call, are calling*
vocant	*they call, are calling*

4. You have now also met all the forms of **sum** (*I am*):

sum	*I am*
es	*you (singular) are*
est	*he/she is, it is, there is*
sumus	*we are*
estis	*you (plural) are*
sunt	*they are*

Homes of the gods

Temples were considered to be the homes of the gods, their physical residences among men. Inside each temple was a statue of the god, which could be seen from outside when the doors were open. However, the temples were closed most of the time; usually people could not go into them as they were considered sacred spaces. Instead, in front of the temples there were altars for sacrifices and offerings. All kinds of people would bring gifts to the gods at their temples: ordinary people, politicians, wealthy individuals, and heads of foreign states.

The grander and more beautiful a temple was, the more it honoured the god to whom it was dedicated. The interiors were lavishly decorated, even though only priests, temple attendants, and the gods themselves would see them. As well as honouring the gods, the temples fulfilled other functions: the Temple of Saturn held the state treasury; the Temple of Vesta held wills and testaments and documents of state such as treaties; some temples even kept money and valuables safe for private citizens. Sometimes the temples were robbed for the gold and valuables they housed.

Remains of a Roman temple in Nîmes, France. You can see clearly where the inner part of the temple would be closed off. The Romans believed emperors became gods after they died, and they were worshipped along with other gods. This temple was dedicated to the imperial family.

LANGUAGE PRACTICE

1. Complete each Latin sentence with the correct ending from the box below to match the English translation. Use each ending once.

   | -ō | -s | -t | -mus | -tis | -nt |

   a. vōs ignem sacrum in templō cūrā... .
   You look after the sacred fire in the temple.

   b. vestīmenta sordida ger... .
   I'm wearing dirty clothes.

   c. Christiānī deōs Rōmānōs nōn adōra... .
   The Christians don't worship the Roman gods.

   d. ad templum ambulā... .
   We are walking to the temple.

   e. tū sorōrem in forō audī... .
   You hear your sister in the forum.

   f. Sabīna vōs in īnsulā vide... .
   Sabina sees you in the apartment block.

ōmina

pompa Capitōlium ascendit. Lūcīlius est in pompā. magna turba pompam spectat, quod imperātor adest. servī animālia dūcunt. animālia mūgiunt et bālant.

pompa ad templum venit. templum est maximum et optimum. Nerō ē lectīcā dēscendit. turba magnum clāmōrem tollit. 5

turba   iō, Nerō! iō, iō, Nerō! nōs tē amāmus.

prō templō, sacerdōs ūnum animal ad āram dūcit. animal est taurus. taurus caput inclīnat. servus caput percutit. sacerdōs cultrum capit et taurum necat. multus sanguis imperātōrem spargit. sacerdōs exta īnspicit. turba est laeta, quod ōmina sunt optima. 10

Nerō templum intrat et simulācrum adōrat. simulācrum est Iuppiter.

Nerō   ō pater! ō rēx Iuppiter!

Nerō ē templō exit.

turba   nōs sumus fēlīcēs! nōs nūmen vidēmus!

imperātor rīdet. 15

Nerō   vōs estis cīvēs optimī! sed vōs nūmen nōn vidētis. ego nōndum sum deus.

Lūcīlius (susurrāns)   vōs estis īnfēlīcēs. vōs deum nōn vidētis, sed hominem perīculōsum.

ōmen *omen, sign*
pompa *procession*
Capitōlium *the Capitoline Hill*
ascendō *I climb*
animal *animal*
mūgiō *I bellow, moo*
bālō *I bleat*
dēscendō *I climb down*
iō! *ho! hurrah!*
amō *I love*
sacerdōs *priest*
āra *altar*
taurus *bull*
caput *head*
inclīnō *I lower*
percutiō *I strike*
culter *knife*
necō *I kill*
sanguis *blood*
spargō *I shower, spray*
exta *entrails*
īnspiciō *I inspect*
simulācrum *statue, image*
Iuppiter *Jupiter*
nūmen *deity*
cīvis *citizen*
nōndum *not yet*
susurrāns *whispering*
homō *man, person*

Sacrifice

One of the most important ways Romans honoured their gods was by making sacrifices to them. Sacrifices ranged from small offerings of food or wine at a shrine in the home to great public ceremonies where dozens of sacrificial animals were slaughtered at the altars of the temples. Sacrifices made by people in their homes included cakes, grapes, little wreaths, or some incense, accompanied by prayers (often asking for specific favours from the gods). Public sacrifices were held on days of significance in the calendar, or when the help of a particular god was desired. These nearly always involved the slaughter of animals, usually cattle, sheep, and pigs. Gods often had a preference for a particular animal: Jupiter, for instance, usually received a white ox, and Juno a white heifer. Extraordinary circumstances could dictate special sacrifices. During the wars against Hannibal, for instance, the Romans promised Jupiter every single animal born that spring, if he gave them protection for five years. If the gods didn't keep their side of the bargain, the sacrifices were not carried out.

Roman relief showing a bull being sacrificed.

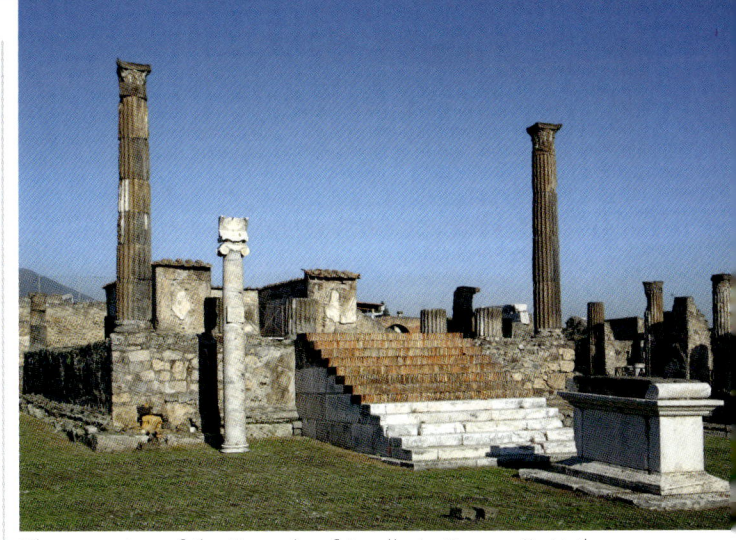

The remains of the Temple of Apollo in Pompeii. At the bottom of the steps leading up to the temple there is an altar, where sacrifices were made.

Animal sacrifices

The same steps were followed meticulously for each sacrifice. If the correct procedure was not followed exactly, the sacrifice could be declared invalid, and the whole ceremony had to be restarted.

1. The animal was consecrated (made holy): to do this the priest in charge sprinkled *mola salsa* (a special mixture of flour and salt prepared by the Vestal Virgins) on the animal's back and wine on its forehead, and passed the sacrificial knife along its back.

2. The animal was slaughtered. A butcher might do this job, or the priest if there was no special butcher available. The animal should consent by lowering its head and showing no panic. For this reason bigger animals like cows would be stunned by a blow to the head first.

3. The animal was laid on its back and its entrails (*exta*) were exposed to the gods, and checked. If no irregularities were found, the sacrifice was deemed successful. However, if there were any abnormalities the sacrifice was aborted and had to restart with a new animal. Sometimes the entrails, especially the liver, were also examined by a soothsayer (*haruspex*). His job was to interpret any omens (messages from the gods).

4. The entrails were then sprinkled with mola salsa and burned on the altar for the gods to receive.

5. The rest of the meat was cooked and eaten in a banquet by the people attending the sacrifice.

LANGUAGE NOTE 3: 3RD DECLENSION NEUTER NOUNS

1. Most third declension nouns are either masculine or feminine. For example, **senātor** (*senator*) is a masculine noun and **nox** (*night*) is feminine. You met the endings of masculine and feminine nouns in Chapters 2 and 3.

2. Some third declension nouns, such as **caput** (*head*) and **animal** (*animal*) are neuter. Their endings are different from those of masculine and feminine nouns. Study the following sentences:

   caput est magnum.
   Its head is large.

   servus caput percutit.
   The slave strikes its head.

   In the singular, both the nominative case and the accusative case have the same form.

   animālia sunt in viā.
   The animals are in the road.

   servī animālia dūcunt.
   Slaves are leading the animals.

   In the plural, both the nominative case and the accusative case end -**a**.

3. Compare the endings of masculine and feminine nouns with neuter nouns in the third declension:

SINGULAR	senator (m.)	night (f.)	head (n.)	animal (n.)
nominative	senātor	nox	caput	animal
accusative	senātōrem	noctem	caput	animal

PLURAL				
nominative	senātōrēs	noctēs	capita	animālia
accusative	senātōrēs	noctēs	capita	animālia

A religious procession from the Ara Pacis.

LANGUAGE PRACTICE

2. Select the correct form of the neuter noun to complete the sentence, then translate.

    a. multa .... in urbe vidēmus.   (forum, fora)
    b. ūnum .... est rotundum.   (templa, templum)
    c. in Subūrā sunt multa ....   (perīcula, perīculum)
    d. quattuor .... ad templum portātis.   (dōnum, dōna)
    e. .... magnum clāmōrem in viā faciunt.   (animālia, animal)
    f. nōs .... tollimus et caelum spectāmus.   (caput, capita)

3. Translate each sentence into Latin by choosing the correct word or phrase from each pair.

    a. *Catia has a sword and hurries to the bar.*
       | Catia | gladium | habēs | sed | ad popīnam | festīnās. |
       | Catiam | gladiōs | habet | et | ad popīnās | festīnat. |

    b. *We are holding gifts and walking to the temple.*
       | vōs | dōnum | tenētis | sed | ad templa | ambulātis. |
       | nōs | dōna | tenēmus | et | ad templum | ambulāmus. |

    c. *You are also coming to the block of flats, because you're looking for a room.*
       | semper | ad īnsulās | vidētis, | quod | cellam | quaerunt. |
       | quoque | ad īnsulam | venītis, | et | cella | quaeritis. |

    d. *The little girls are suddenly running through the city.*
       | parva puella | per urbēs | subitō | currunt. |
       | parvae puellae | per urbem | semper | currit. |

    e. *Nero is present. The crowd is happily praising the emperor.*
       | Nerōnem | adest. | turba | imperātor | lentē | laudāmus. |
       | Nerō | ades. | turbam | imperātōrem | laetē | laudat. |

Private worship

SOURCE 1

May god make Felix Aufidius lucky.
Graffito from Pompeii.

SOURCE 2

At a Roman dinner, after the first course, people used to stay silent until the bit of food that was set aside as an offering was carried to the hearth and put into the fire, and a child had announced that the gods were favourably disposed.
Servius

SOURCE 3

It is the custom of pious travellers, when they pass by a grove or a holy place by the roadside, to say a prayer, to put down an apple as an offering, and to stop for a moment.
Apuleius

SOURCE 4

A statuette of a household god (**Lar**) made from bronze, about 25 cm high.

SOURCE 5

Votive offering of a pregnant woman. Votive offerings were given to the gods in the hope of help (often to cure an illness) or as thanks for a service rendered. This pregnant female terracotta figure suggests that a woman might have made the offering to pray for the safe delivery of her baby.

SOURCE 6

What is more holy, what is more protected by sanctity, than the house of each individual citizen? This is where his altars (**ārae**) are, his hearth fires (**focī**), his household gods, here his sacred rites and ceremonies are held.
Cicero

QUESTION

How do these examples of worship differ from the public rituals of the state religion?

dōna

hōra nōna est. Faustus et fīlia ad īnsulam ambulant. puella servōs vocat.

Sabīna   Lūcriō! Currāx! nōs omnēs ad focum iam convenīmus. vōs dōna habētis?

Lūcriō   certē, nōs dōna habēmus, Sabīna. ecce! dōna sunt tūs et fār et vīnum.   5

familia ad focum convenit. parva simulācra sunt in focō. simulācra sunt Larēs, quod Larēs familiam cūrant. parva lucerna quoque est in focō. Sabīna prope lucernam stat. silentium est. pater vōta facit.

Faustus   vōs Larēs familiam nostram cūrātis. nōs tūs incendimus. nōs fār damus. nōs quoque vīnum …   10

subitō Sabīna clāmat, quod perterrita est.

Sabīna   ei! vestīmenta mea! est incendium!

magnum perīculum est. Lūcriō vīnum iacit et incendium exstinguit. dominus eum laudat, sed ānxius est. ōmina nōn sunt bona.

Faustus   vōta nostra sunt inūtilia. Larēs sunt īrātī.   15

Vocabulary:
- nōnus *ninth*
- ad *at*
- focus *hearth*
- iam *now, already*
- conveniō *I meet*
- tūs *frankincense*
- fār *grain*
- familia *household*
- Lar *household god*
- lucerna *lamp*
- prope *near*
- silentium *silence*
- vōtum *prayer*
- noster *our*
- incendō *I burn*
- iaciō *I throw*
- eum *him*
- bonus *good*
- inūtilis *useless*
- īrātus *angry*

SOURCE 7

*A shrine to the household gods (**larārium**) from a house in Pompeii. A Roman household would have its own lararium.*

Deucalion and Pyrrha

In the earliest times of men, Jupiter, the king of the gods, travelled the earth and saw the impious acts and violent crimes of the human race. In anger he threw down his thunderbolts and released a flood which covered the earth, merging sea and land. Only two people survived, who would recreate the whole human race: Deucalion and his wife, Pyrrha.

- Read or listen to the myth of Deucalion and Pyrrha.

God and man

Ovid was a Roman poet who wrote *The Metamorphoses*, a collection of stories from mythology linked by the theme of transformation. In Ovid's version of the myth of Deucalion and Pyrrha, when Jupiter tells the other gods that he plans to destroy mankind, they are sad. They wonder who will honour their altars with incense. Roman religion was based on the reciprocal relationship between gods and men. Humans offered prayers and sacrifices to the gods, and in return received good fortune from the gods. A lack of offerings and piety would result in punishment.

- Think about other religions. Is there the same reciprocal relationship between gods and men?
- Do you think it is surprising that the gods rely on the offerings of mankind?

Flood myths

Flood myths are common in many cultures around the world. In almost all forms of the myth, the flood is sent by a god or gods as a punishment for mankind. In most versions, after the purge, there is at least one survivor to populate the earth, often after a sacrifice.

- Why do you think the narrative of a flood myth is so common?

SOURCE 1

Look at Source 1. Matsya is one representation of the Hindu god Vishnu. He takes the form of a giant fish with a horn on his head, or he is half-man, half-fish. In the flood myth, he saves Manu by pulling his boat to safety on the top of a mountain.

SOURCE 2

Look at Source 2. In this illustration of the flood myth from the Christian Bible, God watches from above as the flood engulfs mankind.

- How do the depictions of the relationship between god and man differ in the two images?
- How do they compare to the myth of Deucalion and Pyrrha?

Born again

Once Deucalion and Pyrrha had reached safety and thanked the gods with sacrifice, they sought a way to repopulate the earth. They were told they must scatter the bones of their great mother behind them. They understood their great mother was Mother Earth, and threw stones from the ground behind them, from which sprang a new race of men.

SOURCE 3

From here we are a tough race, able to endure hard labour, and so we give proof of the source from which we are sprung.

Ovid

- Look at Source 3. Why do you think the Romans would like the idea that their ancestors were born from stones?

RESEARCH

Find out about:
- Flood myths from other cultures.
- The story of Jupiter and Lycaon.
- The origins of sacrifice.

Chapter 5: aqua

mēns sāna in corpore sānō.
A healthy mind in a healthy body.
Juvenal

febris

nox est calida. nēmō dormit. multī Subūrānī popīnam intrant, ubi
Rūfīna et Quārtilla labōrant. popīna est clāmōsa, quod Subūrānī
bibunt et lūdunt. Subūrānī per diem labōrāre solent, sed per noctem
bibere et lūdere cupiunt. popīnāria et ancilla dormīre cupiunt.
subitō Sabīna appropinquat. 5

'Mānius est aeger, amita!' clāmat Sabīna. 'nōn surgit!'

'quid?' rogat popīnāria. 'ubi est?'

'prope fontem iacet,' respondet puella. 'calidissimus est mendīcus!'

Rūfīna ad fontem venit, ubi Mānius iacet. mendīcus surgere nōn
temptat, quod nimium aeger est. aqua per rīmam fluit et canēs in 10
viā aquam lambunt. Mānius aquam quoque bibere temptat.

nēmō appropinquāre audet, quod mendīcus febrem habet. sed
popīnāria ad Mānium venīre nōn timet. Mānius eam videt et
rīdet. Rūfīna rīdēre cupit, sed lacrimat. lacrimae in mendīcum
cadunt. 15

'valē, Rūfīna,' susurrat Mānius. 'fīnis est.'

mendīcum tollere incipit popīnāria, sed Mānius iam mortuus est.

---

febris *fever*

calidus *hot*
nēmō *no one, nobody*
Subūrānus *inhabitant of the Subura*
lūdō *I play, am at leisure*
soleō *I am accustomed, am used*
cupiō *I want*
appropinquō *I approach*
aeger *sick, ill*
surgō *I get up*
rogō *I ask*
fōns *fountain*
iaceō *I lie down*
respondeō *I reply*
calidissimus *very hot*
temptō *I try*
aqua *water*
fluō *I flow*
lambō *I lick, lap*
audeō *I dare*
eam *her*
lacrimō *I weep, cry*
lacrima *tear*
in (+ acc.) *onto*
valē *goodbye, farewell*
susurrō *I whisper*
fīnis *end*
incipiō *I begin, start*

A public water fountain in Pompeii.

LANGUAGE NOTE 1: 'TO DO' SOMETHING

1. Study the following sentences:

   ego labōrāre temptō.
   I am trying to work.

   Mānius aquam bibere temptat.
   Manius tries to drink the water.

   Rūfīna rīdēre cupit.
   Rufina wants to smile.

   ancilla dormīre cupit.
   The female slave wants to sleep.

2. In each of the Latin sentences above, the verb ending -**re** means 'to do' something. This form of the verb is known as the **infinitive**.

3. The infinitive form of the verb is often found with verbs such as **cupiō** (*I want, desire*), **soleō** (*I am accustomed, used*), **temptō** (*I try*), **audeō** (*I dare*), and **incipiō** (*I begin*).

LANGUAGE PRACTICE

1. Choose the correct form of the verb to complete the sentence, then translate.

   a. Rōmānī rēgem .... nōn solent.   (adōrant, adōrāre, adōrāmus)
   b. vīnum in popīnā .... cupiō.   (bibō, bibunt, bibere)
   c. in Subūrā .... nōn audēs.   (habitāre, habitās, habitāmus)
   d. iuvenēs imperātōrem in forō .... temptant. (audiunt, audiō, audīre)
   e. prīma hōra est, et Sabīna in cellā .... cupit. (legitis, legere, legit)
   f. mendīcī semper in viā .... solent.   (dormiunt, dormīs, dormīre)
   g. nēmō senātōrem īrātum .... audet.   (vituperat, vituperāre, vituperō)
   h. nōs āram prō templō .... temptāmus.   (vidēre, vidēmus, vident)

thermae Nerōniānae

1 Lūcīlius apodȳtērium intrat. hōra octāva est.
Lūcīlius in apodȳtēriō vestīmenta dēpōnit.

2 iuvenis palaestram intrat, ubi amīcōs quaerit.
palaestra est plēna, sed Lūcīlius amīcōs vidēre nōn potest.

3 duo puerī pugnant. Lūcīlius puerōs intentē spectat.

4 ōh! nimium parvus sum. ego pugnāre nōn possum.

5 vah! parvus es, sed Rōmānus. tū vincere potes.

6 Lūcīlius ē palaestrā exit et ad piscīnam ambulat. piscīna quoque est plēna.

7 Lūcīlius est laetus, quod amīcōs audīre potest.

8 amīcī sunt in piscīnā, sed Lūcīlium vidēre nōn possunt. Lūcīlius amīcōs vocat.

9 quid? est Lūcīlius?

in aquā sumus!

nōs tē vidēre nōn possumus!

10 iuvenis currit ...

... et in piscīnam salit.

11 ecce! estis laetī? nunc vōs mē vidēre potestis!

amīcī maximē rīdent.

12 thermae Nerōniānae sunt magnificae.

13 Nerō magnificam domum quoque aedificāre cupit.

14 imperātor novam domum aedificāre nōn potest.

quid dīcis?!

urbs iam est plēna!

15 Nerō omnia facere potest.

LANGUAGE NOTE 2: POSSUM

1. In the picture story **thermae Nerōniānae**, you met all the forms of **possum** (*I am able, I can*). For example:

ego pugnāre nōn possum.	*I am not able to fight.*
Lūcīlius amīcōs audīre potest.	*Lucilius is able to hear his friends.*
vōs mē vidēre potestis.	*You are able to see me.*

   Notice that **possum** is often used with an infinitive.

2. **possum** is made up of the verb **sum** (*I am*) and the adjective **potis** (*able*). Compare the forms of **sum** and **possum**:

sum	*I am*	**pos**sum	*I am able*
es	*you* (singular) *are*	**pot**es	*you* (singular) *are able*
est	*he/she/it is*	**pot**est	*he/she/it is able*
sumus	*we are*	**pos**sumus	*we are able*
estis	*you* (plural) *are*	**pot**estis	*you* (plural) *are able*
sunt	*they are*	**pos**sunt	*they are able*

3. Note that **possum** can be translated as *I am able* or *I can*. For example:

tū vincere potes.		*You are able to win.*
	or	*You can win.*

A bronze statue of a boxer. Note the leather boxing gloves on his hands and the realistic portrayal of his battered face after numerous brutal fights.

The baths

A visit to the baths

Romans believed that regular exercise and bathing were good for health, preventing illness and sometimes providing a cure. A few very wealthy Romans had their own baths at home. But even rich people went to the public baths, because a visit to the baths involved much more than washing. The large *thermae*, such as the Baths of Nero and the Baths of Agrippa, had facilities for sport and leisure activities, including concerts, poetry readings, and lectures. And the baths were a social centre, where you would meet your friends. For many Romans, at least those who had enough free time, a visit to the baths was part of their daily routine.

The working day usually ended at about noon and the main meal was in the late afternoon or early evening. Between midday and evening was the time for visiting the baths. All baths had an *apodȳtērium* (changing room), *frīgidārium* (cold room), *tepidārium* (warm room), and *caldārium* (hot room). Some also had a *palaestra* (exercise ground), a *piscīna* (swimming pool), or a *Lacōnicum* (sauna). There was no set pattern for a visit. Generally, a bather would spend some time in the tepidarium, then go to the caldarium. However, which rooms you went to and which facilities you used would depend on how much time you had, your personal preferences, and, to some extent, how much you could afford. Although entrance to the baths cost very little (and sometimes was even free), some treatments such as massages would be extra.

If you visit Rome, you can see the remains of the huge, elaborate thermae built by the emperors Caracalla and Diocletian in the third and early fourth century AD. Very little now is left of the thermae built by Nero, which Lucilius visits in the story. They opened in AD 62 and were famous for their luxury. The Baths of Nero were on the Campus Martius, near the Baths of Agrippa (named after the friend and adviser of Emperor Augustus); these establishments were open to the public. As well as these large public thermae, there were lots of privately-owned baths all over the city, ranging from the grand and luxurious to the small and grubby, some of them on the ground floor of insulae. This illustration shows a typical bathing complex decorated in the luxurious imperial style.

Who went to the baths?

Most wealthy men would have visited the baths every day. But what about women, the poor, and slaves? Women certainly went to the baths. In the first century AD, men and women could sometimes bathe together unclothed, but it is hard to know how widespread this practice was. There were probably some baths or parts of baths for the use of men or women exclusively, and certain times may have been set aside for women. Some slaves also went to the baths, either to attend their masters or to bathe. As for the poor, they may have bathed less frequently or gone to the baths which had cheaper entrance fees.

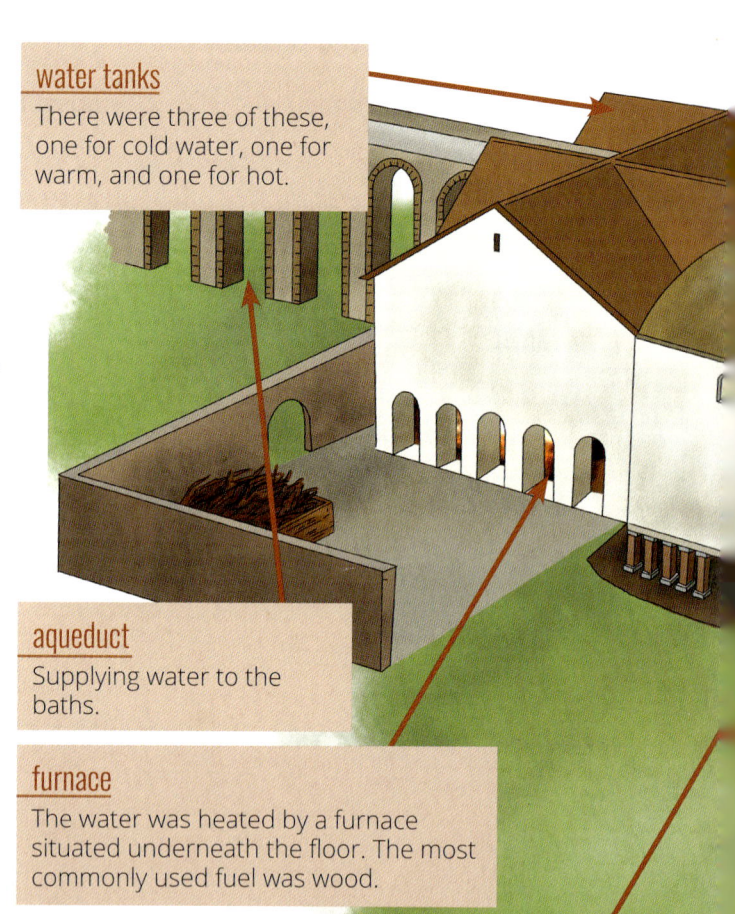

water tanks
There were three of these, one for cold water, one for warm, and one for hot.

aqueduct
Supplying water to the baths.

furnace
The water was heated by a furnace situated underneath the floor. The most commonly used fuel was wood.

Laconicum
A Laconian (Spartan) bath was a hot, dry room, like a sauna, where people would sweat. It had a domed roof, and an opening was left in the centre of the dome. A bronze shield was hung from the top of the dome by chains; this could be lowered and raised to regulate the temperature in the room. The grooves in the ceiling allowed condensation to be channelled down the walls.

Chapter 5: aqua

caldarium
Hot room, with a large, rectangular marble bath, filled with hot water. After sitting and soaking in the hot water, the bather would lie down on a marble slab, either in the caldarium or in an adjoining room. A slave rubbed olive oil into his skin, then scraped off the oil and dirt with a metal instrument called a strigil (*right*). This was followed by a massage. The bather then rinsed himself with water from a stone basin. Finally, if the bather could afford it, he would be anointed with perfume.

apodyterium
Changing room. People undressed here, then gave their clothes to slaves who put them on shelves arranged along the walls. Some people brought a slave to guard their belongings.

piscina
A swimming pool.

latrina
Communal toilet.

frigidarium
The cold room had a circular plunge pool filled with unheated water. Some people finished off their visit to the baths with a dip in the cold pool; others preferred a refreshing cold bath after exercise.

shops and popinae
Visitors to the baths could buy food and drink, and other things they might need for their visit, such as perfume, perfume bottles, and strigils.

tepidarium
Warm room. There were benches around the walls where people could sit and chat while enjoying the warm, steamy atmosphere. Windows high in the walls admitted light and sun.

palaestra
An open space surrounded by a covered walkway. People would go here to exercise before bathing. Exercises included ball games, wrestling, and weightlifting.

peristylium
A covered walkway surrounding the palaestra.

hypocaust
Underfloor heating system. The floor of the baths was suspended on piles of bricks, so that hot air could circulate and provide underfloor heating to the rooms above. Hollow channels in the walls allowed warm air to be drawn up and heat the walls. The Laconicum and the caldarium were nearest to the furnace. The floors of these rooms were so hot that bathers had to wear wooden shoes.

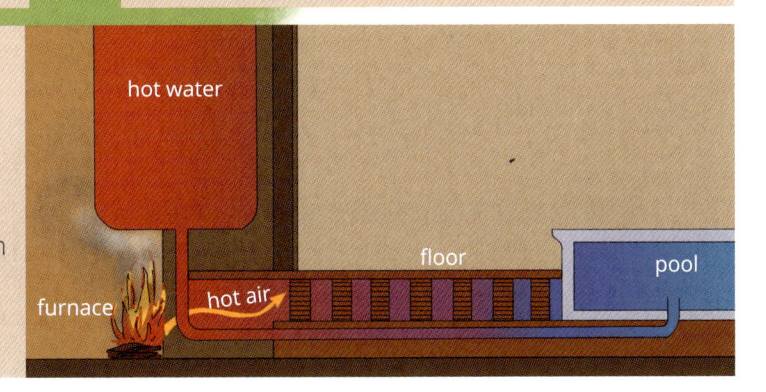

in lātrīnā

Faustus et Giscō lātrīnam vīsitāre cupiunt. Faustus et Giscō lātrīnam intrāre volunt, sed nōn possunt. in lātrīnā mercātōrēs adsunt et negōtium agunt. Subūrānī amīcōs salūtant.

Faustus ego intrāre volō. in viā manēre nōlō!
Giscō certē tū manēre nōn vīs, sed lātrīna est plēna. 5

tandem Giscō et Faustus lātrīnam intrāre possunt. Celer in viā manet.

Faustus ēn, lātrīna est optima. Rōma multās luxuriās habet. tū Rōmae manēre vīs, Giscō?
Giscō vah, Rōma certē est splendida, sed in urbe manēre nōlō. nōs in īnsulā habitāre nōlumus. in fundō rūsticō habitāre volumus. 10
Faustus vērum? Catia Rōmae manēre nōn vult? vōs in Subūrā habitāre nōn vultis, in īnsulā optimā, cum amīcīs optimīs?
Giscō vōs amīcī optimī estis, sed Subūra est perīculōsa. vītam sēcūram volumus. fīlium habēmus … 15
Faustus ego fīliam habeō. Sabīnam prōtegere volō, sed difficile est …
Giscō Sabīna in perīculō est?
Faustus ēheu! senātor aut pecūniam aut fīliam habēre vult …
senex heus! vōs tacēre nōn potestis? compressus sum et nunc quoque ānxius sum! 20

Faustus et Giscō ē lātrīnā exeunt. Celer in viā mingit.

lātrīna toilet

vīsitō I visit
volō I want
negōtium agō I do business
maneō I remain, stay
nōlō I don't want

tandem at last

ēn see!
luxuria luxury
Rōmae in/at Rome
splendidus splendid, sumptuous
fundus farm
rūsticus rural
vērum? really?

vīta life
sēcūrus safe
prōtegō I protect
difficilis difficult

ēheu! oh no! (in despair)
aut … aut … either … or …
heus! hey!
compressus constipated

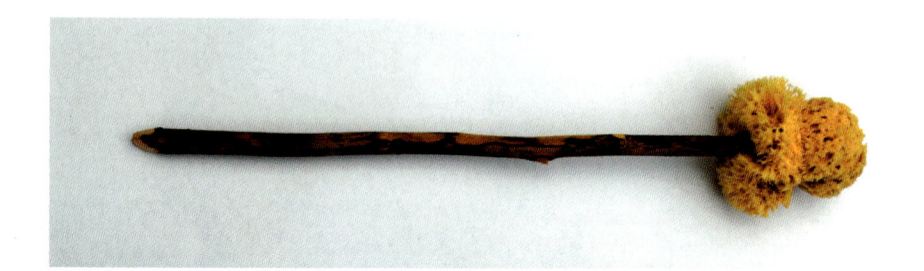

mingō I urinate

*Left: a replica **xylospongium**, sponge on a stick. It's not known whether the Romans used it instead of toilet paper, or to clean the toilet itself.*

QUESTION

What can we learn from this source about the various activities that took place in the baths and the reasons people would visit the baths?

In a letter to a friend, the philosopher Seneca describes the noise from the baths above which he lives:

> I'm surrounded by noise. I live above a set of baths. Imagine the din which makes my ears ache. When the strong lads are working out – or just pretending to work out – I hear their groans as they lift the heavy lead weights, I hear their hissings and harsh gasps as they expel the breath they have been holding in. When my attention turns to an inactive fellow, content with an ordinary, cheap massage, I hear the slap of a hand striking his shoulders. If a ballplayer comes along and begins to count the score, that's it! Add to this, someone starting a fight, and a thief being caught, and someone who likes the sound of his own voice in the bath. Add now, people jumping into the pool with a loud splash. Imagine the shrill cry of the hair-plucker advertising his services by shouting out, and never silent unless he is plucking armpits and making someone else scream for him. Now there's the yelling of the sausage-sellers and cake-sellers and all the bar owners selling their wares, each with his own distinct cry.

Public toilets

Although wealthy Romans had a private toilet in their houses, and some flats probably had toilets on the ground or first floor, most of Rome's population had no access to private facilities; most people had a bucket or pot at home. There were also some public toilets. These had no privacy. People sat next to each other on stone benches arranged in a rectangle or semicircle. Water flowed round their feet in a channel and waste was carried into the sewer.

The public toilets were social spaces where people could chat and issue dinner invitations. We do not know who managed the toilets and cleaned them, and there is no evidence about whether people had to pay to use them.

Instead of toilet paper, Romans may have used a sponge on a stick; after using the sponge they put it into a bucket filled with vinegar or salt water as an antiseptic, ready for the next person to use. Other options would have been dry leaves, scraps of cloth, and even pine cones!

Water supply

> If we consider the distances travelled by the water before it arrives, the raising of arches, the tunnelling of mountains, and the building of level routes across deep valleys, we shall readily admit that there has never been anything more remarkable in the whole world.
>
> Pliny the Elder

In the early days of Rome, people mostly used water from rivers, streams, springs, and wells. Some also collected rainwater from the roofs of buildings in storage jars or tanks under the house.

As the city grew, the Romans constructed aqueducts to bring water from outside sources and springs into the city. The water supplied public baths, fountains, toilets, and some private houses. The aqueducts were an outstanding feat of engineering. They travelled miles, moving the water by gravity alone and maintaining a constant downward gradient. Most of the channels were underground and the Romans used the natural slope of the land as much as possible, sometimes making detours around mountains or valleys to reduce expensive engineering work. Occasionally, however, they tunnelled a direct route through a mountain or crossed huge valleys with multi-arched aqueducts, some of which are still visible today.

Growing demand

By Nero's time Rome was supplied by nine aqueducts which brought into the city an impressive 600,000 m^3 of water every day. This huge volume of water was needed to meet the demand of the hundreds of public fountains and the extravagant public baths which had become a fundamental part of Roman life. The availability of fresh water was abundant even by modern standards. The fresh water gushing day and night from public fountains fulfilled a basic human need and raised the level of hygiene for the entire populace. It also displayed the supremacy of the Romans and their power to control natural resources.

Distribution

When the water reached the city it went straight to water tanks. From here smaller branches of the aqueduct or pipes distributed the water to various public amenities or private houses. Most of the water went to the multitude of public fountains and baths, but individuals could pay to have fresh water piped to their houses. These individuals had to be registered, and paid a fee based on the circumference of the pipe that serviced their property (a fairly inaccurate measure). Tampering and fraud were common, with people illegally tapping the aqueducts or widening their private pipes.

These pipes were often made of lead and some people think that the Romans were affected by lead poisoning. However, because the water flowed constantly and was not still, there was not much build-up of lead in the water. Some pipes would gain a lining of minerals from the water, and therefore were safe from contamination from the lead.

Having water plumbed straight into your house was a luxury few could afford and it was common to find the owner's name cast into the pipe. This inscription translates as 'The most notable lady Valeria Messalina'.

No waste

Any excess from the huge volume of water brought into the city overflowed into Rome's main sewer, the Cloaca Maxima, and into the River Tiber, flushing the city clean of waste.

The remains of the Aqua Claudia, which brought water to Rome. It was completed by Emperor Claudius in AD 52. Its total length was about 43 miles.

LANGUAGE NOTE 3: VOLŌ AND NŌLŌ

1. In the story **in lātrīnā**, you met all the forms of the verb **volō** (*I want, I am willing*). For example:

   ego intrāre volō.
   I want to enter.

   nōs vītam sēcūram volumus.
   We want a safe life.

2. You also saw forms of the verb **nōlō** (*I don't want, I am unwilling*), which is the negative of **volō**. For example:

   ego in urbe manēre nōlō.
   I don't want to stay in the city.

   nōs in īnsulā habitāre nōlumus.
   We don't want to live in an apartment block.

3. Compare the forms of **volō** and **nōlō**. What do you notice about the way **volō** forms its negative?

volō	*I want*	**nōlō**	*I don't want*
vīs	*you* (singular) *want*	**nōn vīs**	*you* (singular) *don't want*
vult	*he/she/it wants*	**nōn vult**	*he/she/it doesn't want*
volumus	*we want*	**nōlumus**	*we don't want*
vultis	*you* (plural) *want*	**nōn vultis**	*you* (plural) *don't want*
volunt	*they want*	**nōlunt**	*they don't want*

   Note that the person endings of **volō** and **nōlō** fit the pattern you met on page 62.

LANGUAGE PRACTICE

2. Complete each sentence by choosing the correct form of the verb, then translate.

   a. pauper sum. multa dōna dare nōn .... (possum, possumus).
   b. Faustus et Lūcriō in īnsulā per diem labōrāre .... (nōn vult, nōlunt).
   c. nēmō sanguinem in viā vidēre .... (vult, volunt).
   d. equum tuum vēndere .... (vīs, vultis), Giscō?
   e. Catia familiam et amīcōs cūrāre .... (potest, possunt).
   f. nōs in viā stāre .... (nōlō, nōlumus). thermās intrāre et negōtium agere .... (volō, volumus).

Sanitation

The Romans went to great lengths to maintain the purity of the water brought into the city. The channels in the aqueducts were covered to prevent contamination from dirt and to keep the water cool. The water was also filtered using settling tanks. However, the quality of water from the nine different aqueducts varied greatly.

When judging the quality of the water, the Romans examined taste, temperature, smell, and appearance. The worst, most dirty water was used for gardens, artificial lakes, and agriculture. The best and purest was used for drinking.

Frontinus was appointed the supervisor of the aqueducts (*cūrātor aquārum*) shortly after the time of our stories. He wrote:

> The job of the curator aquarum is to look after not merely the water supply but also the health and even the safety of the city.

You might assume that, with the aqueducts constantly bringing in fresh water and the Cloaca Maxima flushing away the city's waste, Rome would have been very clean. However, there are records of people on the street being hit by waste thrown from upstairs windows. There is also an inscription from Herculaneum warning that any man caught dumping excrement would be punished.

The Romans also had many practical uses for urine. Far from flushing it away, people were encouraged to relieve themselves or empty their urine into giant clay pots on the street. The collected urine was then put to use in various ways: for cleaning clothes, tanning leather, preparing wool, and even cleaning your teeth! Urine contains ammonia and would actually have worked very well as a cleaning agent.

Eventually, urine became so important as a commodity that Emperor Nero put a tax on the buyers of urine. The phrase *pecūnia nōn olet* (money does not stink), comes from this idea.

A Roman wall painting showing workers in a laundry, hanging clothes to dry.

fuga: pars prīma

multī servī sub thermīs labōrant. calidum et obscūrum est. servī ligna ad fornācēs portant. duo servī susurrant.

'ligna portāre temptō, sed difficile est,' inquit Thellus. 'ligna sunt gravia. mē adiuvāre potes?'

'tē adiuvāre possum,' respondet Galliō. 'et tū mē adiuvāre potes. effugere volō.' 5

'quid? effugere vīs? īnsānus es!' exclāmat Thellus.

'st! custōs tē audīre potest,' Galliō susurrat.

'vah! custōs mē audīre nōn potest. longē abest, et dormīre vult. quōmodo effugere vīs?' rogat Thellus. 10

'per cloācam in aquā sordidā effugere volō,' inquit Galliō. 'sed cloāca portam habet. portam aperīre nōn possum. ūnā tamen eam aperīre possumus.'

'per cloācam effugere nōn potes,' respondet Thellus. 'nimium perīculōsum est. et poenās dare nōlō.' 15

'nēmō tē vidēre potest! obscūrum est! tē ōrō!' susurrat Galliō.

servī portam aperiunt et in cloācam saliunt. custōs sonōrem audit et canēs vocat. canēs vehementer lātrant et servōs per cloācam agitant. Thellus et Galliō canēs audiunt et per tenebrās celeriter currunt.

fuga	*escape*
pars	*part*
sub	*below*
lignum	*log, wood*
fornāx	*furnace*
inquit	*says*
gravis	*heavy*
adiuvō	*I help*
effugiō	*I flee, escape*
īnsānus	*mad, insane*
exclāmō	*I exclaim*
custōs	*guard*
longē	*far off*
absum	*I am away*
quōmodo?	*how?*
cloāca	*sewer*
porta	*gate, grate*
aperiō	*I open*
ūnā	*together*
tamen	*however*
eam	*it*
poenās dō	*I pay the penalty, I am punished*
ōrō	*I beg*
sonor	*noise*
vehementer	*loudly*
tenebrae	*darkness*
celeriter	*quickly*

A Roman hypocaust (underfloor heating system). On the left you can see where the hot air would have flowed through from the furnace.

Rome under attack!

Was Rome always mighty?

For most of its history Rome was at the heart of a vast empire, which kept peace within its borders and successfully defeated external enemies. However, there were moments at which the city of Rome was in danger of disappearing: what made Rome vulnerable?

Marauding Gauls

In 387 BC the Senones, a band of Gauls from northern Italy, defeated the Roman army near Rome, leaving the city almost entirely unprotected. The Romans decided to save what they could of the city: men of fighting age, women, and children took a last stand on the Capitoline Hill. The rest either fled to surrounding villages or, if they were too infirm to move, were left undefended to meet their death.

When the Gauls entered the city, it was quiet and almost empty. They burned and looted what was at hand and killed many of the people still in the city. Then they laid siege to the Capitol. Eventually the Romans were starving and unable to resist any longer. The Gauls and Romans came to an agreement: the Romans would pay 1,000 pounds in weight of gold and the Gauls would go home. The humiliation inflicted by the Gauls was never totally forgotten.

Rome moved on to be the mighty empire we all know, and the city was never attacked again, until ...

The Visigoths

AD 408. The Roman Empire was now in decline. The city of Rome was no longer the capital of the Empire. There were two emperors ruling two halves of the Empire: Emperor Honorius, based in Ravenna (in Italy), was in charge of the West, and his brother Arcadius ruled the East from Constantinople (in modern Turkey).

Groups of Germanic tribes had been slowly infiltrating the Roman Empire. One group, the Visigoths, led by Alaric, crossed into Italy without any difficulties and laid siege to Rome itself. Starving, the people of Rome decided to negotiate for peace. Alaric was not merciful: according to the historian Zosimus, he asked for 'all the gold and silver in the city, all the household goods, and the foreign slaves'. When asked what would be left for the citizens, he replied 'their lives'.

The final payment to liberate Rome was 5,000 pounds of gold and 30,000 of silver, 4,000 silk robes, 3,000 scarlet fleeces, 3,000 pounds of pepper, and some hostages. To pay the sum, individuals had to hand over most of their possessions, but that was still not enough. So the Romans took many of the robes and decorations from the old statues of the gods and even melted some of them down. The siege was lifted, although the peace was not concluded, as the hostages had not been sent to Alaric. He ransacked many of Rome's monuments and enslaved many of its citizens, including the emperor's sister, Galla Placidia.

Rome was sacked again by another foreign people, the Vandals, in AD 455. The Western Empire finally collapsed when Odoacer, an Ostrogoth, removed the last emperor of Rome, Romulus Augustulus, and declared himself King of Italy in 476.

Brennus, the leader of the Gauls, weighs out the spoils.

Chapter 6: servitium

dē cellā

mediā nocte familia dē cellā dēscendit.
marītus sarcinās portat et uxor līberōs dūcit.
omnēs tacitē prōcēdere temptant.

mediā	middle, middle of
dē	from, down from
sarcina	bag
līberī	children
tacitē	quietly, silently

BAU AU
BAU AU AU

sed Celer familiam audit et lātrat. Faustus surgit, et
marītum cum sarcinīs et uxōrem cum līberīs videt.
'ohē!' clāmat Faustus. 'quō festīnātis?'   5
'in cellā obscūrā et sordidā manēre nōn possumus,'
respondet marītus.
'columbae per rīmam volitant et mūrēs per iānuam
currunt.'   10
'cum columbīs et mūribus habitāre nōlumus,' inquit uxor.
'sed pēnsiōnem dēbētis!' clāmat Faustus.
marītus et uxor nihil dīcunt, sed celeriter discēdunt.

quō?	where ... to?
nihil	nothing

hōrā prīmā Faustus cum Lūcriōne ad cellam
ascendit. Lūcriō īnstrūmenta portat.
negōtiātor et servus tēctum reficere
temptant. Celer quoque in cellā labōrat.
canis mūrēs capere temptat.

īnstrūmentum *instrument, tool*
tēctum *roof*
reficiō *I repair*

hōrā quīntā Faustus clāmōrem in viā audit.
magnus servus prō popīnā stat, ubi Sabīna cum ancillā labōrat.

quīntus *fifth*

ubi est pater tuus?

dominus meus pēnsiōnem annuam exspectat.

annuus *yearly, annual*

Sabīna nōn respondet.

servus circumspectat, sed Faustum vidēre nōn potest.
'negōtiātor!' clāmat servus. 'tribus diēbus pecūniam
exspectō!'
servus īrātus Sabīnam intentē spectat.
'pater tuus magnam pecūniam dēbet,' inquit servus.
'es in magnō perīculō!'

circumspectō *I look around*

LANGUAGE NOTE 1: THE ABLATIVE CASE

1. Since Chapter 1 you have been reading sentences like these:

   ego in viā ambulō.
   I am walking in the street.

   Sabīna ē forō currit.
   Sabina runs out of the forum.

   Faustus cum Lūcriōne exit.
   Faustus leaves with Lucrio.

   In this chapter, you have met sentences such as these:

   uxor cum līberīs discēdit.
   The wife is leaving with her children.

   cum columbīs et mūribus habitāre nōlumus.
   We don't want to live with doves and rats.

2. The words in red above are in the **ablative** case. The ablative case is used in a variety of situations. For example, it can be used to mark the place of departure, e.g. **ē forō** (*out of the forum*) or to mark the objects or people with which something happens e.g. **cum līberīs** (*with her children*). The ablative can often be represented in English as *from*, *with*, or *by*.

3. You have now met the following noun endings:

SINGULAR	1st decl.	2nd decl.		3rd decl.	
nominative	puell**a**	amīc**us**	dōn**um**	fūr	caput
accusative	puell**am**	amīc**um**	dōn**um**	fūr**em**	caput
ablative	puell**ā**	amīc**ō**	dōn**ō**	fūr**e**	capit**e**

PLURAL					
nominative	puell**ae**	amīc**ī**	dōn**a**	fūr**ēs**	capit**a**
accusative	puell**ās**	amīc**ōs**	dōn**a**	fūr**ēs**	capit**a**
ablative	puell**īs**	amīc**īs**	dōn**īs**	fūr**ibus**	capit**ibus**

Currāx et Quārtilla

hōrā septimā Currāx et Celer prope popīnam sedent. hodiē Currāx est trīstis et canem mulcet. canis puerum lambit.

Quārtilla Currācem videt et eum ānxiē vocat.

'cūr trīstis es, Currāx?' rogat Quārtilla.

'Giscō et Catia mox ex urbe discēdere volunt,' respondet puer. 'trīstis sum, quod Celer discēdit. Celer amīcus meus est.' 5

'tū multōs amīcōs habēs. ego, māter tua, tē amō, et Faustus ... apud Faustum sēcūrus es,' inquit ancilla.

'māter mea es, sed in popīnā tōtum diem labōrās,' clāmat Currāx. 'in viīs tōtum diem labōrō. nōn sumus hominēs, sed īnstrūmenta.' 10

'st!' susurrat Quārtilla. 'Faustus familiam optimē cūrat et cum Lūcriōne strēnuē labōrat. Sabīna et Rūfīna multās hōrās quoque labōrant. dūra sunt tempora. nōs omnēs diem et noctem labōrāmus.'

'ego nōn sum asinus, māter. Faustus nōn nōs cūrat. Faustus nōs tenet. Rūfīna tē pulsat. ego effugere volō. ego lībertātem volō.' 15

'minimē! perīculōsum est effugere. sī servus effugere temptat ...

subitō vir ad popīnam advenit et Quārtillam intentē spectat. vir, Septimus nōmine, clāmat,

'Rūfīna, vīsne ancillam tuam vēndere?'

---

septimus *seventh*
hodiē *today*
trīstis *sad*

mox *soon*

māter *mother*
apud *at the house of*

optimē *very well*
strēnuē *strenuously, hard*
dūrus *hard, harsh*
tempus *time*
pulsō *I beat, hit*
lībertās *freedom*
sī *if*
vir *man*
nōmen *name*

Slavery in the Roman world

A slave was the property of his or her enslaver, regarded as a commodity that could be bought or sold like a cow or a donkey. Enslaved people had no liberty and no rights. They could not leave their employment and they could not choose what to do, but had to obey the orders of their master. Slave owners had complete control over their slaves, even the power of life and death.

Enslaved people had no right to a family life, were not allowed to marry, and could not own property. They did not even keep their own name; the enslaver would choose a new name for them. In this way, the enslaved person suffered a total lack of freedom and loss of identity.

Enslaved people had many different ethnic backgrounds and were born in various places, including the countries and regions we now call Italy, France, Britain, Spain, Germany, Greece, Egypt, North Africa, and Turkey. They weren't distinguished from free people by skin colour or race, or even by dress or occupation. Slaves and free people often worked alongside each other.

Although the living conditions of slaves varied, what did not vary was the acceptance of slavery. The Romans, and other people who lived around the Mediterranean, regarded slavery as a normal part of life, and there was no movement to abolish it. Even some former slaves would, once they became free, buy slaves of their own.

Slave or servant?

Many enslaved people, like Currax, Quartilla, and Lucrio, were part of a *familia*. This was not the same as a modern family. The Latin word, familia, means household, i.e. all who live in the house. Household slaves lived in their enslaver's house and did the work of domestic servants: cooking, cleaning, attending to the owners of the house, and looking after children. Some worked in a trade or business for or alongside their enslaver.

How were people enslaved?

1. Prisoners of war

The Romans believed that they had the right to enslave people they captured in war. In the second and first centuries BC, Rome was expanding its territory and acquiring an empire. Roman armies captured vast numbers of people in war and took them to Rome to be sold as slaves. The geographer Strabo records one such event from 167 BC:

> Aemilius Paullus [a Roman general] captured seventy cities in Epirus [in Greece] and enslaved 150,000 human beings.

Prisoners of war continued to be a source of slaves, although not in such large numbers. In the first century AD Rome was still conquering territory overseas and enslaving the conquered peoples. After the sack of Jerusalem in AD 70, the victorious Roman army captured thousands of Jews, enslaved them, and brought them to Rome.

Rome

2. Pirates and kidnappers

Some people were enslaved as a result of being captured by pirates or bandits. Pirates took their victims to slave markets, such as one on the island of Delos in the eastern Mediterranean. Slave traders then brought the slaves to Rome and other parts of the Empire. Slave traders also brought slaves from outside the Roman world, for example from sub-Saharan Africa and the region which is now Russia, but these would have formed only a small proportion of the slaves in Rome.

Strabo wrote:

> The slave trade was very profitable, because it was easy to capture slaves. Delos was a large and very rich market, with the capacity to receive and export thousands of slaves in a single day. The reason for this growth in the slave trade is that the Romans had become rich after the destruction of Carthage and Corinth, and began to use large numbers of slaves. The pirates saw how easy it was to make money in this way, so they sprang up all over the place, making raids and trading in slaves.

3. Born a slave

Children of female slaves automatically became slaves themselves. These home-born slaves were known as **vernae**. The Romans regarded vernae as the property of the enslaver. The mother of the child had no rights. The enslaver could decide to sell the mother or the child and thus separate them from each other.

4. Abandoned children

Parents who couldn't afford or didn't want to bring up their children sometimes abandoned babies in rubbish heaps, at crossroads, or in other public places. Anyone could take the infant to bring up as a slave. Even after many years as a slave, a freeborn Roman could legally claim freedom. This would be difficult to prove, but there is some evidence that it did happen.

5. Choosing slavery

Some desperate people even sold themselves into slavery because of extreme poverty or debt. There was no welfare system in the Roman world and for some people life as a slave might have seemed preferable to being a homeless beggar.

The slave market

When a Roman wanted to buy a new slave he might go to the slave market. Every town would have a slave market. There were two in Rome. One was in the Forum Romanum, behind the Senate House. The other was in the Campus Martius. The poet Horace gives an idea of what a slave market might have been like. He imagines a slave dealer speaking to a potential buyer:

> This boy is fair and handsome from head to toe. He can be yours for 8,000 sesterces. A home-born slave, obedient to his master. He has some knowledge of Greek – he's equipped for any art. With moist clay like this you can mould anything! What's more, he will sing – his voice is untrained but it will be a pleasant accompaniment when you are drinking … None of the slave dealers would do this deal for you. And I wouldn't do this favour for everyone.

QUESTIONS

1. What good qualities of the boy does the slave dealer point out?
2. What does this passage tell us about the way Romans regarded the people they enslaved?

LANGUAGE NOTE 2: PREPOSITIONS

1. Study the following sentences:

   Sabīna per urbem festīnat.
   Sabina hurries through the city.

   Mānius est prope fontem.
   Manius is near the fountain.

   Rūfīna ē popīnā currit.
   Rufina runs out of the bar.

   familia dē cellā dēscendit.
   The family comes down from their room.

   Words such as **per** (*through*), **prope** (*near*), **ē** (*from, out of*), and **dē** (*from, down from*) are known as **prepositions**.

2. Some prepositions, such as **per** and **prope**, are followed by the accusative case; others, such as **dē** and **ē**, are followed by the ablative case.

3. You have already met the following prepositions:

   Prepositions + accusative

ad	to, towards
apud	at the house of, among
in	into, onto
per	through
post	after, behind
prope	near

   Prepositions + ablative

ā, ab	by, from
cum	with
dē	from, down from
ē, ex	from, out of
in	in, on
prō	in front of

4. Note that the meaning of **in** depends on whether it is followed by the accusative or the ablative case:

   Faustus **in viam** ambulat.
   Faustus walks into the street.

   Faustus **in viā** ambulat.
   Faustus walks in the street.

Mosaic from Dougga, Tunisia, showing slaves serving food and drink at a Roman feast.

The life of a slave

It is difficult to imagine what life was like for an enslaved person in the Roman world. Almost all the evidence we have is written by enslavers and shows their point of view. The lives of slaves and the extent of the physical suffering they had to endure varied depending on their masters and the type of work the slaves did. Not all enslaved people worked in a household as Currax, Quartilla, and Lucrio did. In the city, some worked in industry or were public slaves. For example, crews of slaves owned by the state looked after the aqueducts and the water supply or worked in public buildings such as temples. In the countryside, many slaves were agricultural labourers. And in provinces such as Spain and Britain, slaves worked in the mines.

On the farms

Wealthy Romans often had huge estates in the countryside outside Rome and in the provinces. Enslaved people managed and farmed these estates. Columella, in a handbook on agriculture, advised how to treat slaves on an estate:

> All careful masters inspect the slaves in the farm prison, to check whether they are properly chained and whether the building is secure. I reward slaves who are hardworking and obedient. To female slaves who have had children I have given time off from work, and sometimes even freedom after they raised several children.

An educated slave

The Romans admired the cultures of some of the nations they had conquered, especially the Greeks. Enslaved Greeks were often skilled workers, such as teachers, doctors, and librarians. In this letter, Pliny praises a slave and worries about his health:

> Encolpius, my reader and a favourite of mine, is sick. How grim it will be for him and what a bitter blow to me if he is unable to study, since studying is his chief accomplishment. Who will read my books and take such pleasure in them as he does?

Domestic slaves

Slaves working in a household were often the victims of brutality, as Romans believed they had the right to punish their slaves with violence. Some Romans were extremely cruel towards their slaves. Seneca records that Emperor Augustus was having dinner with Vedius Pollio when one of Vedius' slaves broke a crystal cup:

> Vedius ordered the slave to be seized and executed in a particularly bizarre way, by being thrown as food to lampreys – he kept some huge ones in his fish pond. Why did he do this? Just to show off his wealth? It was an act of savagery.

At the other extreme, some Romans felt affection for their slaves. Martial wrote this poem expressing his grief for the death of the home-born slave (*vernula*, little verna) he called Erotion:

> Erotion is still warm on her funeral pyre. The cruel law of the Fates has carried her off, my love, my joy, my delight, with her sixth year not yet complete.

In the mines

The worst conditions for enslaved people were in provinces such as Spain and Britain where they worked in the mines. The historian Diodorus Siculus described the terrible sufferings of the people working in the mines in Spain:

> These men exhaust their bodies by working underground day and night, and the mortality rate is high because of the terrible conditions. They are not allowed to pause or rest – the supervisors beat them to force them to continue working. They throw away their lives as a result of these terrible hardships. Some of them survive because of their physical stamina or willpower, and endure their misery for a long time but, because of the extent of their suffering, they prefer death to life.

QUESTION

Although the conditions of their lives varied, what did all enslaved people have in common?

epistula

in Siciliā, Kalendīs Iūliīs, C. Liciniō C. Laecāniō cōnsulibus.

Lūcīlius fīlium Lūcīlium salūtat.

in Siciliā maneō, et prōvinciam administrō. Sicilia nōn est prōvincia magna, et multōs diēs librōs scrībere possum. multās hōrās philosophiam, historiam, et epistulās ab amīcīs legō.

sed epistulae ab urbe mē ānxium faciunt.

amīcōs habēmus et in urbe et in prōvinciīs. multī mē monent. quid facit imperātor, et quid vult facere? Nerō aedificāre cupit sed urbs est plēna. domus nostra est sēcūra?

in temporibus dūrīs vīvimus. imperātor est perīculōsus, perīculōsa est urbs.

lēgātus in Lūsitāniā, nōmine Othō, tribūnum quaerit. tū es iuvenis sapiēns, et tribūnus optimus esse potes. tē iubeō ab urbe statim discēdere, et in Lūsitāniam iter facere. Othō Īdibus Augustīs tēcum convenīre vult.

servī et lībertī fidēlēs domum nostram in urbe administrāre possunt.

valē.

epistula *letter*	ab *from*	iubeō *I order*
cōnsul *consul (leading politician)*	et ... et ... *both ... and ...*	statim *immediately*
prōvincia *province*	moneō *I advise, warn*	iter *journey*
administrō *I manage, administer*	vīvō *I live*	tēcum = cum tē
liber *book*	lēgātus *governor*	lībertus *former slave, freedman*
scrībō *I write*	tribūnus *tribune (officer in the army)*	fidēlis *faithful*
philosophia *philosophy*	sapiēns *wise*	
historia *history*	esse *to be*	

Dates

Kalends: *1st day of the month.*
Ides: *13th or 15th day of the month, depending on the month. In August the Ides were the 13th.*

Romans referred to the year by the names of the two men who were consuls at the time. The consuls held this office for just one year. **Gaius Licinius** and **Gaius Laecanius** were consuls in AD 64.

Lucilius senior

We know about the existence of the older Lucilius through his correspondence with Seneca, the philosopher and adviser to Nero. Their letters are largely about philosophy. In AD 64 Lucilius was governor of the province of Sicily. Lucilius was originally from the Bay of Naples, and he may have written a book on volcanic activity in Sicily called *The Aetna*.

Otho (below)

Otho had been a friend of Nero's but the two had fallen out over Nero's desire to marry Otho's wife, Poppaea. After Poppaea and Otho's divorce, Otho was sent to Lusitania to govern the province, and Poppaea became the new empress of Rome.

Roman letters: epistulae

Romans did not have paper. They usually wrote their letters on papyrus, a material made from reeds grown in Egypt. A well-off man like Lucilius senior probably dictated his letters to a slave. Once the letter was written the papyrus was rolled into a scroll and sealed with wax. Then a slave or freedman took his letters to their recipients across the Empire, to ensure their safe arrival.

Most Latin letters had the same format as modern letters:

1. **date of writing**
   Particularly relevant as post could take a long time to arrive.

2. **a greeting**
   More or less formal, depending on whom one wrote to. What might seem unusual to us is that the greeting might be written in the third person: 'Lucilius greets his son', rather than 'Dear Lucilius'.
   Other examples:
   ◊ **Sabīna salūtem plūrimam dīcit.**
   Sabina sends many greetings.
   ◊ **sī valēs bene est. ego valeō.**
   (can be abbreviated to: SVBEEV)
   If you are well, it is good. I am well.

3. **a farewell**
   There were a number of standard phrases to end a letter, and they could be formal or affectionate.
   Commonly used were:
   ◊ **valē** *goodbye, be well*
   ◊ **optimē valē** *be very well*
   ◊ **cūrā ut valeās** *take care that you are well*

QUESTIONS

1. On which day was the letter written? (line 1)
2. a. Who is writing the letter?
   b. Where is he sending it from?
   c. Who is he writing to?
3. What does Lucilius senior's life seem like, according to the first paragraph of his letter? (lines 3–5)
4. What concerns does Lucilius senior have? (lines 6–11)
5. What is meant to happen on the Ides of August? (lines 14–15)

EXTENSION ACTIVITY

6. Investigate the speed at which letters and people could travel in the Roman world.

fuga: pars secunda

Thellus et Galliō per cloācam currunt. subitō Galliō cadit. servus surgere nōn potest. capiunt eum canēs. Galliō frūstrā pugnāre temptat. fīnis est. servus effugere nōn potest.

procul Thellus comitem vocat. nēmō respondet. servus ē cloācā festīnat et in flūmen salit.

in carcere, custōdēs servum torquent.

'ubi est Thellus?' postulat custōs.

'Thellus est mortuus,' Galliō susurrat.

'Thellus nōn est mortuus. ubi est?' custōs iterum postulat.

'mortuus est,' inquit Galliō. 'corpus in flūmine est.'

'mendāx es,' respondet custōs.

custōdēs servum duās hōrās torquent. tertiā hōrā, custōdēs cautērium ē fornāce extrahunt. cautērium ad Galliōnem portant et caput notant. dolor est intolerābilis. in capite sunt trēs litterae.

trēs diēs et trēs noctēs, Thellus fugit. quārtō diē servus in agrō dormit. hōrā prīmā, duo agricolae eum vident. agricolae Thellum capiunt et eum ad custōdēs dūcunt. custōdēs rīdent. Thellus perterritus est.

frūstrā *in vain, without success*
procul *far off*
5 **comes** *companion, comrade*
in (+ acc.) *into*
flūmen *river*
carcer *prison*
torqueō *I torture*
postulō *I demand*
10 **corpus** *body*

tertius *third*
cautērium *branding iron*
extrahō *I pull out*
notō *I mark*
15 **dolor** *pain*
intolerābilis *unbearable*
littera *letter*
fugiō *I flee*
quārtus *fourth*
ager *field*
agricola *farmer*

Marble relief from Smyrna, in modern Turkey. The two men on the right have been enslaved. They are in chains connected by neck collars.

Seeking freedom

> You have as many enemies as you have slaves.
>
> This Roman proverb is quoted by Seneca. He tells us that the Senate discussed whether all slaves should be dressed in the same way. The senators rejected the proposal, because they feared what would happen if slaves recognized how great their numbers were.

Slave revolts

Large-scale slave rebellions were rare, but when they occurred they could be serious. There were three major slave revolts in the second and first centuries BC. These revolts occurred not in Rome itself, but in Sicily and southern Italy. The most famous was one led by Spartacus, which lasted two years, from 73 to 71 BC. Spartacus and some of his fellow slaves escaped from a gladiator school in Capua, where they were being trained to fight as gladiators (men who fought to entertain an audience), and were then joined by slaves from the large farms in the region. The slaves were eventually defeated by forces from the Roman army.

> The slaves continued to resist until all of them were killed, except for 6,000 who were captured and crucified along the road from Capua to Rome. *Appian*

There is no evidence that any of these slave revolts had the aim of abolishing slavery. The aim of the slaves who rebelled may have been to gain freedom for themselves. However, we have no access to the thoughts and motives of Spartacus and his fellow freedom seekers. The only evidence is the writings of the enslavers.

Running away and resistance

On a much smaller scale, slaves put up resistance in their daily lives by working inefficiently, stealing, or other forms of disruption – if they could do so undetected. Many slaves sought freedom by running away. Some slave owners employed professionals to look for slaves who had sought their freedom, or offered rewards for their return. Others relied on religion or friends:

> Nowadays we believe that our Vestal Virgins have the power by their prayers to make runaway slaves stay where they are as long as they have not gone outside the city. *Pliny the Elder*

In one of his letters, Cicero wrote to a friend asking for help in returning a slave who had sought freedom:

> Dionysius, my slave who looked after my very valuable library, has stolen a large number of books. He thought that he would be punished, so he has run away. He is in your province. My friend Marcus Bolanus and many others have seen him at Narona; but he said that he had been freed by me, and they believed him. If you would arrange for this man to be brought back to me, I can't tell you how grateful I shall be to you. It is an unimportant matter in itself; yet my annoyance is serious.

If they were caught, slaves who had tried to gain their freedom by running away risked harsh punishment: branding on the face, wearing a collar, even death, as Tacitus describes:

> The man was asked his identity. As his statement did not ring true and he was recognized by his master as a runaway slave called Geta, he was crucified, the usual manner of execution for slaves.

Some enslaved people were forced to wear metal collars such as this one. The inscription on the tag says:

> I have run away. Keep me. When you bring me back to my master Zoninus, you will receive a gold coin.

LANGUAGE NOTE 3: TIME

1. Study the following sentences. What is the effect of expressing time in the accusative case?

    Sabīna multās hōrās labōrat.
    Sabina works for many hours.

    trēs diēs et trēs noctēs, Thellus fugit.
    For three days and three nights Thellus flees.

    tōtam noctem dormīs.
    You sleep all night.

    When time is given in the accusative case, it tells us **how long** something lasts for.

2. Now look at these sentences. How does the meaning change when time is expressed in the ablative case?

    mediā nocte familia discēdit.
    The family leaves in the middle of the night.

    hōrā quīntā Faustus clāmōrem audit.
    At the fifth hour Faustus hears a shout.

    tribus diēbus pecūniam exspectō!
    I expect the money in three days.

    When time is given in the ablative case, it tells us **when** something is happening.

LANGUAGE PRACTICE

1. Change the nouns in bold type from singular to plural, or plural to singular, then translate the new sentence.

    a. frāter meus semper ad templum sacrum cum **dōnō** advenit.

    b. fēmina misera cibum in **viā** cum **fīliā** exspectat.

    c. senātor vīnum cārum cum **sorōribus** bibit.

    d. cīvēs īrātī ē **forō** fūrēs agitant.

    e. nēmō rēgēs in **urbibus** vidēre vult.

2. Translate each sentence into Latin by choosing the correct word or phrase from each pair.

   a. *For three hours you worship the goddess in the forum.*
   | hōrā tertiā | deam | in forum | nōs | adōrātis. |
   | trēs hōrās | deās | in forō | vōs | adōrāmus. |

   b. *On the fourth day my mistress walks slowly down from the Capitoline Hill.*
   | quattuor diēs | dominus | lentē | prō Capitōliō | ambulat. |
   | diē quārtō | domina | laetē | dē Capitōliō | ambulās. |

   c. *The old man sleeps behind the shop for one hour.*
   | senex | prope tabernam | hōrā prīmā | dormiunt. |
   | senēs | post tabernam | ūnam hōram | dormit. |

   d. *We don't want to walk into the bar at the second hour.*
   | in popīnam | duās hōrās | laudāre | nōlumus. |
   | in popīnā | hōrā secundā | ambulāre | nōn vultis. |

   e. *For three days I am staying happily among the Suburani.*
   | trēs diēs | ā Subūrānīs | laetē | manēs. |
   | diē tertiō | apud Subūrānōs | frūstrā | maneō. |

Manumission

If you were a slave you might not have to remain enslaved for life. If you were a hardworking slave in a wealthy household you might have been able to earn or buy your freedom. Manumission was a common practice in ancient Rome. The Latin word *manūmissiō* is formed from *manus* (hand) and *missus* (sent). The literal meaning is 'sending from the hand', i.e. 'setting free from control'.

Often slaves were freed after the death of their owner, if he had put this in his will. Some Roman slaves received a small wage or gifts from their owner and they were able to save up this money and use it to buy their freedom. The owner could then use this money to buy a new slave. After being freed, the former slave became a *lībertus* (freedman) or *līberta* (freedwoman).

Some Romans wrote about giving freedom to their slaves as a reward, and describe the friendly relationships they had with their slaves and freedmen. For example, Cicero received this letter from his brother:

My dear Marcus, I am delighted about Tiro. He was much too good for his position and I am very pleased that you preferred that he should be our friend rather than our slave.

It is important to bear in mind, however, that we have no evidence for what Tiro thought about Cicero and their relationship.

It could be in the owner's interest to free his slaves. The Romans used manumission as an incentive to keep slaves working industriously and obediently. Moreover, often slaves were freed once they had reached an age at which they were less productive or had become sick, so owners no longer had the obligation to provide for them.

Laws were introduced to limit the number of slaves who could be granted their freedom. Romans were allowed to free only a proportion of their slaves, and never more than 100, however many slaves they might own.

Most slaves, however, probably never became free. Those working on the large agricultural estates or in the mines had little chance of manumission.

Theseus and the Minotaur

The ancient Greeks told a story about a mythical king, King Minos, who ruled the Mediterranean island of Crete. His wife gave birth to a son who was part-man, part-bull – the Minotaur.

- Find Crete and Athens on the map on pages 2–3.
- Then read or listen to the myth of Theseus and the Minotaur.

SOURCE 1

An image of a man leaping over a bull, from the palace of Knossos in Crete.

SOURCE 2

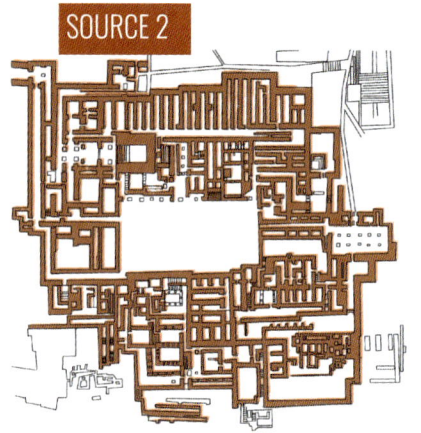

A floor plan of the palace of Knossos.

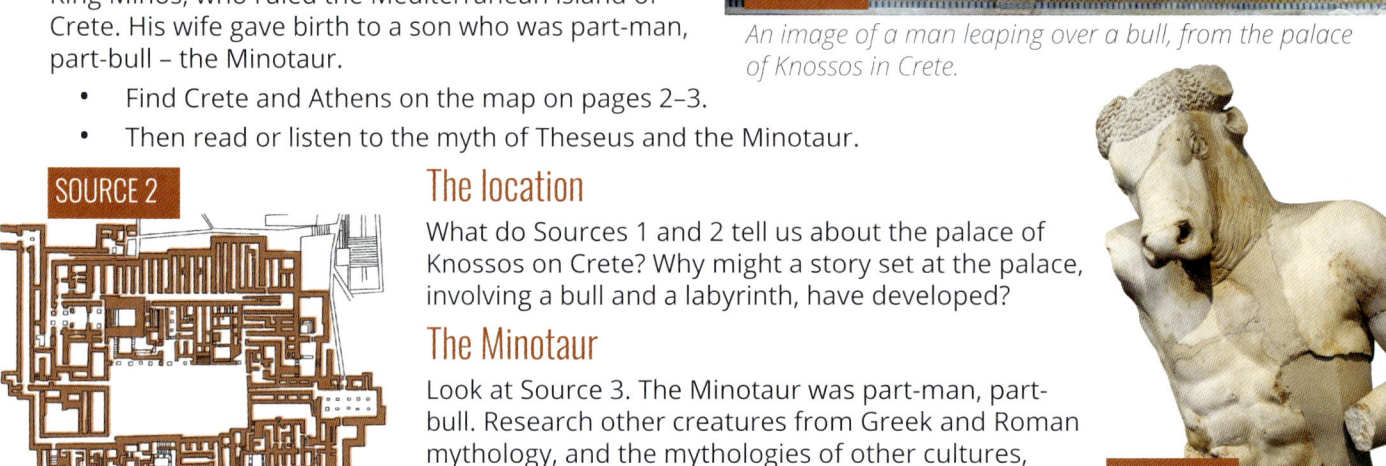

SOURCE 3

Roman statue of the Minotaur.

The location

What do Sources 1 and 2 tell us about the palace of Knossos on Crete? Why might a story set at the palace, involving a bull and a labyrinth, have developed?

The Minotaur

Look at Source 3. The Minotaur was part-man, part-bull. Research other creatures from Greek and Roman mythology, and the mythologies of other cultures, which are part-human, part-animal. Why do you think such creatures hold so much interest for us?

Minoan civilization

Although King Minos was a mythical king, a complex and advanced civilization existed on the island of Crete from about 2700 BC to about 1450 BC. It has been named the 'Minoan civilization' after the mythical king. What can you find out about the civilization? Is it possible that the Minoans really did force Athens, and perhaps other cities, to send hostages every year? Why might the Minoans have required hostages?

Theseus

Look at Source 4. Theseus was the mythical founder of the Greek city of Athens. Why might the Athenians have liked a story about Theseus killing the Minotaur? For the Athenians, what might the Minotaur have symbolized? What else can you discover about Theseus?

Daedalus

Look at Source 5. How is Daedalus connected with the myth of Theseus and the Minotaur? Why did Minos not want to let him go?

SOURCE 4

This Ancient Athenian vase painting shows Theseus killing the Minotaur.

SOURCE 5

Daedalus creates countless winding corridors and is himself hardly able to return to the entrance, so great is the building's deception.

Ovid

RESEARCH

Find out about:
- the mythical King Minos.
- Ariadne (Minos' daughter).
- the role of bulls in sport and culture.
- labyrinths, ancient and modern.

Chapter 7: Londīnium

amīcī

1. Faustus, Giscō et Celer sunt in Forō Boāriō. subitō Celer lātrat. Giscō circumspectat et amīcum cōnspicit.

2. 'dī immortālēs! est Indus!' Giscō clāmat. 'ōlim in Britanniā nōs erāmus mīlitēs.'

3. Giscō! salvē! quid tū in urbe agis?

cum Catiā et Celere in Subūrā habitō.

4. hic est Faustus. Faustus īnsulam in Subūrā cūrat.

5 quid tū in Britanniā agēbās? tū saepe contrā Britannōs pugnābās?

6 ego nōn saepe pugnābam, sed saepe Britannōs adiuvābam.

7 nōs viās ... et pontēs ... et thermās aedificābāmus.

8 et animālia agitābāmus!

9 Britannia est īnsula fluitāns?

10 minimē, sed multa mōnstra in marī saepe vidēbāmus. et in silvīs habitābant fōrmae, partēs hominēs, partēs animālia. avēs mīrābilēs in silvīs cantābant.

11 fābulae! bibere volō. ad popīnam?

dē Britanniā

1. amīcī in popīnā sedent. Catia dē Britanniā rem nārrat.

2. ego prope Londīnium cum parentibus habitābam.

3. pater meus erat ferrārius optimus.

4. māter mea erat artifex mīrābilis.

5. parentēs gladiōs pulchrōs faciēbant.

6 cōtīdiē ego trāns pontem ambulābam.
cōtīdiē ego gladiōs in forō vēndēbam.

7 ōlim mīles pontem custōdiēbat.
mīles negōtiātōrēs spectābat.
mīles erat Giscō.

8 frīgidum erat.
tū laenam viridem gerēbās.

9 minimē! calidum erat.
ego stolam russeam gerēbam!!

10 ego cum sorōre ambulābam.

11 minimē!
tū cum patre ambulābās.

12 vōs cibum et vīnum portābātis.

13 minimē! nōs gladiōs portābāmus et aquam bibēbāmus.

14 pff! sōl lūcēbat. avēs cantābant. tū erās pulchra.

15 et tū es blandus.

Londinium

Soon after the successful invasion of Britannia by the Roman Emperor Claudius in AD 43, the town of Londinium was established. Before the arrival of the Romans there was no settlement there. The area was predominantly pasture and farmland, surrounded by large oak forests, but Londinium was to become the largest city in the new province of Britannia.

Why here?

When Roman troops landed on the south coast, they crossed the River Thames at a narrow point close to the estuary. This became an important gateway to the rest of Britannia. Later a new crossing point was made slightly east, downriver, at a place where ships could dock at high tide to unload. The area, particularly on the south bank of the river, was marshy and liable to flooding; however the two hills on the north bank, Ludgate and Cornhill, were ideal points for building. There was also an abundance of fresh water from the Thames tributaries, such as the Walbrook stream.

Trade

Before the invasion in AD 43, the Britons were already exporting metal, livestock, wool, and cloth to the Roman Empire, and importing food and wine from Gaul. (Gaul is the modern name used for the four provinces of Gallia: Belgica, Lugdunensis, Aquitanica, and Narbonensis.) The Britons lived in tribes, each controlling its own area, and any increase in trading was hampered by the absence of a proper road system, different currencies, and lack of cooperation between the tribes. After the Romans conquered Britannia, they built an impressive network of roads and united the British tribes under a single currency. Importing and exporting increased greatly.

Londinium was originally established around AD 50 as a trading base rather than an adminstrative or military centre. The new network of roads connected it to other parts of Britannia. Here the River Thames was deep enough for large ships to sail up from the sea at high tide. This was a cheaper and more efficient way of transporting goods than by land. From Londinium, the goods could then be distributed by road to the rest of Britannia. Native Britons, along with traders and businessmen from across the Empire, moved to Londinium, drawn by the opportunities in the new trading centre.

The map on the right shows some features of Londinium in about AD 59, superimposed on a map of modern London.

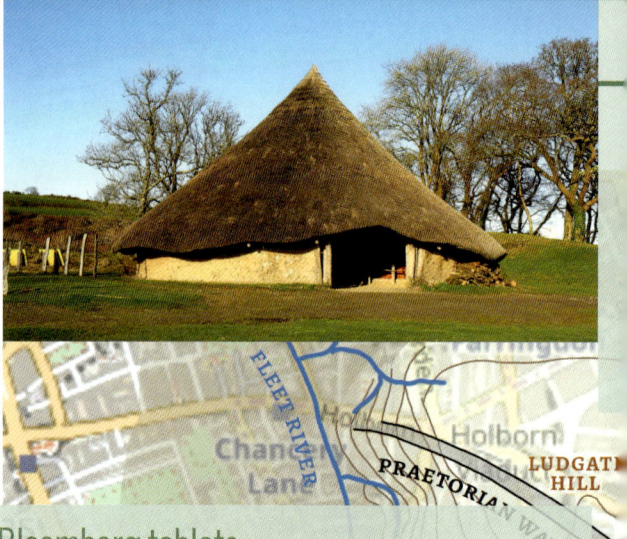

Bloomberg tablets

About 400 writing tablets (pieces of wood which the Romans wrote on) have been found here, preserved by the waterlogged ground around the Walbrook stream. The tablets are named after the company Bloomberg because they were discovered by archaeologists excavating the site of the company's new building. They tell us about the daily life and trades of the earliest Londoners.

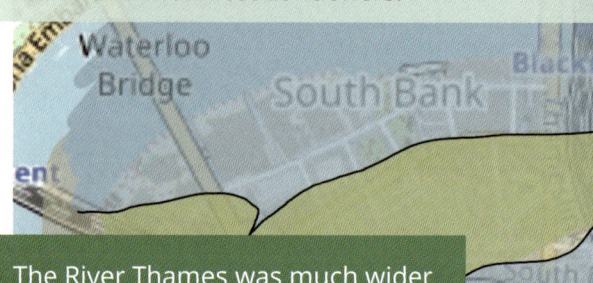

The River Thames was much wider than it is today. At low tide it was about 300 metres wide, 1,000 metres at high tide. It is about 100 metres today at low tide.

North and South

The south bank of the river was a marshy swamp that would be partly underwater at high tide. Roman Londinium was built mostly on the northern bank, but there were some smaller settlements on the south, possibly occupied by local Britons.

Buildings

Native Britons lived in round huts, built using a technique called wattle and daub. This involved constructing wooden frames and filling in the walls with earth and clay. The roofs were thatched with dried grass or reeds.

The first buildings in Roman Londinium were rectangular in shape. There was no local stone so they were built using the same materials as native British huts. They were made quickly, as the town expanded rapidly. The remains of a group of round and rectangular buildings have been found near the Walbrook stream, at Gresham Street.

Temporary fort

Although Londinium was not a military base, there was probably a small garrison of Roman troops in a temporary wooden fort on Cornhill.

The bridge

It is not known when the first bridge was built across the Thames. Evidence for a wooden bridge has been found by archaeologists on the north bank of the river, near modern-day London Bridge, and has been dated to around AD 85–90. Since Londinium grew rapidly as a trading settlement after the invasion of AD 43, it is likely that there was an earlier wooden bridge in a similar location.

Timeline

AD

43	Successful invasion of Britannia by Emperor Claudius.
60	Londinium destroyed by fire and rebuilt as a planned town, north and south of river.
70	Large stone forum, basilica, and amphitheatre constructed.
100	Londinium replaces Camulodunum as capital of Britannia.
120	The great second forum built.
122	Emperor Hadrian visits Londinium.
190	The Romans construct a defensive wall around Londinium.

Surviving section of the city of London Roman wall.

Made in Londinium

The population of the newly established town of Londinium was mixed. The largest group would have been the local native Britons, but there were also the Roman soldiers stationed in the town and an influx of traders and craftsmen attracted by the new opportunities. It is likely that many were from Gaul, but merchants could have come from further away. Within a few decades Londinium had become a cosmopolitan city, the home of skilled craftsmen and a centre of trade and exchange.

Glass

Excavations at a house on Gresham Street recovered a workshop which made glass beads. These were made by melting recycled Roman glass, but using traditional British methods, and their colour and design are typical of beads produced in Britannia before the Roman conquest.

dābes Iūniō cupariō contrā Catullu

You will give [this] to Junius the cooper, opposite [the house of] Catullus.

This is one of the Bloomberg tablets. It gives us an insight into the sorts of job early Londoners might have had. A cooper made wooden barrels which were used instead of amphorae to transport wine and other liquids.

Wool and clothes

After the Roman conquest, wool processing took place on a much larger scale. Spinning and weaving were probably still done at home or in small workshops. Woollen cloth was a British speciality and was dyed using locally available plants such as madder (red), whortleberry or blueberry (blue/purple), woad (blue), or elderberry (grey/purple).

Metalwork and jewellery

Britannia was a rich source of raw metals – gold, silver, iron, lead, and tin – all of which were in high demand across the Roman Empire. Britons were already exporting these materials before the Roman invasion, but the Romans greatly increased the scale of mining.

This iron stamp was used to mark ingots of metal. It is engraved with the letters MPBR, which is thought to stand for **Metalla Prōvinciae Britanniae**: *'the mines of the province of Britannia.' It shows how the Romans exploited Britannia's raw resources on an industrial scale, to be exported to other parts of the Empire.*

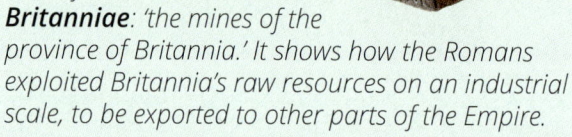

The native Britons were skilled in metalwork before the arrival of the Romans. In Londinium some jewellery was still made in a traditional British style, like the brooch in the shape of a hunting dog on the facing page. This intaglio (*below*), an engraved stone for a ring, shows the winged horse Pegasus. It was probably made by a skilled immigrant jeweller.

- Who do you think this jewellery was made for?

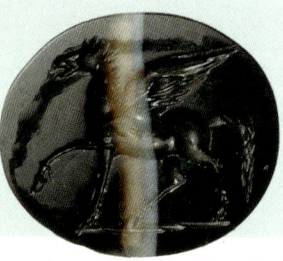

Leather

Evidence for leatherworking has survived well in the waterlogged ground in the Walbrook area of Londinium. Archaeologists have found not only intricately-cut leather shoes (*below*), but also scraps of cut leather and leatherworking tools. It is likely that leatherworking was originally practised in Londonium by skilled immigrant craftsmen.

LANGUAGE NOTE 1: IMPERFECT TENSE

1. Can you spot the difference between these pairs of sentences?

   Catia gladium portat. **Catia gladium portābat.**
   Catia is carrying a sword. *Catia was carrying a sword.*

   And again in these examples?

   nōs prope Londīnium habitāmus. **nōs prope Londīnium habitābāmus.**
   We live near London. *We used to live near London.*

   What is the difference in the form of the Latin verbs? How does that difference affect the meaning of the verbs?

2. The **-ba-** in the ending of the Latin verb indicates that the action was taking place in the past, and was happening for some time. This form of the verb is known as the **imperfect tense**.

3. Look at the imperfect tense of the Latin verb **vocō** (*I call*):

vocā**bam**	*I was calling, used to call*
vocā**bās**	*you* (singular) *were calling, used to call*
vocā**bat**	*he/she/it was calling, used to call*
vocā**bāmus**	*we were calling, used to call*
vocā**bātis**	*you* (plural) *were calling, used to call*
vocā**bant**	*they were calling, used to call*

   Note that the very end of the verb (**-m**, **-s**, **-t**, **-mus**, **-tis**, **-nt**) tells us *who* was carrying out the action and the **-ba-** tells us *when* they were doing it.

4. Now compare these two sentences:

   māter mea est artifex. **māter mea erat artifex.**
   My mother is an artist. *My mother was an artist.*

5. The imperfect tense of **sum** (*I am*) is as follows:

eram	*I was, used to be*
erās	*you* (singular) *were, used to be*
erat	*he/she/it was, used to be*
erāmus	*we were, used to be*
erātis	*you* (plural) *were, used to be*
erant	*they were, used to be*

Brooch in the shape of a hunting dog. You can still see traces of coloured enamel.

Celer

in popīnā Celer prope Giscōnem sedēbat. canis cicātrīcem lambēbat.

'cūr Celer cicātrīcem habet, Giscō?' rogāvit Currāx. 'cicātrix ē vulnere est?'

Giscō rem nārrāvit:

'ingēns aper in silvīs prope Londīnium habitābat. agricolae Britannicī dē aprō erant ānxiī, quod aper in agrīs currēbat et frūgēs dēlēbat. aper vīcōs quoque intrābat et animālia petēbat. Britannī aprum necāre cupiēbant.

'tum agricolae mē ad vēnātiōnem invītāvērunt. Indus quoque aderat. nōs duo equitābāmus et vēnābula portābāmus. Britannī ad vēnātiōnem ambulābant et canēs dūcēbant. ūnus ē canibus erat Celer. mox silvās intrāvimus, ubi aper habitābat. agricolae magnum clāmōrem tollēbant et canēs vehementer lātrābant.

'subitō fragōrem audīvimus. aper aderat et ad Britannōs currēbat. Indus vēnābulum in aprum iactāvit, sed aper vēnābulum vītāvit. equus meus erat perterritus et calcitrābat. ego ad terram praecipitāvī. dē vītā dēspērāvī. ingēns aper nunc mē petēbat.

'sed canēs Britannicī sunt fortēs. ad aprum currēbant. dux erat Celer. postquam Celer aprum petīvit, aper eum vulnerāvit. tum canēs aprum superāvērunt. Celer mē servāvit.'

cicātrīx *scar*

vulnus *wound*

ingēns *huge*
aper *boar*
frūx *crop*
dēleō *I destroy*
vīcus *settlement*
petō *I attack*
tum *then*
vēnātiō *hunt*
invītō *I invite*
equitō *I ride*
vēnābulum *hunting spear*
Britannī *Britons*
fragor *crash, noise*
iactō *I throw*
vītō *I avoid*
calcitrō *I kick out*
terra *ground*
praecipitō *I fall*
dēspērō *I despair*
fortis *brave*
dux *leader*
postquam *after*
vulnerō *I wound*
superō *I overpower*
servō *I save*

Section from the Little Hunt mosaic, in Sicily.

frūctus mīrābilis

Catia rem nārrat.

ōlim in oppidō cum sorōre, nōmine Aucissā, ambulābam. in forō erāmus quod cibum quaerēbāmus. multī īnstitōrēs cibum mīrābilem vēndēbant. ūnus īnstitor appropinquāvit.

'ecce menta et cucumerēs!' īnstitor clāmābat. 'ecce prūna et māla! vōs puellae cunīculōs anteā spectāvistis?'

'certē, īnstitor!' Aucissa clāmāvit. 'sed mālum nōn gustāvī.'

'quid?' īnstitor rogāvit. 'tū mālum nōn gustāvistī? mālum est frūctus dulcissimus!'

tandem ē forō ambulāvimus. Aucissa mentam et multa māla in sportā portābat. prope pontem popīna sordida erat, ubi nautae tōtum diem lūdēbant et bibēbant. mīles pontem custōdiēbat, et prope popīnam stābat. mīles erat Giscō. ingēns nauta Hispānus, postquam Aucissam spectāvit, vehementer clāmāvit, 'ohē, puella! quid in sportā portās?' omnēs nautae rīdēbant.

'vidēre vīs?' ego clāmāvī. tum ego mālum in nautam vehementer iactāvī, sed nauta mālum vītāvit. Giscō mālum nōn vītāvit. mālum mīlitem vulnerāvit. sanguis ē nāsō effluēbat.

ego valdē timēbam, quod mīlitem Rōmānum vulnerāvī. sed mīles rīdēbat. 'cavē, puella! mālum est frūctus perīculōsus!'

Aucissa quoque rīdēbat, et 'cavē, mīles, soror mea est perīculōsa!' clāmāvit.

---

frūctus *fruit*

oppidum *town*
īnstitor *stallholder*

5 menta *mint*
cucumis *cucumber*
prūnum *plum*
mālum *apple*
cunīculus *rabbit*
anteā *before*
10 gustō *I taste*
dulcissimus *very sweet*
sporta *basket*
nauta *sailor*
Hispānus *Spanish*
15

nāsus *nose*
effluō *I flow*
20 valdē *very*

Heavy goods and liquids, including wine and olive oil, were transported in amphorae. These were large pottery containers with two handles, a narrow neck, and a bottom tapering to a point. The spike on the bottom was useful as a third handle for lifting or pouring. A cork or stopper made of fired clay was used to plug the mouth; this was then sealed with mortar. Many of these amphorae were stamped with names or symbols which identify the pottery workshop or its owner. Sometimes the mortar seal was stamped with the name of the merchant. Details of the contents were sometimes painted on the amphora. Many shipwrecks carrying amphorae have been found by archaeologists.

Food

The Romans brought to Britannia new foods and new methods of cooking and farming. Some of the foodstuffs taken for granted in Britain today were introduced by the Romans.

Pre-Roman diet

Native Britons had a simple diet, consisting mainly of bread, a kind of porridge made from grains, vegetables, wild native fruits, and some dairy products. This was supplemented by a little meat and, in some areas, fish. Cattle, sheep, goats, pigs, geese, and hens were kept on farms and the main crops grown were wheat, oats, barley, and rye. Barley was used for brewing beer. Pliny the Elder said that roast goose was 'the richest dish known to the Britons'. Cattle also provided dairy products – milk, cheese, and butter. Romans did not eat butter: they used olive oil for cooking. Honey was used as a sweetener.

Hunting was a popular sport, so the diet included meat such as wild boar, venison, and possibly hare. British hunting dogs were valued so much that they were exported to Rome.

Terracotta cup showing a hunting scene with a stag.

Roman food and drink

For the majority of Britons, especially those outside the towns, there was little change in this simple diet. However, even the lower classes would have benefited from the introduction of a wide range of vegetables and fruits. The upper classes were more influenced by the Roman way of life, and they could afford to eat and drink imported foods.

Even before the invasion, Britons had been importing goods from the nearest parts of the Roman Empire, including wine from Gaul and Italy. After AD 43 trade with the rest of the Roman Empire increased. There was a demand for imported food from Romans who had settled in Britannia, and from the British elite who wanted to show off their status by adopting a Roman way of life.

Introduced by the Romans

Some of the most common fruits and vegetables eaten today in Britain were introduced by the Romans, including onions, turnips, leeks, cabbages, lettuce, peas, and lentils. The only apple growing in Britannia before the conquest was the crab apple. The Romans introduced varieties of eating apple, as well as other fruit and nut trees, including cherry, walnut, and sweet chestnut. Romans were very fond of flavouring their food with herbs, and they brought to Britannia parsley, mint, thyme, garlic, rosemary, sage, and many other herbs.

Animals brought to Britannia by the Romans include pheasant, peacock, guinea fowl, a new breed of sheep, and perhaps even rabbits. Archaeologists have found a rabbit bone at Fishbourne palace on the south coast of Britain, which has been carbon dated to the first century AD.

Documents written in ink on thin sheets of alder wood, dating from about AD 100, have been found at Vindolanda, a military camp near Hadrian's Wall in Northumberland. They include lists of supplies and requests for food, like this shopping list:

... 20 litres of beans, 20 chickens, 100 apples (if you can find any nice ones), 100 or 200 eggs (if they are a good price), 5 litres of fish sauce, 10 litres of olives.

There are also letters mentioning goat's milk, salt, young pig, ham, corn, venison, flour, and pepper. A record of food supplies issued to soldiers includes barley, beer, wine, vinegar, olive oil, and lard.

Oysters

One favourite food the Romans did not have to import was shellfish, especially oysters. Oysters from the British coast were famous. They were so popular that they may have been transported inland live in tanks. Archaeologists have found large quantities of oyster shells on Roman sites.

Trade routes

Heavy goods were transported, as far as possible, by ship. However, sea voyages were dangerous and ships hugged the coast, avoiding the open sea. In the western Empire, navigable rivers such as the Rhône in France were used to take goods from southern France, Italy, or Spain to Britain. The alternative route from Spain around the west coast was longer and more dangerous, and usable only in summer.

The River Rhine was directly opposite the Thames estuary, so it was a good route for carrying goods between Britain and Gaul and Germany.

Olives and olive oil

Olives and olive oil were imported from the Mediterranean, especially southern Spain and North Africa. Broken amphorae have been found at Canterbury.

Fish sauce

Fish sauce (*garum*) was an essential ingredient in lots of Roman dishes. It was similar to the fish sauce used in Vietnamese and Thai cooking today (*nam pla*). Garum was so important that it was made on an industrial scale in many towns in the Empire. Archaeologists have found amphorae for bottling garum near the Roman docks in Londinium, along with traces of the sprats and herring from which it was made.

Recipe: *Put fish guts or small whole fish in a pot and mix with salt. Leave the pot in the sun to ferment for up to two months, shaking it frequently. Strain off the resulting liquid, store it in an amphora, and seal.*

Spices

Some exotic spices were imported from outside the Empire. Pepper came from India, cinnamon from East Africa, and ginger from Southeast Asia.

Dates

Dates were imported from the eastern Empire. Remains of charred dates have been found at St Albans.

Wine

vīta vīnum est Life is wine. *Petronius*

Wine was an important part of Roman culture, and the Britons adopted the Roman love of wine. The wine trade predated the Roman invasion. Archaeologists have found evidence of wine across Britain. Wine was imported from Italy, Spain, and southern France.

QUESTION

What different types of evidence do historians use to find out about life in Roman Britain?

LANGUAGE NOTE 2: PERFECT TENSE

1. Earlier in the chapter we met sentences like these, where the verb is in the imperfect tense:

   ego cum sorōre ambulābam.
   I was walking with my sister.

   mīles pontem custōdiēbat.
   The soldier was guarding the bridge.

2. We have now met sentences such as these:

   ego mīlitem Rōmānum vulnerāvī.
   I wounded a Roman soldier.

   nauta vehementer clāmāvit.
   The sailor shouted loudly.

   subitō nōs fragōrem audīvimus.
   Suddenly we heard a crash.

   The verbs in these sentences are in the **perfect tense**, which is often indicated by **-v-** in the ending.

3. Both the imperfect tense and the perfect tense indicate that the action took place in the past. How would you describe the difference between the meaning of the two tenses?

4. Look at the way the perfect tense of **vocō** (*I call*) is formed:

vocāvī	*I called, have called*
vocāvistī	*you* (singular) *called, have called*
vocāvit	*he/she/it called, has called*
vocāvimus	*we called, have called*
vocāvistis	*you* (plural) *called, have called*
vocāvērunt	*they called, have called*

5. Finally, compare the forms of **vocō** in the following sentences:

Present	**Catia Giscōnem vocat.**	*Catia calls Gisco.*
Imperfect	**Catia Giscōnem vocābat.**	*Catia was calling Gisco.*
Perfect	**Catia Giscōnem vocāvit.**	*Catia called Gisco.*

The Iron Age Britons kept sheep similar to this one, a Soay sheep from the island of Soay off the west coast of Scotland. The Romans introduced a new breed of sheep which was hornless, white-faced, and with short wool.

LANGUAGE PRACTICE

1. Fill each gap using a verb from the box. Then translate each sentence.

bibēbam	accipiēbant	portābāmus	audiēbātis
tenēbās	vēndēbat	adōrābant	gerēbat

   a. cōtīdiē nōs dōna ad templa pulchra ....
   b. vōs maximam turbam in urbe Londīniō ....
   c. soror vestīmenta nova .... et gladiōs in forō ....
   d. tū multum cibum .... , et ego vīnum cārum ....
   e. cīvēs fidēlēs magna praemia .... , quod deōs Rōmānōs ....

2. Add the missing endings to the verbs to match the English translations.

   a. Catia rem mīrābilem dē vītā in Britanniā nārrāv... .
   Catia told an amazing story about life in Britannia.

   b. postquam nōs clāmōrēs audīv... , in viam ambulāv... .
   After we heard the shouts, we walked into the street.

   c. cūr tū frātrēs tuōs hodiē vituperāv... ?
   Why did you criticize your brothers today?

   d. parvae ancillae fūrem īnfēlīcem celeriter superāv... .
   The small slaves quickly overpowered the unfortunate thief.

   e. ego lentē appropinquāv... et equōs in agrō spectāv... .
   I approached slowly and looked at the horses in the field.

   f. cūr vōs per iānuam nōn festīnāv... , postquam fūrem audīv... ?
   Why didn't you hurry through the door, after you heard the thief?

Section of a mosaic from Conimbriga, Portugal.

Romans invading

The Roman Empire was made up of a political centre, Italy, and a periphery of territories called provinces. These provinces had been acquired by Rome over the centuries, some by peaceful means, but the majority by military conquest.

Romans invaded other lands for a range of reasons. For individual commanders or emperors, military victories brought great glory, and often vast personal wealth, as they stole others' possessions for themselves. For the Roman state, conquering territory meant it took control of the people, property, and resources of the area. Many of the people who suffered invasion were then enslaved and sold; those who weren't enslaved were required to pay tax to the Romans. The mineral resources of the invaded territory often included metals, such as gold, silver, iron, and tin, which were both useful and valuable. All of this, combined with other resources such as crops, animals, and timber, amounted to a huge source of income and benefit for Rome.

Background to the invasion of Britain

Claudius was not the first Roman to consider invading Britain. Almost 100 years earlier, Julius Caesar had twice invaded the island (in 55 and 54 BC). However, he and his troops did not stay. Instead, after a series of battles, and having become the first Roman general to lead troops to the largely unknown and mysterious island, he established peace treaties with tribes in the south, and returned to Gaul. Emperor Augustus planned invasions on three separate occasions, but twice events elsewhere in the Empire took precedence, and on the other occasion the Britons appeared ready to make peace. Caligula, too, had made preparations for an invasion, but did not see them through.

Why were the Romans so ambivalent about invading Britain? The ancient historian Strabo, writing at least twenty years before Claudius' invasion, may provide part of the answer. He states that the Britons paid so much money to trade with the Roman Empire, and submitted to Roman influence so easily, that there was little point invading and securing the island: 'some of the British chieftains have made the whole island almost Roman property and the cost of funding our army would outweigh the money that would be gained.' Strabo also noted that violent opposition might be created if the Romans used military force.

So why did Claudius decide to invade? The first two emperors, Augustus and Tiberius, had been proficient military commanders and expanded the Empire significantly. The third emperor, the short-lived Caligula, had been brought up in a military camp. So when Claudius (the fourth emperor) came to power, he knew that a military conquest would be a vital way of displaying his own power.

We know that the British tribes sometimes cooperated with one another, and sometimes fought each other to obtain land, wealth, slaves, and political power. In times of conflict they would ask their neighbours, including the Romans, for help. It so happened that Verica, the leader of a British tribe, was expelled from Britain during an uprising. He appealed to Rome for support. This presented Claudius with a perfect excuse to invade.

The invasion of Britain

In AD 43, two years after becoming emperor, Claudius sent an invading force to Britain, consisting of four legions, under the supreme command of Aulus Plautius. A commander called Vespasian (who years later himself became emperor) was in charge of the Second Legion. The invading Roman army was organized into three sections, landing in different parts of southern Britain in order to divide the British defence.

It took the Romans some time to bring the enemy to battle: the Britons took refuge in swamps, hoping the Romans would run out of provisions and leave. However, Plautius persevered and, with the arrival of Claudius in the final days of the conflict, eventually defeated the Britons in a series of battles. Before the end of the year, the Romans captured the capital of the Catuvellauni, Camulodunum, which they then used as their first capital of Britain. With Camulodunum in Roman hands and south-east Britain secured, Claudius could claim his victory. This first phase of the conquest consolidated Roman power over the southern corner of Britain. However, it would take the Romans a lifetime to extend their control across the island, and work on Hadrian's Wall would not be started for almost eighty years.

> **vēnī vīdī vīcī** – I came, I saw, I conquered.
> The Roman general Julius Caesar said this after his victory in Pontus (in modern Turkey).

Chapter 8: Britannia

Some British tribes lived in hill forts, settlements of round huts surrounded by ditches and high banks, like this one at Maiden Castle in Dorset.

gladius

1. ōlim cum patre labōrābam. pater gladium faciēbat. māter intrāvit.

2. gladius optimus abest, Catia! tū gladium vīdistī?

    ēheu!

3. cūr soror tua discessit?

4. ego attonita eram.

    ego ē vīcō cucurrī et sorōrem quaesīvī.

5. tandem Aucissam prope flūmen invēnī.

6. soror lacrimābat.

7 quid accidit, Aucissa? cūr ē vīcō festīnāvistī?

8 sed Aucissa nihil respondit.

9 tum trēs Britannōs cōnspexī.

10 iuvenēs trāns pontem ambulābant. Aucissam salūtāvērunt. ūnus ē iuvenibus gladium tenēbat.

11 iuvenis gladium magnificum tenet, Aucissa. quis est?

12 amīcus meus est, nōmine Luccus. pater et māter gladium fēcērunt. sed Luccus eum cēpit.

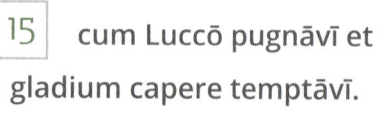

13 tum tōtam rem intellēxī.

14 dēsiste!

sed Luccus nōn dēstitit.

15 cum Luccō pugnāvī et gladium capere temptāvī.

16 sed Luccus ad amīcōs gladium iactāvit.

17 duo amīcī nunc gladium habuērunt. cum gladiō trāns pontem cucurrērunt.

18 Luccum superāvī et sine gladiō ad parentēs dūxī.

LANGUAGE NOTE 1: PERFECT TENSE (CONTINUED)

1. In the last chapter, you saw that the perfect tense is often indicated by **-v-** in the ending of the verb. For example:

   Present tense

   ego sorōrem quaerō.
   I am looking for my sister.

   māter intrat.
   My mother comes in.

   iuvenēs Aucissam salūtant.
   The young men are greeting Aucissa.

   Perfect tense

   ego sorōrem quaesīvī.
   I looked for my sister.

   māter intrāvit.
   My mother came in.

   iuvenēs Aucissam salūtāvērunt.
   The young men greeted Aucissa.

2. Now study these sentences:

   Present tense

   ego ē vīcō currō.
   I am running out of the settlement.

   soror tua discēdit.
   Your sister is leaving.

   amīcī gladium habent.
   The friends have a sword.

   māter et pater gladium faciunt.
   Mother and father are making a sword.

   Perfect tense

   ego ē vīcō cucurrī.
   I ran out of the settlement.

   soror tua discessit.
   Your sister has left.

   amīcī gladium habuērunt.
   The friends had a sword.

   māter et pater gladium fēcērunt.
   Mother and father made a sword.

3. While some Latin verbs use **-v-** to form their perfect tense, some use **-u-** and others form their perfect tense by changing in different ways.

4. When you look up a verb in the dictionary, you are given three parts. For example:

   vocō, vocāre, vocāvī   *call*
   discēdō, discēdere, discessī *leave*

   The first part is the present tense (*I do something*), the second part is the infinitive (*to do something*) and the third part is the perfect tense (*I did something*).

   If you are not sure whether the form of a verb is present or perfect, look up the verb in the dictionary to check.

This Iron Age sword and scabbard were found in the River Thames. The sword is made of iron and the scabbard of bronze. Most British warriors would not have been able to afford a sword.

Britannia

Britain in the Late Iron Age (800 BC–AD 43)

Archaeologists call the period before the Romans conquered Britain the Iron Age, because tools and weapons made of iron were used. In Iron Age Britain people lived in tribes, each tribe having its own land. At the head of most tribes there was a king or queen. Below them were chieftains, who controlled smaller areas within the tribal region. Some tribes lived in family groups in villages and farms scattered about the countryside. Others had settlements known as hill forts: a hill fort was a collection of round huts on top of a hill, surrounded by ditches and high banks.

By the time of the Roman invasion in AD 43, some tribes in the south and south-east had formed sprawling settlements as centres for commerce and industry, such as minting coins, metalworking, and pottery manufacture. But these were not towns in the Roman or the modern sense. There were no permanent stone structures, no public and administrative areas and buildings. Soon after the invasion, the Romans began to unify Britain by building towns linked by a network of roads. As you have seen in Chapter 7, Londinium grew quickly into a commercial centre on a site that had not been an Iron Age settlement. Some other towns were developed in a more organized way. The Romans divided the province of Britain into areas (*cīvitātēs*), so that they could administer it more efficiently. These areas were based on tribal districts. Each *cīvitās* had a capital town, which was the centre of the regional government. These towns were often on, or near, the sites of Iron Age tribal centres or settlements. Other towns grew up around the sites of Roman forts, and a few were built as settlements for retired Roman soldiers (veterans); these were called colonies (*colōniae*).

Celts

The people living in Iron Age Britain before the Roman conquest are sometimes now called Celts. The term 'Celtic' is used also of other peoples of northern Europe and their culture. The main thing these societies had in common is that they spoke a Celtic language. They also shared some cultural and religious practices, and they had a distinctive artistic style. Celtic art used curved and spiral patterns, and stylized depictions of animals were common. You can see some examples of art in the Celtic style on pages 110 and 111.

What was a legion?

The Roman army was divided into units called legions. Under the Empire, there were between twenty-five and thirty-five legions (the number varied), with about 5,000 infantry in each, and 120 cavalry. Each legion was commanded by a legate (*lēgātus*). Below him were ten officers called military tribunes (*tribūnī mīlitum*).

Road network

The Roman army successfully defeated a British force at Camulodunum. Then the army divided: Legion II went south-west; Legion IX went north towards Lindum; Legion XIV and part of XX went north-west; the rest of Legion XX remained in base at Camulodunum.

As the invading legions progressed, they built straight, paved roads. These roads allowed the troops to move quickly. The road network joined major ports on the coast with army camps and Roman towns inland, so that it was easy to bring supplies.

Chapter 8: Britannia   125

The British tribes and Rome

Even before the Roman invasion, life in the different British tribes varied greatly. Some lived in remote hill forts in the mountains. Others, like the Catuvellauni, Trinovantes, and Cantiaci, had close contact with Gaul and were influenced by the Roman world. Unlike most of the people of Iron Age Britain, these tribes cremated their dead, drank wine, and used coins. After initial resistance to the Roman invasion, some tribes, particularly in the south-east, quickly accepted Roman rule and began to adopt a Roman lifestyle, building large towns on the Roman model.

Left: the Great Torc from Snettisham, an Iceni settlement. This gold collar weighs more than a kilogram. Who do you think might have owned it? Why do you think it was buried along with other valuable objects?

What was a province?

A province was a region which the Romans had conquered and made part of their Empire. A high-ranking member of the Roman Senate was in charge as governor of the province. The Roman army set up camps to keep the peace. The native people of the province had to pay taxes to Rome and Roman laws were enforced. Romans could buy land in the provinces.

Key

- Iron Age settlement
- Iron Age hill fort settlement
- Settlement that developed into a Roman town
- New Roman town
- Roman fort

This map shows some of the main features of the province of Britannia in AD 60.

Luccus I

simulatque ad vīcum vēnimus, parentēs vocāvī et tōtam rem nārrāvī. postquam parentēs rem audīvērunt, attonitī erant. tum māter Luccum dē gladiō rogāvit. prīmō Luccus nihil dīxit, sed tandem respondit.

simulatque *as soon as*

prīmō *at first*

1. ad casam vēnī, quod gladiōs vidēre cupiēbam. Aucissa aderat ...

2. quid? tū aderās, Aucissa?

3. ita vērō, māter. aderam. sed gladium trādere nōlēbam. eum cēpit Luccus.

4. quid respondēs, iuvenis?

5. pater meus gladium cupīvit. veterānum Rōmānum occīdere vult.

casa *cottage*
occīdō *I kill*

II

postquam nōs omnēs eum audīvimus, maximē timēbāmus.

pater hercle! pater tuus est īnsānus!

Luccus minimē, senex. pater erat agricola prope Camulodūnum. cum meīs frātribus patrem in agrīs adiuvābam. tum veterānī ad vīcum nostrum vēnērunt. animālia ex agrīs trāxērunt et casās incendērunt. tōtum vīcum dēlēvērunt, quod colōniam aedificāre volēbant. frāter minor erat fortissimus et veterānōs petīvit. sed ūnus ē veterānīs frātrem occīdit.

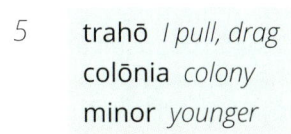

- **trahō** *I pull, drag*
- **colōnia** *colony*
- **minor** *younger*

māter ēheu! certē Rōmānī Britannōs ibi maximē opprimēbant. sed in oppidō Londīniō sunt paucī mīlitēs Rōmānī.

pater cum Rōmānīs nōs Britannī multum negōtium agimus.

Luccus quam stultī estis! Camulodūnum vīdistis? Rōmānī arcum in colōniā aedificāvērunt. in summō arcū est statua. statua est Claudius imperātor. ingēns templum in mediā colōniā aedificant. in templō est alia statua. quoque est Claudius. gentēs Britannicās opprimunt Rōmānī! Britannōs līberāre volō!

- **ibi** *there*
- **opprimō** *I crush, overwhelm*
- **paucī** *few*
- **quam!** *how!*
- **stultus** *stupid*
- **summus** *top (of)*
- **statua** *statue*
- **alius** *another*
- **gēns** *people, race*
- **līberō** *I free, set free*

Luccus ē vīcō ad pontem cucurrit. perterritissima eram.

Camulodunum: Britain's first city

When Emperor Claudius invaded Britain in AD 43, the Roman army pushed back the opposing forces of King Caratacus to his stronghold at Camulodunum. There the Britons were decisively defeated. Then Claudius himself arrived in triumph, leading a force that included elephants. The Romans destroyed the Iron Age fortification and made Camulodunum the capital of their new province.

Army camp to colonia

A large fortress was built straight away. This housed the Twentieth Legion for the first years after the invasion. As the years went on, the legion left, and the fortress was transformed into a town with Roman-style buildings. This was the first time brick buildings were constructed in Britain. The town became a *colōnia*, a settlement for veteran soldiers. The veterans were given land at the end of their service in the Roman legions. The Roman historian Tacitus wrote:

> A colony with a large unit of veterans was established at Camulodunum on territory which had been conquered. This would act as a defence against rebellion and would be a way of making the allies respect our laws.

Some local people were forced off their land to make room for the arrival of large numbers of ex-soldiers. Others, however, found employment in the Roman town and lived in settlements in the surrounding area.

Triumphal architecture

At one end of the town, a large triumphal arch was constructed to commemorate Claudius' victory over the Britons. It was probably similar to the arch Catia and Gisco passed through when they arrived in Rome; this arch commemorated the same victory (see Chapter 2). At the top of the arch in Camulodunum stood a statue of Emperor Claudius. After his death, construction began on a large temple to the Divine Claudius, with a bronze statue of him inside. The local British people financed most of these building projects through the taxes they had to pay to Rome.

Source 1

This tombstone, from Camulodunum, commemorates a Roman cavalry officer called Longinus Sdapeze, who was originally from Bulgaria. It shows the soldier's horse trampling a naked enemy, who is crouching over his shield. Sdapeze would have held a metal weapon (now lost) in his hand.

Source 2

The historian Tacitus wrote this about the Britons' attitude towards the Roman veterans:

> The Britons most bitterly hated the veterans, who had arrived recently in the colony of Camulodunum. For these men were driving people out of their houses, throwing them off their land, and calling them prisoners and slaves. And the violent behaviour of the veterans was encouraged by the serving soldiers, who hoped to behave in a similar way themselves once they retired. A temple to the Divine Claudius had been built and was forever before the eyes of the Britons, as if a stronghold of everlasting tyranny.

QUESTION

How do you think (a) the Romans and (b) the local Britons felt about Camulodunum?

Resist or accept?

Look at these three profiles of British tribal leaders:

1. Togidubnus

Togidubnus was king of the Regni. The Regni was a new tribe created by the Romans to control some of the territory of the Atrebates. Togidubnus was a strong supporter of the Romans. In return for his loyalty to Rome, they made him a client king. This meant that he ruled semi-independently and had the protection of the Roman army. It also secured for the Romans a strategic base for the conquest of south-west Britain.

Togidubnus fully adopted a Roman lifestyle, changing his name to Tiberius Claudius Togidubnus. He built a temple to the Roman gods Neptune and Minerva, and may have built a grand villa near Noviomagus on the south coast. The remains of this villa were found in modern Fishbourne.

3. Caratacus

Caratacus, chief of the Catuvellauni, was the leader of the resistance to the Roman invasion. After he was defeated at Camulodunum, he fled west. He stirred up the Silures and the Ordovices to oppose the Roman advance, but was finally defeated. He escaped and sought protection from the Brigantes. Queen Cartimandua, far from helping him, turned him over to the Romans. He was taken to Rome as a captive, along with his wife, daughter, and brothers. There, they were paraded before the Roman people. Instead of pleading for mercy, Caratacus made a proud speech. Tacitus reports these words: 'If you want to be masters of the world, does it follow that the world should welcome slavery?' Impressed by his courage, Emperor Claudius freed him, along with his family.

2. Cartimandua

Cartimandua, the queen and leader of the Brigantes, was friendly towards the Romans. In exchange for her loyalty, the Romans allowed her to keep her independence and territory. Instead of advancing north, the Roman army concentrated their efforts on the resistance from the west. After she divorced her husband, Venutius, he stirred up unrest within the Brigantes and gathered a force to attack her. The Romans came to her aid and rescued her, but she lost the throne. Venutius became leader of the Brigantes and led the resistance against the Romans.

What did the Britons think of the Roman Empire?

Few people in Iron Age Britain could read and write, so we have only Roman accounts of what the Britons thought of their conquerors. Tacitus reported a speech of the British chief Calgacus, who was defeated by the Roman general Agricola at the Battle of Mons Graupius in Scotland in AD 83. Calgacus addressed his men before the battle:

> The Romans rob, they slaughter, they ravage, and they falsely call this empire. They make a desert and they call it peace. Every day Britain feeds its own servitude.

QUESTIONS

1. What were the benefits of accepting Roman rule?

2. In Tacitus' account, Caratacus says:

   habuī equōs, virōs, arma, opēs.
   I had horses, men, weapons, and wealth.

   The Romans often believed that they were bringing a better way of life to the people they conquered. How does Caratacus reject this idea?

3. If you were a leader of a British tribe, what do you think you would have done?

Druidēs

postquam Catia rem cōnfēcit, Sabīna dīxit, 'Luccus erat iuvenis stultus. in Britanniā omnēs iuvenēs contrā Rōmānōs pugnāre volēbant?'

'minimē, Sabīna,' respondit Giscō. 'multī prīncipēs Britannicī pugnāre nōlēbant, quod pācem cupiēbant.'

'sed Druidēs ad bellum iuvenēs Britannicōs saepe incitābant,' dīxit Indus. 5

'Druidēs vīdistī?' rogāvit Sabīna.

'ubi in Batāviā habitābam, Druidēs nōn vīdī,' respondit Indus. 'sed in Britanniā, sīcut in Galliā, multī Druidēs aderant.'

'dē contrōversiīs inter hominēs et gentēs cōnstituēbant,' inquit Catia.

'Druidēs quoque erant sacerdōtēs,' inquit Giscō. 'in silvīs sacrīs ingēns 10
simulācrum vīmineum faciēbant, et in simulācrum captīvōs pellēbant.'

'postquam simulācrum hominibus vīvīs plēnum erat, Druidēs simulācrum incendēbant,' inquit Indus. 'captīvī vehementer clāmābant, sed effugere nōn poterant.'

'quid accidit?' rogāvit Rūfīna attonita. 15

'mox omnēs captīvī in simulācrō vīmineō periērunt,' susurrāvit Giscō.

'rem mīrābilem nārrāvistis, amīcī,' inquit Faustus.

sed Catia, postquam marītum audīvit, clāmāvit, 'fābulae! Druidēs nōn erant crūdēlēs!' tum Giscō et uxor in popīnā contrōversiam habēbant.

'contrōversia est!' clāmāvit Indus. 'ubi sunt Druidēs?' 20

Druidēs *Druids*

cōnficiō *I finish*

prīnceps *chief, leader*
pāx *peace*

bellum *war*
incitō *I incite, stir up*

ubi *when*
Batāvia *Batavia (in Germania Inferior)*
sīcut *just as, like*
contrōversia *argument, dispute*
inter *among, between*
cōnstituō *I decide*
vīmineus *made of wicker*
captīvus *captive, prisoner*
pellō *I drive, push*
vīvus *alive, living*
pereō *I die, perish*
crūdēlis *cruel*

The Druids

The Druids were a powerful and influential group of people in Iron Age Britain and Gaul. They belonged to the highest rank of society and acted as judges and teachers as well as priests. When the Romans visited and conquered Gaul and Britain, they came into contact with the Druids, and several Romans wrote about their beliefs and practices.

The Druids did not take part in fighting. But their position of authority gave them the ability to organize opposition to the Romans. After the Roman conquest, some Britons, including Druids, fled westwards to the island of Anglesey (the Romans called it Mona), off the west coast. In AD 60 or 61 Suetonius Paulinus, the Roman governor of Britain, attacked this outpost of resistance to Roman rule. The historian Tacitus describes the force that was waiting for the Romans:

> Standing on the shore was the enemy line, thick with weapons and men. Women were running about like Furies, wearing dark clothing, their hair dishevelled, carrying firebrands. And around them were the Druids, pouring out terrible prayers, their hands raised to heaven. They were such a strange sight that the Romans at first, as if their limbs were paralysed, didn't move and offered their bodies to be wounded.

The Romans recovered from their initial shock and defeated the British force. Tacitus continues:

> Then the groves dedicated to barbaric superstitions were cut down; for the Britons thought it was right to stain their altars with the blood of their captives and to find out the will of the gods by examining human entrails.

Tacitus wasn't the only writer to claim that the Druids practised human sacrifice; the belief was widespread among the Romans and was also recorded by Julius Caesar. In contrast to this presentation of the Druids as barbaric, Caesar also described their education system and teachings in a way that shows them in a very different light. They believed that 'souls do not perish, but instead pass from one body to another after death' and they were interested in 'the stars and their movements, the extent of the universe and the earth, the nature of things, and the power of the immortal gods'. Sometimes their training lasted for twenty years. They learnt everything by heart, so no written account of Druidic teachings has survived.

Emperor Claudius banned the Druids on the grounds that human sacrifice was magic and superstition. However, there is no firm evidence to support the claim that the Druids practised human sacrifice: the accusation could have been Roman propaganda.

QUESTION

3. Generally the Romans were tolerant of other religious beliefs and practices. Why do you think that they persecuted the Druids?

This headdress or crown made of bronze was found on the skull of a man in an Iron Age grave. He was buried with his sword and shield. Some priests in Roman Britain more than two hundred years later wore similar crowns. This has given rise to the theory that the man may have been a Druid priest.

QUESTIONS

1. Tacitus gives two examples of 'barbaric superstitions'. In what ways are they (a) similar to and (b) different from Roman religious rites?
2. How do you think a Roman reader would have reacted to this account of the British resistance?

hērōs

ubi ego et Aucissa erāmus minōrēs, hiems frīgidissima erat. Aucissa cum amīcā ad flūmen congelātum cucurrit. Aucissa dīxit, 'ecce, super flūmen ambulāre possum!' longē super glaciem prōcessit. subitō fragōrem audīvērunt. in glaciē erat rīma, et Aucissa repente in aquam frīgidam cecidit. amīca et Aucissa perterritae exclāmābant. 5

mīles Rōmānus puellās audīvit et ad flūmen cucurrit. Aucissam in aquā cōnspexit. statim arma dēposuit. amīca et mīles super glaciem lentē prōcessērunt. 'adsum, puella!' mīles clāmāvit. ad Aucissam veniēbat, sed Aucissa natāre nōn poterat, et sub glaciem ēvānuit. mīles in aquam saluit et quoque ēvānuit. silentium erat. tandem 10
Aucissa et mīles appāruērunt. mīles eam ex aquā in glaciem pepulit. nunc Aucissa in glaciē iacēbat et amīca mīlitem ex aquā trahere temptābat. sed mīles erat nimium gravis, puella nōn valida, glaciēs nōn firma.

hērōs *hero*

hiems *winter*
congelātus *frozen*
super *over*
glaciēs *ice*
repente *suddenly*

arma *arms, weapons*
amīca *friend (female)*
natō *I swim*
ēvānēscō *I disappear*
appāreō *I appear*

validus *strong*
firmus *firm*

LANGUAGE NOTE 2: SUPERLATIVES

1. Study the following sentences:

   Subūra nōn est quiēta, sed cella est quiētissima.
   The Subura isn't quiet, but the room is very quiet.

   māter erat fortis et frāter erat fortissimus.
   My mother was brave and my brother was very brave.

   hiems frīgidissima erat.
   The winter was very cold.

   quiētissima, **fortissimus**, and **frīgidissima** are known as **superlatives**.

2. Superlatives can be translated into English using *very* or *most*, or by adding *-est* to the English word. For example, **cella est quiētissima** can be translated as *the room is very quiet* or *it is the quietest room*.

3. Most superlatives are formed by using **-issim-**, but some are formed differently:

   iter meum erat difficile, sed iter tuum erat difficillimum.
   My journey was difficult, but your journey was very difficult.

   māter gladiōs pulcherrimōs facit.
   My mother makes the most beautiful swords.

LANGUAGE PRACTICE

1. Complete the sentence with the correct verb, then translate.

    a. hōrā quārtā, ad urbem trāns pontem cum amīcīs ....
        (respondī, accidī, cucurrī)
    b. heri Rōmānī frātrem meum .... , quod agrōs nostrōs cupiēbant.
        (dīxērunt, occīdērunt, vēnērunt)
    c. taurum ad forum .... , quod eum vēndere cupiēbātis.
        (vīxistis, fūgistis, dūxistis)
    d. postquam Luccum superāvimus, eum ad parentēs meōs statim ....
        (invēnimus, trāximus, dīximus)
    e. post paucās hōrās, Catia Aucissam sōlam prope flūmen ....
        (invēnit, respondit, accidit)
    f. cūr ā vīcō cum gladiō nostrō subitō .... ?
        (dūxistī, discessistī, vīdistī)

2. Translate these sentences into English.

    a. parentēs īrātissimī erant, quod Luccus gladium cārissimum cēpit.
    b. Aucissa erat trīstissima, sed prīmō nihil dīxit.
    c. frātrēs Britannī erant laetissimī, quod Druidēs contrōversiam difficillimam cōnstituērunt.
    d. amīca mea mīlitem Rōmānum dē aquā frīgidissimā trahere nōn poterat.
    e. multōs diēs comes miserrimus in agrīs habitābat.
    f. fēmina, postquam iter longissimum fēcit, ad urbem pulcherrimam advēnit.

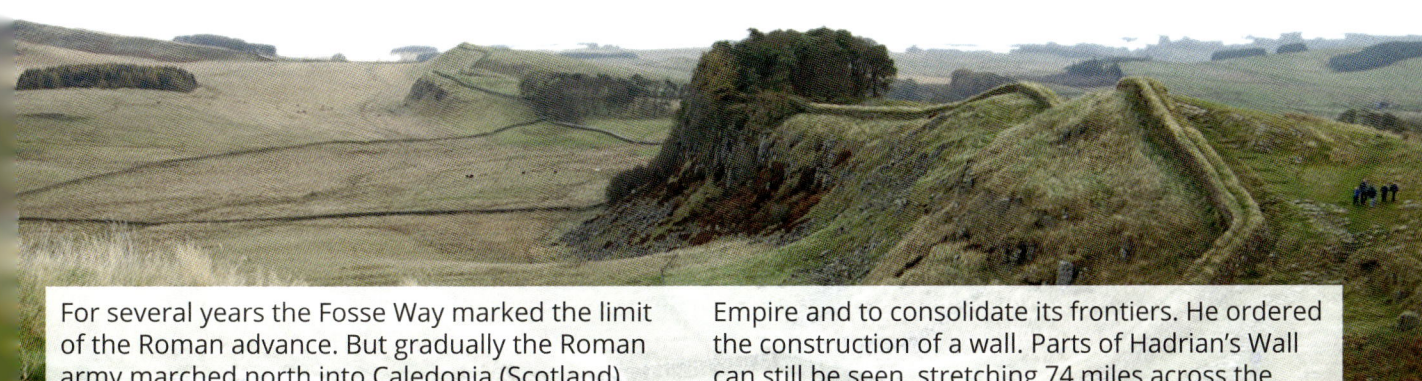

For several years the Fosse Way marked the limit of the Roman advance. But gradually the Roman army marched north into Caledonia (Scotland). Although the Romans defeated the Caledonian tribes at the Battle of Mons Graupius in AD 83, they withdrew without securing their victory.

Forty years later, in AD 122, Emperor Hadrian decided to put an end to the expansion of the Empire and to consolidate its frontiers. He ordered the construction of a wall. Parts of Hadrian's Wall can still be seen, stretching 74 miles across the north of England (*pictured here*).

Although there is evidence that the Romans visited Ireland, which they called Hibernia, it never became part of the Empire.

The Amazons

In ancient mythology the Amazons are a tribe of female warriors. They lived without men and beyond what the ancient Greeks considered the civilized world. It was commonly said that they lived in the East, between modern-day Ukraine and Mongolia. The Amazons fascinated Greek writers and audiences, because they were seen as strange and dangerous, and completely different.

Amazons in stories and art

The Amazons were skilled in battle. Usually they fought on horseback, armed with bow and arrow, and a double-edged axe. They are mentioned in Homer's *Iliad*, an ancient Greek poem about the war between the Greeks and the Trojans. Homer describes them as 'equals of men'. They fight alongside the Trojans, although they do not join the battle until after the end of the poem. Ancient Greek men were both fascinated and appalled by this race of independent fighting women – so different from their mothers, sisters, and wives.

Scenes with Amazons fighting Greeks were common in art, always with the Greeks winning. These mythical battles often represented the Greek wars against the Persians in the fifth century BC. They were a symbol of Greek victory over a foreign invader.

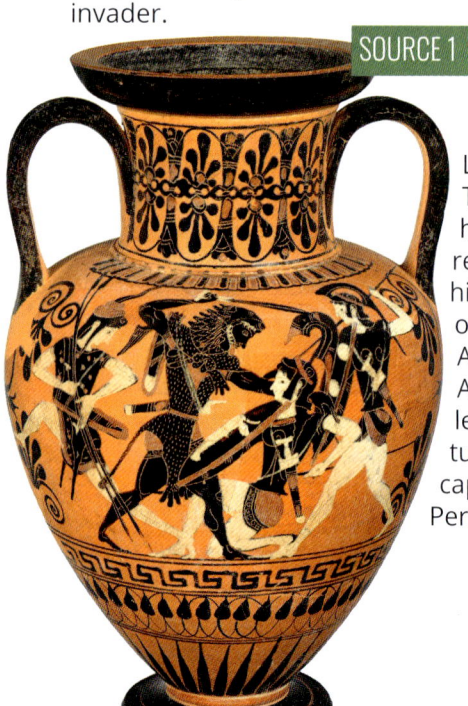

SOURCE 1

Look at Source 1. The Greek hero Hercules, recognizable from his lionskin cape, overpowers three Amazons. The Amazon on the left wears the tunic and leather cap associated with Persian dress.

Amazons in love

Although the Amazons lived apart from men, a particularly popular narrative in mythology was of Amazons falling in love with men. In these stories, the women are depicted as powerful and dangerous, but in the end they always fall in love with a Greek hero.

SOURCE 2

Statue of Achilles and the Amazon Penthesilea, by Bertel Thorvaldsen, 1801.

- Read or listen to one of these stories:
    ◊ Achilles and Penthesilea.
    ◊ Hercules and Hippolyta.
    ◊ Theseus and Antiope.

Men overcoming and dominating women – in love or in war – is a common theme in myths about the Amazons.

- Why do you think this was such a popular theme?

Myth and reality

For a long time it was thought that the Amazons were imaginary. However, archaeologists have found evidence of female warriors among the nomadic tribes who ranged across vast distances from the Black Sea all the way to Mongolia, travelling on horses. These women were buried with bows, arrows, spears, and horses. Some of them appear to have been wounded in battle.

- Research the Siberian Ice Maiden.
- Do you think the mythological Amazons could have been based on someone like this?

QUESTIONS

1. Do you think ancient Greek women would have shared the male view of the Amazons?
2. What do you think about the idea that strong females always give in to love?
3. Can you think of modern-day Amazons in films, books, or reality?

Chapter 9: rebelliō

Camulodūnum I

1 *mediā nocte. in colōniā Camulodūnō.*

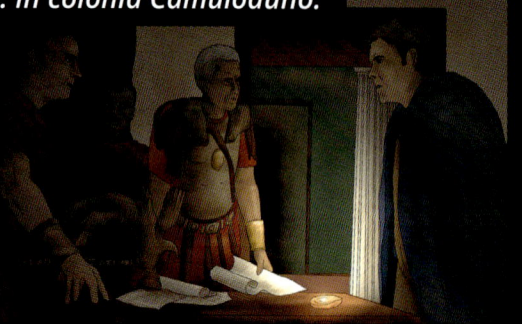

veterānī nūntium vocāvērunt.

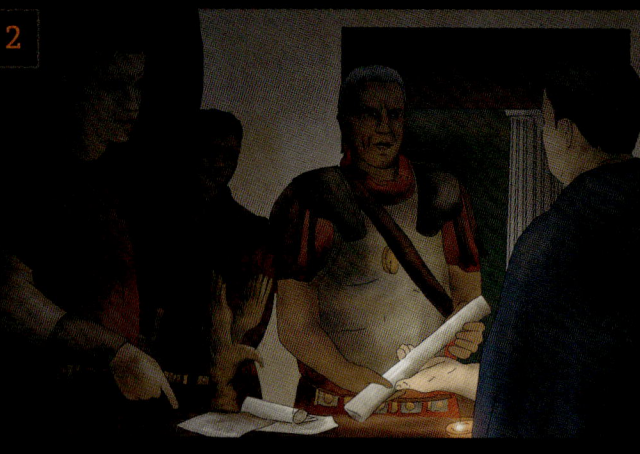

2

veterānī nūntiō epistulam trādidērunt.

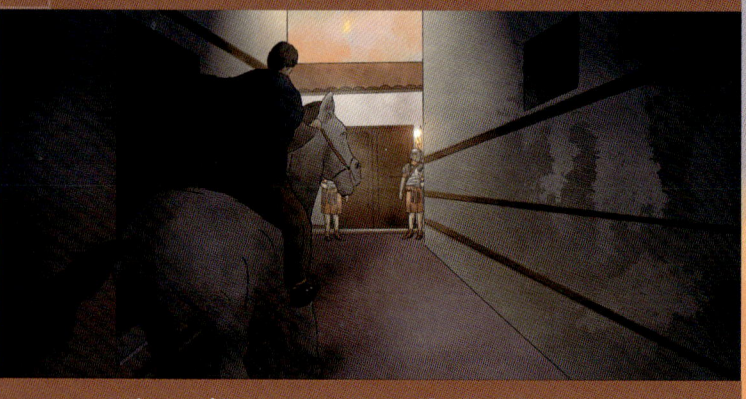

3 *prīmā lūce. in oppidō Londīniō.*

nūntius ad prōcūrātōrem festīnābat.

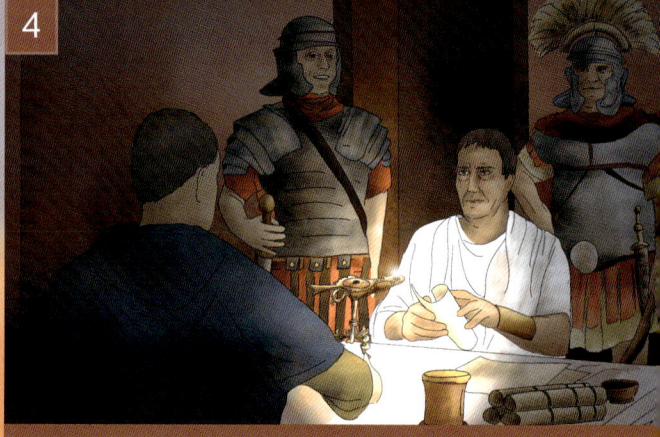

4

nūntius prōcūrātōrī epistulam trādidit.

5 *apud Icēnōs et Trinobantēs.*

mīlitēs Rōmānī mē et fīliās violāvērunt!

cōpiae Britannicae rēgīnam Boudicam audiēbant. Boudica cōpiīs rem gravissimam nūntiābat.

6

iō, Boudica! iō, iō Boudica!

Britannī Boudicae magnum clāmōrem tollēbant.

II

amīcī in popīnā intentē audiēbant. Indus amīcīs rem nārrābat.

'nūntius veterānīs auxilium petēbat,' inquit, 'quod cōpiae Britannicae ad colōniam Camulodūnum celeriter prōcēdēbant. Boudica caedem gravissimam parābat.

'centuriō prope prōcūrātōrem stābat. prōcūrātor centuriōnī epistulam ostendit. tum centuriō prōcūrātōrī cōnsilium dedit: "nōs veterānīs auxilium dare dēbēmus." statim prōcūrātor ducentōs mīlitēs ad colōniam mīsit, sed mīlitibus arma iūsta nōn dedit.'

'quam gravis erat caedēs!' clāmāvit Giscō. 'Britannī erant multī, Rōmānī paucī. postquam cōpiae Britannicae Camulodūnum advēnērunt, Boudica cōpiīs signum dedit. Icēnī et Trinobantēs erant crūdēlēs. virōs, fēminās, līberōs in viīs et domibus occīdērunt. veterānī in templum fūgērunt.

'duōs diēs in templō resistēbant. sed nūlla spēs veterānīs erat. tertiō diē Britannī templum incendērunt. Boudica omnibus Rōmānīs mortem tulit.'

Giscō dīxit, 'tum ad oppidum Londīnium prōcessit Boudica.'

---

auxilium *help*
petō *I beg for*
caedēs *killing, slaughter*
parō *I prepare*
centuriō *centurion (officer in the army)*
ostendō *I show*
cōnsilium *advice, plan*
dēbeō *I ought*
ducentī *two hundred*
mittō *I send*
iūstus *suitable*
resistō *I resist*
nūllus *no*
spēs *hope*
mors *death*
tulī *I brought*

LANGUAGE NOTE 1: THE DATIVE CASE

1. Look at the following sentences. What do you notice about the meaning of the words in red?

    Britannī Boudicae clāmōrem tollēbant.
    The Britons were raising a shout for Boudica.

    veterānī nūntiō epistulam trādidērunt.
    The veterans handed over a letter to the messenger.

    nūntius prōcūrātōrī epistulam trādidit.
    The messenger gave the letter to the procurator.

2. The words in red are all translated in English as *to* or *for*. They are in the **dative case**. The dative case is used primarily to indicate the person for whom an action is carried out.

3. Now look at the order of the words in the Latin sentences above. Can you spot a pattern? The dative noun is often placed between the nominative and the accusative nouns.

LANGUAGE PRACTICE

1. Give the meanings of the following nouns, which are all dative singular.

    For example: marītō   *to/for the husband*

    a. fēminae   e. fīliō   i. mātrī
    b. fīliae   f. deō   j. senī
    c. turbae   g. custōdī
    d. nūntiō   h. hostī

Chain of command

The emperor had overall responsibility for the government of Britannia, but he appointed men to govern the province in his name. The governor would have had experience in politics and a record of military success. In AD 60 the province of Britannia was governed by:

1. The governor: Suetonius Paulinus

The governor's role was primarily military, holding general command over the entire force stationed in the province. He also had other responsibilities, such as maintaining relationships with local chiefs, building roads, conducting religious affairs, and acting as a judge in important legal cases.

2. The procurator: Catus Decianus

The procurator was in charge of the province's financial affairs and reported directly to the emperor. His main duties were collecting taxes and organizing the wages of the soldiers.

3. The legionary commanders

In AD 61 there were four legions stationed in Britannia. Each of these had a commander who answered to the governor.

Heavy hands

Many governors and procurators used their command as an opportunity to exploit the province with high taxes and increase their personal wealth. When Prasutagus, king of the Iceni, died he left half his kingdom to his wife Boudica and half to Emperor Nero. He hoped this generous gesture would satisfy the Romans and secure peace for his people. Instead Catus Decianus took the whole kingdom, and ordered Boudica to be flogged and her daughters to be violated.

The humiliated Iceni rose up under the command of Boudica, and were joined by other tribes who had also suffered at the hands of the greedy Romans. When Suetonius finally faced Boudica's army, he massacred them savagely and inflicted violence in retribution, as Tacitus recorded:

> Although he was outstanding in other respects, his behaviour towards the conquered was arrogant and cruel, as if he were avenging a personal injury.

Catus Decianus, whose greed had initiated the uprising, had already fled to Gaul and was replaced by Gaius Julius Alpinus Classicanus, a Gaul. Subsequently, Suetonius was replaced by Publius Petronius Turpilianus, a less aggressive and more forgiving governor. Under the leadership of Classicanus and Turpilianus, Britannia was pacified without additional punishment: wounded relationships were repaired and towns were rebuilt.

Representing Rome

Provincial governors reported to the emperor, but were usually left to rule independently, particularly in peaceful provinces. Pliny, the governor of Bithynia and Pontus, wrote to Emperor Trajan on many occasions asking for advice and guidance on matters of seemingly little importance. In one of his replies, Trajan wrote:

> I chose you so that, in your wisdom, you might exercise a moderating influence on the customs of that province, and that you might put in place everything that is necessary for the peaceful future of the province.

QUESTIONS

1. Why do you think the Romans chose a man like Turpilianus to replace Suetonius?
2. How do you think the Britons would react to his style of governing?

Septimus revenit

Quārtilla in popīnā dīligenter labōrābat. ancilla erat fessa, quod multīs Subūrānīs cibum offerēbat. Faustus 'vīnum!' clāmāvit. Quārtilla Faustō vīnum trādidit. 'vah!' dīxit Faustus. 'ego bibere volō, sed tū es lenta!'

Quārtilla nihil dīxit. Rūfīna īrāta 'Quārtilla! festīnā!' clāmāvit. cibum ancillae lentae dare nōlō.'

Quārtilla nihil dīxit. ancilla ē popīnā quiētē ambulāvit, et in viā sēdit. Currāx mātrem invēnit. 'cūr tū lacrimās?' puer Quārtillae dīxit. 'vīta est dūra,' Quārtilla fīliō respondit. 'quamquam tōtum diem labōrō, Rūfīna mihi cibum dare nōn vult.'

subitō Septimum in viā cōnspexērunt. vir popīnam intrāvit. 'Septimus est,' inquit Currāx. 'nūper tē emere temptābat. Rūfīnae magnam pecūniam offerēbat, sed domina tē nōn vēndidit. cūr iterum adest?' Quārtilla nihil dīxit.

brevī tempore Septimus īrātissimus ē popīnā exiit. 'domina tua est stultissima,' clāmāvit. 'Rūfīnae plūrimōs dēnāriōs offerēbam, sed tē vēndere nōn volēbat. valē.' Quārtilla nihil dīxit, sed rīdēbat.

'cūr rīdēs, māter?' inquit Currāx. 'vītam novam nōbīs offerēbat Septimus!'

'nōn nōs sed mē sōlam emere volēbat. vīta in Subūrā est dūra, sed hīc tēcum vīvere possum. nōta domina est Rūfīna, Septimus est dominus ignōtus. melius est mihi in popīnā manēre.'

Quārtilla surrēxit et in popīnam festīnāvit. Currāx mātrī nihil dīxit. puer in viā mānsit.

---

reveniō *I return*

dīligenter *carefully*
fessus *tired*
offerō *I offer*

quiētē *quietly*

quamquam *although*

nūper *recently*
emō *I buy*

brevis *short*
plūrimī *very many*
dēnārius *denarius (silver coin)*

hīc *here*
nōtus *known, familiar*
ignōtus *unknown*
melius est *it is better*

LANGUAGE NOTE 2: THE DATIVE PLURAL

1. The sentences below contain examples of the dative plural:

   Boudica cōpiīs signum dedit.
   Boudica gave a signal to her troops.

   nūntius veterānīs auxilium petēbat.
   The messenger was seeking help for the veterans.

   prōcūrātor mīlitibus arma iūsta nōn dedit.
   The procurator didn't give the right weapons to the soldiers.

2. Compare the forms of the dative case with the nominative singular in each declension:

SINGULAR	1st decl.	2nd decl.		3rd decl.	
nominative	puella	amīcus	dōnum	fūr	caput
dative	puellae	amīcō	dōnō	fūrī	capitī

PLURAL					
dative	puellīs	amīcīs	dōnīs	fūribus	capitibus

3. Notice that the forms of the dative are often the same as the ablative:

SINGULAR	1st decl.	2nd decl.		3rd decl.	
ablative	puellā	amīcō	dōnō	fūre	capite

PLURAL					
ablative	puellīs	amīcīs	dōnīs	fūribus	capitibus

LANGUAGE PRACTICE

2. Complete each sentence with the correct form of the noun in brackets, then translate.

   a. ego .... praemium dedī, quod mē adiuvābant. (comitēs, comitibus)

   b. postquam ad āram advēnimus, dominus noster .... dōna obtulit. (deae, dea)

   c. nōs .... gladiōs pulcherrimōs in tabernīs ostendēbāmus. (lībertōs, lībertīs)

   d. tū .... arma gravissima trādidistī, sed contrā Britannōs inūtilia erant. (mīlitī, mīles, mīlitēs)

   e. quod Boudica est dux fortis, nōs .... mortem tulimus. (hostēs, hostibus)

   f. puerī .... cibum parāvērunt, quod iter longum faciēbat. (amīcum, amīcō, amīcus)

The forces

Roman legionary

- Iron helmet
- Body armour: several iron plates with leather straps
- Loose, knee-length tunic, made of wool
- Woollen cloak
- Leather sandals, with nails on the soles
- Socks may have been worn
- Some wore metal leg guards – sometimes only on one leg
- Short, straight-edged stabbing sword (*gladius*), kept inside a scabbard
- Javelin (*pīlum*): wooden shaft with iron tip
- Shield (*scūtum*), made of strips of wood glued together, covered with leather or felt

British warrior

- Woollen cloak
- Woollen tunic
- Trousers
- No breastplate or body armour
- Iron-tipped spear
- Some had a long slashing sword kept inside a scabbard
- Tall oval or rectangular shield, made of wood covered with leather
- Leather sling, for throwing stones
- Blue body paint

> All the Britons dye themselves with woad because it produces a blue colour and this makes them appear more terrifying in battle.
> *Julius Caesar*

Romans	Britons
Highly trained professional army.	Warrior culture; warfare between tribes common before Roman invasion; but no standing army.
From all parts of the Roman Empire.	All native Britons.
Fought as a team; trained in manoeuvres such as standing in line and resisting a charge with their shields, and the tortoise formation.	Fought as individuals. The Romans admired the bravery of the British warriors, but thought they lacked discipline.
Loyalty to legion and comrades. Only men served in the army.	Loyalty to family and tribe. Occasionally some British tribes joined together but in general did not unite against the Romans. Wives and children watched the battle; sometimes women may have led the offensive.
Preferred pitched battle on open ground. Travelled by marching along roads.	Preferred fighting on treacherous terrain – mountains, woods, marshes; guerrilla warfare; raiding parties; attacking marching column from concealed positions.

Why was the Roman army so successful?

In pitched battles on open ground the Roman army was extremely difficult to beat, even when greatly outnumbered. Tacitus says that in the final battle against Boudica almost 80,000 Britons died and about 400 Romans. However, on difficult terrain such as mountains, woods, and marshes the Romans were vulnerable, and the Britons had several successes.

What made the Roman army so successful? First of all, it was a professional army, so soldiers trained and prepared full-time (although they did many other jobs besides fighting). The physical training and weapons practice was strict and rigorous. Soldiers had to go on exercise marches three times a month, wearing armour and carrying heavy packs: their full equipment weighed about 30 kilograms. They were expected to cover 20 miles in five hours.

Preparing for battle

Suetonius, the governor, chose a site for the battle where there was a narrow pass and he had woods to his rear for cover. He had made certain that the enemy was only on the open plain in front of him, so he had no fear of ambush. The legionaries stood close together in lines, with the auxiliary light infantry around them and the cavalry on the wings. In contrast, the Britons, huge numbers of them, darted about in groups all over the field.

Tacitus

QUESTIONS

1. Look at the images of the Roman legionary and the British warrior. Compare their armour and equipment. What advantages and disadvantages did each have?
2. What type of fighting would favour (a) the Britons and (b) the Romans?
3. What other advantages did the British forces have?
4. What other reasons can you think of for the success of the Roman army?

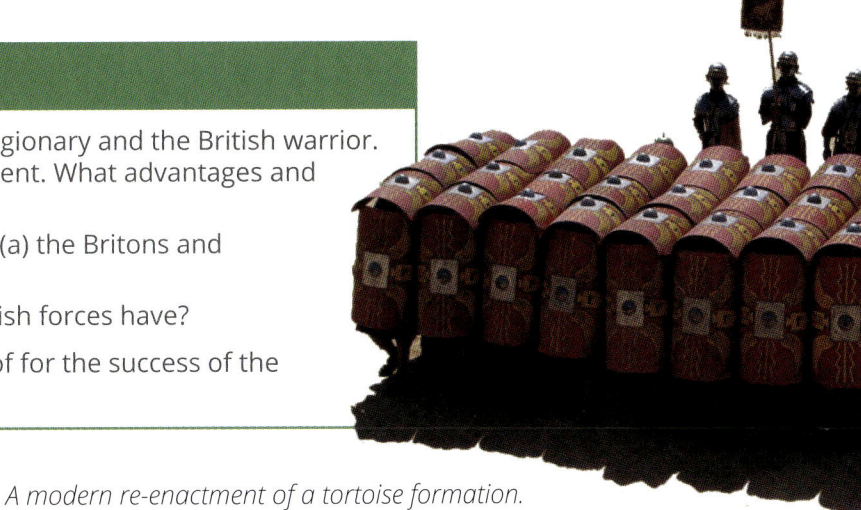

A modern re-enactment of a tortoise formation.

Women and war

Roman authors record how Boudica led the Iceni against the Romans. Cassius Dio describes her delivering a speech to her troops:

> She was very tall, fierce in appearance, with piercing eyes. Her voice was rough and her thick golden hair fell to her hips. She had a great gold necklace and wore a multicoloured tunic and a thick cloak. Grasping her spear, so as to terrify everyone, she spoke.

According to Tacitus, Boudica said that it was normal for Britons to fight under a woman's command. In his description of the final battle between the Romans and the British forces led by Boudica, Tacitus also mentions other British women present at the battle:

> The British forces were so fierce in spirit that they brought their wives to witness their victory; they put them on wagons which they had drawn up on the extreme edge of the plain.

Roman male writers found these fighting women fascinating and glamorous because they were so different from Roman women who did not have such independence.

umbra

in popīnā, amīcī intentē audiunt.

Catia	mox Boudica et cōpiae ad oppidum Londīnium advēnērunt. ubīque erant hostēs. nūlla spēs erat cīvibus. Aucissa erat in oppidō, quod gladiōs in forō vēndēbat. ego cum parentibus ad oppidum festīnāvī. in ponte Giscōnem et Indum invēnimus.
Giscō	trāns pontem hostēs oppidum iam incendēbant. ignēs et flammae tōtum oppidum implēbant. Catia oppidum intrāre voluit. eam retinēre temptāvī. omnēs cīvēs effugiēbant. sed Catiae nōn persuāsī.
Catia	necesse erat nōbīs Aucissae subvenīre. ego cum Giscōne ad forum festīnāvī, et parentēs Aucissam per viās quaerēbant. tandem in forum equitāvimus, ubi Aucissam invēnimus. sanguis ē pectore effluēbat. vehementer lacrimāvī et 'soror, cūr nōn effūgistī?' clāmāvī. 'Boudicam cōnspicere voluī. Luccus ...' sed plūs dīcere nōn poterat. 'quid? quid dīcis, soror?' exclāmāvī. sed Aucissa nōn respondit. soror in bracchiīs meīs periit. nōn potuī ...
Giscō	per flammās et turbās perterritās equitābāmus et parentēs quaerēbāmus. clāmōre viās implēvimus. parentēs iterumque iterumque frūstrā vocāvimus. subitō ante oculōs umbra appāruit.
Catia	māter erat. perterritī erāmus. 'necesse est vōbīs discēdere, columba mea,' dīxit māter. 'valē, mea cārissima.' tum umbra ēvānuit.
Giscō	difficile est nōbīs rem intellegere. sed nūmen aut umbra nōs servāvit.

umbra *shade, ghost*

ubīque *everywhere*

hostis *enemy*
flamma *flame*

persuādeō *I persuade*

necesse *necessary*
subveniō *I help*

pectus *chest*

plūs *more*

bracchium *arm*

impleō *I fill*
iterumque iterumque *again and again*
ante *before, in front of*
oculus *eye*

fuga ex oppidō Londīniō

in popīnā silentium erat. Subūrānī attonitī erant. tandem Rūfīna rogāvit, 'quōmodo ab oppidō effūgistis?'

Rūfīnae respondit Indus, 'pontem contrā hostēs dēfendēbam. nūllum auxilium mihi erat. mox cōpiae Britannicae pontem incendēbant. subitō Catiam et Giscōnem in rīpā cōnspexī.'

'pontem et Indum per turbam vix vidēre poterāmus,' inquit Catia. 'frūstrā pontī appropinquāre temptābāmus. multī hostēs nōs in rīpā opprimēbant. tandem in flūmen saluimus. deinde ingentem fragōrem audīvimus. pōns dēcidit.'

omnēs amīcī Indum spectābant.

'in flūmen saluī,' inquit Indus. 'arma gerēbam. vix ad rīpam ulteriōrem natāre poteram. hostēs tēla in mē iaciēbant. tēla tamen vītāvī, quod sub aquā natābam.'

posteā difficile erat nōbīs iter facere, quod hostēs ubīque erant. per diem dormiēbāmus, per noctem iter faciēbāmus. tandem ad exercitum Rōmānum advēnimus.

dēfendō *I defend*
rīpa *bank (of a river)*
vix *scarcely, hardly*
deinde *then*
dēcidō *I fall down*
ulterior *further, opposite*
tēlum *weapon*
posteā *afterwards*
exercitus *army*

Fenwick Treasure

The Fenwick Treasure (*right*) was found in Colchester (Roman Camulodunum) in 2014 by archaeologists excavating the site of Fenwick's department store. This hoard of gold and silver jewellery and Roman coins was under the floor of a house which had been destroyed by fire. The dating and the absence of any bodily remains suggest that the jewellery and coins were deliberately buried around the time of the Boudican revolt. Among the items are gold earrings, a gold bracelet, and five gold rings. The earrings are hollow gold balls, similar to some which have been found in Pompeii. There is also a silver *armilla*, an award which was given to a retired soldier.

QUESTIONS

1. Who might this treasure have belonged to?
2. Why do you think it was buried?

LANGUAGE NOTE 3: VERBS WITH THE DATIVE CASE

1. Some Latin verbs, because of their meaning, are accompanied by a noun in the dative case. Look at the Latin sentences below. Can their English translations be simplified?

   Catiae nōn persuāsī.
   I was not persuasive to Catia.

   multī Britannī Rōmānīs favēbant.
   Many Britons were giving support to the Romans.

   pontī appropinquāre temptābāmus.
   We were trying to draw near to the bridge.

   Rōmānī Boudicae resistere nōn poterant.
   The Romans weren't able to offer resistance to Boudica.

2. The sentences might more naturally be translated as follows:

   Catiae nōn persuāsī.
   I did not persuade Catia.

   multī Britannī Rōmānīs favēbant.
   Many Britons were supporting the Romans.

   pontī appropinquāre temptābāmus.
   We were trying to approach the bridge.

   Rōmānī Boudicae resistere nōn poterant.
   The Romans weren't able to stop Boudica.

3. Other verbs which are accompanied by the dative case include **imperō** (*order, give an order to*), **parcō** (*spare, give mercy to*), **crēdō** (*trust, give one's trust to*), **placeō** (*please, be pleasing to*), **subveniō** (*help, bring help to*), and **nūbō** (*marry, marry oneself to*).

LANGUAGE PRACTICE

3. Add the missing endings to the nouns to match the English translations.

   a. nōs mendīc... cibum dedimus.
      We gave food to the beggar.

   b. tū sorōr... pecūniam obtulistī.
      You offered money to your sisters.

   c. ego fīli... templum ostendī.
      I showed the temple to my daughter.

   d. rēx imperātōr... captīvōs trādidit.
      The king handed over prisoners to the emperor.

   e. mātrōn... dōna quaerēbātis.
      You were looking for gifts for the ladies.

   f. Britannī cōpi... arma dābant.
      The Britons were giving weapons to their forces.

Why join the army?

There was no compulsory military service in the Roman Empire: men who served as soldiers were volunteers. Being a soldier was considered a prestigious job, and it came with many rewards. Soldiers earned a good wage compared with other professions and were housed and well fed. In addition, the emperors often gave the legions gifts of money to be distributed among the men. While there were dangers associated with warfare, many soldiers saw very little combat, depending on where they were stationed. Instead they spent much of their time constructing roads and buildings, or on administration. Some trained in one of the many trades needed to support an army camp, as, for example, blacksmiths, shoemakers, or butchers. All soldiers were expected to be able to read basic documents, and a discharged soldier had learnt valuable skills during his years of service.

Enlisting

Young men from the age of 16 could sign up for the army. Those wishing to join were vetted to ensure they were healthy, of good character, and freeborn citizens. Preference was given to men who had a trade that would be useful, such as carpenters or smiths. The recruits were given official documentation stating their date of joining; this was important, as the date of their discharge would be calculated from this time. They received their equipment, which included clothing and armour, and completed a rigorous training programme before travelling to join a legion.

Legionary and auxiliary soldiers

Men who were freeborn and citizens of the Roman Empire could join one of the legions. Legionaries usually signed up for a period of twenty-five or thirty years' service. On retirement they received a pension and sometimes some land, often in the province where they had been stationed. Auxiliary soldiers, on the other hand, came from one of the provinces of the Empire where the inhabitants were not automatically citizens. They formed their own smaller divisions, comprised of men from the same province. Auxiliary cohorts often had a specialist skill; they were, for example, archers, cavalry, scouts, or camel riders. Auxiliaries served for twenty-five years before being discharged. They were paid less than legionaries and did not receive a pension or land. However, on retirement they were granted full citizenship, which brought tax exemptions and legal benefits.

QUESTIONS

1. Why do you think it was appealing for young men to join the army?

2. In the stories, Indus is an auxiliary soldier in a **cohors Batāvōrum** (a regiment from Batavia), while Gisco is a legionary. What difference would this make to their status and experience, do you think?

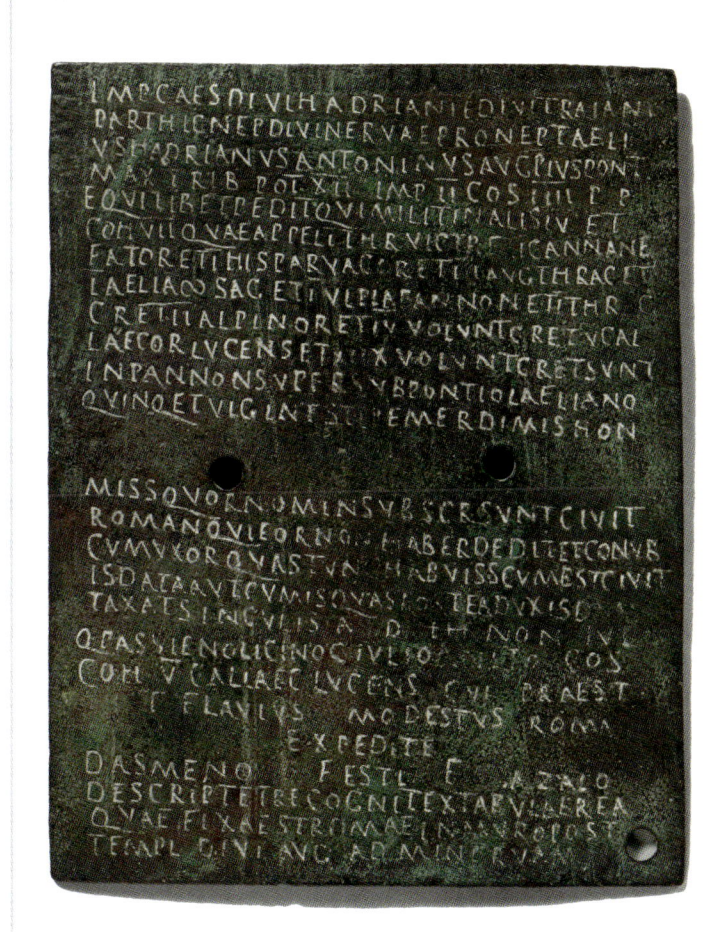

Every auxiliary soldier received a military diploma granting him citizenship upon completing twenty-five years of service in the Roman army. This diploma belonged to a soldier named Dasmenus Azalus, who was discharged in AD 149. It is made of bronze and measures about 13 cm x 10 cm.

proelium

1. imperātor proeliō optimum locum lēgit.
2. Britannī clāmōrem ingentem tollēbant. Boudica prīncipēs et gentēs incitābat.
3. hodiē victōria est nōbīs!
4. vae Rōmānīs!
5. hostēs sunt multī, nōs paucī! necesse est nōbīs cum magnā virtūte pugnāre!
6. imperātor proeliō exercitum parābat. tōtus exercitus imperātōrī magnum clāmōrem sustulit.
7. cōpiae Britannicae ad exercitum Rōmānum fortiter currēbant.
8. imperātor signum dedit.

imperātor *general*
proelium *battle*
locus *place*
victōria *victory*
vae! *woe!*
virtūs *courage, virtue*

fortiter *bravely*

9   prīmō mīlitēs in Britannōs pīla iēcērunt.

10 deinde equitēs hastīs Britannōs occīdērunt.

pīlum *javelin*
eques *horseman;*
 pl. = cavalry
hasta *spear*

11
tum et mīlitēs et auxiliārēs
gladiīs hostēs oppugnāvērunt.

12 mox exercitus Rōmānus Britannicās cōpiās dēlēvit.

auxiliāris *auxiliary soldier*
oppugnō *I attack*

Giscō in mediā caede ego Luccum
cōnspexī. iuvenī īnfēlīcī parcere
prīmō volēbam. tum gladium
cōnspexī. īrātissimus eram.
'sceleste!' clāmāvī.
iuvenem occīdī.

parcō *I spare*
scelestus *wicked*

Resistance

Boudica was not the only leader to resist Roman invasion. Across Europe, North Africa, and the Middle East, people fought for their freedom.

Caesar in Gaul

In 59 BC, there were two Roman Gallic provinces: Gallia Cisalpina and Gallia Transalpina. The rest of Gaul was home to free, independent peoples. They were not, however, a cohesive country, but a collection of tribes (with leaders elected for their military prowess).

In 58 BC Julius Caesar became the governor of the two provinces, and travelled there with four legions. Once there, he levied two more legions, so had about 30,000 legionaries and 4,000 auxiliary troops. Caesar began by supporting some Gallic tribes against threats from their enemies (for instance, from Germanic tribes across the Rhine, or from other Gallic tribes). He led a number of summer campaigns that allowed his legions to move north into the Gauls' territory. He increased his power by demanding taxes, food, and hostages.

Vercingetorix

However, in 52 BC resentment among the Gauls grew. They felt that they were paying far too high a price for Roman help. Gathered under a new leader, Vercingetorix, they rebelled against the Romans.

Vercingetorix tried to overcome some of the traditional problems of large Gallic armies: disorganization, lack of cohesion and discipline, and poor supplies. He started the rebellion in winter, while Caesar was away in Cisalpine Gaul and his legions were dispersed in their winter quarters. However, Caesar reacted quickly, and rapidly reassembled his army. After several defeats for the Gauls, and one at Gergovia for the Romans, Caesar's army was closing in on the Gauls.

This statue of Vercingetorix was set up in 1865 at the presumed site of Alesia.

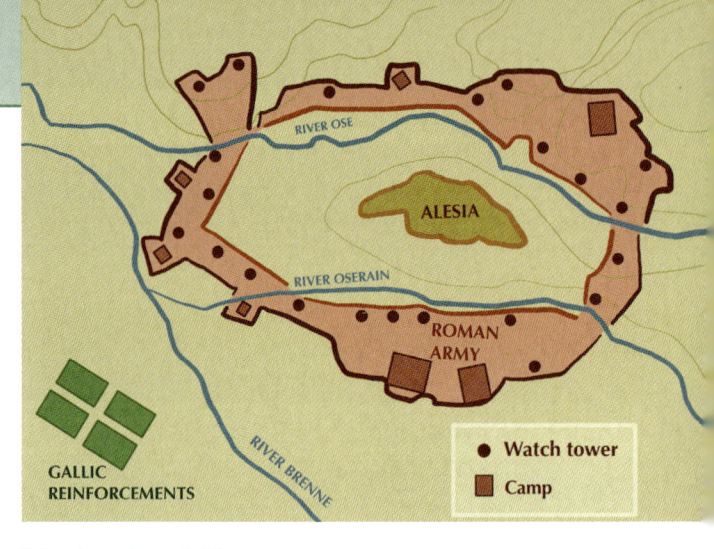

The battle of Alesia

Vercingetorix and his 80,000 men decided to withdraw to the well-fortified hilltop town of Alesia. Caesar, calculating that a force of so many soldiers, together with the local population, would soon run out of food, decided to lay siege to Alesia. Noticing what was happening, Vercingetorix dispatched his cavalry to seek reinforcements across Gaul.

Caesar ordered three sets of ditches to be dug, completely encircling the town of Alesia, and beyond these he constructed a rampart and wall 3.5 metres high, with defensive turrets at regular intervals. The siege works were vast, stretching for 10 miles.

Then, in order to defend his troops against the reinforcements Vercingetorix had called for, Caesar ordered a second set of defensive works to be built, facing the opposite direction. These fortifications ran for 13 miles. The Romans had provisions to last about a month. They positioned themselves in between the two sets of fortifications, and waited.

One episode shows the utter cruelty of the siege: as provisions were decreasing in the town, Vercingetorix ordered all the inhabitants who couldn't fight (children, women, old people, and the sick and injured) to leave the walled town. Caesar refused to allow them through the Roman fortified area, either for fear of an attack or to demonstrate his power. Whatever the reason, they were left to starve in no-man's land.

Finally, the Gallic relief force arrived, and the main battle began. The Romans were significantly inferior in number, and the battle was harshly fought, but the Romans' military training and experience prevailed. Vercingetorix was taken prisoner and, five years later, was paraded through the streets of Rome in Caesar's triumphal procession, before being publicly executed. After the fall of Alesia, Gallic resistance to Caesar was broken. The conquest of Gaul was completed the following year.

Chapter 10: Aquae Sūlis

pāx Rōmāna

sōl lūcēbat.
in valle erat nebula. nebula dēnsa dē palūde surgēbat.
in palūde erant aquae. aquae calidae dē terrā surgēbant.

vir ad palūdem stābat et dēnārium novum tenēbat.

vir, nōmine Antigonus, dēnārium novum   5
per nebulam dēnsam iēcit.

dēnārius in aquās calidās cecidit.

Giscō rem nārrat.

Antigonus, postquam dēnārium in aquās calidās iēcit, mihi appropinquāvit. locum intentē spectābat, ubi labōrābam. deinde 'locus est bonus, Giscō,' inquit. 'thermīs locum bonum lēgistis.' 'certē, sumus fēlīcēs,' Antigonō respondī. 'aquae sunt bonae. saxum est bonum. lignum bonum ē silvīs proximīs ferimus. et Britannī et Rōmānī bene labōrant.'

'vōs mīlitēs estis amīcī bonī Britannīs,' inquit Antigonus. 'ubi ego mīles eram, multae gentēs Britannicae erant hostēs Rōmānīs.'

'multōs annōs contrā gentēs Britannicās bellum gerēbāmus,' dīxī. 'nunc decōrum est nōbīs pācem in Britanniā habēre.'

tum tubam audīvimus. nōs omnēs – et operāriī et mīlitēs – statim tacuimus et ad āram parvam convēnimus. sacerdōtēs ad āram parvam prōcessērunt et sacrificium deae Sūlī Minervae fēcērunt. tum tōta turba – et Britannī et Rōmānī – vōtum deae Sūlī Minervae fēcit.

10 **proximus** *nearest, next to*
ferō *I carry, bring*
bene *well*
annus *year*
bellum gerō *I wage war*
15 **decōrum** *proper, right*
tuba *trumpet*
operārius *workman*
sacrificium *sacrifice, offering*
20 **Sūlis** *Sulis (local Celtic goddess)*
Minerva *Minerva (Roman goddess)*

magnum perīculum

Indus rem nārrat.

thermae, ubi Giscō labōrābat, erant novae. templum prope thermās novās simul aedificāre coepimus. decōrum erat nōbīs templum magnificum aedificāre, quod aquae calidae erant sacrae. fabrī erant Gallī, operāriī erant Britannī et servī erant captīvī ē gentibus Britannicīs. 5

cōtīdiē viae novae erant plēnae. multa plaustra ad locum, ubi strēnuē et dīligenter labōrābāmus, veniēbant. alia saxum portābant, alia lignum. puerī saepe ad plaustra conveniēbant, quod prō praemiō operāriōs adiuvāre volēbant. ūnum ē puerīs bene meminī.

parvus puer nōs semper adiuvābat. īnstrūmenta portābat et cibum 10 ferēbat. ōlim, ubi mūrōs exstruēbāmus, cāsus dīrus erat. plaustrum saxa ingentia portābat; puer prope plaustrum labōrābat. subitō magnum fragōrem audīvimus. ūnum ē saxīs dē plaustrō cecidit et puerum percussit.

'ei mihi!' exclāmāvit puer miser. in perīculō dīrō erat. in magnō dolōre 15 sub saxō ingentī iacēbat.

'Giscō! Inde!' clāmāvit Antigonus. 'necesse est vōbīs puerum adiuvāre!'

ego et Giscō ad puerum miserum cucurrimus, sed saxum tollere nōn poterāmus. Celer vehementer lātrābat. tum ūnus ē captīvīs Britannicīs ad nōs festīnāvit. captīvus erat ingēns et validus. ingēns captīvus saxum 20 cum summā difficultāte sustulit et puerum līberāvit.

ingentī captīvō dīxit Giscō, 'tibi grātiās agō. puerum servāvistī. tibi lībertātem prōmittō.'

simul *at the same time*
coepī *I began*
faber *craftsman*
Gallus *a Gaul*
plaustrum *cart*
alia ... alia ... *some ... others ...*
prō *for, in return for*
meminī *I remember*
mūrus *wall*
exstruō *I build*
cāsus *accident*
dīrus *dreadful*
ei mihi! *argh!*

difficultās *difficulty*
grātiās agō *I give thanks*
prōmittō *I promise*

Aquae Sulis

The hot spring

Aquae Sulis (modern Bath) lies where the Fosse Way crosses the River Avon. It grew into an important town in the Roman Empire because of its sacred springs. Still today 1,170,000 litres of hot water (46°C), rich in minerals, rise up out of the ground, as they have done for thousands of years. It is likely that, for a long time before the Romans came, the Britons living nearby had regarded the spring as a holy place whose waters had healing properties.

Winning hearts and minds

Soon after the invasion of Britain in AD 43, the Roman army was campaigning against the Silures. It is possible that soldiers injured in the fighting came to recuperate in the healing waters of the spring. As you learned in the previous chapter, after the suppression of Boudica's revolt, the new governor and procurator took a gentler approach to governing Britain. They wanted to win over the native Britons and encourage them to adopt a Roman way of life. One way they did this was by building Roman-style towns and amenities in the territory they had already conquered.

At Aquae Sulis they began to construct a religious, health, and leisure complex on the site of the sacred spring. In our stories Gisco and Indus are working on the first stages of this building project in AD 62; it was completed by AD 76.

The temple

The hot spring was at the centre of the complex. The Romans, like the Britons, thought the spring was a holy place. On one side they built a temple to Sulis Minerva. Sulis was a local British goddess and Minerva was the Roman goddess of healing. By joining the names together, the Romans encouraged the Britons to associate Sulis with the Roman goddess. The area around the temple and spring was the sacred courtyard. In the middle of the courtyard was an altar, where sacrifices were made.

The baths

On the other side of the spring, a huge set of public baths was constructed. There were three warm baths, using water from the naturally hot spring. Later another set of baths was added, heated by a hypocaust; here there was a caldarium, a tepidarium, and a frigidarium.

The spring overflow

Roman engineers designed a plumbing and drainage system which can still be seen today. Hot water from the spring was carried to the baths in lead pipes, using the flow of gravity. The original Roman drain carries surplus water from the spring, which then flows into the River Avon. Archaeologists have made some important discoveries in the drain, including thirty-four gemstones and a tin mask.

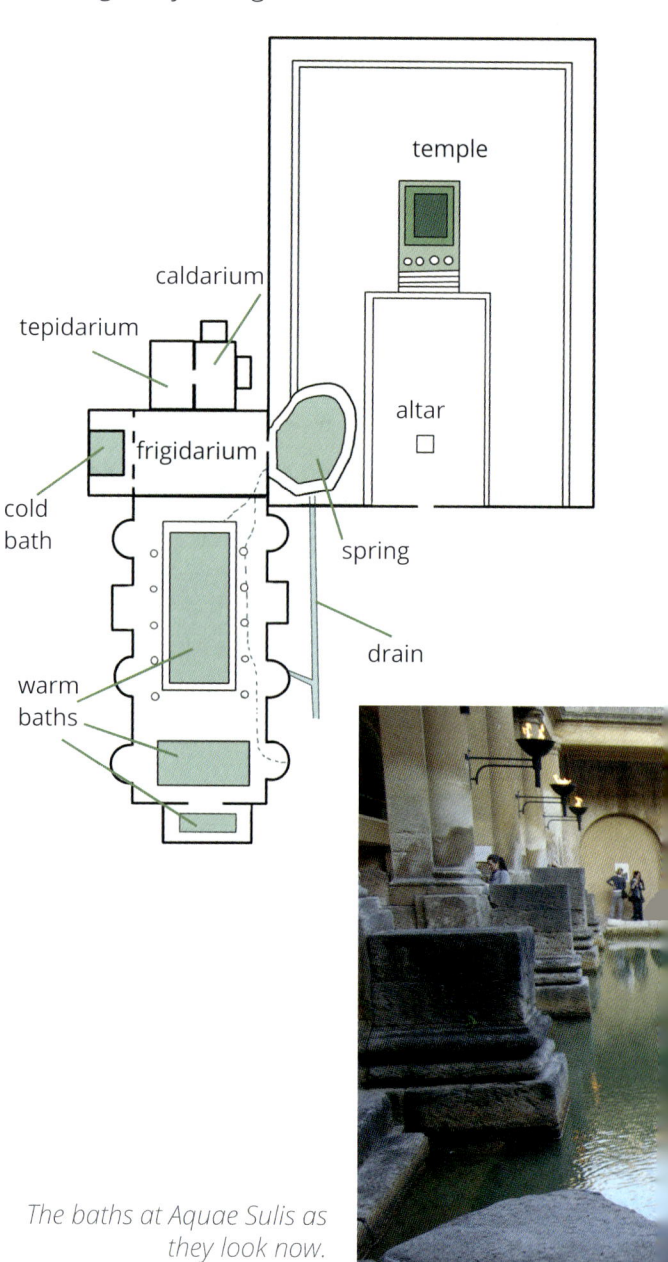

The baths at Aquae Sulis as they look now.

Visitors and their offerings

Aquae Sulis grew into an important religious centre. People travelled there to worship the goddess, to visit the spring and the baths, and to seek a cure for their ailments. They made sacrifices to Sulis Minerva (sometimes just called Sulis), dedicated altars to her, and threw offerings into the sacred spring. Romans offered presents to the gods in the hope of receiving an answer to a prayer, or thanking them for a prayer which had been granted.

Part of the handle of a metal dish which might have been used for offering holy water. Archaeologists have found many dishes like this in the spring. They have the letters **DSM** *on them, which is short for* **deae Suli Minervae**. *What do you think the words mean?*

PRISCUS
TOUTI FILIUS
LAPIDARIUS
CIVES CARNU
TENUS SULI
DEAE VOTUM SOLVIT
LIBENS MERITO

Priscus, son of Toutius, stonemason, from the Carnutes tribe, willingly and deservedly fulfils his vow to the goddess Sulis.

Dedication to the goddess Sulis by a stonemason from Gaul.

DEAE
SVLIMI
NERVAE
SVLINVS
MATV
RI FIL
V S L M

To the goddess Sulis Minerva, Sulinus son of Maturus willingly and deservedly kept the promise he made.

The abbreviation VSLM = **votum solvit libenter merito**

◊ Find a letter written backwards.
◊ Find an 'i' written above another letter.
◊ Find some letters that are joined together.

Sulinus set up this altar to Sulis Minerva. He had made a promise and kept it. We don't know what the promise was. Perhaps he had promised to set up the altar if his prayer was granted.

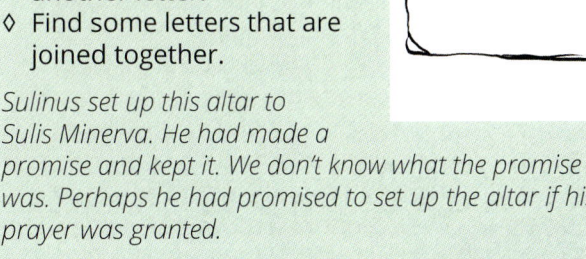

QUESTION

Why did people come to Aquae Sulis?

Think of as many reasons as you can.

Different gods

The Roman state religion was polytheistic. The Romans worshipped many gods and had no problem with adding more. As the Roman Empire expanded, the Romans merged local gods and goddesses with their own. In doing so, they encouraged the conquered peoples to identify with Roman customs and peacefully accept a Roman way of life.

nōmina alia aliīs gentibus

'Different names to different peoples.' This is how Pliny the Elder expressed the idea that different peoples worshipped the same gods, but gave them different names. Often the gods that were merged shared characteristics, but they did not have to match perfectly.

Sulis Minerva

Sulis: The local goddess of the thermal springs. Her name probably derived from a Celtic word for 'sun'.

Minerva: The Roman goddess of wisdom, medicine, and crafts.

The natural springs were a sacred place for the native Iron Age Britons. They associated the hot spring, with its bubbling and mineral-rich waters, with the goddess Sulis.

Although there is no evidence of any shrine or settlement, coins from the late Iron Age have been found in the spring. This suggests that people in the Iron Age probably worshipped Sulis, the goddess of the spring. The name the Romans gave the town, Aquae Sulis, means Waters of Sulis.

The grand temple and bathing complex were constructed in honour of Sulis Minerva, the fusion of the British and Roman goddesses. This was a powerful strategic decision by the occupying Roman force. The native Britons would continue to worship Sulis, assimilated with the Roman Minerva, and therefore would be likely to accept and respect the Roman-style complex.

Bronze head of Sulis Minerva, probably from the statue inside the temple at Aquae Sulis.

Hadad and Jupiter

Hadad was the god of storm and rain in the ancient Semitic and Mesopotamian religions. He was depicted as a bearded man, often holding a club and a thunderbolt.

When the Romans conquered Damascus, in Syria, in 64 BC, they assimilated Hadad with Jupiter, the Roman god of thunder and the king of the gods. They commissioned the local architect Apollodorus to design a new temple for Hadad-Jupiter. He copied the symmetry and scale of Roman temples, but kept much of the original Semitic design.

Isis

Isis was the Egyptian mother goddess and had been worshipped from around 3000 BC. Private shrines to Isis were set up in Rome from about the first century BC, and her cult was gradually accepted into Roman religion.

As her popularity grew, Isis was given new titles. She was sometimes referred to as 'having 10,000 names'. In a novel by Apuleius, the main character, Lucius, is visited by Isis, who says:

> The whole world worships my single divinity, in many forms and various rituals, and under different names. The Phrygians call me the Pessinuntican mother of the gods, the Athenians call me Minerva, the Cypriots Venus, the Cretans Diana, the Sicilians Stygian Proserpina, the Eleusinians Ceres. Some call me Juno, others Bellona, and others Hecate. The Ethiopians and the Egyptians call me by my true name, Queen Isis.

QUESTION

Do you agree with Pliny that people worship the same gods but under different names?

LANGUAGE NOTE 1: 1ST AND 2ND DECLENSION ADJECTIVES

1. Study the following sentence:

    subitō fragōrem audīvimus.
    Suddenly we heard a crash.

    Look at the word **fragōrem**.
    i. What case (nominative, accusative, dative, ablative) is it?
    ii. Is it singular or plural?
    iii. Look up **fragor** in the dictionary: is it masculine, feminine, or neuter?

2. Now look at this sentence:

    subitō magnum fragōrem audīvimus.
    Suddenly we heard a big crash.

    magnum (*big*) is an **adjective** and describes **fragōrem**. Look at the ending of **magnum**. **fragōrem** is accusative, singular, and masculine, so **magnum** is also accusative, singular, and masculine.

3. Finally study this sentence:

    nōs viās bonās aedificābāmus.
    We were building good roads.

    viās is accusative, plural, and feminine. **bonās** describes **viās**, so **bonās** is also accusative, plural, and feminine.

4. Latin adjectives change their endings to match the noun they describe in **case**, **number** (singular or plural), and **gender**.

5. Adjectives like **magnus** and **bonus** can change their endings as follows:

SINGULAR	*masculine*	*feminine*	*neuter*
nominative	**bonus**	**bona**	**bonum**
accusative	**bonum**	**bonam**	**bonum**
dative	**bonō**	**bonae**	**bonō**
ablative	**bonō**	**bonā**	**bonō**

PLURAL			
nominative	**bonī**	**bonae**	**bona**
accusative	**bonōs**	**bonās**	**bona**
dative	**bonīs**	**bonīs**	**bonīs**
ablative	**bonīs**	**bonīs**	**bonīs**

Because the masculine changes like **amīcus**, the feminine like **puella**, and the neuter like **dōnum**, adjectives such as **magnus** and **bonus** are known as **1st and 2nd declension adjectives**.

senex ignōtus

Catia rem nārrat.

Giscō et Indus, ubi oppidum pulchrum cum Britannīs aedificābant, laetī erant, quamquam labor erat dūrus. duōs annōs ibi habitābāmus. annō prīmō ē Giscōne concēpī. laetissima eram.

simulatque Giscōnī rem fēlīcem nūntiāvī, vir laetus

'ō mea pulchra Catia!' clāmāvit. 'quam fēlīx sum! laeta es, mea columba?'

'certē,' respondī, 'laetissima sum.'

tum Giscōnī ōsculum dedī. Celer lātrābat. dominus rīsit et 'ōsculum quoque cupis, Celer?' rogāvit. 'hahae! quam fidēlis es!'

Giscō, postquam canem fidēlem mulsit, ad labōrem laetē rediit. intereā ego ad fontem sacrum ambulāvī, quod Mātribus Sūleviīs vōtum facere volēbam. Celer fidēlis mēcum ambulābat.

ubi ad fontem stābam, senem ignōtum cōnspexī. senex vestīmenta sordida gerēbat et tabulam parvam tenēbat. fūrtim circumspectābat. Celer senem miserum intentē spectābat, et vehementer lātrāvit. senex, postquam canem ferōcem audīvit, perterritus ā fonte cucurrit. tabula parva dē manū cecidit.

tabulam sustulī. perterrita vōtum malum lēgī:

Sūlī equitem Numidicum dēvoveō

eques Numidicus fīlium meum necāvit

labor work
concipiō I conceive, become pregnant

ōsculum kiss

hahae! ha ha!
redeō I go back, return
intereā meanwhile
Sūleviae Suleviae (Celtic goddesses)
mēcum = *cum mē*
tabula curse tablet
fūrtim secretly, like a thief
ferōx fierce
ā = *ab*
manus hand
malus bad, evil
eques horseman
Numidicus Numidian
dēvoveō I curse

A Roman curse tablet (Source 1 on the facing page).

Curses

A curse tablet is a small piece of lead or pewter, flattened into a thin flexible sheet, with a smooth surface. You would scratch your curse on the sheet with a metal stylus, then roll it up and throw it into the spring. The lettering is sometimes of very poor quality, suggesting that an illiterate person was copying letters. Some of the inscriptions are just scratches imitating letters. It is likely that there were people who made a living from inscribing curses on tablets and selling them.

One hundred and thirty curse tablets have been found in the spring at Aquae Sulis. Similar curse tablets have been found in other parts of Britain and all over the Roman Empire. Often they use formulae which we would think of as magic: writing the words backwards or using nonsense words such as **bescu**, **berebescu**, and **bazagra**. Some uses of magic were outlawed in the Roman world. In Chapter 8 you read that Emperor Claudius banned the Druids on the grounds that human sacrifice was magic. The presence of these curse tablets in a sacred place shows that the distinction between religion and magic was not always clear-cut.

SOURCE 1

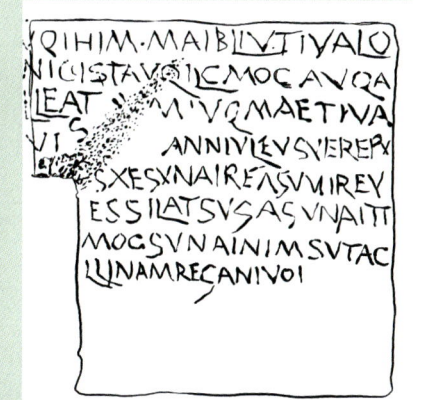

QU[I] MIHI VILBIAM IN[V]OLAVIT SIC LIQUAT COM[O] AQUA ..... EL[LA] M[U]TA QUI EAM [INVOL] AVIT ... VELVINNA EX[S]UPEREUS VERIANUS SEVERINUS AUGUSTALIS COMITIANUS MINIANUS CATUS GERMANILL[A] IOVINA

May he who stole vilbia (?) from me become liquid as water. May she who stole [or devoured] her become dumb ... Velvinna Exsupereus ... (a list of names follows)

Some people think that Vilbia is a woman's name. Others think that the word refers to an object which has been stolen.

◊ The words are in the correct order, but each word is written backwards. Can you see MIHI and VILBIAM in the first line?

SOURCE 2

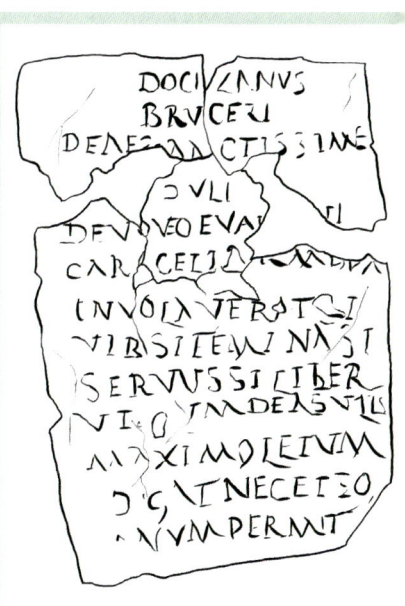

DOCILIANUS BRUCERI DEAE SANCTISSIMAE SULI DEVOVEO EUM QUI CARACALLAM MEUM INVOLAVERIT SI VIR SI FEMINA SI SERVUS SI LIBER ...

Docilianus son of Brucerus to the most holy goddess Sulis. I curse whoever stole my hooded cloak – whether man or woman, slave or free. May the goddess Sulis inflict death on him and not allow him to sleep or have children now or in the future until he has brought my cloak back to her temple.

SOURCE 3

Docimedis has lost two gloves. He asks that the thief should lose his mind and eyes in the goddess' temple.

QUESTIONS

These sources are examples of the curse tablets from the spring at Aquae Sulis.

1. What do the curses have in common?
2. Does it seem strange to you that religion is used to bring harm to people?

LANGUAGE NOTE 2: 3RD DECLENSION ADJECTIVES

1. Study the following sentences:

   Quārtilla fēminās trīstēs spectābat.
   Quartilla was watching the unhappy women.

   senex canem ferōcem audīvit.
   The old man heard the fierce dog.

   In the first sentence, **fēminās** is accusative, plural, and feminine. **trīstēs** describes **fēminās**, so **trīstēs** is also accusative, plural, and feminine.

   In the second sentence, **canem** is accusative, singular, and masculine. **ferōcem** describes **canem**, so **ferōcem** is also accusative, singular, and masculine.

2. Adjectives such as **trīstis** and **ferōx** change their endings as follows:

SINGULAR	masculine/feminine	neuter	masculine/feminine	neuter
nominative	trīst**is**	trīst**e**	ferōx	ferōx
accusative	trīst**em**	trīst**e**	ferōc**em**	ferōx
dative	trīstī		ferōcī	
ablative	trīstī		ferōcī	

PLURAL				
nominative	trīst**ēs**	trīst**ia**	ferōc**ēs**	ferōc**ia**
accusative	trīst**ēs**	trīst**ia**	ferōc**ēs**	ferōc**ia**
dative	trīst**ibus**		ferōc**ibus**	
ablative	trīst**ibus**		ferōc**ibus**	

   Because the masculine and feminine change like **fūr**, and the neuter like **caput**, adjectives such as **trīstis** and **ferōx** are known as **3rd declension adjectives**.

3. Adjectives can come either before or after the noun they describe, although adjectives of size and quantity (such as **magnus** and **omnis**) are more likely to come before their noun.

vōx crūdēlis

vōtum malum diū cōgitābam. nocte dormīre nōn poteram. nōnnūllās hōrās in lectō iacēbam. Giscō dormiēbat. tum surrēxī. summum perīculum sēnsī. domum circumspectāvī, sed nihil vīdī. vīcus erat quiētus. Celer dormiēbat. itaque ad lectum redībam.

subitō manus mē tenuit. tum pugiōnem cōnspexī. dē pugiōne 5
cadēbat sanguis. 'custōdem Rōmānum iam necāvī,'
susurrāvit vōx crūdēlis. 'canem saevum tuum sopōrāvī.
nunc equitem Numidicum scelestum petō.'
Giscōnem ē somnō excitāre volēbam, sed
exclāmāre nōn audēbam. 10

deinde rēs mīrābilis accidit. dē manū
cecidit pugiō sanguineus. cum magnō
clāmōre vir ignōtus periit. tum vōcem
nōtam audīvī: 'es tūta, Catia.' Indus
prope senem mortuum stābat. 15
gladium magnificum tenēbat.

diū	*for a long time*
cōgitō	*I think, consider*
nōnnūllī	*some, several*
lectus	*bed*
sentiō	*I feel, notice*
itaque	*and so, therefore*
pugiō	*dagger*
vōx	*voice*
saevus	*savage*
sopōrō	*I drug*
somnus	*sleep*
excitō	*I wake up*
sanguineus	*bloody*
tūtus	*safe*

LANGUAGE PRACTICE

1. Translate the following sentences, taking care to pair the adjectives with the appropriate nouns.
   a. multōs annōs mīlitēs nostrās thermās aedificābant.
   b. Rōmānī bonam pācem habēre cupiēbant.
   c. contrā hostēs crūdēlēs Luccus vīcum dēfendēbat.
   d. dē plaustrō grave saxum subitō cecidit.
   e. captīvus īnfēlīcem puerum servāvit.
   f. tandem senex saevus custōdem vīdit.

2. Select the correct form of the adjective to fill the gap, then translate the sentence.
   a. Giscō et Indus in .... popīnā sedēbant.   (parvō, parvā, parvīs)
   b. Druidēs dē contrōversiīs .... cōnstituērunt.   (difficilibus, difficilēs, difficilis)
   c. .... līberī deae vōta dedērunt.   (omnēs, omnī, omnibus)
   d. ego Lūcīliō epistulam .... mīsī.   (brevis, breve, brevem)
   e. praemia amīcīs .... dabāmus.   (fidēlis, fidēlēs, fidēlibus)
   f. cōtīdiē tū cum .... frātribus labōrābās.   (laetus, laetīs, laetōs)

Military life

Roman camp at Aquae Sulis

In about AD 44 the Roman force arrived in the area which was to become the town of Aquae Sulis. They met no resistance from the local British tribe. The Dobunni had been trading with the Roman Empire for decades and accepted the Romans peacefully. The Romans built a wooden fort there to protect the strategically important crossing point of the River Avon, about 800 metres away from the spring. It was an important location, on the Fosse Way, ready to protect the Roman terrritory to the east and continue the assault against the Silures to the west.

The vicus

The arrival and construction of a Roman camp attracted craftsmen and traders. Settlements grew organically next to Roman camps. Here native Britons, foreign merchants, and Roman veterans lived and interacted with the soldiers in the camp. In this way early Roman Aquae Sulis was shaped by military needs.

*We can see the Latin word **vīcus** in many place names in Britain. It was adapted in Old English to become wic, wick, wich, or wych. Some examples of places which grew from Roman settlements are Hackney Wick, Gatwick, Aldwych, Dulwich, Norwich, and Ipswich.*

Vindolanda

The fort at Vindolanda was on the northern frontier of the Roman Empire in Britannia. When it was first built in the 80s AD it was a wooden structure, but it was later rebuilt in stone. Just outside the walls of the military fort was a vicus which also contained a bathhouse.

What makes the site of Vindolanda special is the discovery of over four hundred wooden tablets, preserved in the waterlogged ground of a rubbish heap in the corner of the commander's house. Most of these are from AD 97–103. Although they were written a few decades after our stories are set, the picture they paint of daily life in a Roman camp would not have changed significantly.

The tablets are made of thin slivers of wood between 1 and 3 millimetres thick, about the size of a postcard. They give us an insight into the lives of ordinary soldiers, usually not mentioned in historical texts. From the tablets we can also see how the soldiers interacted with the local people.

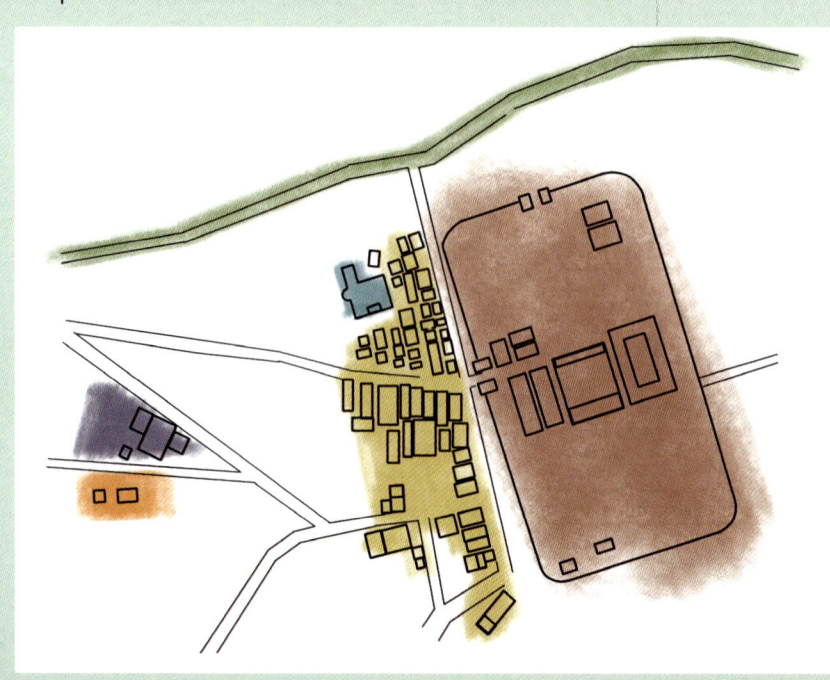

Key

red: army camp
yellow: vicus
blue: bathhouse
purple: temples
orange: industrial area
green: road

Work duties

One tablet from Vindolanda records the duties of the soldiers at the camp:

> Of 343 men present, twelve were making shoes, eighteen were building the bathhouse, some were out collecting lead, clay, and rubble. Others were assigned to the wagons, the kilns, the hospital, and to plastering duty.

Trajan's column

Trajan's column is a huge monument in Rome, built to commemorate Emperor Trajan's defeat of the Dacians (in modern Romania). The continuous image carved on stone winds twenty-three times round the column from the base to the top and depicts scenes from the conquest.

Although it depicts a military campaign, there are relatively few scenes of battle. Instead we can see tasks carried out by the soldiers.

QUESTION

Look at these images from Trajan's column. What are the soldiers doing?

Everyday life

The Vindolanda tablets and other artefacts found at the site allow us to see the more intimate relationships within the camp and the preoccupations of the people who lived there.

Flavius Cerialis

Flavius Cerialis was the commander of the camp from about AD 97. His family was allowed to live within the camp. Archaeologists have found a party invitation to his wife Lepidina from her friend at a nearby camp:

> Greetings from Claudia Severa to Lepidina. On 11 September, sister, for my birthday, I ask you to come and visit us, to make the day more enjoyable for me, if you are free.

Other soldiers would also have had contact with their families. This lucky soldier received a parcel containing some essentials and a note from his family:

> I have sent you ... pairs of socks from Sattua, two pairs of sandals and two pairs of underpants. Greet all your messmates with whom I pray that you live in the greatest good fortune.

Games and passing the time

Life in an army camp was not all about battles and training. Many soldiers saw little military combat. Instead they built roads and infrastructure for the conquered territory. In their free time, soldiers played games and gambled with dice. These dice are made of ivory and glass.

The people of Roman Britain

D[IS] M[ANIBUS] REGINA LIBERTA ET CONIUGE BARATES PALMYRENUS NATIONE CATVALLAVNA AN XXX

To the spirits of the dead, for Regina his freedwoman and wife, of the Catuvellaunian tribe, aged 30, Barates, a Palmyran by birth [set this up]
Regina the freedwoman of Barates, alas.

Most of the inscription is in Latin; the last line is in Palmyrene (Aramaic). Barates was from Palmyra in Syria.

This tombstone was found at Arbeia (South Shields), a fort near the eastern end of Hadrian's Wall. In the late second century AD Arbeia was a busy port and supply base for the troops stationed on Hadrian's Wall. Near to the fort there would have been a small civilian settlement occupied by traders and workmen who supplied the needs of the soldiers, veterans who had settled there rather than returning to their native lands, and the families of the soldiers. Officially, Roman soldiers were not allowed to marry, but they often formed relationships with local women, as Gisco did with Catia. After discharge a soldier could marry, and any children he already had would become Roman citizens.

A multilingual society

The Iron Age Britons spoke a language (more precisely, several variants of a language) which historians call Brittonic. The Roman conquest introduced to Britain not just the Latin language, but also the languages of the Empire. People came to Britain from all over the Empire, as soldiers, traders, slaves, and administrators, and they brought with them their languages, such as Greek, the languages of the Gallic and Germanic tribes, and the languages of the Near East. For these people Latin was their common language.

The curses from Aquae Sulis are almost all written in Latin. The curse on this tablet (*right*) is intriguing because it is in a language which isn't Latin. It could be a British language.

QUESTIONS

Look at the maps of the Empire (pages 2–3) and Britannia (page 125). Find Syria, and the territory of the Catuvellauni.

1. Both Regina and Barates were far from home. How might they have felt about living in Arbeia? How might they have come to live so far from their places of birth?

2. What can we learn from this tombstone about the people who were living in Britain in the second century AD?

valē

Catia	annō secundō nūntium fēlīcem accēpimus. praefectus ab exercitū Giscōnem dīmīsit. itaque nōs ā Britanniā discēdere cōnstituimus.	**praefectus** *commander* **dīmittō** *I release, discharge*
Giscō	nūntium trīstem simul accēpimus. Antigonus ā morbō ignōtō periit.	**nūntius** *message, news* **morbus** *illness*
Sabīna	quōmodo tū ad urbem Rōmam advēnistī, Inde?	

Indus respondēre coepit, sed subitō Lūcriō popīnam intrāvit et Faustō appropinquāvit. dominō susurrāvit servus, 'omnia parāvī.'

Faustus necesse est tibi ab urbe discēdere, fīlia mea.

The pediment of the temple at Aquae Sulis, with its original colours shown. The carved head is thought to be based on the Gorgon's head, a symbol of the goddess Minerva.

QUESTION

As you learned in the previous chapter, the Britons burned the temple of Claudius at Camulodunum, yet they accepted the temple at Aquae Sulis. Why do you think the reactions were so different?

The Gorgons

The Gorgons were three sisters in Greek mythology. They were such terrifying monsters that anyone who looked at their faces was turned to stone. Often they were portrayed with glaring eyes and protruding tongues, snakes in their hair, beards, tusks, and golden wings.

The inside of a Greek drinking cup from the sixth century BC, decorated with a Gorgon's face.

SOURCE 1

SOURCE 3

A fifth-century BC Greek painting from a vase.

- Look at Source 1. What features of a Gorgon does this painting have? Why might the painter have chosen to decorate a drinking cup in this way?
- Similar images were often used by the Greeks on armour such as shields and breastplates. Why was that appropriate?

Medusa and Perseus

The most famous of the Gorgons was Medusa. She is often depicted with snakes in her hair, but with the face and body of a young girl. King Polydectes ordered Perseus to bring him the head of Medusa. With the help of the gods, Perseus was able to decapitate Medusa with his sword while she was asleep. But even after death Medusa's gaze retained its power, so Perseus put the head in a bag and eventually gave it to Minerva.

- Read or listen to the story of Perseus and Medusa.
- How was Perseus helped by the gods? What did they give him?
- How are Perseus and Medusa presented in this statue?

A nineteenth-century sculpture, showing Perseus with the head of Medusa.

SOURCE 2

- What parts of the story of Perseus and Medusa are being depicted in Source 3?

Study Sources 1, 2, and 3.

- Compare the way Gorgons are depicted in these three images.

Minerva and the Gorgon

Minerva (called Athena by the Greeks) was the goddess of war. She was often shown wearing a helmet and a breastplate, which was sometimes decorated with the image of a Gorgon's head.

- Look at the pediment of the temple at Aquae Sulis on page 165. Why do you think that some people think the figure in the middle is a Gorgon?

Petrification

If you are petrified, you are, literally, turned to stone. Petrification ('turning into stone') comes from the Latin words *petra* (rock) and *faciō* (make).

- Petrification is a punishment in myths and stories from many cultures. Why do you think it is such a common theme?
- Imagine what it would mean to be turned to stone. How might it be different from being dead?
- Why is it such a frightening and terrible punishment?

RESEARCH

Find out about:
- the winged horse Pegasus.
- Perseus and Andromeda.
- other female monsters in mythology, e.g. Scylla, the Sirens, the Sphinx, the Harpies.
- people being turned to stone in other myths.

Chapter 11: mare

Ostia

nox erat. urbs erat quiēta. paucī hominēs per urbem ambulābant.
nōs per viās urbis celeriter prōcēdēbāmus.

Sabīna   cūr festīnāmus?
Lūcriō   pater tuus senātōrī magnam pecūniam dēbet.
Rūfīna   Faustus senātōrem maximē timet. servus
           senātōris tē quaerit.   5

postquam Lūcriō mē ad Forum Boārium
dūxit, flūmen per tenebrās vīdī.
tum scapham ascendimus.

trēs hōrās per flūmen nāvigābāmus,   10
tum ad portum vēnimus. portus Rōmae,
nōmine Ostia, iam erat clāmōsus.
multī operāriī ibi labōrābant.

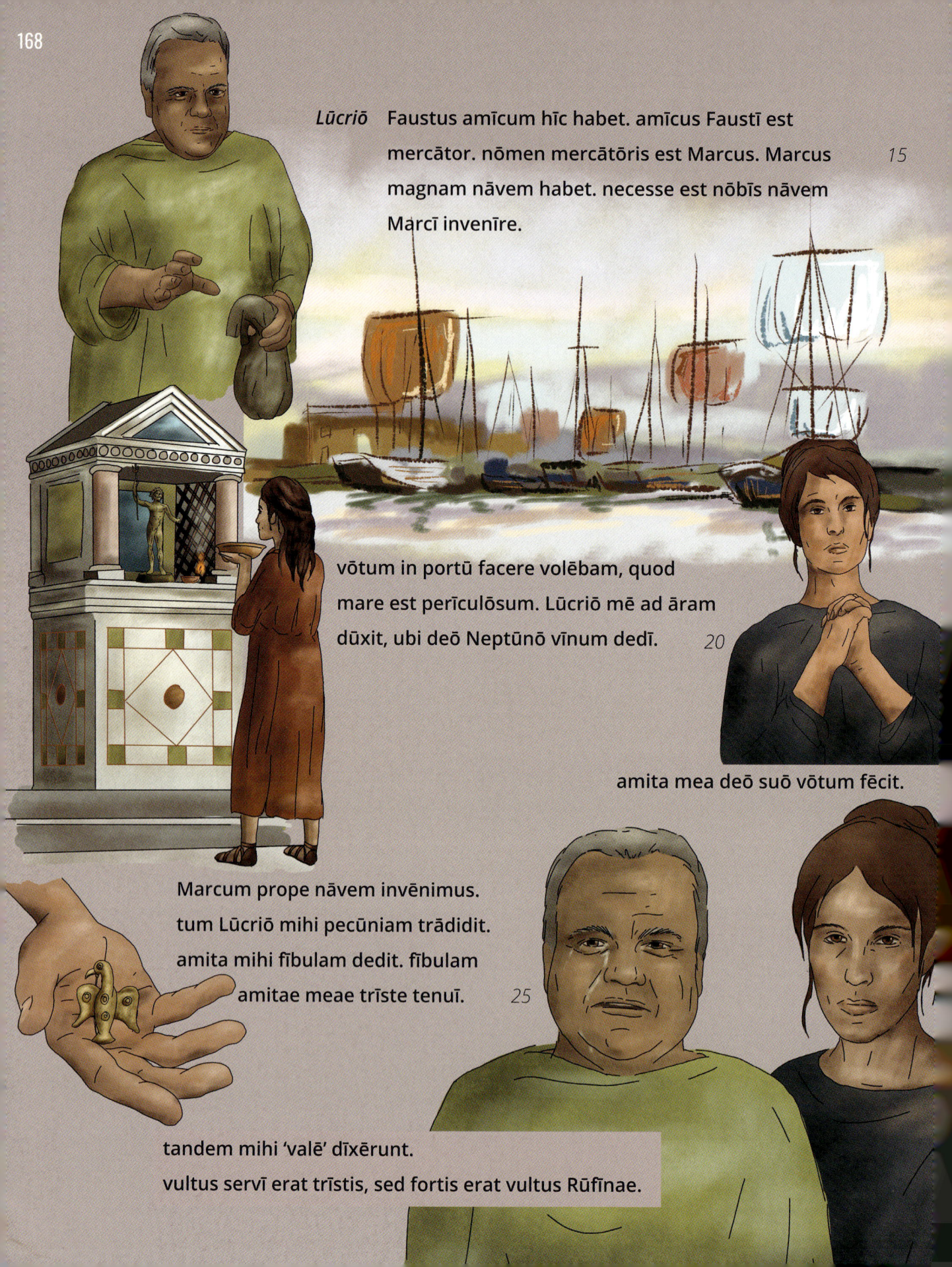

Lūcriō Faustus amīcum hīc habet. amīcus Faustī est
mercātor. nōmen mercātōris est Marcus. Marcus
magnam nāvem habet. necesse est nōbīs nāvem
Marcī invenīre.

vōtum in portū facere volēbam, quod
mare est perīculōsum. Lūcriō mē ad āram
dūxit, ubi deō Neptūnō vīnum dedī.

amita mea deō suō vōtum fēcit.

Marcum prope nāvem invēnimus.
tum Lūcriō mihi pecūniam trādidit.
amita mihi fībulam dedit. fībulam
amitae meae trīste tenuī.

tandem mihi 'valē' dīxērunt.
vultus servī erat trīstis, sed fortis erat vultus Rūfīnae.

Romans and the sea

If you look at the map on pages 2–3 you will see that the Roman Empire hugs the coast of the Mediterranean Sea, from Lusitania and Mauretania in the west to Syria in the east, with the city of Rome at the centre. The Romans called the Mediterranean *Mare Nostrum* (Our Sea) as well as *Mare Internum* (Internal Sea).

Oceanus and the gods of the sea

Romans believed that the Mare Internum, along with all the rivers, flowed into a great sea that surrounded the world, which they called Oceanus. Britannia was beyond Oceanus, which added to its mystery and strangeness in the eyes of Romans, especially before the conquest.

The poet Horace wrote this in 13 BC:

> **bēluōsus quī remōtīs**
> **obstrepit Ōceanus Britannīs**
> monster-filled Oceanus
> who roars round the far-off Britons

Oceanus was worshipped as a god. In this mosaic (*below*) he has lobster claws sprouting from his head, while dolphins and other fish are swimming out of his beard. The mosaic was made to decorate the floor of a grand villa in Cordoba, in Spain.

Neptune (the equivalent of the Greek Poseidon) was the main sea god worshipped by the Romans. His festival, the Neptunalia, was celebrated on 23 July and he had a temple on the Campus Martius in Rome. There were temples and statues of Neptune all over the Empire. For example, this inscription is from a temple in Chichester (Noviomagus) in Britain.

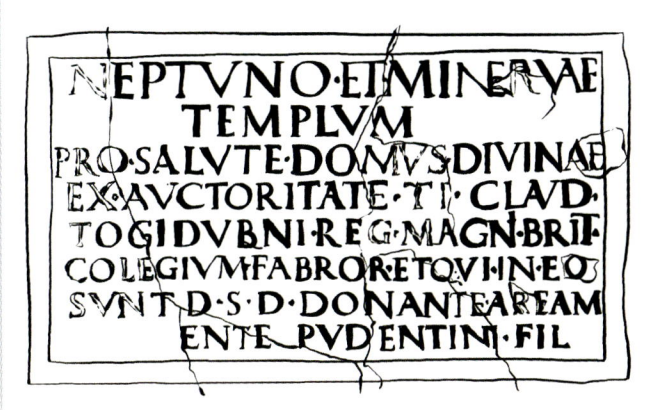

NEPTVNO·ET·MINERVAE
TEMPLVM
PRO·SALVTE·DOMVS·DIVINAE
EX·AVCTORITATE·TI·CLAVD·
TOGIDVBNI·REG·MAGN·BRIT·
COLEGIVM·FABROR·ET·QVI·IN·EO
SVNT·D·S·D·DONANTE·AREAM
ENTE·PVDENTINI·FIL

QUESTIONS

1. Which two gods is the temple dedicated to?
2. Why might these two gods have been chosen?

Before setting out on a voyage travellers gave offerings and prayers to Neptune, asking for a safe journey. And again, when they arrived safely at their destination, they would make more offerings and prayers of thanksgiving. Read these two excerpts from plays by Plautus. Why have the speakers been to sea?

> I give thanks to Neptune, my patron, who lives in the fish-teeming salt sea, for bringing me home from his dwelling, weighed down with my catch and with my boat safe.

> I give thanks to Neptune and to the Tempests because I am returning home safe, my business successful. And also to Mercury, who has helped me in my business affairs and quadrupled my fortune with profits.

Right: underwater archaeologists found this statue of Neptune in the River Rhône at Arles (Arelate) in the south of France.

ad Galliam

nōnnūllōs diēs nāvigābam. nāvis animālia ad amphitheātra Galliae
ferēbat. Marcus erat benignus, sed sōla eram. mox artificem
iuvenem cognōscēbam. nōmen artificis erat Alexander. Alexander
quoque erat sōlus. familia Alexandrī in Lūsitāniā habitābat.

Sabīna	ecce, terra! estne Gallia?	5
Alexander	minimē, Sabīna. est īnsula Corsica.	
Sabīna	quālis īnsula est Corsica?	
Alexander	īnsula magna et perīculōsa est, ubi latrōnēs saevī in montibus habitant.	

amphitheātrum *amphitheatre*
benignus *kind*
sōlus *lonely*
cognōscō *I get to know*
-ne *(marks a question)*
quālis? *what sort of?*
latrō *robber*
mōns *mountain*

tum nauta vetus nōbīs appropinquāvit. barba nautae erat longa, 10
vultus rūgōsus.

nauta   hodiē mare est quiētum. mihi placet. placetne tibi, puella?
Sabīna   certē, mihi placet. mare est pulchrum. sed ānxia sum.
vīdistīne mōnstra in marī? vīdistīne pīrātās?
nauta   multās fābulās nautārum dē mōnstrīs audīvī, 15
sed mōnstra numquam vīdī – nisi elephantōs et
crocodīlōs et hippopotamōs! hahae!
fābulīs dē mōnstrīs nōn crēdō.
sed ōlim manus pīrātārum
nāvem meam petīvit. 20

quid? pīrātaene tē petīvērunt? ubi accidit?

vetus *old*
barba *beard*
longus *long*
rūgōsus *full of wrinkles*
placet *it is pleasing, it pleases*
pīrāta *pirate*
numquam *never*
nisi *except*
elephantus *elephant*
crocodīlus *crocodile*
hippopotamus *hippopotamus*
crēdō *I believe*
manus *gang*

LANGUAGE NOTE 1: THE GENITIVE CASE

1. Look at the way the words **nauta**, **amīcus**, and **urbs** change in these sentences:

   nauta nōbīs appropinquāvit. barba **nautae** erat longa.
   A sailor approached us. The beard of the sailor was long.

   amīcus nāvem habet. nōmen **amīcī** est Marcus.
   A friend has a boat. The name of the friend is Marcus.

   urbs erat quiēta. per viās **urbis** prōcēdēbāmus.
   The city was quiet. We were going through the streets of the city.

   The words **nautae** (*of the sailor*), **amīcī** (*of the friend*), and **urbis** (*of the city*) are all examples of the **genitive case**.

2. The genitive case can be represented in English in two ways. For example:

   barba nautae erat longa.   *The beard of the sailor was long.*
                              or   *The sailor's beard was long.*

3. Think of two different ways to translate the words in bold below:

   nōmen īnsulae est Corsica.

   nōs **nāvem Marcī** quaerēbāmus.

   tū **pecūniam fūris** invēnistī.

The first sailors

These extracts from two Latin poems tell us about how some Romans felt about the sea and sailing.

1. Ovid is speaking about his girlfriend, who is preparing to go on a voyage:

   If only the first ship, the Argo, had sunk
   and no more seagoing ships were ever made …
   Look, Corinna is leaving her familiar bed and
      household gods
   and is preparing to go on treacherous paths.

2. Horace expresses amazement at the daring of the first person who ever set sail, braving the dangers of the sea. The poem continues:

   God, in his wisdom, separated
   the land from the sea – they are not compatible.
   But he wasn't successful; unholy boats
   still cross the waters they shouldn't touch.
   Humans are in a hurry to commit every
      forbidden sin.

The language of the sea

You have met the word *mare* for 'sea'. This isn't the only word the Romans had for the sea.

unda/undae *wave/waves*   **altum** *the deep*
frētum *narrow channel*   **sal** *salt*
vada *the shallows*   **marmor** *marble*
aequor *level surface of the sea*
pontus *a Greek word for 'sea'*

- Why do you think the Romans had so many words for the sea?
- How many words for 'sea' can you think of in English?

QUESTIONS

1. What different attitudes to the sea and sailing are shown in these poems?
2. Can you think of any things people do nowadays that the Romans would have regarded as impossible or unnatural?

Underwater archaeology

More than a thousand shipwreck sites have been found in the western Mediterranean, mostly off the French coast, dating between 100 BC and AD 100. Some of these ships were very large, able to carry heavy cargo.

A large merchant ship discovered off the coast near Toulon in southern France is one of the largest ancient ships ever found under the sea: it was about 40 metres long and 9 metres wide, with two masts. It was carrying a cargo of wine and pottery when it sank in about 75–60 BC. Archaeologists found amphorae stamped with the name of the potter, Publius Veveius Papus, who had a workshop in the wine-exporting area of Terracina in southern Italy, not far from Rome. After the excavation the ship was reburied in sand and left on the seabed.

In 2004 archaeologists found a river barge (*above*) in the mud at the bottom of the River Rhône at Arles in southern France. The boat had sunk with its cargo of building stones from a quarry less than 10 miles north of the town. The mud in the river had protected the boat from decay, but the water had damaged the wood. As a result, the whole boat was soft and spongy, held together only by the water of the river. It would disintegrate if the water evaporated. Conservationists found a solution. They soaked the wood for months in polyethylene glycol, then freeze-dried it. But the barge had to be cut into sections so that it would fit into the freeze-dryers. The whole process took two years.

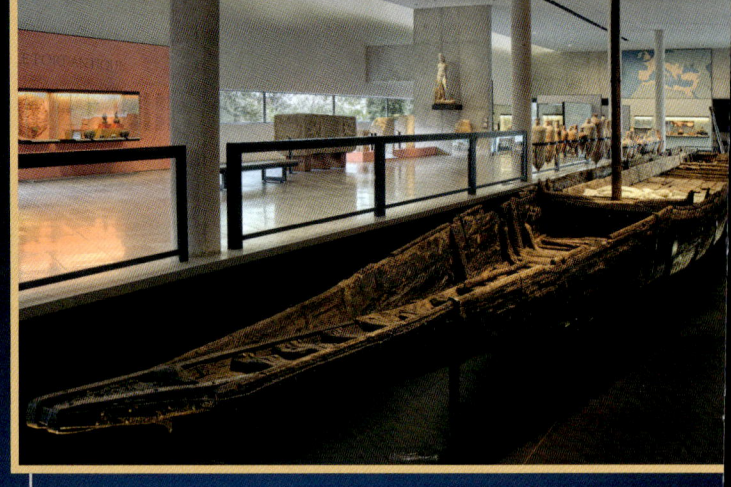

Roman Arelate (modern Arles) was nearer the sea than it is nowadays, because the mouth of the River Rhône has silted up and moved the coastline out. It was one of three great harbours in southern Gaul: the others were Massalia (modern Marseille) and Narbo (modern Narbonne). Ships sailed upriver from the Mediterranean or via a canal which linked Arelate with Massilia. Goods were then unloaded and transported from Arelate up the Rhône on barges. This was the supply route for the north of the Empire, including the legions stationed in Britannia.

RESEARCH

Find out about other discoveries made by underwater archaeologists. What techniques do they use to preserve what they find?

Navigation and maps

The Romans did not have compasses or charts; instead, they navigated by careful observation of their surroundings. They learned astronomy from the Phoenicians, an ancient civilization which originated in modern-day Lebanon. They applied this knowledge to navigate the sea at night, using the stars to find which direction was north. They also used the position of the sun at midday and the direction of the winds.

> The helmsman keeps watch all night long and observes the movement of the stars. *Petronius*

In general, the Romans sailed close to the coast to avoid straying off course. They also used landmarks on the mainland or the many islands of the Mediterranean to navigate their route. When sailing close to the coast, they used a device called a sounding line to avoid hitting rocks or sandbanks. A sounding line was a heavy bell-shaped mass, usually made of lead, attached to a rope. Sailors would hang it over the side of the ship and let it fall to the bottom of the sea to estimate the depth of the water.

The first sailing directions for coastal trips were written in Greek and described voyages within the Mediterranean. These directions listed landmarks that sailors could follow to stay on course and warned of dangers along the way. Later directions, in Latin or Greek, covered trips along the Atlantic coast of Africa and past the Persian Gulf to India and beyond.

Roman geography

Without planes or satellites to record the earth from above, creating a precise map was incredibly difficult. Generally, the Romans were more concerned with making their maps practical, rather than accurate – just like the London Underground map where stations are positioned relatively, but the distances between them are completely wrong. Roman maps are effective for following a route from point A to point B, but give no real sense of the distances between.

Strabo's *Geographica*

Strabo was a Roman geographer, who came originally from Greece. He wrote his *Geographica* between AD 14 and 37. His work, which included maps, was a history and description of the known world. It focused on people and cultures, as well as geographical features.

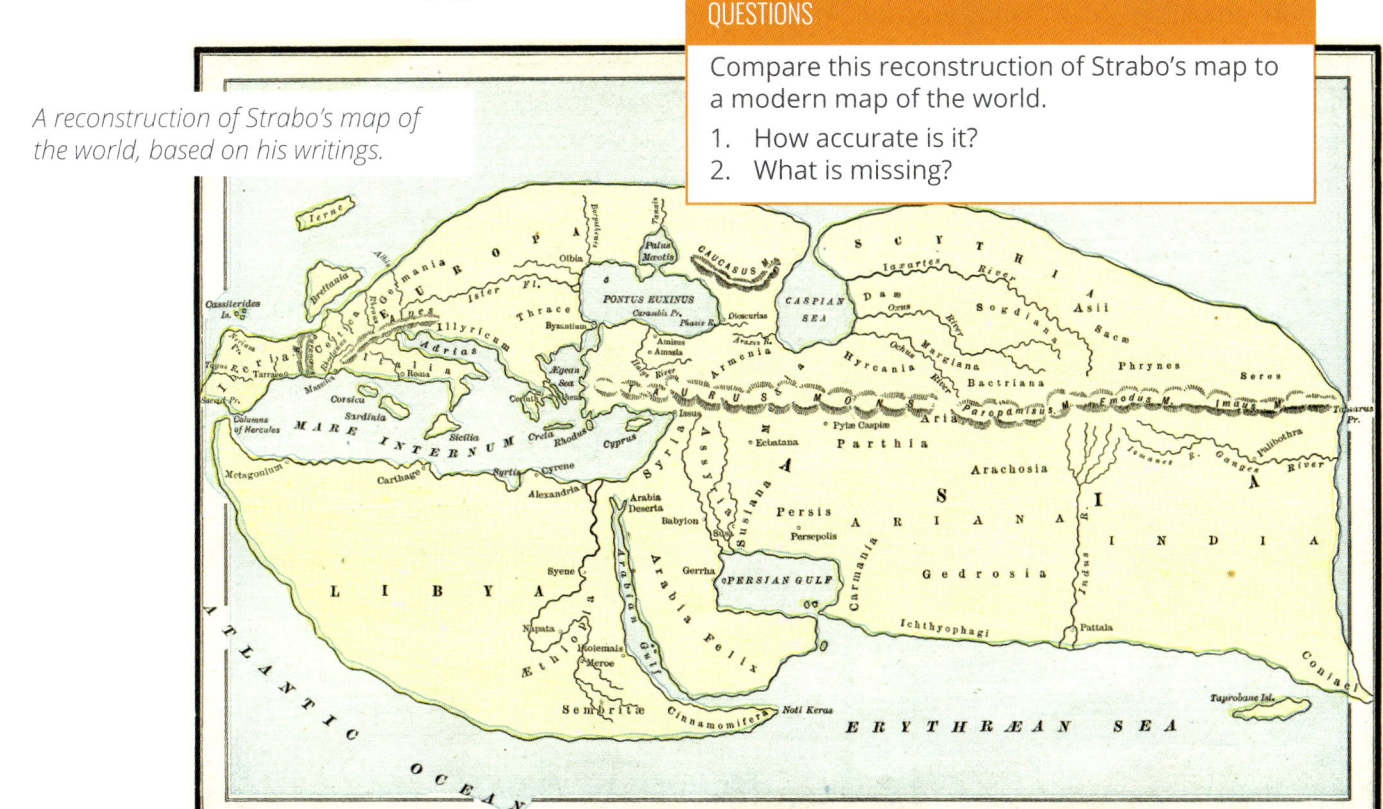

A reconstruction of Strabo's map of the world, based on his writings.

QUESTIONS

Compare this reconstruction of Strabo's map to a modern map of the world.
1. How accurate is it?
2. What is missing?

pīrātae

tum nauta fābulam mīrābilem dē pīrātīs nārrāvit.

'rem bene meminī. cum patre meō iter longum faciēbam. multae amphorae erant in nāve – vīnum ad Āfricam ferēbāmus – et inter nautās erant nōnnūllī senēs iuvenēsque. prope īnsulam Siciliam, ubi multī pīrātae habitābant, nāvigābāmus. subitō pater exclāmāvit: "ecce nāvis! sunt pīrātae! sunt fūrēs!"

'mox manus fūrum saevōrum nāvem nostram oppugnāvit et superāvit. nōs omnēs perterritī erāmus. aliī pīrātīs frūstrā resistēbant, aliī ā pīrātīs fugere temptābant. clāmōrēs senum et iuvenum perterritōrum nāvem implēbant. pater meus sub multitūdine amphorārum mē cēlāvit.

'dux pīrātārum nautīs duōbus appropinquāvit et exclāmāvit, "nunc vōs estis captīvī nostrī. quantam pecūniam in nāve habētis?"

'nautae respondēre nōlēbant. itaque dux scelestus eōs statim occīdit. tum corpora duōrum nautārum in mare iēcit. pīrātae pecūniam per tōtam nāvem quaerere coepērunt. ūnus pīrāta amphorīs appropinquāvit. perterritus cucurrī. tum ante oculōs pīrātārum et captīvōrum in mare dēsiluī. patrem nōn iterum vīdī.'

mihi attonitae susurrāvit Alexander, 'nautae perīcula nārrāre gaudent.'

amphora *amphora, jar*
Āfrica *Africa (Roman province in what is now North Africa)*
-que *and*
aliī ... aliī ... *some ... others ...*
multitūdō *large number, crowd*
cēlō *I hide*
duo *two*
quantus? *how big? how much?*
eōs *them*

dēsiliō *I jump*
gaudeō *I rejoice*

Dangers at sea

Piracy was a big problem in the Mediterranean in the first century BC, but by the time of our stories it was under control. Emperor Augustus established a navy, with fleets based at several points on the coasts of Italy, Gaul, and Egypt. One of the duties of these fleets was to suppress piracy.

Pirates still operated in the Red Sea. The *Travellers' Guide to the Red Sea*, an ancient handbook for merchants and sailors, advises ships to sail down the middle of the Red Sea, avoiding coming close to shore, to escape being detected by pirates.

Pirates would seize the cargo of a ship and kill the crew and passengers, or sell them into slavery. If the passengers were wealthy or important, the pirates would ransom them.

SOURCE 1 In this extract from Vergil's *Aeneid*, the hero of the poem, Aeneas, is sailing from Sicily to Italy when the goddess Juno sends a storm to destroy his fleet:

> Suddenly the clouds snatch away both sky and daylight
> from the Trojans' eyes; black night lies over the sea.
> The poles thunder and the sky flashes with repeated lightning,
> and everything threatens the crew with immediate death.
> As Aeneas is praying, a screeching blast from the North Wind
> strikes the sail head-on, and lifts the waves up to the stars.
> The oars shatter. Then the prow turns and offers its side
> to the waves. A sheer mountain of water presses against it in a mass.
> Some men are dangling on the crest of a wave; for others, the water gapes open
> and reveals the seabed between the waves; the water seethes with sand.
> The South Wind snatches up three ships and hurls them onto hidden rocks.
> The East Wind drives three ships from the deep sea
> onto the shallow sandbanks, a pitiful sight,
> smashes them into the shallow water, and surrounds them with a pile of sand.

SOURCE 2 Propertius is lamenting the death of Paetus, a young merchant who drowned at sea:

> Money, it's you who are the cause of life's stress;
> because of you we set out early on the road that leads to death.
> When Paetus spread his sails for Alexandria,
> it was you who overwhelmed him – three, four times – in a furious sea.
> For, in pursuit of you, the poor boy lost his life at a young age,
> and now floats as unfamiliar food for far-off fish.
> Paetus, your mother is unable to give you the proper rites of a loving burial,
> or put you in the tomb with your family ashes.
> But now the sea birds stand over your bones,
> now for you the whole Carpathian Sea is your tomb.

QUESTIONS

Look at Source 1.
1. Does reading this passage help you imagine what it feels like to be caught in a storm at sea?
2. How does Vergil use detail and images to make the storm seem exciting and frightening? Pick out some examples to support your ideas.

Look at Source 2.
3. Why do you think the Romans considered dying at sea to be a terrible fate?

LANGUAGE NOTE 2: THE GENITIVE PLURAL

1. The sentences below contain examples of the genitive plural:

   dux pīrātārum nōbīs appropinquāvit.
   The leader of the pirates approached us.

   ante oculōs captīvōrum in mare dēsiluī.
   Before the eyes of the prisoners I jumped into the sea.

   clāmōrēs senum nāvem implēbant.
   The shouts of the old men were filling the ship.

2. Compare the forms of the genitive case with the nominative singular in each declension:

SINGULAR	1st decl.	2nd decl.		3rd decl.	
nominative	puell**a**	amīc**us**	dōn**um**	fūr	caput
genitive	puell**ae**	amīc**ī**	dōn**ī**	fūr**is**	capit**is**

PLURAL					
genitive	puell**ārum**	amīc**ōrum**	dōn**ōrum**	fūr**um**	capit**um**

3. There is a chart of all the noun endings you have met on page 272.

This mosaic from Sicily is called The Great Hunt. It shows wild African animals being hunted and put onto ships to be taken to Rome.

tempestās I

1. mare erat quiētum. lūna surgēbat. sed vultus Sabīnae erat gravis.

2. esne ānxia, Sabīna?

3. ego sum sōla, Alexander.

4. nōnne familia tua in Galliā tē exspectat?

5. minimē. Marcus mē ad Galliam dūcit, ubi familia eius mē exspectat. familia mea in Subūrā habitat, et dē salūte patris meī timeō.

tempestās *storm*
lūna *moon*
nōnne? *surely?*
eius *his, her, its*
salūs *safety*

II

mediā nocte vōx Alexandrī Sabīnam ē somnō excitāvit:

'tempestās appropinquat, Sabīna!'

puella fessa surrēxit et circumspectāvit.
ventus iam erat validus.

mox multum pluēbat. 5

deinde **fulgēbat**
et *vehementer*
tonābat.

Sabīna mare ānxiē spectāvit.
nunc undae altae ubīque erant. 10
fragor undārum altārum eam terruit.

tum undae altissimae nāvem percutere
coepērunt. omnēs in nāve erant perterritī. aliī
deum Iovem ōrābant, aliī deum Neptūnum.
nautae valdē timēbant, et clāmōrēs 15
animālium – leōnum elephantōrumque –
nāvem implēbant.

ventus *wind*	tonābat *it was thundering*
multum *much*	unda *wave*
pluēbat *it was raining*	altus *high, deep*
fulgēbat *there was lightning*	terreō *I frighten*
	leō *lion*

subitō ingēns unda nāvem percussit.

ei mihi!

omnis spēs salūtis aberat. 20

Alexander manum puellae vix tenēre potuit.

ūnā ad nāvem diū haerēbant.
nōnnūllās hōrās ventus erat validissimus.
sed tandem vīs ventī sēdāvit. nāvis ad portum 25
Galliae, nōmine Arelātē, lentē advēnit.

haereō *I cling*
vīs *force*
sēdō *I settle, calm down*
Arelātē *Arles (town in southern France)*

LANGUAGE NOTE 3: -NE AND -QUE

1. In this chapter, you have met **-ne**. Can you explain what it does? Why do you think the Romans added it to the first word in the sentence?

   est Gallia.
   It's Gaul.

   estne Gallia?
   Is it Gaul?

   pīrātae tē petīvērunt.
   Pirates attacked you.

   pīrātaene tē petīvērunt?
   Did pirates attack you?

2. You have also met **-que**, which is an alternative to **et** (*and*). Can you explain where it is placed?

   cibum et vīnum cupiēbant.
   cibum vīnumque cupiēbant.
   They wanted food and wine.

   leōnēs audīvī et elephantōs ingentēs vīdī.
   leōnēs audīvī elephantōsque ingentēs vīdī.
   I heard lions and saw huge elephants.

Travelling by sea

In the Roman world people often travelled long distances, despite the discomfort, dangers, and time which this involved. Soldiers, traders, skilled craftsmen and artists, students and teachers, and government officials (sometimes with their wives and households) undertook long journeys all over the Roman Empire. Sabina's journey from Ostia to Arelate would have taken about nine days in July.

When deciding whether to go by road or sea, travellers had to weigh up several factors: cost, time, weather, the season of the year, and comfort. A sea voyage was generally preferred to an overland journey because it was cheaper and took less time, even if the distance was greater. The Mediterranean Sea is relatively calm for part of the year, but in winter sailing is dangerous, and rocky outcrops around islands are always a risk. There was a sailing season, from March to October. Outside these months sailing was less frequent, although it was still possible.

There were no passenger ships. Instead, people travelled on merchant ships. Either they slept on deck or the ships put into shore and the passengers slept in tents or inns.

Pliny travelled from Rome to Bithynia, on the south coast of the Black Sea (which Romans called Pontus Euxinus), in AD 110, to take up the post of governor of the province. He wrote to Emperor Trajan to update him on his journey:

> I am reporting to you that I am at Ephesus with all my staff, having sailed round Cape Malea* despite being held back by opposing winds. Now I intend to make for my province, partly by coastal ships and partly by carriage. For, while the intense heat discourages overland travel, the continual winds are a deterrent to going by sea.

* Cape Malea, at the south-eastern tip of Greece, was notoriously dangerous for ships.

QUESTIONS

1. Find Bithynia and Ephesus on the map of the Roman Empire (pages 2–3).
2. What difficulties and dangers of travel does Pliny mention, (a) by land and (b) by sea?

LANGUAGE PRACTICE

1. Choose the genitive form of the noun to complete each sentence, then translate.
   a. Boudica erat dux et rēgīna .... (Britannōs, Britannōrum, Britannīs)
   b. pater .... Giscōnem occīdere temptāvit. (Luccō, Luccī, Luccus)
   c. nēmō pecūniam .... invenīre potuit. (puella, puellam, puellae)
   d. manus .... nōs ē vīcō discēdere iussit. (mīlitēs, mīlitibus, mīlitum)
   e. turba .... prope templum conveniēbat. (fēminārum, fēminās, fēminīs)
   f. pācem et spem .... petīvimus. (pāx, pācis, pācem)

2. Rewrite the following sentences using **-que** instead of **et**, then translate.

   For example: Rūfīna et Lūcriō ad portum Sabīnam dūxērunt.
   Rūfīna Lūcriōque ad portum Sabīnam dūxērunt.
   Rufina and Lucrio took Sabina to the port.

   a. Lūcriō pecūniam et cibum ferēbat.
   b. ego ad portum vēnī et nāvem invēnī.
   c. altōs montēs et flūmina magna in Corsicā vīdimus.
   d. Sabīna cum nautā veterī et iuvenī artifice nāvigābat.

3. Use **-ne** to change each statement into a question, then translate the question.

   For example: pīrātae crūdēlēs sunt.
   pīrātaene crūdēlēs sunt?
   Are the pirates cruel?

   a. Rūfīna in popīnā labōrat.
   b. tū in urbe habitāre vīs.
   c. līberī silvam sine patre intrāvērunt.
   d. animālia tempestātem timent.

In this mosaic you can see two merchant ships, sea creatures, including a whale and a dolphin, and shells.

Pirates in the Mediterranean Sea

Pirates in the Mediterranean Sea

Pirates, robbers of the sea, had long been a problem in the ancient Mediterranean. It was only when the Roman Empire became strong enough to control the whole Mediterranean that being a pirate became so dangerous that it was no longer an attractive means of making money. Before that, in the first century BC, piracy was such a serious nuisance for the Romans, and interfered so regularly with traffic across the sea, that it endangered trade and vital food supplies to Rome. The pirates mostly operated from bases on the wild and rugged coast of Cilicia.

Caesar captured by pirates

In 75 BC, at just 25 years old, Julius Caesar was captured by a crew of pirates. When they demanded a ransom to release him, Caesar laughed at them. They clearly had no idea who he was. Feeling that the ransom demand was too low for someone of his status, Caesar replied that he would pay more than twice the amount they had asked for. While his men went to gather the money for the ransom, he spent about forty days in the hands of the pirates. He exercised with them, told them to be quiet when he wanted to sleep, and read his own poetry to them, to show how unconcerned he was about being captured. He also jokingly promised the pirates that, once he was freed, he would find them, capture them, and crucify them. And that is exactly what he did. Once he regained his freedom, he quickly put together a fleet, captured the pirates when they were anchored, and crucified them all.

This marble bust of Julius Caesar was made in 1514.

Pompey and the pirates

According to the ancient biographer Plutarch, the power of the pirates increased when civil wars between the Romans in the first century BC left the seas unguarded. The number of pirate ships grew to over a thousand, and they felt so secure in their power that they attacked not only ships, but also coastal cities and islands, demanding huge ransoms for their release. In 68 BC pirates even attacked Ostia, 15 miles from Rome, burning the military fleet stationed there. The impact on trade was so bad that the Romans were faced with famine.

Stone portrait of Pompey, 50 BC.

The Romans then voted to give a special command to one of their best generals (Pompey the Great) to rid the sea of pirates. Pompey was granted enormous power: 500 ships, 120,000 troops, 5,000 cavalry, and as much money as he needed. He was also given complete *imperium* (power) over all Roman territory within 50 miles of the coast, for a period of three years.

Pompey accomplished the task in one single campaign in 67 BC, or at least so it was presented in ancient times. Modern scholars think that he may just have reduced the threat to a manageable size. Starting in the west, he is said to have cleared the Mediterranean as far as Sicily within forty days, and to have finished the job within three months. Trade across the Mediterranean increased immediately and so the price of food dropped, making Pompey extremely popular with the people of Rome.

This Roman coin, decorated with the prow of a ship, commemorates the achievements of Pompey the Great.

Chapter 12: incendium
fūmus

1. Lūcriō et Rūfīna nāvem Marcī diū spectābant.

2. tum scapham ascendērunt et ad urbem Rōmam trīste redīre coepērunt.

3. lacrimāsne, domina?

4. minimē! aliquid in oculō habeō. nihil est.

5. scapha lentē prōcēdēbat. mox in caelō fūmum dēnsum cōnspexērunt.

6. Rōmam spectā, domina! caelum spectā!

7. pff. nōlī timēre, Lūcriō! saepe in urbe sunt incendia.

8. *Lūcriō*
spectā intentē et audī, domina! magnum est incendium. multae avēs ab urbe volitant.

fūmus *smoke*
aliquid *something*

post trēs hōrās, Forō Boāriō appropinquāre coepērunt. difficile erat eīs prōcēdere, quod multae scaphae nāvēsque flūmen implēbant.

"ohē, nauta! scapham movē!"

"heus, tū! fūnem cape!"

"nautae! vōs dormītis? nāvem movēte!"

"nōlīte currere, līberī! scapham lentē ascendite!"

"serve, nūntium ad marītum mitte! tūtī sumus."

"incendia spectāte!"

"nautae, audīte intentē! nūntium ad portum Ostiae mittite. auxilium rogāte!"

moveō *I move*
fūnis *rope*

flammae

postquam ad Forum Boārium advēnimus, ego et Rūfīna ad Subūram statim festīnāvimus. in aliīs partibus urbis nūllum incendium erat, sed in aliīs partibus, fūmus dēnsissimus viās implēbat. flammae maximae multās domōs dēlēbant. violentia ventī et inertia hominum incendia augēbant. aestus flammārum in viīs angustīs erat intolerābilis. 5

tandem ad Forum Rōmānum advēnimus, fessī et ānxiī. tum rem terribilem audīvī et vīdī: templum et domus virginum Vestālium ardēbant. nōnnūllae virginēs Vestālēs etiam nunc in domō erant. vigilēs, cīvēs, servī servāre temptābant virginēs. equī sīphōnēs 10 ad incendium trahēbant. ubīque clāmōrēs hominum et equōrum hinnītus aurēs nostrās implēbant.

'currite, servī!' clāmābant vigilēs. 'plūs aquae portāte! domum, templum, virginēs Vestālēs prōtegite! deōs prōtegite! nōlīte timēre!'

'Lūcriō, vigilēs adiuvā! virginēs servā!' inquit Rūfīna. 'ego ad Subūram 15 eō. Faustum quaerere volō.'

statim vigil 'ohē, tū!' clāmāvit. 'aquam in domum fer! virginēs Vestālēs quaere!' perterritus et immōtus stetī. 'nōlī timēre, serve! deī tē exspectant! fortēs Fortūna adiuvat!'

vigil mē verberāvit. exclāmāvī. iterum vigil mē verberāvit. ad terram 20 dēcidī. dolor per tōtum corpus ruēbat. surrēxī, aquam tulī, et in domum quam celerrimē ruī. sed fervor, flammae, fūmus mē statim superāvērunt. vix spīrāre poteram. iterum dēcidī. nōn surrēxī.

violentia	*violence*
inertia	*inaction*
augeō	*I increase*
aestus	*heat*
angustus	*narrow*
terribilis	*terrible*
ardeō	*I burn*
etiam	*even*
vigil	*fireman*
sīphō	*fire engine, pump*
hinnītus	*neighing*
auris	*ear*
eō	*I go*
immōtus	*motionless*
Fortūna	*Fortune (goddess)*
ruō	*I rush*
quam celerrimē	*as quickly as possible*
fervor	*heat*
spīrō	*I breathe*

Fighting the fire

On the night of 18 July AD 64 a fire broke out in Rome. It spread rapidly throughout the city, moving easily between the tightly packed buildings, many of which were made of wood. The fire burned for nine days almost continuously, and when the ashes cooled only four of the fourteen regions of the city were left unscathed.

Rome had a permanent fire brigade, which had been created by Emperor Augustus in AD 6. Their official name was *vigilēs urbānī* (watchmen of the city), but they were commonly known by their nickname, *sparteolī* (little bucket-carriers). In AD 64 the brigade numbered about 4,000 men, who were freedmen; two hundred years later there were 7,000 vigiles. They lived in barracks which were distributed around the city and they stored their equipment in depots.

The vigiles patrolled the city, especially at night, on the lookout for fires. They may also have been responsible for maintaining law and order, but this always came second to prevention and control of fires. They carried buckets and axes. Other equipment included ladders, hooks, poles, and blankets soaked in water or vinegar. The vigiles would rush to the site of a blaze, then form a line to the nearest source of water, a fountain or tank, and pass buckets of water from hand to hand. Often they could not extinguish the flames directly, so they tried to control the spread of the fire by demolishing the building:

> The firemen broke down the door suddenly and began to create uproar with their water and axes.
>
> *Petronius*

When Pliny was governor of Bithynia, there was a fire in the city of Nicomedia. He wrote to Emperor Trajan about the lack of firefighting equipment:

> There was no publicly provided pump, no bucket, in short no equipment for putting out fires. I have given orders that these things shall be provided in the future.

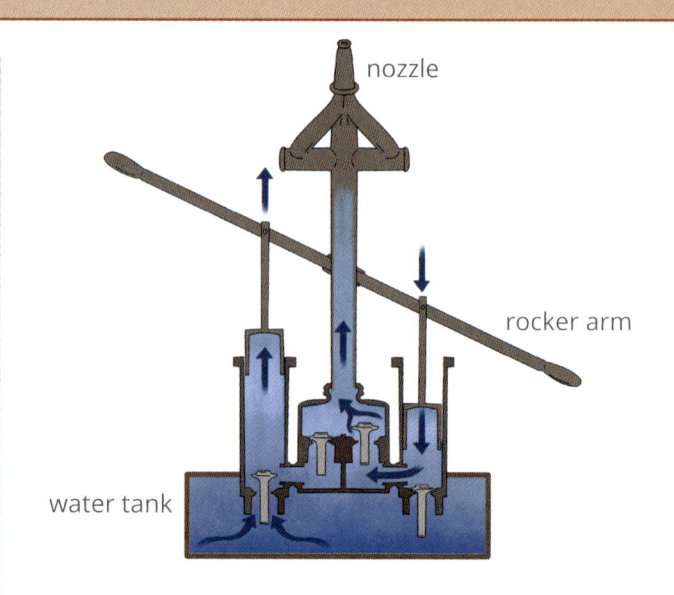

A diagram of a Roman water pump.

The first fire engine?

Ctesibius was a Greek who lived in Alexandria in Egypt in the third century BC. He discovered that compressed air could be used as a source of power and invented the water pump (*sīphō*) to raise water to a height. Three hundred years later another Alexandrian, Hero, developed this idea to invent the first fire engine. The pump was worked by two men, pushing down each side of a rocker arm alternately, like a seesaw. The nozzle could be adjusted so that you could aim the stream of water at a particular spot. The water pump could have been mounted on wheels and pulled by horses.

Some of Hero's inventions remained at the stage of theory and were never manufactured. Archaeologists have found remains of pumps, although they can't tell whether they were used for putting out fires or for other purposes such as drawing water up from a well.

QUESTIONS

1. What can you deduce from Pliny's letter about the equipment used in Rome for fighting fires?
2. What equipment do modern firefighters have which Romans lacked?
3. How might a pump have been used to control a fire? Would it have been more effective than buckets of water?

LANGUAGE NOTE 1: GIVING ORDERS

1. In the sentences below, the Latin words for *look!*, *move!*, *send!*, and *listen!* each have two forms. Can you explain why?

   Rūfīna, caelum spectā!
   Rufina, look at the sky!

   amīcī, incendium spectāte!
   Friends, look at the fire!

   ohē, nauta! scapham movē!
   Hey, sailor! Move your skiff!

   nautae! nāvem movēte!
   Sailors! Move your boat!

   serve, nūntium ad marītum mitte!
   Slave, send a message to my husband!

   servī, nūntium ad portum Ostiae mittite!
   Slaves, send a message to the port of Ostia.

   audī, domina!
   Listen, mistress!

   audīte intentē, nautae!
   Listen carefully, sailors!

2. The form of the Latin verb used for giving orders is called the **imperative**. It changes depending on whether one person or more than one person is being told to do something.

3. In the singular the imperative ends in a single vowel (the infinitive without **-re**) and in the plural it ends **-āte**, **-ēte**, **-ite**, or **-īte**.

4. Now look at the following sentences:

   nōlī timēre, Lūcriō!
   Don't be afraid, Lucrio!

   nōlīte currere, līberī!
   Don't run, children!

   Orders not to do something use **nōlī** or **nōlīte** followed by the infinitive. **nōlī** and **nōlīte** are the imperatives of **nōlō**, so mean *be unwilling* (to do something).

Vesta and Vulcan

For the Romans fire was a divine power which could be both protective and destructive. You have read about Vesta, the goddess associated with the sacred flame of Rome, on page 58. She represented the fire of the hearth and home. Vulcan, on the other hand, was the god of fire as a violent, and sometimes destructive, force. He had an annual festival on 23 August, the Vulcanalia, and people offered prayers and sacrifices to him to ward off fires. Vitruvius, who wrote about architecture, said that Vulcan's temples should be built outside the city, to draw the god of fire away.

Vulcan was also the god of volcanoes and blacksmiths. The word 'volcano' comes from his name.

A marble relief of the god Vulcan, from Herculaneum.

incendium in Subūrā

in urbe

incendium per viās tōtae urbis nunc ruēbat. flammae tabernās, popīnās, īnsulās violenter cōnsūmēbant. Subūrānī per viās fūmōsās ruēbant. mātrōnae līberīs haerēbant. dominī servōs vocābant. omnēs effugere temptābant.

violenter *violently*
fūmōsus *smoky*

prō popīnā

Catia ad popīnam festīnābat. Quārtillam prō popīnā cōnspexit. 5

'ubi est īnfāns?' ancilla perterrita rogāvit.

'nōnne tū eum cūrās?' exclāmāvit Catia.

Currāx perterritus fēminās spectāvit. 'īnfāns in īnsulā dormiēbat ...', puer susurrāvit.

Catia ferōciter exclāmāvit, et ad iānuam īnsulae cucurrit. 10

ferōciter *fiercely*

'tēcum veniō, īnsula est perīculōsa!' ancilla exclāmāvit. 'hīc manē, mī fīlī.'

in īnsulā

mātrōna et ancilla īnsulam intrāvērunt et per fūmum ascendēbant. īnsula obscūra erat et fēminae mūrōs cellārum vix vidēre poterant. lentē prōcēdēbant. in tabulātō secundō prōcēdere nōn potuērunt, quod trabs conlāpsa erat. flammae nunc ubīque erant. Catia dēspērābat, sed Quārtilla trabem cum magnā difficultāte sustulit. 'festīnā!' Quārtilla exclāmāvit. Catia breviter dubitāvit, sed clāmōrem īnfantis audīvit, et 'nōlī timēre, Quārtilla!' dīxit, 'reveniō!' Catia sub trabem rēpsit, et in tabulātum tertium festīnāvit. subitō ingēns fragor resonāvit.

15

tabulātum *floor, storey*
trabs *beam*
conlāpsus *collapsed*
breviter *briefly*
dubitō *I hesitate*
rēpō *I crawl*
resonō *I resound*

in viā

in viā Currāx īnsulam ānxiē spectābat. subitō Giscō advēnit et 'dīc mihi, ubi est uxor? ubi est fīlius?' rogāvit.

20

'in īnsulā sunt, domine. īnfāns ...', servus dīcere coepit. tum Currāx et Giscō ingentem fragōrem audīvērunt. Giscō puerum rapuit et celeriter cucurrit. tōta īnsula in viam cecidit.

rapiō *I grab*

LANGUAGE NOTE 2: VOCATIVE CASE

1. Look at the words in red in the following sentences:

   ubi es, puella?
   Where are you, girl?

   ubi estis, puellae?
   Where are you, girls?

   amīce, spectā caelum!
   Friend, look at the sky!

   amīcī, spectāte caelum!
   Friends, look at the sky!

   labōrāsne, fūr?
   Are you working, thief?

   labōrātisne, fūrēs!
   Are you working, thieves?

2. Latin uses the **vocative** case for someone who is being spoken to.

3. The vocative case has exactly the same form as the nominative case, except in the singular of the second declension, where **-us** becomes **-e** and **-ius** becomes **-ī**:

   Faustus est in popīnā.
   Faustus is in the bar.

   Fauste, quid tū in popīnā facis?
   Faustus, what are you doing in the bar?

   fīlius Quārtillae in viā currit.
   Quartilla's son is running in the street.

   hīc manē, fīlī!
   Stay here, son!

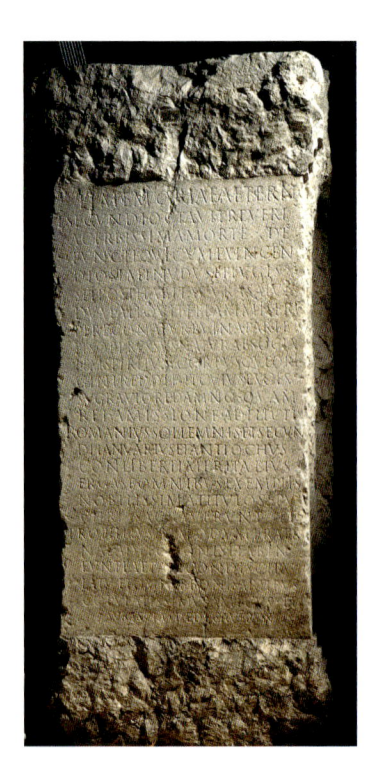

Lucius Secundus Octavius

This tombstone is from Trier in Gaul. It was set up by a group of friends in memory of Lucius Secundus Octavius, who died in a fire. The inscription reads:

To the Gods of the Dead, and to the eternal memory of Lucius Secundus Octavius of Trier, who has suffered a most cruel death. He escaped half-naked from a fire, then, putting aside concern for his own safety, he was trying to save something from the flames when he was crushed by a falling wall and returned his friendly spirit and his body to the earth. Affected more greatly by his death than by the loss of their property, Romanius, Sollemnis, Januarius, and Antiochus, Secundus' fellow freedmen, have memorialized on the inscription of this tomb his most noble qualities, which he displayed towards them with all kinds of proof.

DISCUSSION

Think about what this inscription tells us about Lucius Secundus Octavius and the friends who set up his tombstone.

Fuel and fire

> We cannot help but marvel that almost nothing is made without using fire. Fire takes some sand and, depending on the place, turns out glass or silver, cinnabar or lead, paint pigments or medicines. It is fire that melts stones into copper, fire that produces iron and moulds it, fire that purifies gold, fire that hardens the stones that hold our houses up.
> *Pliny the Elder*

All technology relies on energy. As the Empire grew and cities evolved, more and more energy was required to provide and maintain the luxuries of a civilized Roman lifestyle on a large scale. The Romans relied heavily on fire in most technological processes and imported large amounts of wood and coal. Just as they tamed water (see Chapter 5), the Romans harnessed the destructive nature of fire and used its power to fuel their Empire.

WOOD – Wood was the primary source of fuel. By AD 64 Italy was almost completely stripped of its forests. For this reason Rome had to import timber from the northern parts of its Empire. Archaeological evidence indicates that the more energy-packed charcoal (the black residue left after burning wood) was used in the manufacturing of glass and metals. Charcoal provides about twice as much energy as raw wood and burns evenly with little smoke.

COAL – The use of coal was confined to areas where it was available locally. Archaeological remains have shown coal being used in settlements and forts in Britain and around the River Rhine. Burning coal could produce very high temperatures so it was often used in iron workshops.

VEGETABLE WASTE – Olive pits, acorns, seeds, small branches, and straw were also used as fuel. They would have been used locally on country estates, where the residues of crop processing and food production were used to heat the villa and baths.

PETROLEUM – The word 'petroleum' comes from the Latin words *petra* (rock) and *oleum* (oil). The Roman geographer Strabo writes about naphtha, a black oil which was found in Babylon:

> If naphtha is brought near a flame it catches fire; if you smear it on something and bring it near a fire, then it too bursts into flames; and it is impossible to put these flames out with water (for they burn even more violently), unless a great amount is used.

Industry

Producing pottery, glass, and iron requires high temperatures of up to 1,100°C in furnaces or kilns. To reach these temperatures large amounts of charcoal or coal were needed, so the centres of these industries were often located close to sources of fuel. In the time of the Roman Empire, demand for these products increased and small, local industries expanded. Items began to be mass-produced and fine pottery, ironware, and glassware were exported across the Empire.

Left to right: a glass jug; a glass drinking cup made using a mould-blowing technique – the cup is signed in Greek 'by Ennion'; a green glass bowl; a terracotta beaker.

Solar power

One sign of luxury was a really hot bath. Seneca commented on the excessive temperatures of the imperial baths in Rome:

> The baths used to be heated to a temperature suitable for use and for health, not the heat that has recently become fashionable, like a real fire!

A huge amount of wood was required to reach these high temperatures. One estimate calculates that heating the caldarium of a single bath consumed over 100 tonnes of wood per year. Local resources were running out and prices were increasing, so instead the Romans turned to solar energy to heat their baths. They built bath complexes with huge glass windows and glazed the outside of the walls to trap the sun's rays, orientating the baths to face south-west.

After the fire

Rebuilding the city

Tacitus generally paints a very hostile picture of Nero. However, in his account of the immediate aftermath of the fire he reports that the Emperor introduced measures to relieve the plight of the homeless and destitute. He erected temporary shelters in the Campus Martius and his own gardens. He ensured supplies of food were shipped from Ostia and neighbouring towns, and reduced the price of grain. Later, Nero saw to the rebuilding of Rome. The narrow, winding, haphazard alleys were replaced with a more organized, open layout of streets. Nero contributed to the construction of insulae from his own money. New regulations were introduced aimed at reducing the risk of fire. Height limits were placed on buildings and there had to be open areas between them to stop the spread of fire. Everyone had to keep equipment in their homes for putting out fire. Nero also made sure more watchmen were employed to safeguard the water supply, because people had been siphoning off water to their own homes.

Compensation

There was no buildings insurance in Rome. Instead, people who had lost property relied on the generosity of the emperor or friends for compensation. After the fire of AD 64, Nero gave owners grants to rebuild insulae and houses. Emperor Tiberius had compensated the owners of insulae after fires in AD 27 and 36. More informally, sometimes houseowners relied on contributions from friends. This system could be abused, as Martial indicates in this poem:

> You bought a house, Tongilianus,
> for 200,000;* a disaster that is only too frequent in this city took it from you.
> Gifts poured in, amounting to a million sesterces.
> Might you be suspected of having set fire to your own house, Tongilianus?

*This was very cheap for a house in Rome.

QUESTIONS

1. Why were fires so frequent and so destructive in Rome? Think of as many reasons as you can.
2. What did some of the emperors do to prevent the outbreak of fires and to help the victims? What do you think their motives were?

Finding a scapegoat

There was a rumour that Nero was responsible for the fire, despite his aid to the victims and his plans for rebuilding the city. In order to shift suspicion from himself, Nero needed to find a scapegoat (someone to blame). He blamed the Christians. The Christians were already unpopular because they refused to join in with Roman religious ceremonies and worship Roman gods, so they were a minority who could easily be picked on. Christians in Rome were rounded up and punished in abominable ways: torn to pieces by dogs, or put on crosses and set on fire as human torches.

There may have been no evidence at all that some Christians were guilty of arson. On the other hand, there was a Christian prophecy that Christ would come to earth again and this event would be marked by fire. It is possible that some Christians, believing that this prediction was coming true, lit fires to add to the blaze.

Domus Aurea

Nero used the fire as an opportunity to build an extravagant new palace: the *Domus Aurea* (Golden House). It covered the Palatine and the Esquiline Hills, as well as the area in between them. In addition, he commissioned the Colossus, a huge bronze statue of himself, over 30 metres high.

The walls of the palace were painted with intricate frescoes, and the floors and even the ceilings were covered with mosaics of precious stones and ivory. To top it all, it had a golden roof. There were 300 large rooms, and it seems that the entire building was dedicated to entertainment and receiving guests. The domed ceilings, made from concrete, had never been seen before. Overall, the palace was an extraordinary feat of architecture and engineering.

There is evidence that the common people were invited into the extensive gardens of the palace. There are no archaeological remains of walls or fences around the grounds at all. Indeed two temples that had been destroyed in the fire were rebuilt within its grounds.

> The palace was so large that it had a triple colonnade a mile long. There was also a lake, like a sea, surrounded by buildings that represented cities. In addition to this, there was vast countryside, ploughed fields, vineyards, pastures, and woods, with many wild and tame animals. In the rest of the house, everything was completely covered with gold leaf and decorated with jewels and mother-of-pearl. There were dining rooms with ceilings made from panels of ivory, which could rotate and scatter flowers down onto the guests. There were also pipes to sprinkle the guests with perfumes from above.
>
> *Suetonius*

A digital reconstruction of Nero's Domus Aurea, complete with the lake and an enormous statue of the Emperor.

QUESTION

How do you think the inhabitants of Rome might have reacted to the new palace?

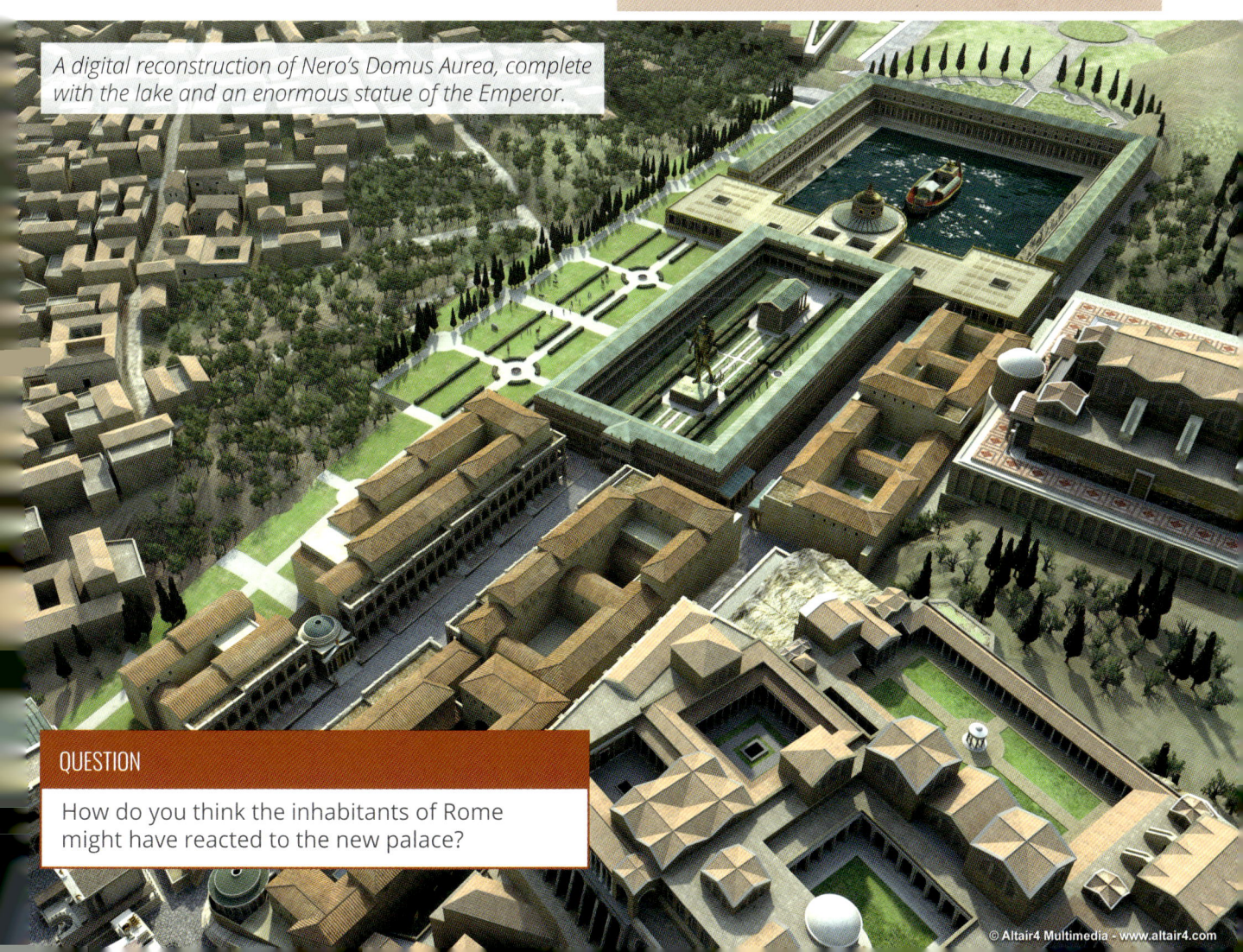

fūrēs

Chīlō ad fontem festīnābat. aqua nōn aderat in fonte, sed via prope fontem plēna Subūrānōrum perterritōrum erat. aliī aquam quaerēbant, aliī familiam vocābant. via erat fūmōsa et vōcēs Subūrānōrum raucae erant.

raucus hoarse

Chīlō	heus, Procle! hīc sum!	5
Proclus	Chīlō! tūtus es, amīce?	
Chīlō	certē sum tūtus. et tū?	
Proclus	omnia āmīsī, Chīlō. incendium cellam meam dēlēvit. necesse est nōbīs quam celerrimē effugere.	
Chīlō	vah! ego nihil āmīsī, quod nihil habuī! audī, amīce. effugere nōn dēbēmus. ecce, omnēs sunt perterritī. omnēs effugiunt. mercātōrēs tabernās nōn dēfendunt. quid dīcis?	10
Proclus	mercātōrēs nōn adsunt ...	
Chīlō	venī, mī amīce!	15

mī vocative of meus

amīcī per viās festīnābant, et tabernās intrābant. pecūniam, bona, statuās abstulērunt. nēmō eīs obstitit. in ūnā tabernā lībertus aderat. simulatque fūrēs cōnspexit ē tabernā cucurrit. in aliā tabernā duae ancillae aderant, sed fūrēs eās terruērunt et fēminae effūgērunt. in ūnā popīnā amīcī vīnum et cibum invēnērunt. fūrēs vīnum ex amphorīs bibēbant. subitō vōcem īrātam audīvērunt.

bona goods
auferō I steal

20

vir	heus, vōs! quid facitis? dēsistite!	
Chīlō	abī, stulte. fuge!	

abeō I go away

sed vir nōn effūgit. Chīlōnem petīvit et amphoram ē manū rapere temptāvit. Chīlō amphoram in virum iēcit. amphora caput virī percussit. vir in pavīmentum dēcidit. fūrēs ē popīnā exiērunt. vir immōtus in pavīmentō popīnae iacēbat. multus sanguis ē capite fluēbat. periit Faustus.

25

pavīmentum floor

LANGUAGE PRACTICE

1. Translate each sentence into Latin by choosing the correct word or phrase from each pair.

    a. *Brothers, carry water to the forum!*

frāter,	aquam	ad forum	portā!
frātrēs,	aqua	ā forō	portāte!

    b. *My friend, praise the words of the king!*

mī amīce,	laudā	verbum	rēgum!
meus amīcus,	laudāte	verba	rēgis!

    c. *Fireman, order the slaves to enter the apartment blocks!*

vigil,	servum	īnsulīs	intrāre	iubēte!
vigilēs,	servōs	īnsulās	intrāte	iubē!

    d. *Show the book to your companions, sister!*

librum	comitī	ostendite,	sorōrēs!
librōs	comitibus	ostende,	soror!

    e. *Find the enemy and kill them, soldiers!*

invenī	hostēs	et eōs	interfice,	mīles!
invenīte	hostium	et eum	interficite,	mīlitēs!

    f. *Write a letter to your mother and send a gift, my son!*

epistulās	ad mātrēs	scrībite	dōnumque	mittite,	mī fīlī!
epistulam	ad mātrem	scrībe	dōnaque	mitte,	meus fīlius!

2. Rewrite the sentences below, changing the words in bold type from dative singular to dative plural, or vice versa. Then translate the new sentence. For example:

    veterānī **nūntiō** epistulam trādidērunt.
    veterānī **nūntiīs** epistulam trādidērunt.
    The veterans handed over a letter to the messengers.

    a. heri prīncipēs **rēgī** arma pulchra obtulērunt.
    b. proelium incipere volēbāmus, sed **cōnsulibus** persuādēre nōn poterāmus.
    c. prīmō īnfēlīx rēgīna **cōnsiliō** cōpiārum nōn crēdidit.
    d. **Rōmānīs mīlitibus** saepe resistēbās, posteā tamen poenās dedistī.
    e. prīmā lūce pugnāvistis et **mātrōnae fīliae**que auxilium tulistis.

What caused the Great Fire of Rome?

In the wake of the disaster, people tried to find someone to blame. Even now, almost 2,000 years later, the cause of the fire is hotly debated.

Arson or accident? What do you think?

1. The ancient sources

Source 1: Suetonius
AD 69 – 122

As if he were offended by the ugliness of the old buildings and the narrow, crooked streets, Nero set fire to the city. He did this so openly that some ex-consuls did not stop his slaves, even though they caught them on their property with torches. There were some granaries near the Golden House. Nero particularly wanted the land they occupied, so they were first demolished by military machines before being set on fire, because their walls were made of stone. For six days and seven nights the destruction raged, and people were forced to look for shelter in monuments and tombs.

Source 2: Cassius Dio
AD 155 – 235

Nero decided to bring about what, no doubt, he had always wanted – to destroy the whole city during his lifetime. Therefore, he secretly sent out men who pretended to be drunk, with instructions to set fire, at first, to one or two or even a few buildings in different parts of the city. People were desperate; they couldn't find the source of the fires or put them out, though they were constantly aware of many strange sights and sounds.

Many houses were destroyed because there was nobody to help save them. Many others were set on fire by the men who came to help; for the vigiles, who were more interested in looting than in putting out fires, lit new ones.

Source 3: Tacitus
AD 56 – 120

Disaster followed – whether accidental or by the Emperor's treachery was uncertain (writers have recorded both explanations). It was more serious and more frightening than all the disasters which have happened to this city through the violence of fires. The fire started in the part of the Circus Maximus next to the Palatine and Caelian Hills, where there are shops containing flammable merchandise. Instantly it became fierce. Fanned by the wind, it whipped through the length of the Circus. For here there were no houses or temples surrounded by solid walls; no other obstacle lay in its path. The furious blaze ran first over level ground, then rose up to the hills, before again devastating the area below. It outstripped all attempts to stop it, because of the speed of its destructive advance and because the city was vulnerable, owing to the narrow, twisting lanes and irregular blocks which characterized old Rome.

Nobody dared fight the fire. Many people were opposing efforts to put out the flames, repeatedly shouting out threats. Others were openly throwing in torches and yelling that 'they had their orders'. Either they wanted more freedom to loot or else they were under orders.

QUESTION

Tacitus reports that some people deliberately tried to make the fire spread and prevent it being controlled.

What **two** possible motives does he suggest that these people had?

2. The modern experts

Expert A - Gerhard Baudy
Professor

(In Rome, Christians were circulating prophecies.) 'In all of these oracles, the destruction of Rome by fire is prophesied, that is the constant theme: Rome must burn. This was the long-desired objective of all the people who felt subjugated by Rome.'

Expert B - Andrea Carandini
Archaeologist

'For instance, there are serious scholars who now say that the fire was not Nero's fault. But how could he build the Domus Aurea without the fire? Explain that to me. Whether or not he started the fire, he certainly profited from it.'

Expert C - Eric Varner
Art historian

'It seems unlikely that Nero would have started the Great Fire of AD 64, because it destroyed his palace, the Domus Transitoria, a huge, villa-like complex that stretched from the Palatine to the Esquiline.'

3. The suspects

Nero
Nero was known for his cruelty and eccentricities. Could he have been driven by a mad rush of power and a desire to see his city burn? Or was it a means to clear land for his new palace, the Domus Aurea?

The Christians
They didn't join in with the Roman state religion. Perhaps they had even heard the prophecy that Rome would burn? Or were they just an easy target as a hated minority?

An accident
Fires in Rome were common. Buildings were made of flammable materials and stood too close together. Could an innocent oil lamp or brazier have started the blaze, which then spread with a breeze and the summer heat?

Arson
Could the fire have been started or spread by someone looking to profit from it?

Your decision

Consider everything you have read about the fire in this chapter and what you know about the city of Rome.

1. What evidence is available?
2. How reliable are the sources?

Prometheus

SOURCE 1

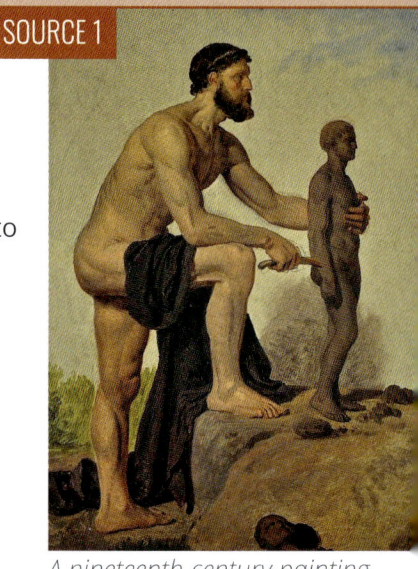

Life. And the four priorities for life: shelter, water, fire, and food. The ancient Greeks told a story about how humans first came into being, and first came to have fire. Prometheus, a Titan, created people out of nothing more than clay from the ground. He loved his new creations so much that he stole precious fire from Zeus to help them keep warm.

- Listen to or read the myth of Prometheus.
- Look at Source 1. In what ways is this similar to, and different from, how you imagined Prometheus with one of his creations? What do, and don't, you like about the painting? How similar to Prometheus is his creation?

A nineteenth-century painting showing Prometheus moulding one of his creations.

SOURCE 2

- Look at Source 2. Describe what you see in the image.

The creation of humans

Almost all cultures tell stories about how humans came to exist. Which can you think of? How similar and different are they to each other? What, if anything, do they have in common with the way Prometheus created humans? How do you explain the existence of humans?

SOURCE 3

God created mankind in his own image, in the image of God he created them; male and female he created them. God blessed them and said to them, 'Be fruitful and increase in number.'

The Bible

- Study Source 3. Do you think God/the gods created people to look like Him/them, or do we create gods to look like us?

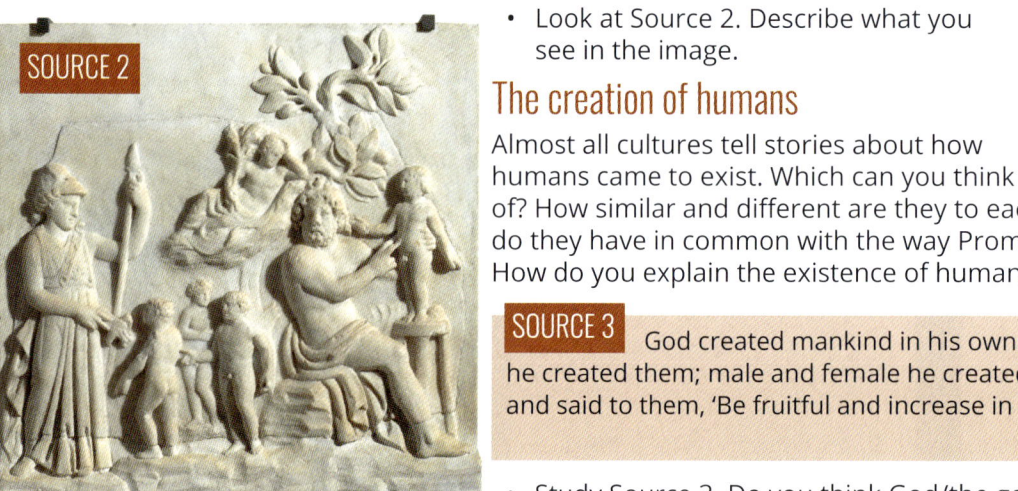

Roman third-century AD stone carving.

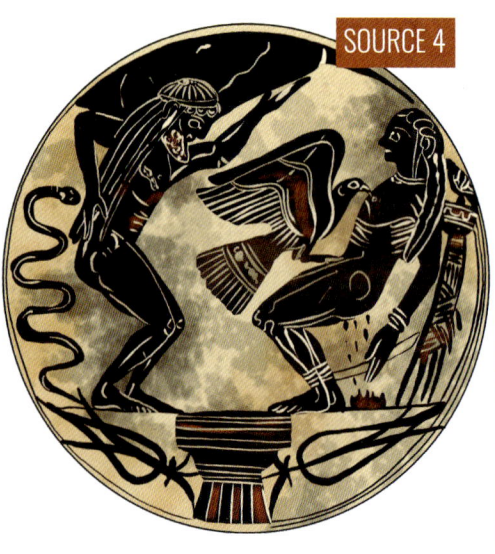

A drawing of an ancient Greek bowl showing an eagle pecking out Prometheus' liver.

SOURCE 4

Fire

Humans are the only creatures with the ability to control fire, and doing so allows us to stay warm, cook, ward off predators, be active in the dark, work metal, build machines, and run engines. Find out how long archaeologists think humans have been able to control fire, and how we first obtained it. What would life be like without it?

Defying the gods

Prometheus was willing to suffer perpetual torture to help humanity. Was he fighting for human rights against an oppressive ruler? A thief defying a direct instruction? How do you see Prometheus? Look at Source 4. Besides Prometheus, who else is being punished in the image?

RESEARCH

Find out more about:
- Pandora.
- other myths where characters are punished for their actions.
- the ancients' view of the liver.

Chapter 13: Arelātē
prīmā lūce

1. puella ad āram stat.

2. puella, quae ad āram stat, est Sabīna.

3. Sabīna per viās colōniae ambulat.

quī, quae, quod *who, which*

4 līberōs canēsque videt.

5 līberī, quī in viā lūdunt, sunt clāmōsī.
canēs, quī in viā iacent, dormiunt.

6 in colōniā est theātrum.

7 theātrum, quod est in colōniā, est pulchrum.

theātrum *theatre*

8 in viā sunt cīvēs et servī. servus, quī pānem portat, Sabīnam salūtat.

9 tandem Sabīna ad pistrīnum venit.

minimē, Sabīna!
hōra prīma est.

vōs dormītis?

nōs labōrāmus!

pānis *bread*
pistrīnum *bakery*

How to build a Roman town
10 EASY STEPS

Follow these steps to build your own Roman-style town.

STEP 1: CHOOSE A LOCATION

> When building a city, the first thing to do is choose a healthy location. It should be on high ground, not affected by fog or frost; its climate should be neither too hot nor too cold, but moderate.
> *Vitruvius*

Sometimes the Romans built upon existing settlements in the territory they conquered, as at Arelate and Camulodunum; at other times they built new towns from scratch, as at Londinium. The advantage of a previously uninhabited location (a greenfield site) was that there was less risk of opposition from the local population who might not like the changes. For example, as you learned in Chapters 8 and 9, in Camulodunum some of the local people resented the arrival of the Romans. However, often the best sites had already been used by the native peoples.

STEP 3: ROADS

Roman towns built from scratch were constructed on a grid plan so all roads intersected at right angles. For Romans, the straighter the road the better. Consider how you can connect your new town to the road system of the Empire so that trade is easier and communications are faster. And within your town you'll want to build new roads or improve existing ones. You'll have to use the materials available to you locally to build your road. Efficient drainage and a level surface are key.

STEP 4: WALLS AND GATES

The walls around your city should have wide foundations and towers at regular intervals. At the top, the wall should be wide enough for two armed men to pass each other and the distance between the towers should not be further than you can shoot an arrow in case you are attacked. The towers should be round, not square, so they are stronger.

> Public buildings have three purposes: defence, religion, community. Buildings for defence are walls, towers, and gates, designed to protect the town's inhabitants against enemy attacks. Religious buildings are the shrines and temples of the immortal gods. Buildings for communal use are gates, fora and marketplaces, baths, theatres, colonnades, and similar. Since they are for public use, they should be located centrally.
> *Vitruvius*

STEP 2: WATER SUPPLY

Water is essential. Roman engineering enabled water to be carried for miles in aqueducts. However, find a spot with fresh water nearby and you save yourself time and money in construction and maintenance. Open streams, rivers, and lakes are the obvious sources of fresh water, but other sources can be found under the ground. Look for willows and rushes to indicate an underground source nearby.

What goes in must come out, so think about a way to remove waste from the city. Roman towns often had underground sewers, and cities close to large rivers used them to dispose of most of their waste directly.

The Pont du Gard, a Roman aqueduct and bridge in France.

STEP 5: CIVIC BUILDINGS

Start with the focal point of the city, the forum. Build the forum in the centre of the town and with it a basilica and the other buildings which make up the civic centre.

STEP 8: ENTERTAINMENT

All good Roman towns had a large theatre. Build a circus and an amphitheatre as well, for greater impact and to provide more opportunities for entertainment.

The amphitheatre at El Djem, Tunisia.

STEP 7: SANITATION

You've got fresh flowing water, so add some pipes to reach the wealthier houses. Don't forget to build enough fountains at street corners, and public toilets for the ordinary people. Personal hygiene was important to the Romans and wealthier people bathed once a day. Build bath complexes and a palaestra to keep your inhabitants in good condition.

STEP 6: PLEASE THE GODS
(PERHAPS THE MOST IMPORTANT)

Now you have the beginnings of a town, it is vital to please the gods. Place temples to the gods who protect the city somewhere with a high vantage point. Keep Mercury in the forum to help business, Apollo near the theatre, and put Vulcan's temple far outside the city walls to draw away the risk of fire.

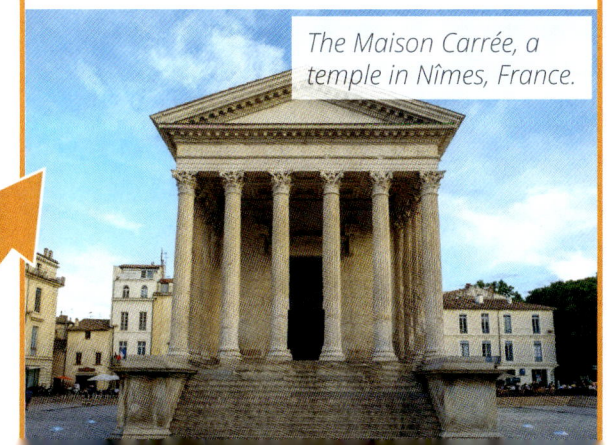

The Maison Carrée, a temple in Nîmes, France.

STEP 9: HOUSES AND SHOPS

You have the key features of your Roman town. Now fill in the space with houses, shops, and workshops – grand houses for the rich and small apartments for the poor.

STEP 10: GIVE IT A NAME

Roman towns were often named after their founders or benefactors. This was commonly an emperor, so many colonies carried the name of the emperor or a member of his family. These were commonly used:

- Colonia Iulia
- Colonia Claudia
- Colonia Augusta

Finally, choose a name for your Roman town.

QUESTIONS

1. What features does a Roman town have which a modern town lacks?
2. What features does a modern town have which you wouldn't find in a Roman town?

Arelate

Arelate (modern Arles) was on the River Rhône, in the Roman province of Gallia Narbonensis. The modern city is about 25 miles from the sea, but in Roman times it was a few miles nearer. The town was built at the lowest point at which the river could be crossed. You have already read a little about Arelate in Chapter 11 (page 172).

Arelate was originally a Greek town. When Julius Caesar was fighting in Gaul in 49 BC he used Arelate as a base for building warships to use against Massilia (modern Marseille). Three years later Arelate became a colonia, when Caesar settled veterans of the Sixth Legion there, taking some of the territory that had been occupied by Massilia. In return for their military support against Massilia, Caesar gave the people of Arelate Roman citizenship.

LANGUAGE NOTE 1: RELATIVE CLAUSES

1. In the sentences below, look at the clauses in red. Who or what do the clauses refer to?

    puella, quae ad āram stat, est Sabīna.
    The girl, who is standing at the altar, is Sabina.

    servus, quī pānem portat, Sabīnam salūtat.
    The slave, who is carrying bread, greets Sabina.

    theātrum, quod est in colōniā, est pulchrum.
    The theatre, which is in the colony, is beautiful.

2. In the first sentence **quae ad āram stat** relates to **puella** (*the girl*).
   In the second sentence **quī pānem portat** relates to **servus** (*the slave*).
   In the third sentence **quod est in colōniā** relates to **theātrum** (*the theatre*).

3. The clauses are known as relative clauses, because they relate to someone or something.

4. Identify the relative clauses in the following sentences. To which Latin word does each relative clause refer?

    Marcus, quī magnam nāvem habēbat, Sabīnam laetē salūtāvit.

    in viā est plaustrum, quod ligna et saxa portat.

    colōnia, quae est in Galliā, templa pulchra habet.

    Sabīna Neptūnō, quī est deus maris, vīnum dedit.

The remains of a large bakery from Pompeii. You can see the millstones where the corn was ground. The oven is on the left.

in pistrīnō

Sabīna pistrīnum intrāvit et clāmāvit, 'salvēte! Poppille! Letta! adsum!'

in pistrīnō Poppillus, quī erat pistor et senex, pānem parābat. sua uxor rūgōsa, quae erat Letta, eum adiuvābat. Sabīnam simul vocāvērunt: 'venī ad nōs, cāra puella!'

Poppillō et Lettae appropinquāvit Sabīna. eīs ōsculum dedit. 5

ānser quoque erat in pistrīnō. animal ferōx, quod magnum clāmōrem tollēbat, puellam intentē spectābat.

'salvē, Manlī!' Sabīna ānserī dīxit. 'tūne domum nostram dīligenter custōdīs?'

Manlius tamen immōtus stetit. 10

tum exiit ānser. deinde Poppillus pānem calidum ad mēnsam tulit, Letta frīgidam aquam. quamquam Sabīna in pistrīnō labōrāre incipiēbat,

'sedē nōbīscum, Sabīna,' eī simul dīxērunt. 'cōnsūme et bibe.'

'vōbīs grātiās agō,' eīs respondit Sabīna. 'semper benignissimī estis. trēs mēnsēs mē iam cūrāvistis.' 15

'tē cūrāre gaudēmus,' dīxit Letta. 'diū sōlī habitāvimus. nec līberī nec servī nōbīs sunt, nisi ille ānser.'

subitō clangōrem ānseris in viā audīvērunt, tum magnum clāmōrem iuvenis. 20

'ohē, pistor! ubi es? ānser saevus tuus mē petit!'

Alexander in pistrīnum cucurrit. artifex, quī erat perterritus, vix spīrābat. omnēs trēs, quī ad mēnsam sedēbant, statim surrēxērunt.

Sabīna, quae paene rīdēbat, clāmāvit, 'salvē, Alexander! nōlī timēre! vīsne pānem emere?' 25

intereā Letta marītō suō susurrābat, 'puellam vidēre sōlum vult.'

'minimē!' respondit Alexander, quī multum ērubēscēbat. 'vōs omnēs invītāre ad theātrum volō.'

pistor baker
ānser goose
mēnsa table
mēnsis month
nec ... nec ... neither ... nor ...
ille that
clangor honking
paene almost
emō I buy
sōlum only

in theātrō

ingēns turba erat in theātrō, quod diēs fēstus erat. Alexander Sabīnaque ad summum gradum ascendērunt. Poppillus Lettaque, postquam ad duōs iuvenēs tandem pervēnērunt, inter eōs sēdērunt.

mē miserum! Sabīnam aut vidēre aut audīre vix possum! 5

gradus *step, row*
perveniō *I arrive, reach*

Poppillus	(*fessus*) ōh mihi! hic gradus est altus! senēs, quī in prīmō gradū sedent, sunt fēlīcēs!
Sabīna	sed aspectus est magnificus! ecce, scaenae frōns!
Alexander	nōnne emblēmata, quae sunt in scaenae fronte, vidētis?
Sabīna	ita vērō. 10
Poppillus	minimē, iuvenis! oculī meī nōn sunt validī.
Alexander	ūnum ex emblēmatibus, quae Sabīna vidēre potest, ego fēcī.
Sabīna	ōh! est pulcherrimum!
Poppillus	emblēma, quod indicās, vidēre nōn possum.
Letta	st, vōs trēs! tubae signum dant! 15

scaenae frōns *stage building*
emblēma *mosaic*
indicō *I point out*

chorus et pantomīmus, quōs multī spectātōrēs ardenter exspectābant, scaenam intrāvērunt. fābula, quam chorus nārrābat, erat dē Pȳramō et Thisbā. prīma persōna, quam pantomīmus agēbat, erat Pȳramus. deinde pantomīmus persōnam Thisbae ēgit.

Poppillus	chorum audīre nōn possum. aurēs meae nōn sunt validae.	20
Letta	nihil est, mī lepus. fābulam bene nōvistī. spectā pantomīmum! prīmō Pȳramus, quem Thisba amat, ad mūrum stat. deinde Thisbam per rīmam vocat.	
Alexander	pst! Sabīna!	
Letta	nunc Thisba Pȳramō respondet.	25
Sabīna	quid est, Alexander?	
Letta	Pȳramus Thisbaque iam cōnsilium capiunt …	
Alexander	mūrus, quī nōbīs obstābat, abest!	

amor semper vincit.

chorus *chorus*
pantomīmus *mime performer*
ardenter *eagerly*
Pȳramus et Thisba *Pyramus and Thisbe (star-crossed lovers)*
persōna *character*
agō *I act*
lepus *hare; darling*
nōvī *I know*

cōnsilium capiō *I make a plan*

amor *love*

The theatre

In Chapter 3 you learned that theatrical performances were part of the entertainment at some religious festivals. These performances took place in open-air theatres, which are some of the largest and most impressive Roman buildings. There was a large theatre at Arelate, probably built in the time of Augustus. Some towns, for example Rome and Pompeii, also had smaller, roofed theatres.

The theatres in Gaul, and in other provinces of the Roman Empire, were modelled on those in Rome. But the government in Rome did not pay for them. Community buildings such as theatres were paid for by wealthy local people at their own expense.

The entertainment started early in the morning and lasted all day, with several plays being performed. As these were festival days, shops were closed and no business was done in the forum, so people were free to spend the day at the theatre. Everyone could go – men, women, and children; free people and slaves; freedmen and freedwomen. A patron (*patrōnus*), who was a wealthy citizen, paid the expenses (actors, musicians, dancers, scenery, costumes), and admission was free.

> **QUESTION**
>
> Why do you think rich people would pay for theatres to be built and plays to be performed?

Plays and performers

The audiences enjoyed comedies, tragedies, and pantomimes. Sabina and her friends are watching a pantomime, which was a particularly popular kind of performance. Despite the name, this was nothing like the pantomimes performed nowadays. The Roman pantomime was a mixture of opera and ballet, performed by a single actor, a *pantomīmus*. The word 'pantomimus' is derived from two Greek words, and means 'acting everything'. The plots of pantomime were taken from myths and legends, such as the story of Pyramus and Thisbe. The pantomimus played all the parts; he or she would silently mime and dance. The pantomimus was accompanied by musicians and a chorus, who sang the words of the story.

Troupes of performers travelled from town to town. Most of the actors were men. They were often Greeks, either enslaved people or freedmen. The actors wore masks, probably made of linen, covered with plaster, and painted. Wearing a mask enabled the actor to play more than one character; he would show a change of character by changing his mask. Another advantage was that the features on the masks were exaggerated, so that members of the audience at the back of the theatre would find it easier to identify the characters.

orchēstra

The *orchēstra* was a semicircular paved space in front of the stage. 'Orchestra' is a Greek word which means 'dancing-place'; in a Greek theatre, the chorus danced and sang in the orchestra. In a Roman theatre, there were two or three rows of wooden seats for leading citizens such as local magistrates.

cavea

The seating area was arranged in a semicircle around the orchestra, with stone seats rising in tiers. The best seats at the front were reserved for the richer, more important citizens. The theatres at Arelate and the nearby town of Arausio (modern Orange) had thirty-three rows and could hold about 6,000 to 8,000 people. The cavea was uncovered, but awnings (*vēla*) could be drawn over on ropes and pulleys to protect the audience from rain or sun.

altars

Plays often had scenes set at an altar. The theatre at Arelate had two altars to Apollo, the god of music. One was on the stage and the other was in the orchestra.

scaenae frōns

The stage building behind the stage was as high as the auditorium. There were three or five doors, which served as entrances and exits to and from the stage. The *scaenae frōns* was elaborately decorated with columns, marble, mosaic, carvings, and niches holding statues of gods, goddesses, and emperors. Statues of Emperor Augustus and Venus, the goddess of love, decorated the theatre at Arelate. The theatre at Arausio had a statue, possibly of Augustus, in a niche above the centre of the stage, and above the central door there was a carving of centaurs, mythical creatures which are half-man and half-horse.

scaena

The stage was a high, wide platform, covered with a roof.

The theatre at Orange is one of the best preserved Roman theatres. In this illustration, a photograph of the theatre as it is now is overlaid with a drawn reconstruction of the theatre in Roman times.

sub vesperum

	sub vesperum *towards evening*

sub vesperum spectātōrēs in theātrō stābant, gaudēbant, vehementer plaudēbant. post scaenam tamen āctōrēs, fessī et calidissimī, sedēbant aquamque frīgidam bibēbant. inter āctōrēs erat senex, nōmine Gabrus, quem cēterī valdē amābant. lentē surgere temptāvit, sed statim ad pavīmentum dēcidit. cēterī ad eum festīnāvērunt. 5

āctor *actor*

cēterī *the others*

Darius labor āctōris est dūrus, Gabre, et diēs sunt longī. quamquam optimus āctor erās, nunc nimium vetus es. nōbīs inūtilis es. manēre apud nōs diūtius nōn potes.

diūtius *longer*

Gabrus ita vērō, Darī. quamquam difficile est mihi nūntium, quem tū fers, audīre, stultus tamen nōn sum – rem 10 intellegō. senex sum. sed nūllōs familiārēs habeō. nēmō mē cūrat. amīcī meī, quōs valdē amō, vērum mihi dīcite. quōmodo nunc vīvere possum?

familiāris *relative*
vērum *truth*

āctor prīmus senex es, Gabre, et labōrāre nōn potes. necesse est tibi in viīs prope tabernās mendīcāre. 15

mendīcō *I beg*

āctor secundus minimē! in oppidō proximō sunt multae popīnae, in quibus fābulās mīrābilēs nārrāre potes.

Darius ecce, Gabre! praemium, quod hodiē patrōnus nōbīs dedit, accipe! paucōs diēs bene vīvere potes!

patrōnus *patron (who pays for the show)*

omnēs vīve ac valē, amīce! 20

ac *and*

Gabrus bene vīvite ac valēte, amīcī.

eā nocte Gabrus sub aquaeductū sōlus dormiēbat.

eā nocte *that night*
aquaeductus *aqueduct*

QUESTIONS

What do you think happens to Gabrus next? Read these two options and discuss which you think is more likely. Alternatively, write your own ending.

a. fūrēs duo Gabrum et pecūniam eius cōnspexērunt. māne senex, quī frīgidus et ānxius erat, quoque pauper erat.

māne *in the morning*

b. māne tamen duo frātrēs eum invēnērunt. 'tūne Gabrus es? sī tibi placet, nōbīscum venī. multōs annōs tū omnibus multum gaudium tulistī. nunc familiae nostrae placet tē cūrāre.'

LANGUAGE NOTE 2: RELATIVE PRONOUNS

1. Look at **quae** and **quī**, the words for *who*, in the following sentences. Why do you think they have different forms?

   puella, quae ad āram stat, est Sabīna.
   The girl, who is standing at the altar, is Sabina.

   servus, quī pānem portat, Sabīnam salūtat.
   The slave, who is carrying bread, greets Sabina.

   quae and **quī** are both forms of the **relative pronoun**. **quae** is feminine because it relates to **puella** (*the girl*). **quī** is masculine because it relates to **servus** (*the slave*).

2. Now compare **quae** and **quam** in the following sentences.

   puella, quae ad āram stat, est Sabīna.
   The girl, who is standing at the altar, is Sabina.

   puella, quam Alexander videt, est Sabīna.
   The girl, whom Alexander sees, is Sabina.

   quae and **quam** both relate to **puella** (*the girl*). In the first sentence, **quae** is nominative, because the girl is standing at the altar. In the second sentence, **quam** is accusative, because Alexander sees her.

3. The most common forms of the relative pronoun are given below. A chart of all the forms is on page 275.

SINGULAR	*masculine*	*feminine*	*neuter*
nominative	**quī**	**quae**	**quod**
accusative	**quem**	**quam**	**quod**

PLURAL			
nominative	**quī**	**quae**	**quae**
accusative	**quōs**	**quās**	**quae**

An incense burner in the shape of a comic actor sitting on an altar. The actor is wearing a comic mask.

Making bread

Bread was consumed in huge quantities throughout the Roman Empire. For the majority of the population, bread was an essential part of the diet. Grain and flour production were enormous industries, and bakeries were thriving businesses.

Grain was grown across the Empire, and particularly in those regions where the soil and climate were favourable. Most of the grain consumed in the city of Rome was grown in North Africa, then shipped across the Mediterranean. The grain was then ground into flour in mills. Some houses had their own hand-powered mills, and sizeable towns had several larger mills, often driven by donkeys. The animals were harnessed to the mill, and walked round in circles to turn the rotating stones that ground the grain. Some mills produced finer flour than others, and the quality of the bread varied greatly.

Bakers (*pistōrēs*) used the flour to make loaves of bread that they baked in ovens. Towns had many bakeries of various sizes. Archaeologists have found thirty-one bakeries in Pompeii, a medium-sized town in southern Italy. Some bakeries had their own shops; others sold their bread to other shops or market stalls. A few bakers ran very big businesses and could make a fortune, such as the freedman Eurysaces, whose tomb survives in Rome.

The tomb of Eurysaces the baker, in Rome (first century BC). The circular holes perhaps represent grain-measuring vessels or kneading basins.

Industrial milling: Barbegal

A huge water-powered mill complex has been found at Barbegal, about five miles from Arelate. Sixteen waterwheels were set in two parallel rows on a steep hillside. A nearby aqueduct supplied them with water from above. The wheels powered grain mills that had the capacity to produce enough flour to feed about 10,000 people daily (approximately a third of the total population of Arelate). It's not certain whether the flour produced by these mills was used by local people to make bread, or whether it had another purpose. One theory is that the mill may have supplied flour to make *pānis nauticus*, a dry bread that could be stored for a long time and was used to feed sailors on ships travelling long distances. The Barbegal mill is the largest Roman watermill so far discovered, and one of the most impressive mechanical constructions from the ancient world.

Above: a reconstruction of the Barbegal mill.

LANGUAGE PRACTICE

1. Change the forms of **sum** from present tense to imperfect tense, then translate the new sentence. You may wish to use the chart on page 278 to help you.

    a. Sabīna **est** trīstissima, quod sōla **est**.

    b. quamquam **sum** iuvenis, fortissima tamen **sum**.

    c. in theātrō āctōrēs ad**sunt**. itaque in pistrīnō nōn **sumus**.

    d. quamquam crūdēlissimī **estis**, amīcī tuī **sunt** fidēlēs.

    e. Poppillus et Letta per tōtum diem ab**sunt**. laetissimī **sunt**.

    f. chorum audīre nōn pot**es,** quod senex **es**.

2. Choose the correct form of the relative pronoun to complete each sentence, then translate.

    a. animālia, ... Alexander audīre poterat, erant ānserēs.
    (quae, quem, quod)

    b. caelum, ... fūmōsum est, intentē spectā!
    (quās, quod, quōs)

    c. taberna, ... frāter noster intrāvit, vestīmenta nova vēndēbat.
    (quōs, quam, quī)

    d. deinde artificem, ... emblēma cōnficiēbat, cōnspeximus.
    (quem, quae, quod)

    e. statuās pulcherrimās, ... fabrī in theātrum portābant, spectāre volumus.
    (quem, quōs, quās)

    f. quōmodo imperātōris equōs, ... in montibus altīs āmīsī, invēnistis?
    (quae, quōs, quam)

Mosaic of a theatrical tragic mask from the House of the Faun in Pompeii.

Pyramus and Thisbe

Pyramus and Thisbe were a young couple who lived next door to each other in the ancient city of Babylon. Although they were in love, their families did not approve of their relationship and would not allow them to marry. Pyramus and Thisbe would talk to each other through a crack in the wall between their two houses. They decided to meet and run away together secretly, but their plan ended in tragedy.

- Read or listen to the story of Pyramus and Thisbe.

Aetiological stories

Aetiological myths and stories are used to explain the origins and causes of natural phenomena which are not understood. Read Source 1:

> **SOURCE 1**
> And tree, you who now cover the poor body of one man with your branches, and soon will shade two, keep the signs of our death and always bear fruit that is dark in colour as is fitting for this grief, a memorial of our double death.
> *Ovid*

In Ovid's account of the story of Pyramus and Thisbe, he explains that the mulberry tree, under which Pyramus and Thisbe died, has red berries because of their blood.

- Why do you think humans make up stories that explain things in the world that they do not understand?

A sculpture of Pyramus and Thisbe, made in 1775.

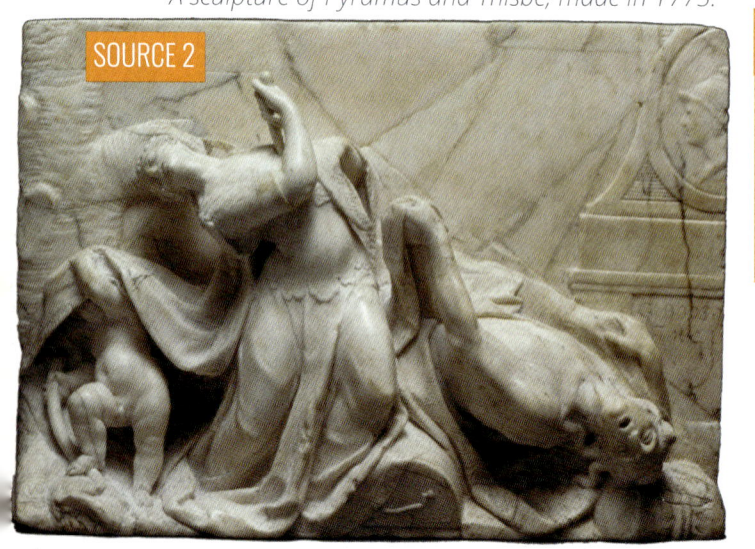

SOURCE 2

'Star-cross'd lovers'

The story of Pyramus and Thisbe has inspired many other stories that are still well known today. The most famous is probably Shakespeare's *Romeo and Juliet*. Source 3 is an extract from this play.

> **SOURCE 3**
> Two households, both alike in dignity
> In fair Verona, where we lay our scene
> From ancient grudge break to new mutiny
> Where civil blood makes civil hands unclean.
> From forth the fatal loins of these two foes
> A pair of star-cross'd lovers take their life
> Whose misadventured piteous overthrows
> Do with their death bury their parents' strife.
> *Shakespeare*

Look at Sources 2 and 3.

- What do you think the phrase 'star-cross'd lovers' means?
- Why do you think the tragedy of the star-cross'd lovers is so popular in literature, art, and drama?

Forbidden love

The parents of Pyramus and Thisbe forbade their relationship because of a family feud. Modern reworkings of the story give many other reasons why the couple can't be together.

- Think of examples of forbidden love from modern literature, drama, and film.
- Why do you think forbidden and secret love is often seen as more romantic?

> **RESEARCH**
>
> 1. Find other stories from mythology or more modern sources that are aetiological.
> 2. Shakespeare also told the story of Pyramus and Thisbe in *A Midsummer Night's Dream*. Read this version of the story.

Chapter 14: artifex

in officīnā fabrōrum

1. Sabīna in viā ambulābat, ubi officīnae fabrōrum erant. in ūnā ex officīnīs Alexander cum servīs labōrābat. Sabīna erat laeta, quod artificem cōnspexit.

2. salvē, Alexander!

3. salvē, Sabīna! intrā officīnam! opus novum meum tibi ostendere cupiō.

officīna *workshop*
opus *work*

4. Alexander laetus eī respondit.

5. vōsne emblēmata, quae sunt in forō, iam cōnfēcistis?

6. ita vērō, in forō diū labōrāvimus. heri pavīmentum prope basilicam, quae est in forō, cōnfēcimus. hodiē in officīnā labōrāmus, quod opus novum parāmus. crās in thermīs labōrābimus.

heri *yesterday*
crās *tomorrow*

7. artifex Sabīnae opus ostendit.

8 *Alexander* in mediō pavīmentō erit imāgō pulchra. in imāgine erunt fōrmae, partēs hominēs partēs piscēs, et alia animālia maris.

imāgō *picture*
piscis *fish*

9 *Sabīna* opus est optimum! nautaene et Sīrēnēs in imāgine erunt?

Sīrēn *Siren (a mythical creature: part-bird, part-woman)*

10 hahae! tūne nōs adiuvāre vīs?

11 ita vērō. hodiē Poppillum Lettamque adiuvō. sed crās vōs adiuvābō. tūne mē docēbis?

12 certē, crās tē docēbō. nōn difficile erit tē docēre. mīrābilis artifex eris.

doceō *I teach*

LANGUAGE NOTE 1: THE FUTURE TENSE

1. Can you spot the difference in the verbs in these pairs of sentences?

   in thermīs labōrāmus.
   We are working in the baths.

   in thermīs labōrābimus.
   We shall work in the baths.

   And again in these sentences?

   ego amīcum doceō.
   I am teaching my friend.

   ego amīcum docēbō.
   I shall teach my friend.

   What is the difference in the form of the Latin verbs? How does that difference affect the meaning of the verbs?

2. The **-bō** and **-bi-** in the ending of the Latin verbs indicate that the action will take place in the future. This form of the verb is known as the **future tense**.

3. Look at the future tense of **vocō** (*I call*):

vocābō	*I shall call*
vocābis	*you* (singular) *will call*
vocābit	*he/she/it will call*
vocābimus	*we shall call*
vocābitis	*you* (plural) *will call*
vocābunt	*they will call*

   Note that the very end of the verb (**-ō**, **-s**, **-t**, **-mus**, **-tis**, **-nt**) tells us *who* will carry out the action and the **-b-**, **-bi-**, or **-bu-** tell us *when* they will do it.

4. Now compare these two sentences:

   imāgō pulchra est in pavīmentō.
   A beautiful image is in the floor.

   imāgō pulchra erit in pavīmentō.
   A beautiful image will be in the floor.

5. The future tense of **sum** (*I am*) is as follows:

erō	*I shall be*
eris	*you* (singular) *will be*
erit	*he/she/it will be*
erimus	*we shall be*
eritis	*you* (plural) *will be*
erunt	*they will be*

Creating mosaics

Mosaics covered floors, walls, and arches in public and private buildings in the Roman world. They were particularly suitable for decorating floors because they were strong and hard-wearing.

Above: pattern from a mosaic floor in Conimbriga, in Portugal.

Right: mosaic of Neptune and his wife Amphitrite, from a house in Herculaneum.

Preparing the floor

The Roman architect Vitruvius gives a description of how to lay mosaic floors well. He recommends starting with a timber base, then a two-level concrete floor (one rough layer and one smooth layer), which should be 'laid to rule and level'. Mosaics were made of small stones called *tesserae*. These stones were pressed into the concrete, then polished to smooth them down further, as Vitruvius instructs: 'the edges of the tesserae should be completely smoothed off, or the work will not be properly finished.' The cracks between the tesserae were filled with grout made of lime and sand.

QUESTION

Which materials do you think were used for the tesserae of the mosaics on this page?

Laying the mosaic

Simple mosaic floors could be laid directly with pegged lines or with guidelines scored into the concrete. Some examples of these guidelines have survived. Complicated designs, however, were probably pre-prepared in panels; the whole panel was then laid in place. The panels were made by gluing the tesserae onto a piece of fabric in a wooden frame, on which the design had been drawn in reverse image. These whole panels were then put in place on the prepared floor. Some mosaics show obvious errors where pre-prepared panels were fitted into the rest of a mosaic.

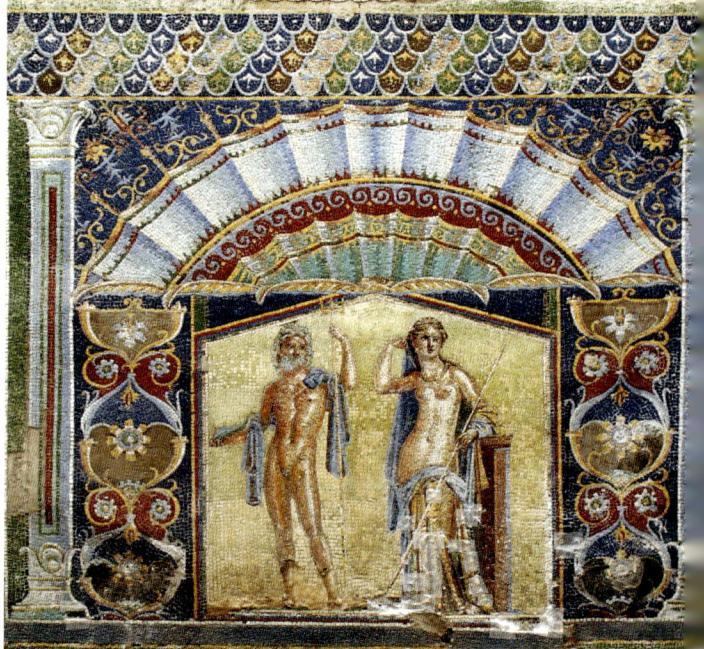

tesserae

Most tesserae were made from local natural stone, cut bricks, tiles, or pottery, which were cut to the right size. These tesserae were therefore predominantly in natural colours such as white, black, brown, and orange. The contrast between the different-coloured tesserae could bring out patterns well. Some more exotic materials such as marble, glass, precious stones, and even gold were used as well for their brighter colours. The smaller the tesserae were cut, the more detailed the mosaics could be. As there was no paint involved, Roman mosaics look as bright now as when they were made.

Quality & fashion

Not all mosaics were made to the same standard of workmanship. Some were small and simple, made out of one or two colours only, with straightforward borders. Others included intricate geometric patterns, small details, vivid colours, and artistic use of shading and composition. The cost of a mosaic varied wildly as a result, and skilled mosaicists made a very good living and were in high demand. Certain mosaic designs appear to have gone in and out of fashion, too: in France and Italy in the first century AD, for instance, black and white mosaics became widespread. It is unlikely that this was to do with reducing cost (though the tesserae used were easier to source), since these mosaics are found in very large houses, including the villa of Emperor Hadrian. Instead, this was probably the current fashion.

Mosaic of the Minotaur in the labyrinth, from Conimbriga in Portugal.

Mosaic makers

Very little is known about the people who made the beautiful mosaics we see today. Most ancient writers were not interested in craftsmen and have left us almost no record of their lives. Sometimes the art or work itself is praised, but the creator remains anonymous. Ancient writers, such as Pliny, praised famous artists and sculptors, but the trade of mosaic making was seen as a practical craft, tied to the construction of the building itself, rather than a true art form.

A whole team of craftsmen worked together to create a mosaic. The lead craftsman would draft the design and do the most intricate work, such as the faces, while less skilled craftsmen and apprentices would work on the borders.

Some mosaic makers left their signature within the design itself by including their name or a trademark symbol, such as a bird, in all their designs. One gravestone of a mosaic maker, set up by his son, reads:

> In many cities I exceeded all others in my skill, which I got from the gifts of Athena.

His son Proklos, who set up the gravestone, is described as being equally skilled. This is a rare insight into the lives of these craftsmen, who travelled around from city to city, perhaps gaining recognition for their work and passing the trade to their children and apprentices.

When archaeologists excavate a site they often lift mosaics and take them to museums. Sometimes they find markings in the cement underneath where the craftsmen sketched out the drawing in advance. At the Lod mosaic, in Israel, archaeologists have even found footprints of the ancient artists imprinted in the cement.

Subject matter

Mosaics had a wide range of subject matter. Mythological scenes were popular, inspired by the Greek tradition. Imagery from nature, hunting scenes, abstract patterns, exotic or common animals, foods, and gods were all found. The location of a mosaic could influence its subject (sea gods in bathhouses, foodstuffs in dining rooms), but did not need to.

QUESTIONS

1. Look at the mosaics in this chapter. What do you think they can tell us about the tastes of the owners, and the space in which they were created?
2. Which aspects of life in the Roman world do these mosaics illuminate?

autumnus

autumnus erat. Sabīna etiam nunc in thermīs labōrābat. magnam imāginem delphīnī cum Philētō, quī erat ūnus ē servīs Alexandrī, faciēbat.

Sabīna	emblēmata paene cōnfēcimus, Philēte! laeta sum! omnēs cīvēs Arelātēnsēs nōs laudābunt.
Philētus	ego sum laetior quam tū! fortasse nunc Alexander mē nōn diūtius verberābit. heus, ubi est Alexander?
Sabīna	nesciō. heri epistulam ā parentibus, quī in Lūsitāniā habitant, accēpit. dē cōnsiliō parentum cognōvit.
Philētus	quid est cōnsilium eōrum?
Sabīna	nesciō. mihi nihil dē eō dīxit, sed Alexander est laetissimus.

illō tempore, Alexander advēnit et Sabīnam vīdit.

Alexander	*(sibi susurrāns)* Sabīna est tam pulchra! est pulchrior quam omnēs fēminae in Galliā! eam amō, eam semper amābō!
Sabīna	quid dīxistī? nōn tē audīre possum.
Alexander	Sabīna, imāgō est tam pulchra! imāgō est pulchrior quam omnēs imāginēs in Galliā! eam amō!
Sabīna	sōlum est imāgō delphīnī! nihilōminus, quid mē rogāre vīs?
Alexander	maximī mōmentī est.
Sabīna	Alexander, quid est?
Alexander	Sabīna, tūne eris mea … ? ōh, ānxius sum!
Sabīna	ānxior sum! quid est, Alexander?
Alexander	Sabīna, tūne eris mea … ministra?
Sabīna	quid?
Alexander	ei! mox in Lūsitāniā labōrābimus. tē mēcum venīre volō. tibi placet?

autumnus *autumn*
delphīnus *dolphin*

Arelātēnsis *of Arles*
quam *than*
fortasse *perhaps*
nesciō *I don't know*

sibi *to himself*
tam *so*

nihilōminus
  nevertheless
mōmentum
  importance

ministra *employee, assistant*

Mosaic pattern books

Although the design and subject matter of mosaics vary widely, there are recognizable patterns and shared features across the Roman Empire. These similarities have led archaeologists to believe that there were standard pattern books which mosaic makers would work from. Clients could choose a particular scene or pattern that was fashionable at the time, just as one might now choose wallpaper or tiles.

Fishbourne Palace, England. About AD 160.

Conimbriga, Portugal. Second to third century AD.

Sanctuary of Artemis, Ephesus, Turkey. About AD 200.

Boutria (ancient Acholla), Tunisia. AD 150–170.

QUESTIONS

1. What similarities and differences can you see in these mosaics from across the Empire? Think about: colour, subject matter, style, and layout.
2. How do you think these designs would have travelled and become popular?

manēre aut abīre

Poppillus ad Lūsitāniam cum Alexandrō iuvene nāvigābis, Sabīna?

Sabīna incerta sum. emblēmata facere gaudeō, sed vōs duōs relinquere nōlō. post mortem patris, vōs mē cūrāvistis. nunc vōs estis parentēs meī.

Poppillus pff! hīc in aeternum manēbis? sī tū ad Lūsitāniam ībis, tū 5
terrās mīrābilēs vidēbis. hīc senectūs ac mors tē exspectant.

Letta quid? nōn tacēbis, Poppille? Sabīnam terrēbis! mē audī, Sabīna. necesse est tibi verba mea dīligenter cōgitāre (nec stulta verba quae Poppillus murmurat). iūnior multō es quam nōs senēs. carpe diem! orbem terrārum trānsī! in ūnā colōniā tōtam vītam 10
ēgī. laeta eram, sed nunc laetior sum, quod tē cognōvī. et sī tū cum Alexandrō nāvigābis, laetissima erō.

Sabīna ille vult mē esse suam ...

Poppillus uxōrem?

Sabīna minimē. suam ministram. 15

Letta quid? nihil dē amōre dīxit?

Sabīna dē amōre nec ille nec ego dīcimus.

Letta numquam dē amōre dīcitis? numquam? sine dubiō tē amat et cūrābit, Sabīna. amāsne tamen eum?

Sabīna fortasse eum nunc amō. fortasse mē amat. sed eum semper 20
amābō? mē semper amābit?

Poppillus quandō Alexander ac servī abībunt?

Sabīna paucīs diēbus nāvigābunt.

subitō Sabīna surgit.

Letta quō īs? 25

Sabīna ad templum Minervae eō. necesse est mihi deam adōrāre ac verba vestra cōgitāre.

post paucās hōrās, Sabīna revēnit.

Poppillus salvē, puella. manēre aut abīre cōnstituistī?

---

incertus *uncertain*
relinquō *I leave*

in aeternum *forever*
senectūs *old age*

iūnior *younger*
murmurō *I mutter*
multō *much, by far*
carpō *I enjoy, use*
orbis terrārum *world*
trānseō *I cross*
agō *I spend (time)*

sine dubiō *without doubt*

quandō? *when?*

vester *your*

LANGUAGE NOTE 2: COMPARISON

1. Look at the following pairs of sentences. Can you see how the form of the adjective in the first sentence changes in the second sentence? How does its meaning change?

   laeta sum.
   I'm happy.

   ego sum laetior quam tū.
   I'm happier than you.

   ānxius sum.
   I'm worried.

   ānxior sum.
   I'm more worried.

   Sabīna est pulchra.
   Sabina is beautiful.

   Sabīna est pulchrior quam omnēs fēminae in Galliā!
   Sabina is more beautiful than all the women in Gaul!

   laetior, **ānxior**, and **pulchrior** are known as **comparative** adjectives.

2. Comparative adjectives are often translated using *more* or by adding *-er* to the English word. When **quam** is used with a comparative adjective, it means *than*.

3. Note that comparative adjectives change their endings in a similar way to third declension adjectives and nouns:

   spectātōrēs laetiōrēs erant quam āctōrēs.
   The spectators were happier than the actors.

   līberīs miseriōribus cibum dedimus.
   We gave food to the more unfortunate children.

4. You have now met both the comparative and the superlative forms of adjectives:

Positive	Comparative	Superlative
laetus (happy)	**laetior** (happier)	**laetissimus** (happiest)
trīstis (sad)	**trīstior** (sadder)	**trīstissimus** (saddest)
pulcher (beautiful)	**pulchrior** (more beautiful)	**pulcherrimus** (most beautiful)

5. A small number of adjectives have irregular comparative and superlative forms. For example:

Positive	Comparative	Superlative
bonus (good)	**melior** (better)	**optimus** (best)
magnus (big)	**maior** (bigger)	**maximus** (biggest)

   See page 274 for other irregular comparative and superlative adjectives.

in metallō

Lūcīlius nunc est tribūnus mīlitum in Lūsitāniā. cum servō suō metallum in Tarracōnēnsī prōvinciā vīsitat. cūrātor metallī eōs per metallum dūcit.

cūrātor metalla magna in Lūsitāniā administrās?

Lūcīlius ita vērō. hoc tamen metallum maius est quam omnia in Lūsitāniā. 5

cūrātor sine dubiō, hoc metallum est maximum! ecce, tibi omnia dēmōnstrābō.

metallum *mine*
Tarracōnēnsis *of Tarraconensis*
cūrātor *manager*
maior, maius *bigger*

dēmōnstrō *I show, point out*
cavō *I hollow out*

cūrātor nunc servī hunc montem cavant.    mox servī trabēs verberābunt …

anteā   **posteā**

... et sīc montem dēlēbunt.   10

sīc *so, in this way*

ubi saxa dūriōra sunt, ignēs et aqua ea dēlēre possunt.

hīc aqua, quae ex aquaeductibus effluit, saxa aurō permixta ē monte fert.

aurum *gold*
permixtus *mixed*

Lūcīlius	rēs mīrābilēs mihi ostendis. multum aurum cōtīdiē invenītis? 15
cūrātor	plūs aurī inveniēbāmus quam in hīs temporibus.
Lūcīlius	cūr minus aurī nunc adest?
cūrātor	nesciō, tribūne.

subitō servus sordidus exclāmāvit.

servus sordidus bene scīs, sceleste! multum aurum invenīmus, sed aurum ēvānēscit! nōs servī diē et nocte labōrāmus sub monte. sub monte labor dīrus necābit nōs. coniūrātiō tamen est, tribūne! rogā cūrātōrem dē Cantabrō! rogā eum ubi plaustra ...

tum custōdēs servum capiunt.

cūrātor mendāx! servī quī dēspērant fābulās scelestās semper nārrant ...

Lūcīlius certē, et eōs sevēriter pūnīre dēbēs. servī quī dominum timent sunt servī fidēlēs.

cūrātor ita vērō, Lūcīlī. ēn, haec īnstrūmenta vidēs?

sciō *I know*

coniūrātiō *plot, conspiracy*
Cantaber *Cantaber*

sevēriter *severely*
pūniō *I punish*

Tīrō, ī per metallum. servōs dē Cantabrō rogā. tōtam rem intellegere volō ...

LANGUAGE PRACTICE

1. Translate each sentence into Latin by choosing the correct word or phrase from each pair.

   a. *Tomorrow we will consider your leader's plan.*
      | heri | cōnsilium | ducem | tuum | cōgitābunt. |
      | crās | cōnsiliō | ducis | tuī | cōgitābimus. |

   b. *Soon our soldiers will terrify the enemy in battle.*
      | ita | nōs | mīles | hostēs | in proeliō | terrēbimus. |
      | mox | nostrī | mīlitēs | hostium | in proelium | terrēbunt. |

   c. *Will you sail across the sea for many days?*
      | tūne | trāns mare | multīs diēbus | nāvigābis? |
      | egone | sub marī | multōs diēs | nāvigābō? |

   d. *There will never be a girl more beautiful than Sabina.*
      | paene | puella | pulchrior | quoque | Sabīnae | erit. |
      | numquam | puer | pulcher | quam | Sabīna | eris. |

   e. *When will Alexander whisper the words which Sabina wants to hear?*
      | quandō | Alexandrum | verbum, | quae | Sabīnam | dīcere | volunt, | susurrābit? |
      | cūr | Alexander | verba, | ubi | Sabīna | audīre | vult, | susurrābitis? |

   f. *Will you hurry at first light to the city, or will you stay in the mountains?*
      | nōnne | prīmā lūce | ad urbem | festīnābit | nec | in montibus | manēbitis? |
      | vōsne | prīma lūna | per urbem | festīnābitis | aut | in montēs | manēbit? |

2. Translate the following sentences into English.

   a. saxa graviōra dūriōraque mox dēlēbimus.

   b. Alexander emblēmata, quae maiōra erunt quam cētera in oppidō, facit.

   c. nēmō est stultior quam imperātor quī audīre nōn vult.

   d. quamquam labor erit difficilior, maiōra erunt praemia.

   e. rēgīna, quae erat senior quam prīncipēs, quoque sapientior et fortior erat.

   f. vestrīne comitēs fidēliōrēs vōs adiuvābunt?

   g. spectātōrēs āctōrēs meliōrēs post fābulam laudābunt.

   h. equus tuus est minor quam meus, sed saepe celerior est.

Mining at Las Médulas

The Roman Empire depended heavily on metals. Iron, tin, copper, silver, and gold were mined throughout the Empire and used for construction, machinery, military equipment, coins, jewellery, and other purposes. Possibly the largest mining operation in the Empire was the gold mine at Las Médulas, in Spain.

The landscape at Las Médulas still shows the effects of Roman mining. One technique widely used there was known as *ruīna montium* (mountain collapsing): entire mountains were systematically collapsed to reach the gold deposits underground.

The power of water

The Romans developed a variety of mining techniques which used hydraulic power (the power of water). You have read about the watermill at Barbegal in Chapter 13. At Las Médulas, seven aqueducts were constructed to feed a series of basins and waterways.

Remains of a rock-cut aqueduct at Las Médulas.

Aerial view of the Las Médulas site, showing the effects of mountain collapsing.

Mining techniques

1. Prospecting with water

Aqueducts and rivers fed into reservoirs where water was stored. These reservoirs were then emptied to release an avalanche of water over a hillside. The water swept away the top layer of soil to reveal veins of gold for mining.

2. Sluicing

Where gold deposits were on the surface (mixed in with mud, silt, and rubble), water power was used to shift huge quantities of soil, and then sift them for gold. Aqueducts or rivers fed into a series of stepped basins that gradually filtered out gold from loose soil and debris. The basins were lined with rosemary, a spiky bush. The chunks of gold got caught in the bushes, while mud, silt, and sand passed through them. Workers could then collect the bushes and pick out the gold by hand.

3. *ruina montium*: mountain collapsing

This technique was used at Las Médulas, where gold deposits were found deep underground, beneath hills that were at some points about 100 metres high. A network of tunnels was cut into the mountain. Workers then deliberately cut the beams supporting the tunnels, so that the tunnels caved in, causing the whole mountain to collapse (as in **in metallō**). A flood of water was then released from a reservoir above. The force of the water washed away all the debris, to expose the gold deposits below.

4. Breaking up tougher rocks

Where the ground was too hard to mine with pickaxes, miners used fire and water to blow up the rocks. They lit fires at the base of the rock to heat the stone, then suddenly cooled the stone down by dousing it with water (or sometimes vinegar). The sudden drop in temperature caused the rock to crack or explode, as in the story **in metallō**.

5. Draining mines

As a result of the extensive use of water in the mines, as well as groundwater coming up from below, there was a constant need to drain the tunnels. Bailing out by hand with buckets was the simplest way to do this. However, more advanced techniques included the use of a series of water wheels to remove water from the mines, such as this one (*left*) found in the Rio Tinto copper mine in southern Spain.

Part of a wooden wheel used to drain a mine.

Working conditions in the mines

> The men dig tunnels through the mountains, working by lamplight. For months the miners cannot see the sunlight, and the tunnels collapse suddenly, crushing the workmen.
> *Pliny the Elder*

Thousands of people must have worked at the Las Médulas mine in various jobs: from low-skilled physical labourers to advanced engineers in charge of tunnelling machinery and hydraulic systems. The vast majority of work in mines was done by slaves, though prisoners of war, convicts, and poor freeborn labourers also formed part of the workforce. For these men, working in the mines was extremely dangerous and they usually died young; the physical labour was exhausting, the poor air quality in the underground tunnels ruined their lungs, and accidents were very common.

Women

Roman historians wrote about many women, but they were typically women who, like the historians themselves, were from wealthy or aristocratic families. Their stories can tell us much about what Romans expected from such women, and in particular *mātrōnae* (married women).

Lucretia

Some wealthy young Romans were discussing their wives. As none could agree whose wife was best, they went home to check what their wives were up to. Most of the women were idly chatting and dining with their friends, but Lucretia was busy spinning wool and weaving. Not only was she properly occupied, but she immediately fulfilled her duties, producing food and wine for her husband and his friends. Her husband, Collatinus, was very proud of her, but Tarquinius, the king's arrogant son, fell in love with her.

One night, Tarquinius returned alone to visit Lucretia, with the intention of seducing her. At first she received him kindly as a guest, but when he tried to seduce her, she repeatedly refused. Finally, Tarquinius said he would kill her and a male slave, and place the slave naked next to her. He would then pretend he had found them committing adultery and had killed them. As Lucretia could not accept her reputation being insulted, she submitted to Tarquinius. Once he left, she sent for her husband and father. In front of them she explained what had happened, and then took her own life, ignoring the pleas of her family, who tried to reassure her that she had done nothing wrong.

Sempronia

The historian Sallust wrote about Sempronia, a wealthy lady who was involved in a conspiracy to kill the consuls of 63 BC and overturn the Republic. There were many positive things about Sempronia: she was from a good family, was well-married, and was a mother. She was also educated in Greek and Latin, played the lyre, danced well, wrote poetry, and had a witty way with words. However, her dancing was so good that it was better than was appropriate for a respectable woman! It seems that being too good at some activities was not acceptable: why should a proper Roman matrona dance and play so well? The implication is that Sempronia was performing the role of an entertainer rather than of a mother of the house. This is not the only criticism that Sallust levels at Sempronia: she was also lacking in modesty and chastity (she went after men more than they pursued her), she spent money extravagantly, often refused to pay her debts, broke her word, and was even involved in murder. We can't be sure that Sempronia actually did any of these things, but her story indicates what Romans thought was, and was not, acceptable behaviour for aristocratic women.

Agrippina

Agrippina was sister, wife, and mother of emperors (Caligula, Claudius, and Nero respectively), and therefore probably the most powerful woman of her age. She lived during violent times when the first imperial family was establishing itself, and she had to navigate very dangerous waters. According to Roman historians she was beautiful, extremely ambitious, and ruthless. We are told that she had an incestuous relationship with her brother, who sent her into exile, and that she poisoned her third husband, Emperor Claudius, so that her son, Nero, could become emperor in AD 54. As Nero was only about 16, she exerted an enormous influence over her son, but he soon started to resent her power and ordered her execution in AD 59.

As a modern reader, one gets the impression that Roman historians believed Agrippina deserved what she got, and it is difficult to separate historical fact from obvious prejudice. Probably Agrippina's greatest failure in the eyes of Roman historians was that her ambition, in particular her manipulation of Claudius and Nero, moved her out of the sphere allotted to women into that of male power. However, when no other option was open, what else could a capable and ambitious woman do?

A marble portrait of Agrippina made in about AD 50.

Chapter 15: vīlla

in culīnā

1. crās tribūnus mīlitum hanc vīllam vīsitābit. cēnam splendidam tribūnō parābimus. nōs omnēs dīligentissimē labōrābimus.

2. ille tribūnus oculōs pulchrōs habet.

3. quid tū dīcis?

culīna kitchen
vīlla country house, house
cēna dinner
dīligentissimē very carefully

4. silentium erat.

5. amīca mea dīcit tribūnum oculōs pulchrōs habēre.

6. cēterī multum rīdēbant.

7. tacēte, vōs omnēs! certē audiō tribūnum oculōs pulchriōrēs quam vōs habēre.

in hortō

hortus *garden*

8 servī ancillaeque nōn sōlum in culīnā vīllae sed etiam in hortō occupātī sunt.

9 ohē, comes! dā mihi auxilium! difficile est mihi hās amphorās in vīllam portāre.

10 tū stulte! numquam dīligenter labōrās! auxilium tibi dare nōn possum. necesse est mihi plūs cibī ab hortō ferre.

11 tūne dīcis mē neglegenter labōrāre?

12 tūne nōn intellegis mē occupātum esse?

13 ohē! bellumne geritis, vōs duo? dēsistite! dominus noster semper est īrātus ubi videt servōs nōn dīligenter labōrāre.

occupātus *busy*
neglegenter *carelessly*

Country estates

Cantaber owns a large house in Conimbriga and a country villa and estate about six miles outside the town. Wealthy men in Rome and the provinces often owned country houses, and some owned the surrounding farmland as well. Land was expensive, but it was a good investment for those who could afford it. Usually the owner did not maintain the farm himself. Some rented the land to tenant farmers who then had to pay the owner with a share of their produce. Often slaves worked the land; a freedman supervised them and kept everything running smoothly. Some landowners bought the adjoining farms, creating huge complexes known as *lātifundia*. Romans relied on the labour of enslaved people to farm these latifundia.

On a country estate there would be a main house for the owner and his family and guests. There would also be land for crops and animals, accommodation for slaves, a bathhouse, granary, and gardens.

An imagined reconstruction of the country estate known as the villa Rabaçal near Conimbriga in Portugal, based on the archaeological remains.

Idealization of the farmer

For peasants and tenant farmers, working the land was necessary for survival. Among wealthy Romans (who would never have to work the land themselves), the farmer's life was sometimes idealized. Cicero said:

> Of all the jobs from which we get some profit, none is better than agriculture, none more productive, none more pleasant, none more fitting for a free man.

Country living

Some country estates, like Cantaber's, were close to towns and their owners would visit for a few days, enjoying a brief relief from the bustling city. Others were further away, and wealthy Romans might stay there for the summer months to escape the heat of the city. For sophisticated Romans, having a country retreat was a necessary part of the good life. It was a place to enjoy leisure time in the fresh air: reading, horse-riding, walking, and hunting. However, they brought with them every amenity and comfort of the town and passed their time in the height of luxury.

Conimbriga

Conimbriga was a town in the Roman province of Lusitania (modern Portugal and western Spain). It is the best preserved Roman city in Portugal, although it was not the largest. When the Romans conquered the area in 163 BC they kept the name of the original settlement: Conimbriga means 'high rocky citadel', referring to the location of the town on a plateau. In the late first century BC the town was remodelled in the Roman style. This included building a forum, baths, and a large surrounding wall with gates giving access from the main roads.

Honey bees

Although no beehives have survived from Roman times (they were made of biodegradable materials), many Roman authors wrote about beekeeping. The Romans did not have sugar; instead they used honey as a sweetener. The production of honey was not the only benefit of beekeeping. The wax was also used to make writing tablets and for medicinal purposes.

Fish ponds

Freshwater fish ponds in the gardens of country estates provided fish to eat, but they also housed luxury pet fish. Some Romans are reported to have become extremely attached to these expensive fish. Antonia (the mother of Emperor Claudius) is even said to have attached earrings to her favourite eel!

Snails

Snails were a special delicacy for the Romans. They were kept in pens in the garden and fattened on grain and aromatic herbs. The practice of farming snails is called heliculture, from the Greek word 'helix', which means spiral.

Gardens

Gardens were practical spaces. At any size, in the town or in the countryside, they were a source of fresh fruit, vegetables, and herbs for the household. In towns, people living in insulae might have had a window box for a few herbs; only wealthier houses had space for a garden. Outside the town, houses could have large gardens and grow a wide variety of produce. Some richer households even had greenhouses where they could grow more exotic fruit out of season.

The garden at the Getty Villa in California is a reconstruction of a Roman garden.

Decorative gardens

By the time of our stories, wealthy Romans valued gardens more for decoration than for practicality. Gardens became an opportunity to display one's wealth with exotic plants, water features, and statues. The garden paradises Romans created were not only private spaces for the owner of the house to relax in; they were also designed to impress guests. They were often in the centre of the house and could open onto a small garden room (*exedra*) which was used for entertaining guests. A skilled slave, called a *topiārius*, had the job of trimming the bushes and hedges into decorative shapes.

Garden archaeology

Garden archaeology is still a new branch of study. Analysis of seeds, along with evidence from literature and art, helps determine which plants were grown in Roman gardens. Roses, lilies, and rosemary were some of the favourites. Other physical remains allow archaeologists to reimagine the layout of the gardens. For example, holes in the earth show where plants were planted, and sometimes remains of water systems, fences, and trellises survive. Archaeologists have also found flower pots in Roman gardens; these help them reconstruct the location of plants. They have even compared the DNA of Roman grape seeds to modern ones to find out more about ancient agricultural practices.

in vīllā Cantabrī

prope ātrium Lūcīlius et Tīrō susurrant. vultus tribūnī est gravis.

Lūcīlius	putō Cantabrum ab illō metallō aurum auferre.
Tīrō	(*attonitus*) sed, domine –
Lūcīlius	tacē, Tīrō! ī quam celerrimē per hanc vīllam. servōs dē Cantabrō rogā.

exit servus. Lūcīlius ātrium intrat, ubi duo artificēs emblēmata faciunt. prīmō tribūnus est ānxius: artificēsne eum Tīrōnemque audiēbant? deinde cōnspicit ūnam artificem vultum suum intentē spectāre.

Lūcīlius	hercle! tē agnōscō! salvē … ?
Sabīna	… Sabīna. hic est Alexander, quī est meus … magister.
Lūcīlius	Gāius Lūcīlius Iūnior, tribūnus mīlitum, sum. quid accidit, Sabīna? proximō annō Rōmae habitābās. nunc videō tē in Lūsitāniā habitāre.
Sabīna	in incendiō Rōmae exspīrāvit pater. dē vītā amitae meae, quae est Christiāna, dēspērō.
Lūcīlius	audiō Christiānōs esse in magnō perīculō.
Sabīna	certē, Lūcīlī. audī. tē iuvāre possum. servī dīcunt plaustra horreīs mediā nocte appropinquāre. servī quoque dīcunt hominēs plaustra horreaque custōdīre.
Lūcīlius	grātiās maximās tibi agō, Sabīna! necesse est mihi rem Cantabrī cognōscere.

Lūcīlius exit.

Alexander	(*īrātus*) esne īnsāna, Sabīna? Cantaber est vir magnī imperiī. et nōbīs et familiae meae multum nocēre potest.
Sabīna	tūtī erimus, Alexander. putō tribūnum esse virum magnae virtūtis.
Alexander	(*īrātior*) amāsne hunc tribūnum?
Sabīna	(*īrātissima*) quid? stultior quam asinus es, Alexander!

ātrium *reception room, entrance hall*
putō *I think*

agnōscō *I recognize*
magister *employer*

exspīrō *I die*

iuvō *I help, assist*
horreum *barn, granary, warehouse*

imperium *power*
noceō *I harm*

LANGUAGE NOTE 1: STATEMENTS, DIRECT AND INDIRECT

1. Since Chapter 1 you have seen statements like these:

   Sabīna in Lūsitāniā habitat. *Sabina is living in Lusitania.*
   senex dīligenter labōrat. *The old man is working carefully.*

   These are known as **direct statements**: the author gives us information about Sabina and the old man directly.

2. In this chapter you have met sentences like these:

   dīcit Sabīnam in Lūsitāniā habitāre. *He says Sabina to live in Lusitania.*
   = *He says that Sabina is living in Lusitania.*

   putāmus senem dīligenter labōrāre. *We think the old man to work carefully.*
   = *We think that the old man works carefully.*

   These are known as **indirect statements**: the author gives us information about Sabina and the old man indirectly, through what a character says or thinks.

3. Look at the sentences below. What case do **Lūcīlius** and **puella** become when they move from the direct to the indirect statements? What happens to **habet** and **mittit**?

   Direct statement

   Lūcīlius oculōs pulchrōs habet.
   Lucilius has lovely eyes.

   puella nūntium mittit.
   The girl is sending a message.

   Indirect statement

   dīcit Lūcīlium oculōs pulchrōs habēre.
   She says Lucilius to have lovely eyes.
   = *She says that Lucilius has lovely eyes.*

   sciunt puellam nūntium mittere.
   They know the girl to be sending a message.
   = *They know that the girl is sending a message.*

   Indirect statements use an **accusative and infinitive** construction. The accusative usually comes immediately after the verb of saying, thinking, or perceiving. The infinitive often comes at the end of the sentence.

4. You may find indirect statements after verbs such as **dīcō** (*say*), **putō** (*think*), **audiō** (*hear*), **sentiō** (*notice*), **videō** (*see*), and **cognōscō** (*learn*).

5. When translating an indirect statement, it may be helpful to translate it first literally, then more naturally. It can also help to use *that* after the verb of saying, thinking, or perceiving, e.g. *They say that ... , I hear that ... .*

cēna

nōnā hōrā multī hospitēs magnificam cēnam in vīllā Cantabrī cōnsūmēbant. Lūcīlius proximus Cantabrō recumbēbat. ūnus ex hospitibus clāmāvit saltātrīcēs triclīnium intrāre, deinde omnēs exclāmābant plaudēbantque. Lūcīlius tamen ad Cantabrum sē vertit.

'ubi in prōvinciā Tarracōnēnsī iter faciēbam, metallum vīsitāvī,' inquit Lūcīlius. 'cūrātor mihi nūntiāvit metallum esse maximum in prōvinciā.' 5

Cantaber, quī servum vīnum ferre iubēbat, clāmāvit, 'vah! num dē metallīs cognōscere cupis, tribūne? cōnsūme glīrēs et plūs vīnī bibe!'

'quantum aurum dē metallō cōtīdiē trahis, Cantaber?' rogāvit Lūcīlius. 'sciō tē prō Nerōne illud metallum administrāre.' 10

'vērum? quid nescīs, tū callide?' Lūcīliō susurrāvit Cantaber, quī īram suam vix cēlābat. 'nōnne scīs custōdēs meōs aurum in plaustrīs ad monētam imperātōris rēctā dūcere? cognōvistīne tamen illa plaustra esse paene inānia? etiam melius est mihi fundōs administrāre quam metalla.' 15

Lūcīlius nihil respondit, quod crēdidit Cantabrum mendācem esse.

intereā Alexander et Sabīna in culīnā vīllae sedēbant. Alexander dulcis 'dīxī tē īnsānam esse, Sabīna,' inquit. 'sciō mē longē errāre. potesne mihi ignōscere?'

'certē, tibi ignōscō, Alexander,' eī respondit Sabīna. 'īrāta eram, quod 20 putāvistī mē tribūnum amāre. intellegō tamen Cantabrum esse perīculōsum. rēs est gravis. erō comes fidēlis nōn sōlum cōnsiliōrum tuōrum sed etiam omnium perīculōrum.'

---

hospes *guest*
recumbō *I recline, lie down*
saltātrīx *dancer*
triclīnium *dining room*
sē *himself*
vertō *I turn*
num? *surely ... not?*
glīs *dormouse*

callidus *clever*
īra *anger*
monēta *mint (coin factory)*
rēctā *directly, straight*
inānis *empty*

dulcis *sweet, pleasant*
errō *I make a mistake*
ignōscō *I forgive*

Dormice were a popular delicacy. One recipe was roasted dormouse, glazed in honey and rolled in poppy seeds. The jar on the right is a **glīrārium**, an earthenware vessel used for keeping and fattening dormice. The side has been cut away to show the interior. The wall is pierced with holes and inside there is a ledge which spirals from the rim to the base. Varro wrote:

> Dormice are fattened in jars, which many people keep inside their villa. Potters make these in a very different form from other jars; they have ridges along the sides and a hollow for holding food. Acorns, walnuts, or chestnuts are put inside; a cover is placed on top and the dormice grow fat in the dark.

LANGUAGE NOTE 2: INDIRECT STATEMENTS – PERFECT MAIN VERBS

1. Study the following pairs of sentences:

   Present tense main verb

   dīcit Sabīnam in Lūsitāniā habitāre.
   He says Sabina to live in Lusitania.
   = He says that Sabina **is** living in Lusitania.

   putāmus senem dīligenter labōrāre.
   We think the old man to work carefully.
   = We think that the old man **is** working carefully.

   Perfect tense main verb

   dīxit Sabīnam in Lūsitāniā habitāre.
   He said Sabina to live in Lusitania.
   = He said that Sabina **was** living in Lusitania.

   putāvimus senem dīligenter labōrāre.
   We thought the old man to work carefully.
   = We thought that the old man **was** working carefully.

2. Notice how the translation of the indirect statement changes when it is introduced by a verb in the perfect tense.

LANGUAGE PRACTICE

1. Translate the following direct and indirect statements.
   a. Sabīna Lūcīlium amat.
   b. Alexander putat Sabīnam Lūcīlium amāre.
   c. Alexander stultus est.
   d. Sabīna dīcit Alexandrum stultum esse.
   e. comes cēnam magnificam cōnsūmit.
   f. lībertus cognōscit comitem cēnam magnificam cōnsūmere.
   g. hostēs ferōcēs bellum saepe gerunt.
   h. mīlitēs sciunt hostēs ferōcēs bellum saepe gerere.
   i. puerī plūs pecūniae quaerunt.
   j. nēmō sentit puerōs plūs pecūniae quaerere.

2. Translate the following direct and indirect statements.
   a. rēx hominēs līberat.
   b. ducēs audīvērunt rēgem hominēs līberāre.
   c. labor est dūrus.
   d. intellēximus labōrem esse dūrum.
   e. rēgīna in proeliō frūstrā pugnat.
   f. prīncipēs scīvērunt rēgīnam in proeliō frūstrā pugnāre.
   g. nōs auxilium ad amīcōs mittimus.
   h. nūntiāvimus nōs auxilium ad amīcōs mittere.
   i. puer ē vīllā festīnat.
   j. sēnsistis puerum ē vīllā festīnāre.

Dinner parties

surgite: iam vēndit puerīs ientācula pistor
Get up: now the baker is selling breakfast to boys.
Martial

Romans ate three meals a day:

ientāculum (breakfast), was bread, possibly with some cheese.

prandium (lunch) was eaten at about midday. It was just a snack, perhaps bread and cheese and some vegetables.

cēna (dinner) was the main meal of the day. Generally this was eaten in the late afternoon or early evening, while it was still daylight. For most people it was a simple meal, often a takeaway, as you learned in Chapter 1 (pages 18–19). Rich Romans sometimes gave dinner parties which started later, lit by lamplight, because they could afford lamps or torches. The word for dinner party or banquet is *convīvium* – literally a living together or get-together. The host and his guests often met in the baths beforehand, and some people went to the baths in the hope of receiving an invitation to dinner. Business associates, political contacts, and the host's freedmen would be invited, as well as friends and family.

Preparing and serving the meal

When the guests arrived, a slave would take off their shoes and wash their feet, then take them to the dining room (*triclīnium*). Slaves cooked and served the food. They cut it up beforehand, then the guests served themselves from a central table, using their fingers or a spoon. Guests often brought their own napkins (*mappae*), and used them later as doggy bags for taking away leftovers. The food was served on expensive tableware made of silver, glass, and bronze.

Often the food was intended to impress the guests and provide a spectacle as well as being tasty. Exotic produce such as peacock and flamingo was served because of its rarity and high cost, and elaborate recipes were invented.

QUESTIONS

1. Look at Sources 1 and 2. Which menu is more elaborate and which is more simple?
2. What impression of their own tastes and lifestyle do you think the hosts want to give?

SOURCE 1

Listen to the menu; there's nothing bought in the market. From my farm at Tivoli, a plump little goat, the most tender of the herd, which has not yet tasted grass, with more milk than blood in its veins; wild asparagus which the farm manager's wife picks after she's finished her spinning; big, warm eggs, wrapped in straw – along with their mothers; grapes, preserved for half a year, but as fresh as they were on the vine; Syrian pears and fragrant apples.
Juvenal

SOURCE 2

A guest at a dinner party is describing some of the dishes that were served. He notes how the host explained in detail where the ingredients came from and how they were cooked. The dishes included:

- wild boar, served with spiced turnips, lettuce, radishes, water-parsnips, and pickled fish.
- oysters, fillets of plaice, turbot – all of these cooked in new ways.
- lamprey with prawns, and a dressing of olive oil from Venafrum from the first pressing, fish sauce made from Spanish mackerel, five-year-old wine (Italian not Greek), white pepper, vinegar made from fermented grapes from Lesbos, and rocket.
- crane's legs, goose liver (from a goose fed on figs), shoulder of hare, blackbird, and pigeon.

Horace

A blue, glass drinking cup and a bronze serving fork. Although the Romans did not use forks to eat, larger forks, like this one, were used to serve the food.

The dining room

One of the most important rooms in a town house or country villa was the triclinium, the dining room. This was where wealthy Romans entertained their guests with lavish dinner parties. The word 'triclinium' comes from the Greek for 'three couches'. The dining room was called the triclinium because the main items of furniture were three couches, arranged on three sides of one or several small tables. Rich Romans reclined on couches to eat at their dinner parties, lying on their left side and resting on cushions. Each couch had room for three people. The reclining arrangements reflected the importance of the guests. One of the couches was for the guests of honour, while another was for the least important. Some couches were permanent: they were made of stone, with sloping surfaces, and would be covered with mattresses and cushions. There were also wooden and bronze couches which could be moved around. Some grand houses had a separate open-air summer triclinium. These rooms were lavishly decorated with wall paintings and mosaic floors.

Entertainment

At some banquets there was music, played on the flute or lyre. Other entertainment included singing, dancing, acrobatic displays, or recitals of poetry.

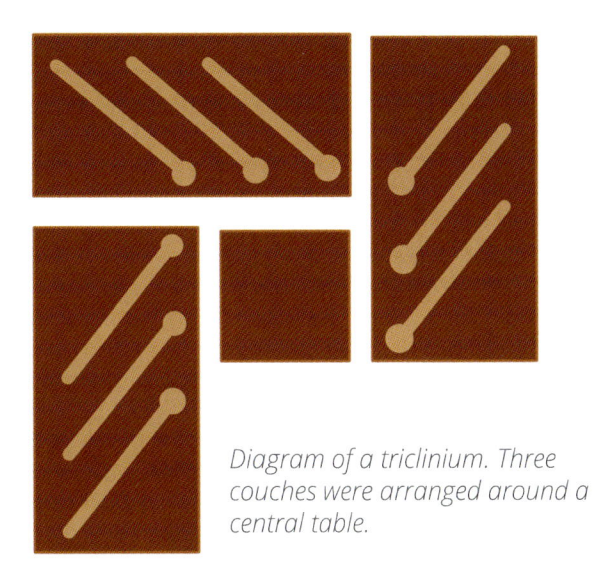

Diagram of a triclinium. Three couches were arranged around a central table.

Wall painting with a scene from a dinner party.

Menus

ab ōvō usque ad māla
from egg to apples
Horace

Dinner was usually three courses, and this saying was used to mean 'from start to finish'.

gustātiō: appetizers, e.g. eggs, olives, snails, cheese, vegetables.
mēnsae prīmae: first course, e.g. meat or fish dishes with various sauces.
mēnsae secundae: dessert, e.g. fruit, nuts, sweet things.

Wine, mixed with water, was drunk during the meal.

Recipes

Several authors wrote about the food at dinner parties. The most valuable source is a cookery book by Apicius, which was probably compiled in the fifth century AD. Cato, who lived about 200 BC, wrote a handbook on farming which includes some recipes.

gustātiō

Olive paste
Remove the stones from green, black, or mixed olives. Chop the olives. Add oil, vinegar, coriander, cumin, fennel, and mint. Put in a dish, cover with oil. Serve.

Cabbage or broccoli
Boil the cabbage or broccoli. Season with cumin, garum, wine, and oil. Add pine nuts and raisins.

mēnsae prīmae

Poached ostrich
First, make a stock. Put into a pot: pepper, mint, cumin seeds, leeks, celery seeds, dates, honey, vinegar, sweet wine, water or stock, a little olive oil. Bring to the boil and add the ostrich pieces. Simmer until the meat is done. Remove the ostrich pieces and strain the broth. Thicken the broth with flour, pour over the pieces of cooked ostrich in a serving dish, and sprinkle with pepper. Add garlic during the cooking if you like.

Fish in a coriander crust
Put salt and coriander seeds in a mortar and crush finely. Roll the fish fillets in the mixture. Put them in a dish, cover, and cook in the oven. When cooked, remove the fish, sprinkle with vinegar, and serve.

mēnsae secundae

Stuffed dates
Remove the stones from the dates. Stuff with a nut or nuts and ground pepper. Sprinkle the outside with salt and cook in honey.

QUESTIONS

1. Compare these recipes with those in a modern cookery book or magazine. What similarities and differences do you notice?
2. Would it be possible for a modern cook to make these dishes? What difficulties would you have if you tried to make them at home?

LANGUAGE NOTE 3: INDIRECT STATEMENTS – SĒ OR EUM?

1. What do you think might be the difference in meaning in these two sentences?
    a. **Lūcīlius scit sē magnam pecūniam habēre.**
       Lucilius knows that he has a lot of money.
    b. **Lūcīlius scit eum magnam pecūniam habēre.**
       Lucilius knows that he has a lot of money.
2. **sē** refers to the subject of the main verb, i.e. Lucilius, whereas **eum** refers to someone else. So sentence **a.** means Lucilius knows that he himself has a lot of money, while sentence **b.** means Lucilius knows that someone else has a lot of money.
3. Latin always uses **sē** to refer to the subject of the main verb, whether it's a man, a woman, or a number of people. **eum**, **eam**, **eōs**, and **eās** are used as appropriate to refer to others.

LANGUAGE PRACTICE

3. Choose the correct pronoun to match the English meaning.

    a. Lūcīlius dīxit ..... ē vīllā discēdere.   (sē, eum)
       Lucilius said that he (himself) was leaving the villa.
    b. Alexander putat ..... Sabīnam amāre.   (sē, eum)
       Alexander thinks that he (someone else) loves Sabina.
    c. Sabīna scit ..... nūllam pecūniam habēre.   (sē, eam)
       Sabina knows that she (herself) has no money.
    d. Rōmānī cognōvērunt ..... arma parāre.   (sē, eōs)
       The Romans learned that they (others) were preparing their weapons.

A Roman wall painting showing two men preparing food.

post cēnam

mediā nocte Lūcīlius in lectō iacēbat, sed nōn dormiēbat. subitō vōcem Tīrōnis per fenestram audīvit.

'age, domine!' susurrāvit Tīrō, quī in hortō vīllae stābat. 'ancilla dīxit plaustra horreō appropinquāre.'

Lūcīlius statim surrēxit et ad iānuam cubiculī festīnāvit. Tīrō tamen 'nōlī per vīllam īre, domine!' inquit. 'anteā cognōvī lībertōs cubiculum tuum custōdīre.'

itaque Lūcīlius dē fenestrā cubiculī in hortum tacitē dēscendit, et cum Tīrōne per hortum prōcēdēbat.

age! *come!*

cubiculum *bedroom*

brevī tempore tribūnus servusque ad horreum advēnērunt et post
mūrum sē cēlāvērunt. prīmō vīdērunt servōs saccōs frūmentō plēnōs
ē plaustrīs trahere. lībertus ingēns et ferōx, quī hūc illūc ambulābat,
servōs saccōs in horreum portāre iubēbat. servī, postquam ad plaustra
rediērunt, gravēs arcās accēpērunt. arcās quoque in horreum cum
magnā difficultāte trahēbant. tum Lūcīlius et Tīrō duōs custōdēs, quī
inter sē susurrābant, audīvērunt.

prīmus custōs	quot arcae iam sunt in horreō?
secundus custōs	nesciō, comes. sed putō dominum esse laetum. amīcus meus dīxit eum arcās in horreō aperīre et ex arcīs multum aurī tollere.

subitō manus ignōta Lūcīlium rapuit. tribūnus servusque audīvērunt
vōcem lībertī ingentis. ille ferōciter dīxit, 'nōlīte resistere nōbīs, vōs duo.'
tum custōdēs ad Cantabrum eōs dūcere iussit.

saccus *sack, bag*
frūmentum *corn, grain*
hūc illūc *here and there*
arca *crate, strongbox*

quot? *how many?*

Civil War

Civil War in the Late Republic

As mentioned in Chapter 3, the Republic in the first century BC was plagued by vicious civil wars. As the Empire grew larger, keeping control of distant provinces required strong armies led by capable commanders. Two of those commanders were Marius and Sulla.

Marius (157–86 BC)

Marius championed the poor. He restructured the army, changing it from a part-time citizen force to a full-time professional one. All Roman citizens, including the poor, could find reliable employment and careers as legionary soldiers. When these professional soldiers retired, they received money from their commander, and a plot of land in a conquered region. That money was provided by the generals themselves (not by the state), and therefore close bonds developed between soldiers and their commanders. The power and influence of individual Roman generals, with loyal armies behind them, increased greatly.

In addition to reshaping the army, Marius was a very successful general. He was credited with the victory against the Numidian king Jugurtha and with stopping two German tribes from threatening the Roman provinces of southern Gaul (and perhaps Italy itself).

Marius' political career was also groundbreaking: he was the first man to be consul for five years in a row (104–99 BC), and in total he was elected consul seven times. This success may help to explain how he came to believe that he was the only man entitled to take the lead in Rome's battles and politics.

Sulla (c.138–78 BC)

Sulla was an aristocrat and one of Marius' quaestors (subordinate officers). In 88 BC he was himself elected consul, and was given command of a Roman army fighting in the East. However, Marius was jealous of Sulla's opportunity to prove himself. He convinced one of the tribunes to persuade the Popular Assembly to remove Sulla's command and give it to him. Sulla did not accept the Assembly's decision. He took his army and marched against Rome, as an external enemy would have done, and forced the Romans to give him back his command. He then returned to fight in the East.

While Sulla was away from Rome, Marius and his faction slaughtered a number of Sulla's supporters. In 86 BC Marius obtained the last of his seven consulships, together with a man called Cinna. Although Marius died at the beginning of the year, Cinna continued the violence against Sulla's supporters. Sulla returned from the East and marched on Rome for a second time. He was appointed dictator, executed Marius' and Cinna's supporters, and confiscated their property. Once he had achieved his revenge, he undid any laws created by Marius and his allies which undermined the aristocracy and the Senate. He then resigned his post and retired to live a private life.

Marius and Sulla therefore both broke the traditional constitution of Rome: Marius was consul repeatedly; Sulla led an army against his own city of Rome. Both headed factions which killed fellow Roman citizens. Powerful commanders who came after them now had an example to follow. Marius and Sulla had set precedents for continued consulships, marching on Rome with armies, and killing fellow citizens. These actions were all to be repeated in the decades to come.

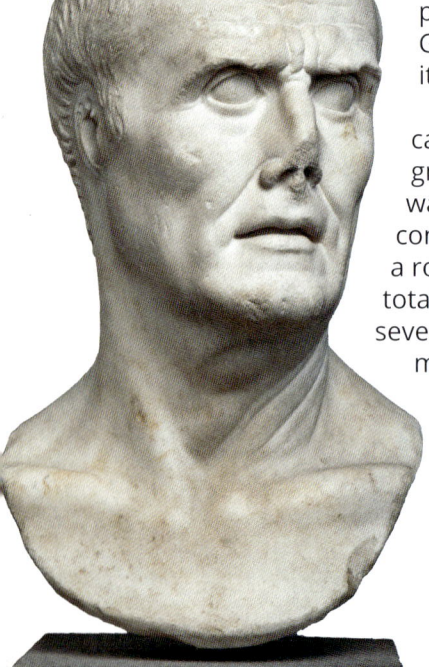

Chapter 16: nūptiae

familia Alexandrī

1. haec fēmina est Hettia, māter Alexandrī.

2. hic vir est Maelō. Maelō est pater Alexandrī.

3. hī virī sunt servī, quōs Maelō in forō ēmit. servī laterēs faciunt.

later *brick*

4. hī sunt frātrēs Alexandrī, quī quoque laterēs faciunt.

5. hae fēminae, quae vestīmenta parant, sunt sorōrēs Alexandrī.

6 Maelō! Alexander adest!

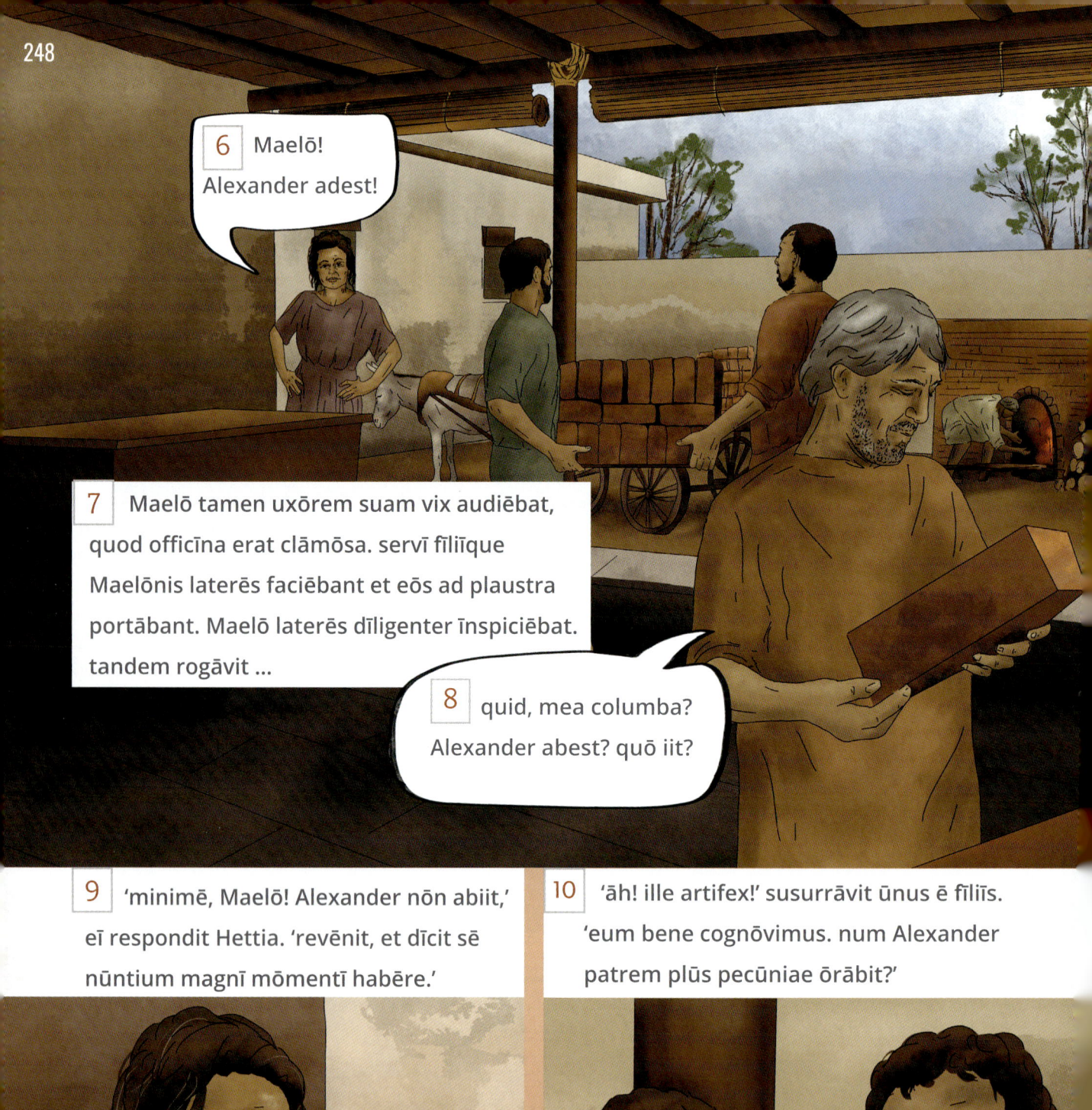

7 Maelō tamen uxōrem suam vix audiēbat, quod officīna erat clāmōsa. servī fīliīque Maelōnis laterēs faciēbant et eōs ad plaustra portābant. Maelō laterēs dīligenter īnspiciēbat. tandem rogāvit ...

8 quid, mea columba? Alexander abest? quō iit?

9 'minimē, Maelō! Alexander nōn abiit,' eī respondit Hettia. 'revēnit, et dīcit sē nūntium magnī mōmentī habēre.'

10 'āh! ille artifex!' susurrāvit ūnus ē fīliīs. 'eum bene cognōvimus. num Alexander patrem plūs pecūniae ōrābit?'

āh! *ah!*

pater ānxius

prīmā lūce postrīdiē, ubi Alexander cum parentibus sedēbat, eīs multa dē Sabīnā nūntiābat. māter Alexandrī multō laetior quam marītus suus erat. illa gaudēbat, sed hic ānxiē

'quālis puella est illa Sabīna?' rogāvit. 'unde venit? quis est pater eius?'

eī Alexander trīste respondit patrem eius esse mortuum. tum dīxit Sabīnam esse Subūrānam et multō fidēliōrem quam puellās in oppidō Conimbrīgā.

'Sabīna dīligenter labōrat. lānam cōtīdiē facit. emblēmata eius sunt magnifica. domum optimē servābit. Sabīnam in Galliā relinquere nōluī. eam in mātrimōnium dūcere volō. tandem pecūniam habeō. nunc līberōs et uxōrem habēre volō.'

tandem Maelō sēnsit fīlium uxōrem bonam legere.

'sed eam amās?' rogāvit māter.

'sine dubiō, māter. iam tibi dīxī,' eī respondit Alexander. 'et sub vesperum eam rogābō.'

postrīdiē on the following day

unde? from where?

Subūrānus from the Subura
Conimbrīga Conimbriga (town in Lusitania)
lāna wool
in mātrimōnium dūcō I marry

Brickmaking was an important industry in Conimbriga. This ceramic brick is inscribed with the words: **AVE MAELO** *(Greetings, Maelo). It is one of several which record Maelo as the owner of a factory which made bricks.*

ānulus

Alexander per viās festīnāvit. tandem parvam officīnam fūmōsam intrāvit, ubi ferrārius dīligenter labōrābat, et dē ānulō rogāvit. 'ecce, ānulus est parātus,' eī respondit ferrārius, et Alexandrō eum trādidit.

ānulus ring
parātus ready

vestīmenta

1 paucōs post diēs, tōta familia Maelōnis occupāta erat, quod diēs nūptiālis appropinquābat. Hettia et fīliae vestīmenta nūptiālia faciēbant. id quod Hettia faciēbat erat flammeum.

2 diēs nūptiārum meārum optimus erat.

3 certē, soror! quam pulchra erās.

4 diē nūptiārum tuārum sīcut rēgīna eris, Sabīna.

nūptiālis *nuptial, wedding*
id quod *that which*
flammeum *bridal veil*
nūptiae *wedding*

5 iō, rēgīna Sabīna!

6 omnēs quattuor laetē rīdēbant.

porcus fugitīvus

"cavēte, omnēs!"

"nōlīte porcō appropinquāre!"

frātrēs Alexandrī per forum
ruēbant clāmābantque.
porcum fugitīvum, 5
quī graviter grundiēbat et
celeriter currēbat, frūstrā
agitābant. turba attonita
clāmōrem eōrum audīvit.

porcus *pig*	graviter *heavily*
fugitīvus *runaway*	grundiō *I grunt*

per tōtam urbem frātrēs porcum 10
quaesīvērunt, tum dēspērābant. 'nōnne
aliquis eum abstulit?' sibi dīxērunt.
tandem invēnērunt animal īnfēlīx, quod in
vestīmentīs nūptiālibus sē cēlābat.

LANGUAGE NOTE 1: THIS AND THAT

1. In the sentences below, what do **hic**, **haec**, **hōs**, and **hās** all have in common?

   hic vir est Maelō.
   This man is Maelo.

   haec fēmina est Hettia.
   This woman is Hettia.

   hōs gladiōs vēndimus.
   We are selling these swords.

   hās amphorās movēre temptō.
   I'm trying to move these amphorae.

2. **hic**, **haec**, **hōs**, and **hās** are all forms of **hic**, meaning *this* (in the singular) and *these* (in the plural). Like other adjectives, **hic** changes its form to match the case, number, and gender of the noun described.

3. In these sentences, what do **ille**, **illa**, **illōs**, and **illās** all have in common?

   ille artifex pecūniam ōrābit.
   That artist will ask for money.

   quālis puella est **illa** Sabīna?
   What sort of girl is that Sabina?

   illōs virōs saepe sentiēbāmus.
   We often used to noticed those men.

   illās amphorās movēre nōn potes.
   You can't move those amphorae.

4. **ille**, **illa**, **illōs**, and **illās** are all forms of **ille**, meaning *that* (in the singular) and *those* (in the plural). Again, the form changes to match the case, number, and gender of the noun described.

5. Now look at these sentences:

   hic est Faustus.
   This (man) is Faustus.

   haec est Sabīna.
   This (girl) is Sabina.

   ille nihil dīxit.
   That man said nothing.
   or *He said nothing.*

   illam nōn amō.
   I don't like that woman.
   or *I don't like her.*

   Forms of **hic** and **ille** can be used on their own to refer to people or things.

6. There is a chart of all the forms of **hic** and **ille** on page 275.

The tomb of a wool merchant. The decoration shows different stages of wool production.

Wool and weaving

The majority of clothes were made from wool. However, wealthy Romans also had access to linen from Egypt and Syria, and even silk all the way from China. The production of woollen clothes was a long and time-consuming process.

1. Getting the fleece

The Romans kept many different breeds of sheep, which were valued for the colour and quality of their fleece. The Roman author Varro even described sheep being given leather jackets to protect their wool! By the time of our stories, it was common to cut the fleece off the sheep using iron shears like these.

2. Preparing the wool

The fleece from a sheep contains an oily substance called lanolin, as well as mud and dirt. Before the fleece could be spun into thread, it was washed to remove any impurities and combed to separate the fibres so that the spun thread would be even.

If the fleece was to be dyed, it was done at this stage. The Romans used various plants and shells to obtain a wide variety of colours. Saffron, a bright orange dye, was harvested from the crocus flower. It was used to dye a Roman bride's veil (*flammeum*). Pliny the Elder describes another plant, called radicula:

> It releases a juice often used when washing wool, and it is quite wonderful how much it adds to the whiteness and softness of wool.

3. Spinning the thread

The main tools for spinning wool into thread were the distaff and spindle. The bottom of the spindle was attached to a whorl, a heavier wheel which was spun around. The prepared wool was rolled into a ball and placed on the end of a distaff which was held in the left hand. The spinner drew fibres from the wool and twisted them in her right hand, winding them around the spindle, which hung down from the distaff. The weight of the whorl aided the spinner in drawing the fibres out and winding them round the spindle. The illustrations to the stories on pages 247 and 250 show Alexander's sisters spinning and weaving.

4. Weaving

The threads were then woven together on a loom. Most garments were simple in shape, either rectangular tunics or semicircular cloaks, but weaving an item of clothing of the right size required practice and skill.

Factory production

Originally all clothes were woven at home, but by the time of our story textiles were being produced in workshops. Even the poorer classes normally bought their clothing, which was produced locally. Wealthier Romans would buy luxury textiles from across the Empire and beyond.

The province of Asia was a centre of the textile industry and, on its west coast, the city of Miletus was well known for its fine wool exports. Miletus' coastal position provided a direct trade route to Rome but also granted access to a precious purple dye, extracted from a particular type of sea snail, the murex. This dye was known as Tyrian purple because it was produced in Tyre, in modern Lebanon. It was used for the edging on the togas of the most senior senators. Laodicea, near Miletus, was a great exporter of clothes. Evidence of the wide-reaching textile trade is found on a gravestone from Lugdunum, in Gaul, which was set up to Iulius Verecundus, a *negōtiātor Laodicēnārius* – a trader in cloth goods from Laodicea.

A bronze distaff and a decorated glass whorl.

Pallade plācātā lānām mollīre puellae discant et plēnās exonerāre colōs.

With the blessing of Pallas [Minerva], let girls learn to soften wool and unwind the full distaffs.

Ovid

cōnsilium

intereā Lūcīlius, quem mīlitēs custōdiēbant, in vīllā Cantabrī sedēbat. duo virī prō eō stābant. alter erat Cantaber, quī īram cēlāre nōn poterat, alter Othō, lēgātus prōvinciae Lūsitāniae. Othō tribūnum intentē spectābat sed nihil dīcēbat. Cantaber tamen Lūcīlium ferōciter 'cūr mediā nocte errābās per hortum meum cum illō servō, iuvenis?' rogāvit.

'cūr necesse est tibi cēlāre tantum aurum tam dīligenter, Cantaber?' rogāvit tribūnus. 'unde aurum abstulistī? quō id mittis? num tantam pecūniam dēbēs?'

ubi Cantaber Lūcīlium vituperābat, Othō vīdit comitem īram temperāre nōn posse. igitur Cantabrō 'dēsiste, mī amīce,' graviter inquit. 'tempus est breve.' tum ad tribūnum sē vertit, et dulcis 'multum cognōvistī, mī Lūcīlī,' inquit. 'bene ēgistī et fēlīciter. audī nunc meum cōnsilium, quod tibi libenter offerō.'

deinde lēgātus Lūcīliō dīxit imperium Rōmānum in maximō perīculō esse, et 'Nerō nōn sīcut imperātor sed sīcut rēx agere cupit,' inquit. 'quālis prīnceps urbem suī populī et domōs suōrum cīvium incendit? vīsne illī virō īnsānō crūdēlīque imperium relinquere?'

Othō, postquam sēnsit Lūcīlium dubitāre, rogāvit, 'nescīsne mortuum esse Senecam, patris tuī amīcum cārum? hōc annō Nerō eum coēgit suā manū perīre. itaque aurum, quod Cantaber in horreō cēlat, mihi est. legiōnēs parāre iam coepī. cum hīs legiōnibus legiōnēs illīus mōnstrī oppugnābō. adiuvābisne mē? ingēns praemium tibi erit.'

alter ... alter ... the one ... the other ...

tantus so much
id it

temperō I control, restrain
igitur therefore
fēlīciter successfully
libenter willingly, gladly
imperium empire
prīnceps emperor
populus people

cōgō I force, compel
suā manū by his own hand
legiō legion

LANGUAGE NOTE 2: HIM, HER, IT, THEM

1. Study the use of the words in red in the following sentences:

   frāter meus clāmābat. vōs omnēs eum audīvistis.
   My brother was shouting. You all heard him.

   Sabīna est in vīllā. eam vocābō.
   Sabina is in the villa. I shall call her.

   imāgō est tam pulchra. eam emere volō.
   The image is so beautiful. I want to buy it.

   duae fēminae aderant, sed fūrēs eās terruērunt.
   Two women were present, but the thieves terrified them.

   postquam laterēs fēcērunt, nōs eōs ad plaustra portāvimus.
   After they made the bricks, we carried them to the carts.

   quis est pater eius?
   Who is her father? or *Who is his father?*

   unde aurum abstulistī? quō id mittis?
   Where did you steal the gold from? Where are you sending it to?

2. The words in red are all forms of the pronoun **is**, **ea**, **id**. Latin uses them to refer to someone or something that has previously been mentioned.

3. **is**, **ea**, **id** changes its form to match the gender and number of whatever it is referring to. Its case depends on its own role in the sentence.

4. There is a chart of all the forms of **is**, **ea**, **id** on page 275.

LANGUAGE PRACTICE

1. Use the chart of **is**, **ea**, **id** on page 275 to translate the word(s) in bold into Latin.

   a. The boys often helped us. We liked **them** very much.
   b. You saw **her** yesterday in the forum.
   c. They led **him** towards the Subura.
   d. The sisters often met at our house. I knew **them** well.
   e. Give the food **to her**.
   f. The money belonged to the actors. We gave it back **to them**.
   g. My mother was an excellent artist. This is **her** sword.
   h. The brothers bought the pig in the market. It is **their** animal.

Marriage

For Romans there was no official legal or religious wedding ceremony. Simply by living together a couple declared their agreement to be husband and wife. However, people who wanted to celebrate their marriage could choose from various traditions and ceremonies. The main reason for getting married was to have legitimate children who would continue the family line and inherit the family property or business. Among the upper classes marriage was often for political reasons. Men made political alliances through marriage. But marriage was also viewed as a partnership between a couple who wanted to live together harmoniously, and some people married for love.

Most of our knowledge of Roman marriage refers to the upper classes. We know much less about marriage among ordinary people and the poor. There is also very little evidence from the wife's point of view, because most of the sources are written by men. The subject is also complicated by the fact that conventions, attitudes, and laws changed over the years.

Generally the youngest age for marriage was twelve for girls and fourteen for boys, although the average ages were higher. Young girls often married much older men who had been widowed. Although in upper-class families marriages were often arranged, a father could not force his son to marry a particular wife. By law a woman had to give her consent, but the only grounds she had for refusal were that the bridegroom was morally unfit.

There were two kinds of marriage. In marriage *cum manū* (with control) the woman passed from her father's family and guardianship to her husband's, and her property then belonged to her husband. By the first century AD marriage *sine manū* (without control) was the norm, except in some upper-class families. The woman stayed under the guardianship of her father and owned her own property.

A gold engagement ring from the third century AD. Its small size suggests that it was given to a young girl.

Dowry

It was traditional for the woman's family to give a dowry to the husband, although this may not have applied to the poorest members of the population. The dowry was a payment in the form of money, property, or land. It was intended to be a contribution towards the cost of maintaining the new household. During the marriage the dowry and any income it generated were the property of the husband. When he died or the couple divorced, all or part of the dowry was returned to the wife's family. This was a way of protecting the woman financially, and made it easier for her to remarry.

A large dowry was an important factor in securing a desirable husband. Pliny wrote the following, in a letter to a friend whose daughter was about to get married:

> Since your daughter is about to marry that most successful man Nonius Celer, and since his position requires a certain amount of elegance, she must show respect for her husband's status by having clothes and an escort of slaves which make her look suitably distinguished. I am also aware that your resources are limited, so I am offering to contribute to your expenses. As though I were a second father to the girl, I am giving you 50,000 sesterces.

Pliny

Engagement

The marriage was often preceded by an engagement. This involved agreements between the two families about property and dowries. The man gave the woman a ring made of gold or iron, which she wore on what is now known as the ring finger of her left hand. There was a belief that a nerve ran directly from this finger to the heart.

> When the human body is cut open a very delicate nerve is found, which starts from the finger next to the smallest finger and runs to the heart. It is therefore appropriate that this finger, which is connected directly to the body's most vital organ, should be given the ring.

Aulus Gellius

QUESTION

Why do you think the woman wore an engagement ring and the man did not?

LANGUAGE PRACTICE

2. Choose the correct word in the brackets to complete the sentence, then translate. You may wish to use the chart on page 275 for help.

   a. nōs .... hominem in vīllā numquam vīdimus. (hunc, hanc, hōs)
   b. nōnne .... fēmina Alexandrō nūbere vult? (hās, hic, haec)
   c. vōsne .... montēs sine cibō et aquā ascendistis? (illōs, illa, illius)
   d. verba .... puellae intentē audīvimus. (hic, huius, hōs)
   e. frātrēs .... porcum per tōtam urbem Conimbrīgae quaesīvērunt. (illō, illum, illās)
   f. tandem Maelō cum .... virīs ad officīnam revēnit. (hunc, hīs, hōs)
   g. .... dīxit sē Alexandrum amāre. (illōs, illās, illa)
   h. mox .... cognōvī quod saepe in urbe clāmōrēs sustulērunt. (illōs, illius, illō)

Divorce

Divorce was easy and frequent among the upper classes. (We don't have evidence for the lower classes.) A divorce could be by mutual agreement, or either the husband or the wife could make the decision.

Marriage laws

Emperor Augustus introduced laws to encourage marriage and having children, because the birth rate had fallen, especially in the wealthier classes. There were penalties for remaining single: for example, single people had to pay higher taxes and could not inherit property. There were also rewards for married couples who had three or more children. In addition, Augustus brought in laws to punish adultery as a crime.

Julia, daughter of Augustus

Julia, the daughter of Emperor Augustus, was married three times to men chosen for her by her father to promote his political interests. Augustus had no surviving male children. Therefore, he married Julia to men who would be suitable heirs. Julia's first marriage, when she was 14, was to Marcus Claudius Marcellus, her cousin, who was about 17. Three years later Marcellus died, and Julia was married to Agrippa, Augustus' friend and trusted general, the man Augustus saw as his successor. Julia was 18 and Agrippa was in his late forties. When Agrippa died, Augustus arranged for Julia to marry Tiberius, her stepbrother, Augustus' preferred heir. When Julia was accused of being unfaithful, Tiberius divorced her. She was banished by her father and spent the rest of her life in exile.

Marble bust of Julia.

Husbands and wives

Most of the evidence we have about the relationships between husbands and wives is from tombstones, letters, and literature. Almost all of this was written by men.

Look at Sources 1 and 2.

> **SOURCE 1** A funerary inscription set up by a wife for her husband:
>
> > To the spirits of the dead
> > for Quintus Sittius Flaccus
> > centurion of the 1st cohort,
> > tribune of the 10th praetorian cohort,
> > Anicia Caecilia, daughter of Marcus,
> > set up this monument
> > for her most excellent husband.

> **SOURCE 2** A funerary inscription set up by a husband for his wife:
>
> Stranger, what I say is brief. Stop and read it. This is the unlovely tomb of a lovely woman. Her parents named her Claudia. She loved her husband with all her heart. She gave birth to two sons. One of them she leaves on earth, the other she placed beneath the earth. Her conversation was charming and her movements were graceful. She looked after the house. She made wool. I have spoken. Go.

QUESTIONS

1. For what achievements does Anicia Caecilia praise her husband?
2. For what qualities is Claudia remembered by her husband?

In praise of women

> **SOURCE 3** A funeral speech by a son for his mother:
>
> The eulogies of all good women are simple and almost the same since there's a limited number of ways to describe their natural goodness and self-control. It is enough that they have all done the same good deeds which merit a fine reputation. And because it is hard to find new ways to praise a woman since women's lives have little variation, it is necessary to remember the virtues they share so that none is omitted; for this might devalue the rest.

> **SOURCE 4** A funerary inscription set up by a man for his young wife:
>
> Here I lie, a married woman, Veturia, wife of Fortunatus and daughter of Veturius. I lived for just twenty-seven years, and I was married for sixteen years. I had only one lover and husband. I gave birth to six children, but only one survived. Titus Iulius Fortunatus, centurion of the Second Legion, set this up for his loyal and virtuous wife.

> **SOURCE 5** Part of a funerary inscription set up by a man in praise of his wife, Turia:
>
> Why should I list all your domestic virtues: your loyalty, obedience, friendliness, reasonableness, skill at working wool, religion without superstition, demure dress, modesty of appearance? Why dwell on your love for your relatives, your devotion to your family? You have shown the same care to my mother as you did to your own parents, and have taken care to secure an equally peaceful life for her as you did for your own family, and you have innumerable other merits in common with all married women who care for their good name.

QUESTIONS

3. How much do these sources tell us about the individuals who are commemorated?
4. How reliable do you think funerary inscriptions and speeches are as a source?

An ideal match

SOURCE 6

Part of a funerary inscription from Rome. Both Hermia and his wife were freed slaves.

> Lucius Aurelius Hermia, freedman of Lucius, a butcher from the Viminal Hill.
> This woman, who has gone before me by fate, pure in body, was my one and only wife, loving possessor of my heart. She lived as a faithful wife to a faithful husband, with equal devotion on both sides. She never deserted her duty because of greed.

SOURCE 7

An extract from an essay by Plutarch called *Advice to the Bride and Groom*:

> A man should not choose a wife with his eyes or by counting how much money she has. Instead his decision should be based on how well they will live together as partners.

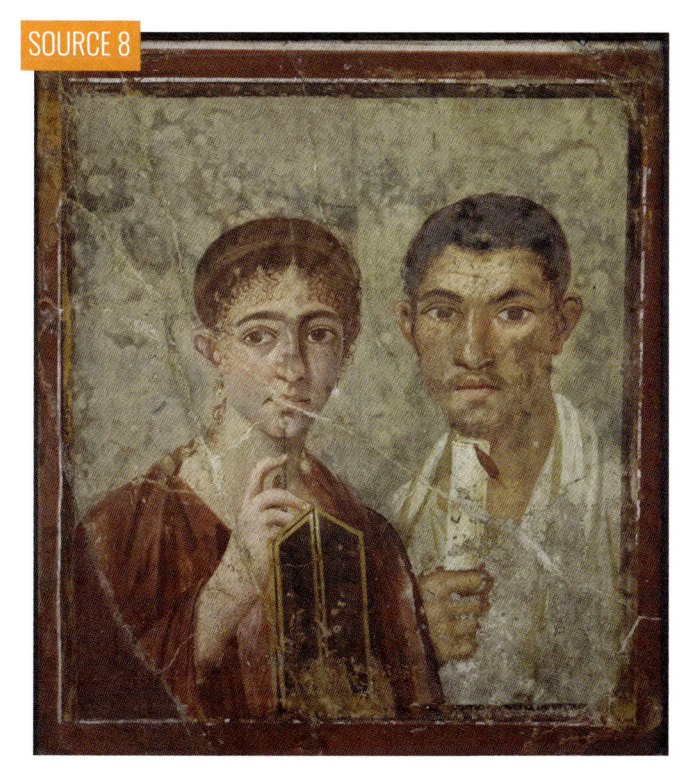

SOURCE 8

SOURCE 9

Pliny wrote this letter to a friend. His friend's niece was 14 years old and Minicius was in his early thirties:

> You ask me to look out for a husband for your niece. Minicius Acilianus is available. He is very energetic and hard-working, but still extremely modest. He has a noble appearance, with a rosy complexion and a handsome build. He is a senator, and behaves in a way which is suited to his rank. I think that these qualities shouldn't be disregarded. I don't know whether I should add that his father is rich. Money has to be taken into account when making a marriage contract.

Left: Terentius Neo, the owner of a bakery, and his wife, in a wall painting from their house in Pompeii.

QUESTIONS

5. Look at Sources 6–8. What do they reveal about what Romans considered to be an ideal marriage?
6. Look at Source 9. What qualities does Pliny think should be looked for in a husband?
7. How honest do you think these attitudes to marriage are?

diēs nūptiālis

diēs nūptiārum erat. familia Alexandrī nūptiās celebrābat.

Sabīna tunicam albam flammeumque gerēbat. servī porcum ad parvam āram dūxērunt, ubi Maelō sacrificium nūptiāle fēcit. tum deae Iūnōnī precēs obtulit.

Maelō	vōbīs omnibus nūntiō hanc virginem esse uxōrem huius virī. 5

omnēs clāmābant, 'fēlīciter! fēlīciter!'

Alexander Sabīnae manum dextram tenēbat, et eī ōsculum dedit.

Sabīna	tantum gaudeō quod tū mē in mātrimōnium dūcere cupis, Alexander.

post nūptiās cēna splendida erat. posteā māter Alexandrī facēs sacrās 10
deae Cererī incendit, et sorōrēs eās tulērunt. omnēs Sabīnam ad
Alexandrum dūxērunt. Alexander prō iānuā stābat.

Alexander	quis es? unde vēnistī?
Sabīna	ubi tū es Gāius, ego sum Gāia.

frātrēs clāmābant rīdēbantque: 'Alexander, fēlīciter!' 15

tunica *tunic*

precēs *prayers*

virgō *girl, young woman*

dexter *right*

tantum *so much*

Cerēs *Ceres (goddess of agriculture)*

The ceremony

The Roman wedding was a mixture of religious and private rituals. There was no official legal ceremony or licence required. Most important was the consent from both parties (although in some cases this could be from the bride's father rather than the bride). We have very little evidence for lower-class weddings, but it is likely they had similar but less elaborate festivities.

Preparations

The first task was to choose a lucky day for the ceremony. The *Kalendae* (first day of the month), *Nōnēs* (nine days before the Ides), and *Īdēs* (the fifteenth or thirteenth day) of each month, and the day following each of them, were unlucky. So was all of May and the first half of June. Festival days were also a bad choice, as it was likely that friends and family would be busy.

The night before her wedding, the bride dedicated objects from her childhood to her family Lares. These might be her toys or clothes, a symbol of what she was leaving behind.

On the day itself the bride was dressed by her mother or female relatives. She wore a simple, long, white or orange tunic, which was only worn once. The tunic was bound by a belt tied in a special knot, the knot of Hercules. Only her new husband was allowed to undo the knot. Hercules had fathered many children and this ritual was supposed to secure the fertility of the couple. The bride's hair was arranged into a special style. Using a bent iron spearhead, her hair was divided into six parts, and then twisted up into a cone and crowned with flowers which she had picked herself. The origins of this ritual are not understood. The bride was then covered with the flame-coloured veil (*flammeum*) which reached down to her feet. Sometimes she also wore orange shoes.

The marriage

There were variations on the Roman wedding ceremony. The most formal was presided over by the Pontifex Maximus, but this was reserved for only a few couples from the upper classes. Most ceremonies involved lighting a torch to the goddess Ceres, in hope of the couple's fertility. Pliny the Elder wrote that a torch made of wood from the may tree was best, because it bore many fruits. There was then a sacrifice – a pig was a common choice – and the bride and groom sometimes exchanged gifts. This was followed by a marriage feast at the bride's house.

Then came the most important part of the day. First the bride was snatched from her mother, with a show of force. This was called the *raptiō* and was a tradition which mimicked the earliest Roman weddings. According to legend, the early Romans stole the local Sabine women to become their brides. The poet Catullus describes the raptio, addressing Hesperus (the Evening Star) and Hymen, the god of marriage:

> Hesperus, you can tear the daughter from her mother's arms,
> and give the virgin girl to the passionate youth.
> O Hymenaeus Hymen, O Hymen Hymenaeus!

The bride was then escorted to her new home, surrounded by a crowd of well-wishers singing crude wedding songs. This procession, the *dēductiō*, was a public act and was an important symbol of the bride's consent. Behind the bride were carried the spindle and distaff, tokens of her domestic life. The groom also scattered nuts on the ground, a sign that he was giving up his childish ways.

When they reached her new home, the groom lifted the bride across the threshold to prevent her tripping – a bad omen. She then made the vow:

ubi tū Gāius, ego Gāia.
Where you are Gaius, I am Gaia.

And the doors closed behind the newly-weds.

ad lūcem

puer aeger in lectō iacet. febrem gravem habet. prope lectum sedet
Rūfīna. pōculum tenet. lacrimae eius in puerum cadunt.   *pōculum* cup

Rūfīna   tolle caput, mī lepus! bibe!

LANGUAGE PRACTICE

3. Choose the correct word in the brackets to complete the sentence, then translate. You may wish to use the chart on page 275 for help.

   a. Lūcīlius et Tīrō aderant. custōs .... in hortō vīdit.   (eās, eōs, eum)
   b. postquam frātrēs Alexandrum vīdērunt, ... laetē salūtāvērunt.   (ea, eum, eam)
   c. simulatque Sabīna vīllam intrāvit, Hettia flammeum .... ostendit.   (eī, eōs, eās)
   d. est nūlla pecūnia in tabernā. ubi .... cēlāvistī?   (ea, eum, eam)
   e. Lūcīlius effugere voluit. custōs tamen bracchium .... rapuit.   (eīs, eius, eō)
   f. sorōrēs Alexandrī rīdēbant. Hettia clāmōrēs .... audīvit.   (eōrum, eārum, id)
   g. quamquam fīliae tuae nōn crēdō, verba .... cōgitābō.   (eius, eum, eam)
   h. mox amīcī revēnērunt. tum.......... dōna obtulī.   (eum, eās, eīs)

4. Translate each sentence into Latin by choosing the correct word or phrase from each pair.

   a. *We often said that the freedmen were working for a long time.*
      nōs   semper   dīcimus   lībertōs   diū   labōrābant.
      vōs   saepe   dīcēbāmus lībertī   vix   labōrāre.

   b. *For three days the Romans resisted the fierce Britons in vain.*
      tribus diēbus   Rōmānī   Britannōs   ferōcibus   frūstrā   resistēbant.
      trēs diēs   Rōmānōs   Britannīs   ferōcēs   fortiter resistēbāmus.

   c. *I decided to leave the city without food and to travel across the mountains.*
      ad urbem   sine cibum   discēdere   aut   trāns montēs   prōcēdere   convēnī.
      ab urbe   sine cibō   dūcere   ac   trāns montibus   prōmittere cōnstituī.

   d. *However, the queen always kills her enemies if she can.*
      rēx   tamen   hostēs   saepe   necat,   sī poterat.
      rēgīna   tandem   hostibus semper   necāvit, sī potest.

   e. *Although they know life is short, they do not fear death.*
      quoque   scīvērunt   vītam   brevem   est,   mortem   nunc   timent.
      quamquam   sciunt   vīta   brevis   esse,   mortis   nōn   timēbunt.

   f. *'Where are you going?' 'We are going to the house which is near the wood.'*
      'quō   īmus?'   'ad   vīllās,   quās   prope   silvae   erit,   īmus.'
      'cūr   itis?'   'ā   vīllam,   quae   post   silvam   est,   itis.'

Arachne

Arachne, the daughter of a cloth-dyer, created more beautiful weaving work than any other woman. She claimed her skill was entirely her own, rather than due to the gods' gifts. When the goddess Athena heard of this, she paid Arachne a visit.

- Now read or listen to the story of Arachne.

Hubris

The ancient Greek word 'hubris' refers to the behaviour of humans who defied the authority of the gods. Often acts of hubris involved people believing themselves to be equal to the gods. In the end, the overconfident mortal usually brought about their own downfall or was punished by a god for their arrogance.

- Look at Source 1. What do you think Arachne's hubris is precisely?
- And what is her punishment?

> **SOURCE 1**
> You could see she was taught by Athena. However, the girl herself denied this and she was offended at the idea of having such a teacher. 'Let Athena compete with me,' she said, 'and I won't at all deny it if she defeats me.'
>
> *Ovid*

Look at Source 2.

- Which part of the story does this painting show?
- Why do you think the painter chose to represent this part?

Jealous gods

In many Greek myths, the gods display a human temperament, and they're just as prone to jealousy, anger, or pride as mortals. Do you think the Greek gods model good behaviour, and are they fair and just in their dealings with mortals? What does the story of Arachne tell you about the relationship between gods and humans?

> **RESEARCH**
>
> 1. Find other stories in Greek mythology that involve hubris (for instance: Niobe, Icarus, Oedipus).
> 2. Find out who the goddess Nemesis was, and what her connection was to hubris.
> 3. Can you think of stories from other times that involve hubris?

SOURCE 2

Reference

Vocabulary for learning	266
Order of information in Latin sentences	270
Nouns	272
Uses of the cases	273
Adjectives	274
Adjectives/Pronouns	275
Numbers	276
Verbs	277
Irregular verbs	278
Expressions, mottoes, and abbreviations	279
English to Latin dictionary	280
Latin to English dictionary	282
Ancient authors	297
Timeline	300

VOCABULARY FOR LEARNING

Chapter 1

dormiō	I sleep
ego	I
frāter	brother
hōra	hour
in	in, on
īnsula	block of flats
labōrō	I work
legō	I read
meus	my
nōn	not
pater	father
rīdeō	I laugh, smile
servus	slave, enslaved person (male)
tū	you (singular)
turba	crowd
ubi?	where?
via	street, road, way
sum	I am
es	you (singular) are
est	(he/she/it) is

Chapter 2

cadō	I fall
cibus, cibum, m.	food
dūcō	I lead, take
et	and
fīlia, fīliam, f.	daughter
fīlius, fīlium, m.	son
forum, forum, n.	forum, marketplace
habeō	I have, hold
habitō	I live
intrō	I enter
magnus	big, large, great
pecūnia, pecūniam, f.	money, sum of money
quaerō	I search for, look for, ask
quoque	also, too
salūtō	I greet
sed	but
spectō	I look at, watch
videō	I see
vīnum, vīnum, n.	wine
vocō	I call

Chapter 3

ambulō	I walk
amīcus, amīcum, m.	friend
ancilla, ancillam, f.	slave, enslaved person (female)
clāmō	I shout
clāmor, clāmōrem, m.	shout, shouting, noise
cum	with
currō	I run
dīcō	I say, speak, tell
equus, equum, m.	horse
festīnō	I hurry
gladius, gladium, m.	sword
īnfēlīx	unlucky, unhappy
laetus	happy
multus	much, many
omnis	all, every
per	through, along
prīmus	first
senātor, senātōrem, m.	senator
urbs, urbem, f.	city
vincō	I conquer, win, am victorious

Chapter 4

ad	to, towards; at
adsum	I am here, I am present
deus, deum, m.	god
dominus, dominum, m.	master
dōnum, dōnum, n.	gift, present
laudō	I praise
nōs	we, us
parvus	small
perīculum, perīculum, n.	danger
perterritus	terrified
puella, puellam, f.	girl
quod	because
rēx, rēgem, m.	king
Rōmānus	Roman
subitō	suddenly
templum, templum, n.	temple
teneō	I hold, keep, possess
tollō	I raise, lift up, hold up
veniō	I come
vōs	you (plural)

Chapter 5

aqua, aquam, *f.*	water
audiō, audīre	hear, listen to
cupiō, cupere	want, desire
custōs, custōdem, *m.f.*	guard
dēbeō, dēbēre	owe
dō, dare	give
effugiō, effugere	escape
iuvenis, iuvenem, *m.f.*	young person
maneō, manēre	remain, stay
nēmō, nēminem	no one, nobody
nōlō, nōlle	don't want, refuse
nox, noctem, *f.*	night
portō, portāre	carry, bear, take
possum, posse	can, am able
pulcher	beautiful, handsome
respondeō, respondēre	reply
taceō, tacēre	am silent, am quiet
timeō, timēre	fear, am afraid
vēndō, vēndere	sell
volō, velle	want, wish, am willing

Chapter 6

ā, ab + *abl.*	from, away from
capiō, capere	take, catch, capture, adopt (a plan)
diēs, diem, *m.*	day
discēdō, discēdere	depart, leave
ē, ex + *abl.*	from, out of
exspectō, exspectāre	wait for, expect
faciō, facere	make, do
iam	now, already
in + *acc.*	into, onto
inquit	says
marītus, marītum, *m.*	husband
māter, mātrem, *f.*	mother
prope + *acc.*	near
rogō, rogāre	ask, ask for
sedeō, sedēre	sit
stō, stāre	stand
tōtus	whole
trīstis	sad
tuus	your (**singular**), yours
uxor, uxōrem, *f.*	wife

Chapter 7

appropinquō, appropinquāre, appropinquāvī	approach, come near to
cūr?	why?
epistula, epistulam, *f.*	letter
homō, hominem, *m.*	man, person
ingēns	huge
īnsula, īnsulam, *f.*	island; block of flats
mīles, mīlitem, *m.*	soldier
minimē	no
nārrō, nārrāre, nārrāvī	tell, relate
nauta, nautam, *m.*	sailor
nunc	now
ōlim	once, some time ago
pars, partem, *f.*	part
puer, puerum, *m.*	boy
pugnō, pugnāre, pugnāvī	fight
rēs, rem, *f.*	thing, story
saepe	often
silva, silvam, *f.*	wood, forest
tum	then
vehementer	loudly, violently, strongly

Chapter 8

agō, agere, ēgī	do
bibō, bibere, bibī	drink
cōnspiciō, cōnspicere, cōnspexī	catch sight of, notice
dē + *abl.*	from, down from; about
domus, domum, *f.*	house, home
eam	her; it
eum	him; it
gerō, gerere, gessī	wear
iaceō, iacēre, iacuī	lie down
incendō, incendere, incendī	burn, set on fire
mox	soon
nihil	nothing
noster	our
porta, portam, *f.*	gate
postquam	after
prōcēdō, prōcēdere, prōcessī	go along, proceed
senex, senem, *m.f.*	old person
surgō, surgere, surrēxī	get up
tandem	at last, finally
trāns + *acc.*	across

Chapter 9

adveniō, advenīre, advēnī	arrive
cīvis, cīvem, *m.f.*	citizen
difficilis	difficult
domina, dominam, *f.*	mistress, lady
gravis	heavy; serious
hostis, hostem, *m.*	enemy
imperātor, imperātōrem, *m.*	emperor, general
īrātus	angry
iter, iter, *n.*	journey, route, way
lacrimō, lacrimāre, lacrimāvī	cry, weep
līberī, līberōs, *m. pl.*	children
medius	middle, middle of
nūntius, nūntium, *m.*	messenger; message, news
paucī, *pl.*	few, a few
petō, petere, petīvī	attack; seek, beg, ask for
sanguis, sanguinem, *m.*	blood
statim	immediately, at once
trādō, trādere, trādidī	hand over, hand down
vir, virum, *m.*	man
vīta, vītam, *f.*	life

Chapter 10

accipiō, accipere, accēpī	accept, take in, receive
alius, alia, aliud	another, other
annus, annum, *m.*	year
bonus, bona, bonum	good
contrā + *acc.*	against
dea, deam, *f.*	goddess
deinde	then
ferō, ferre, tulī	bring, carry, bear
fidēlis, fidēlis, fidēle	loyal, faithful, trustworthy
iaciō, iacere, iēcī	throw
locus, locum, *m.*	place
miser, misera, miserum	poor, unfortunate
novus, nova, novum	new
nūllus, nūlla, nūllum	no, not any
occīdō, occīdere, occīdī	kill
pāx, pācem, *f.*	peace
pereō, perīre, periī	die, perish
quam ... !	how ... !
sacer, sacra, sacrum	sacred, holy
sub + *acc.* or *abl.*	under, below, beneath

Chapter 11

absum, abesse, āfuī	am out, absent, away
accidō, accidere, accidī	happen
altus, alta, altum	high, deep
bene	well
dux, ducis, *m.*	leader
flūmen, flūminis, *n.*	river
fortis, fortis, forte	brave
frūstrā	in vain, without success
fugiō, fugere, fūgī	run away, flee
hodiē	today
ibi	there
inveniō, invenīre, invēnī	find
itaque	and so, therefore
mare, maris, *n.*	sea
nāvigō, nāvigāre, nāvigāvī	sail
nāvis, nāvis, *f.*	ship
prō + *abl.*	in front of; for
saevus, saeva, saevum	savage, cruel
sōlus, sōla, sōlum	alone, only, lonely, on one's own
ubi	where? where, when

Chapter 12

caelum, caelī, *n.*	sky, heaven
caput, capitis, *n.*	head
corpus, corporis, *n.*	body
crūdēlis, crūdēlis, crūdēle	cruel
dēleō, dēlēre, dēlēvī	destroy
diū	for a long time
iānua, iānuae, *f.*	door, doorway
iterum	again
mittō, mittere, mīsī	send
offerō, offerre, obtulī	offer
quis? quid?	who? what?
redeō, redīre, rediī	go back, come back, return
Rōma, Rōmae, *f.*	Rome
servō, servāre, servāvī	save, protect, keep, look after
stultus, stulta, stultum	stupid, foolish
superō, superāre, superāvī	overcome, overpower
taberna, tabernae, *f.*	shop, inn
terra, terrae, *f.*	ground
trahō, trahere, trāxī	drag, draw, pull
vōx, vōcis, *f.*	voice, shout

Chapter 13

coepī	*began*
cōnsūmō, cōnsūmere, cōnsūmpsī	*consume, eat*
intellegō, intellegere, intellēxī	*understand, realize*
inter + *acc.*	*among, between*
ita vērō	*yes, absolutely*
labor, labōris, *m.*	*work*
longus, longa, longum	*long*
mūrus, mūrī, *m.*	*wall*
nōmen, nōminis, *n.*	*name*
parō, parāre, parāvī	*prepare*
post + *acc.*	*after, behind*
praemium, praemiī, *n.*	*prize, reward, profit*
quamquam	*although*
quī, quae, quod	*who, which*
quōmodo?	*how? in what way?*
semper	*always*
summus, summa, summum	*highest, greatest, top (of)*
suus, sua, suum	*her, his, its, their (own)*
tamen	*however*
vīvō, vīvere, vīxī	*live, am alive*

Chapter 14

amō, amāre, amāvī	*love, like*
amor, amōris, *m.*	*love*
cōgitō, cōgitāre, cōgitāvī	*think, consider*
cōnficiō, cōnficere, cōnfēcī	*finish*
cōnsilium, cōnsiliī, *n.*	*plan, idea, advice*
cōnstituō, cōnstituere, cōnstituī	*decide*
dīrus, dīra, dīrum	*dreadful*
eōs	*them*
fēmina, fēminae, *f.*	*woman*
mōns, montis, *m.*	*mountain*
mors, mortis, *f.*	*death*

nec
    nec ... nec ...
	and not, nor, neither
	    neither ... nor ...

necō, necāre, necāvī	*kill*
nesciō, nescīre, nescīvī	*don't know*
numquam	*never*
ostendō, ostendere, ostendī	*show*
tempus, temporis, *n.*	*time*
terreō, terrēre, terruī	*frighten*
verbum, verbī, *n.*	*word*

Chapter 15

anteā	*before*
bellum, bellī, *n.*	*war*
cēna, cēnae, *f.*	*dinner, meal*
cēterī, cēterae, cētera, *pl.*	*the rest, the others*
cognōscō, cognōscere, cognōvī	*get to know, find out, learn*
comes, comitis, *m.f.*	*comrade, companion*
eō, īre, iī	*go*
etiam	*even, also*
ferōx, *gen.* ferōcis	*fierce, ferocious*
hortus, hortī, *m.*	*garden*
intereā	*meanwhile*
iubeō, iubēre, iussī	*order*
lībertus, lībertī, *m.*	*freedman, former slave*
multum	*much*
nōnne?	*surely?*
nūntiō, nūntiāre, nūntiāvī	*announce, report*
putō, putāre, putāvī	*think*
sē	*himself, herself, itself, themselves*
simulatque	*as soon as*
vīlla, vīllae, *f.*	*country house, house*

Chapter 16

ac	*and*
auferō, auferre, abstulī	*steal, carry off*
brevis, brevis, breve	*short, brief*
cēlō, cēlāre, cēlāvī	*hide*
hic, haec, hoc	*this, he, she, it*
ille, illa, illud	*that, he, she, it*
imperium, imperiī, *n.*	*empire; power*
legō, legere, lēgī	*read; choose*
lūx, lūcis, *f.*	*light, daylight*
ōrō, ōrāre, ōrāvī	*beg, beg for*
prīnceps, prīncipis, *m.*	*chief; emperor*
quō?	*where to?*
rapiō, rapere, rapuī	*seize, grab*
rēgīna, rēgīnae, *f.*	*queen*
resistō, resistere, restitī + *dat.*	*resist*
reveniō, revenīre, revēnī	*come back, return*
sciō, scīre, scīvī	*know*
sentiō, sentīre, sēnsī	*feel, notice*
sī	*if*
sine + *abl.*	*without*

ORDER OF INFORMATION IN LATIN SENTENCES

1. In a Latin sentence information tends to come in a standard order. Familiarity with that order can help you to read and understand Latin.

2. In general, expect the nominative first, then accusative, and then verb. For example:

   sorōrēs   gladiōs   vēndēbant.
   sisters   swords   they were selling

   The sisters were selling swords.

3. If the nominative does not need to be stated, expect accusative, verb:

   gladiōs   vēndēbant.
   swords   they were selling

   They were selling swords.

4. If there is no accusative, then expect nominative, verb:

   sorōrēs   currēbant.
   sisters   they were running

   The sisters were running.

5. Adverbs, and phrases describing the action, are usually immediately before the verb:

   sorōrēs   gladiōs   in forō   vēndēbant.
   sisters   swords   in the forum   they were selling

   The sisters were selling swords in the forum.

6. A dative noun is usually between the nominative and accusative:

   sorōrēs   cīvibus   gladiōs   in forō   vēndēbant.
   sisters   to the citizens   swords   in the forum   they were selling

   The sisters were selling swords to the citizens in the forum.

7. Adjectives may appear before or after the nouns they describe:

   sorōrēs   cīvibus   gladiōs   pulchrōs   in forō   vēndēbant.
   sisters   to the citizens   swords   beautiful ones   in the forum   they were selling

   The sisters were selling beautiful swords to the citizens in the forum.

   Adjectives of size or number are usually before the noun they describe:

   sorōrēs   cīvibus   multōs   gladiōs   in forō   vēndēbant.
   sisters   to the citizens   many   swords   in the forum   they were selling

   The sisters were selling many swords to the citizens in the forum.

8. Genitives usually follow the nouns they describe:

>   **sorōrēs** **cīvibus** **gladiōs** **parentum** **in forō** **vēndēbant.**
>   *sisters* *to the citizens* *swords* *of their parents* *in the forum* *they were selling*
>
>   *The sisters were selling their parents' swords to the citizens in the forum.*

9. Relative clauses also often follow the nouns they describe:

>   **Sabīna,** **quae** **paene** **rīdēbat,** **Alexandrō** **appropinquāvit.**
>   *Sabina* *who* *almost* *was laughing* *to Alexander* *drew near*
>
>   *Sabina, who was almost laughing, drew near to/approached Alexander.*

10. Indirect statements use an accusative and infinitive construction. The accusative usually comes immediately after the verb of saying, thinking, or perceiving. The infinitive often comes at the end of the sentence:

>   **servī** **dīcunt** **hominēs** **plaustra** **custōdīre.**
>   *slaves* *say* *men* *carts* *to guard*
>
>   *The slaves say that men are guarding the carts.*

11. As you become familiar with the usual word order, you may notice when the author departs from that order to emphasize a particular word or point:

>   **Mānium** **in viā** **invēnimus** **mortuum.**
>   *Manius* *in the street* *we found* *dead*
>
>   *We found Manius in the street. He was dead.*
>
>   **servum** **Rūfīna** **videt.**
>   *slave* *Rufina* *sees*
>
>   *It's the slave that Rufina sees.*

Sometimes Latin authors used a symmetrical order of words:

>   **clāmōrēs** **hominum** **et** **equōrum** **hinnītus**
>   *shouts* *of men* *and* *of horses* *neighing*
>
>   *the shouts of men and the neighing of horses*

Latin authors were also fond of using three parallel examples, as well as removing words such as **et**:

>   **vigilēs,** **cīvēs,** **servī** **servāre** **temptābant** **virginēs.**
>   *firemen* *citizens* *slaves* *to save* *were trying* *young women*
>
>   *The firemen, citizens, and enslaved people were trying to save the young women.*

Latin verbs are sometimes omitted if they can be understood from elsewhere in the sentence:

>   **mīles erat nimium gravis, puella nōn valida, glaciēs nōn firma.**
>
>   *The soldier was too heavy, the girl (was) not strong, the ice (was) not firm.*

	First declension	Second declension		
	feminine	masculine	masculine	neuter
SINGULAR				
nominative	puella	amīcus	puer	dōnum
accusative	puellam	amīcum	puerum	dōnum
genitive	puellae	amīcī	puerī	dōnī
dative	puellae	amīcō	puerō	dōnō
ablative	puellā	amīcō	puerō	dōnō
PLURAL				
nominative	puellae	amīcī	puerī	dōna
accusative	puellās	amīcōs	puerōs	dōna
genitive	puellārum	amīcōrum	puerōrum	dōnōrum
dative	puellīs	amīcīs	puerīs	dōnīs
ablative	puellīs	amīcīs	puerīs	dōnīs

	Third declension			
	masculine	feminine	feminine	neuter
SINGULAR				
nominative	fūr	nox	urbs	caput
accusative	fūrem	noctem	urbem	caput
genitive	fūris	noctis	urbis	capitis
dative	fūrī	noctī	urbī	capitī
ablative	fūre	nocte	urbe	capite*
PLURAL				
nominative	fūrēs	noctēs	urbēs	capita
accusative	fūrēs	noctēs	urbēs	capita
genitive	fūrum	noctium	urbium	capitum
dative	fūribus	noctibus	urbibus	capitibus
ablative	fūribus	noctibus	urbibus	capitibus

The vocative case has exactly the same form as the nominative case, except in the singular of the second declension, where -**us** becomes -**e** and -**ius** becomes -**ī**. For examples see page 190.

* The ablative singular of **mare** (*sea*) ends -ī: marī.

USES OF THE CASES

nominative	**amīcus** labōrat.	The **friend** is working.	The noun carrying out the action.
vocative	salvē, **Faustē**!	Hello, **Faustus**!	Speaking to someone.
accusative	puella **amīcum** laudat.	The girl praises her **friend**.	The noun receiving the action.

	puella ad **amīcum** ambulat.	The girl walks towards her **friend**.	With some prepositions, e.g.
			    ad (*towards*)
			    per (*through*)
			    trāns (*across*)
			    in (*into*)

	puella **multās hōrās** dormiēbat.	The girl was sleeping **for many hours**.	How long something lasts for.
genitive	nōmen **amīcī**	the **friend's** name the name **of the friend**	Possession: of, 's.
dative	puella **amīcō** dōnum dat.	The girl gives a present **to her friend**.	to
	necesse est **amīcō** labōrāre.	It is necessary **for the friend** to work.	for
	puella semper **amīcō** crēdit.	The girl always trusts her **friend**.	Some verbs are used with a noun in the dative case.

ablative	puella cum **amīcō** in **forō** ambulat.	The girl is walking with her **friend** in the **forum**.	in, on, by, with, from, at
			Often with a preposition, e.g.
			    in (*in, on*)
			    cum (*with*)
			    ā/ab (*from, by*)
			    ē/ex (*out of*)

	mediā nocte canis lātrāvit.	**In the middle of the night** the dog barked.	The time when something happens.
	hōrā prīmā puella surgit.	**At the first hour** the girl gets up.	

	First and second declension			Third declension			
	masculine	*feminine*	*neuter*	*masculine/feminine*	*neuter*	*masculine/feminine*	*neuter*
SINGULAR							
nominative	bonus	bona	bonum	trīstis	trīste	ingēns	
accusative	bonum	bonam	bonum	trīstem	trīste	ingentem	ingēns
genitive	bonī	bonae	bonī	trīstis		ingentis	
dative	bonō	bonae	bonō	trīstī		ingentī	
ablative	bonō	bonā	bonō	trīstī		ingentī	
PLURAL							
nominative	bonī	bonae	bona	trīstēs	trīstia	ingentēs	ingentia
accusative	bonōs	bonās	bona	trīstēs	trīstia	ingentēs	ingentia
genitive	bonōrum	bonārum	bonōrum	trīstium		ingentium	
dative	bonīs			trīstibus		ingentibus	
ablative	bonīs			trīstibus		ingentibus	

COMPARATIVE AND SUPERLATIVE ADJECTIVES

Positive		Comparative		Superlative	
laetus	*happy*	laetior	*happier*	laetissimus	*happiest, very happy*
pulcher	*beautiful*	pulchrior	*more beautiful*	pulcherrimus	*most beautiful, very beautiful*
trīstis	*sad*	trīstior	*sadder*	trīstissimus	*saddest, very sad*
dīves	*rich*	dīvitior	*richer*	dīvitissimus	*richest, very rich*
facilis	*easy*	facilior	*easier*	facillimus	*easiest, very easy*

IRREGULAR FORMS

Positive		Comparative		Superlative	
bonus	*good*	melior	*better*	optimus	*best, very good*
magnus	*big*	maior	*bigger*	maximus	*biggest, very big*
malus	*bad*	pēior	*worse*	pessimus	*worst, very bad*
multus	*much*	plūs	*more*	plūrimus	*most, very much*
parvus	*small*	minor	*smaller*	minimus	*smallest, very small*

ADJECTIVES/PRONOUNS

SINGULAR	masculine	feminine	neuter	masculine	feminine	neuter
nominative	hic	haec	hoc	ille	illa	illud
accusative	hunc	hanc	hoc	illum	illam	illud
genitive		huius			illius	
dative		huic			illī	
ablative	hōc	hāc	hōc	illō	illā	illō

PLURAL						
nominative	hī	hae	haec	illī	illae	illa
accusative	hōs	hās	haec	illōs	illās	illa
genitive	hōrum	hārum	hōrum	illōrum	illārum	illōrum
dative		hīs			illīs	
ablative		hīs			illīs	

SINGULAR	masculine	feminine	neuter	masculine	feminine	neuter
nominative	is	ea	id	quī	quae	quod
accusative	eum	eam	id	quem	quam	quod
genitive		eius			cuius	
dative		eī			cui	
ablative	eō	eā	eō	quō	quā	quō

PLURAL						
nominative	eī	eae	ea	quī	quae	quae
accusative	eōs	eās	ea	quōs	quās	quae
genitive	eōrum	eārum	eōrum	quōrum	quārum	quōrum
dative		eīs			quibus	
ablative		eīs			quibus	

	I	we	you (singular)	you (plural)	himself, herself, themselves
nominative	ego	nōs	tū	vōs	
accusative	mē	nōs	tē	vōs	sē
genitive	meī	nostrum	tuī	vestrum	suī
dative	mihi	nōbīs	tibi	vōbīs	sibi
ablative	mē	nōbīs	tē	vōbīs	sē

NUMBERS

1	I	ūnus, ūna, ūnum
2	II	duo, duae, duo
3	III	trēs, trēs, tria
4	IIII or IV	quattuor
5	V	quīnque
6	VI	sex
7	VII	septem
8	VIII	octō
9	VIIII or IX	novem
10	X	decem
50	L	quīnquāgintā
100	C	centum
500	D	quīngentī
1,000	M	mīlle

1st	prīmus, a, um
2nd	secundus, a, um
3rd	tertius, a, um
4th	quārtus, a, um
5th	quīntus, a, um
6th	sextus, a, um
7th	septimus, a, um
8th	octāvus, a, um
9th	nōnus, a, um
10th	decimus, a, um

The numbers 4–10, 50, and 100 do not change their endings.

The numbers 1–3 change their endings as follows:

	masculine	feminine	neuter	masculine	feminine	neuter	masculine	feminine
nominative	ūnus	ūna	ūnum	duo	duae	duo	trēs	tria
accusative	ūnum	ūnam	ūnum	duōs	duās	duo	trēs	tria
genitive		ūnīus		duōrum	duārum	duōrum		trium
dative		ūnī		duōbus	duābus	duōbus		tribus
ablative	ūnō	ūnā	ūnō	duōbus	duābus	duōbus		tribus

VERBS

	1st conjugation	2nd conjugation	3rd conjugation	4th conjugation	3rd/4th conjugation
	call	*hold*	*send*	*hear*	*take*
PRESENT (*I call, am calling, etc.*)					
I	vocō	teneō	mittō	audiō	capiō
you (sing.)	vocās	tenēs	mittis	audīs	capis
he, she, it	vocat	tenet	mittit	audit	capit
we	vocāmus	tenēmus	mittimus	audīmus	capimus
you (pl.)	vocātis	tenētis	mittitis	audītis	capitis
they	vocant	tenent	mittunt	audiunt	capiunt
FUTURE (*I shall call, etc.*)					
I	vocābō	tenēbō			
you (sing.)	vocābis	tenēbis			
he, she, it	vocābit	tenēbit			
we	vocābimus	tenēbimus			
you (pl.)	vocābitis	tenēbitis			
they	vocābunt	tenēbunt			
IMPERFECT (*I was calling, used to call, etc.*)					
I	vocābam	tenēbam	mittēbam	audiēbam	capiēbam
you (sing.)	vocābās	tenēbās	mittēbās	audiēbās	capiēbās
he, she, it	vocābat	tenēbat	mittēbat	audiēbat	capiēbat
we	vocābāmus	tenēbāmus	mittēbāmus	audiēbāmus	capiēbāmus
you (pl.)	vocābātis	tenēbātis	mittēbātis	audiēbātis	capiēbātis
they	vocābant	tenēbant	mittēbant	audiēbant	capiēbant
PERFECT (*I called, have called, etc.*)					
I	vocāvī	tenuī	mīsī	audīvī	cēpī
you (sing.)	vocāvistī	tenuistī	mīsistī	audīvistī	cēpistī
he, she, it	vocāvit	tenuit	mīsit	audīvit	cēpit
we	vocāvimus	tenuimus	mīsimus	audīvimus	cēpimus
you (pl.)	vocāvistis	tenuistis	mīsistis	audīvistis	cēpistis
they	vocāvērunt	tenuērunt	mīsērunt	audīvērunt	cēpērunt
PRESENT INFINITIVE (*to call, etc.*)					
	vocāre	tenēre	mittere	audīre	capere
IMPERATIVE (*call!, etc.*)					
singular	vocā	tenē	mitte	audī	cape
plural	vocāte	tenēte	mittite	audīte	capite

IRREGULAR VERBS

PRESENT	I am	I am able	I go	I want	I don't want	I bring
I	sum	possum	eō	volō	nōlō	ferō
you (sing.)	es	potes	īs	vīs	nōn vīs	fers
he, she, it	est	potest	it	vult	nōn vult	fert
we	sumus	possumus	īmus	volumus	nōlumus	ferimus
you (pl.)	estis	potestis	ītis	vultis	nōn vultis	fertis
they	sunt	possunt	eunt	volunt	nōlunt	ferunt

FUTURE	I shall be	I shall be able	I shall go
I	erō	poterō	ībō
you (sing.)	eris	poteris	ībis
he, she, it	erit	poterit	ībit
we	erimus	poterimus	ībimus
you (pl.)	eritis	poteritis	ībitis
they	erunt	poterunt	ībunt

IMPERFECT	I was	I was able	I was going	I used to want	I was unwilling	I was bringing
I	eram	poteram	ībam	volēbam	nōlēbam	ferēbam
you (sing.)	erās	poterās	ībās	volēbās	nōlēbās	ferēbās
he, she, it	erat	poterat	ībat	volēbat	nōlēbat	ferēbat
we	erāmus	poterāmus	ībāmus	volēbāmus	nōlēbāmus	ferēbāmus
you (pl.)	erātis	poterātis	ībātis	volēbātis	nōlēbātis	ferēbātis
they	erant	poterant	ībant	volēbant	nōlēbant	ferēbant

PERFECT	I have been	I have been able	I went	I wanted	I didn't want	I brought
I	fuī	potuī	iī	voluī	nōluī	tulī
you (sing.)	fuistī	potuistī	iistī	voluistī	nōluistī	tulistī
he, she, it	fuit	potuit	iit	voluit	nōluit	tulit
we	fuimus	potuimus	iimus	voluimus	nōluimus	tulimus
you (pl.)	fuistis	potuistis	iistis	voluistis	nōluistis	tulistis
they	fuērunt	potuērunt	iērunt	voluērunt	nōluērunt	tulērunt

PRESENT INFINITIVE	to be	to be able	to go	to want	not to want	to bring
	esse	posse	īre	velle	nōlle	ferre

IMPERATIVE			go!		be unwilling!	bring!
singular			ī		nōlī	fer
plural			īte		nōlīte	ferte

EXPRESSIONS, MOTTOES, AND ABBREVIATIONS

A.D.	annō dominī	*in the year of the Lord*
a.m.	ante merīdiem	*before midday*
ad lib	ad libitum	*as you desire*
c.	circā	*about, approximately*
cf.	confer	*compare (with)*
C.V.	curriculum vītae	*course of life*
e.g.	exemplī grātiā	*as an example*
et al.	et aliī	*and the other people*
etc.	et cētera	*and the other things*
ibid.	ibidem	*in the same place (in a book)*
i.e.	id est	*that is*
n.b.	notā bene	*note well*
p.m.	post merīdiem	*after midday*
p.s.	post scrīptum	*after writing*
Q.E.D.	quod erat demonstrandum	*(that) which had to be proved*
R.I.P.	requiēscat in pāce	*rest in peace*
S.P.Q.R.	Senātus Populusque Rōmānus	*the Senate and the People of Rome*
v. or vs.	versus	*against, facing*

ad hoc	*as necessary; temporary*
ālea iacta est. (*Julius Caesar*)	*The die has been thrown.*
alibī	*in another place*
bonā fide	*genuine; in good faith*
carpe diem! (*Horace*)	*Seize the day!*
cōgitō ergō sum.	*I think, therefore I am.*
cui bonō?	*to whose benefit?*
dē factō	*in reality*
dē iūre	*according to the law, in theory*
ē plūribus ūnum	*out of many, one*
fortibus Fortūna favet.	*Fortune favours the brave.*
in sitū	*in (the original) place*
mea culpa	*my own fault*
mēns sāna in corpore sānō. (*Juvenal*)	*A healthy mind in a healthy body.*
modus operandī	*a way of doing something*
pecūnia nōn olet.	*Money doesn't stink.*
per capita	*each person*
per sē	*in/by itself*
prīmus inter parēs	*a first among equals*
prō bonō (pūblicō)	*for the public good*
quid prō quō	*one favour in return for another*
quis custōdiet ipsōs custōdēs? (*Juvenal*)	*Who will guard the guards?*
rēs pūblica	*the public situation, the state*
status quō	*the existing situation*
summā cum laude	*with great glory*
vēnī, vīdī, vīcī. (*Julius Caesar*)	*I came, I saw, I conquered.*
viā	*by way of*
vice versā	*the other way around*
vōx populī	*the voice of the people*

ENGLISH TO LATIN

able, I am	possum, posse, potuī
across	trāns + acc.
adopt (a plan), I	capiō, capere, cēpī
advice	cōnsilium, cōnsiliī, n.
afraid, I am	timeō, timēre, timuī
against	contrā + acc.
alive	vīvus, vīva, vīvum
alone	sōlus, sōla, sōlum
along	per + acc.
always	semper
am, I	sum, esse, fuī
among	inter + acc.
and	et; -que
anger	īra, īrae, f.
angry	īrātus, īrāta, īrātum
announce, I	nūntiō, nūntiāre, nūntiāvī
arms	arma, armōrum, n. pl.
arrive, I	adveniō, advenīre, advēnī
ask, I	rogō, rogāre, rogāvī
ask for, I	petō, petere, petīvī; rogō, rogāre, rogāvī
at	ad + acc.
at last	tandem
at once	statim
attack, I	oppugnō, oppugnāre, oppugnāvī; petō, petere, petīvī
away from	ā, ab + abl.
bad	malus, mala, malum
bear (= carry), I	portō, portāre, portāvī
beautiful	pulcher, pulchra, pulchrum
beg (someone), I	petō, petere, petīvī
between	inter + acc.
big	magnus, magna, magnum
boy	puer, puerī, m.
build, I	aedificō, aedificāre, aedificāvī
by	ā, ab + abl.
call, I	vocō, vocāre, vocāvī
can, I	possum, posse, potuī
capture, I	capiō, capere, cēpī
care for, I	cūrō, cūrāre, cūrāvī
carry, I	portō, portāre, portāvī
catch, I	capiō, capere, cēpī
catch sight of, I	cōnspiciō, cōnspicere, cōnspexī
children	līberī, līberōrum, m. pl.
come, I	veniō, venīre, vēnī
command	imperium, imperiī, n.
commander	lēgātus, lēgātī, m.
conquer, I	vincō, vincere, vīcī
country (= homeland)	patria, patriae, f.
country (= land)	terra, terrae, f.
country house	vīlla, vīllae, f.
crowd	turba, turbae, f.
cruel	saevus, saeva, saevum
cry, I	lacrimō, lacrimāre, lacrimāvī
danger	perīculum, perīculī, n.
daughter	fīlia, fīliae, f.
dear	cārus, cāra, cārum
decide, I	cōnstituō, cōnstituere, cōnstituī
deep	altus, alta, altum
defend, I	dēfendō, dēfendere, dēfendī
demand, I	postulō, postulāre, postulāvī
despair, I	dēspērō, dēspērāre, dēspērāvī
dinner	cēna, cēnae, f.
do, I	faciō, facere, fēcī
drag, draw, I	trahō, trahere, trāxī
dreadful	dīrus, dīra, dīrum
drink, I	bibō, bibere, bibī
empire	imperium, imperiī, n.
enter, I	intrō, intrāre, intrāvī
even	et
evil	malus, mala, malum
expect, I	exspectō, exspectāre, exspectāvī
ex-slave	lībertus, lībertī, m.
fall, I	cadō, cadere, cecidī
fear, I	timeō, timēre, timuī
few, a few	paucī, paucae, pauca
field	ager, agrī, m.
fight, I	pugnō, pugnāre, pugnāvī
finally	tandem
find, I	inveniō, invenīre, invēnī
first	prīmus, prīma, prīmum
flee, I	fugiō, fugere, fūgī
food	cibus, cibī, m.
for a long time	diū
forum	forum, forī, n.
freedman	lībertus, lībertī, m.
friend	amīcus, amīcī, m.
frighten, I	terreō, terrēre, terruī
from (= away from)	ā, ab + abl.
from (= out of)	ē, ex + abl.
garden	hortus, hortī, m.
gate	porta, portae, f.
generous	benignus, benigna, benignum
gift	dōnum, dōnī, n.
girl	puella, puellae, f.
give, I	dō, dare, dedī
god	deus, deī, m.
goddess	dea, deae, f.
good	bonus, bona, bonum
great	magnus, magna, magnum
greet, I	salūtō, salūtāre, salūtāvī
ground	terra, terrae, f.
guard, I	custōdiō, custōdīre, custōdīvī
hand over, hand down, I	trādō, trādere, trādidī
handsome	pulcher, pulchra, pulchrum
happy	laetus, laeta, laetum
hard	dūrus, dūra, dūrum
have, I	habeō, habēre, habuī
hear, I	audiō, audīre, audīvī
help	auxilium, auxiliī, n.
help, I	adiuvō, adiuvāre, adiūvī
hide, I	cēlō, cēlāre, cēlāvī
high	altus, alta, altum
hold (= have), I	habeō, habēre, habuī
hold (= keep), I	teneō, tenēre, tenuī
homeland	patria, patriae, f.
hour	hōra, hōrae, f.
house	vīlla, vīllae, f.
hurry, I	festīnō, festīnāre, festīnāvī
husband	marītus, marītī, m.
idea	cōnsilium, cōnsiliī, n.
immediately	statim
in	in + abl.
inn	taberna, tabernae, f.
into	in + acc.
invite, I	invītō, invītāre, invītāvī
keep (= possess), I	teneō, tenēre, tenuī
keep (= protect), I	servō, servāre, servāvī
kill, I	necō, necāre, necāvī

kind	benignus, benigna, benignum
kingdom	rēgnum, rēgnī, n.
land	terra, terrae, f.
large	magnus, magna, magnum
lead, I	dūcō, dūcere, dūxī
leave, leave behind, I	relinquō, relinquere, relīquī
letter	epistula, epistulae, f.
life	vīta, vītae, f.
like, I	amō, amāre, amāvī
listen to, I	audiō, audīre, audīvī
live, I	habitō, habitāre, habitāvī
living	vīvus, vīva, vīvum
lonely	sōlus, sōla, sōlum
long	longus, longa, longum
look after, I	cūrō, cūrāre, cūrāvī; servō, servāre, servāvī
look at, I	spectō, spectāre, spectāvī
love, I	amō, amāre, amāvī
maid	ancilla, ancillae, f.
make, I	faciō, facere, fēcī
make for, I	petō, petere, petīvī
man	vir, virī, m.
many	multus, multa, multum
marketplace	forum, forī, n.
master	dominus, dominī, m.
meal	cēna, cēnae, f.
messenger	nūntius, nūntiī, m.
miserable	miser, misera, miserum
mistress	domina, dominae, f.
money	pecūnia, pecūniae, f.
much	multus, multa, multum
my	meus, mea, meum
near	prope + acc.
new	novus, nova, novum
news	nūntius, nūntiī, m.
no (= not any)	nūllus, nūlla, nūllum
not	nōn
not any	nūllus, nūlla, nūllum
notice, I	cōnspiciō, cōnspicere, cōnspexī
often	saepe
on	in + abl.
only	sōlus, sōla, sōlum
onto	in + acc.
out of	ē, ex + abl.
overcome, overpower, I	superō, superāre, superāvī
place, I	pōnō, pōnere, posuī
plan	cōnsilium, cōnsiliī, n.
possess, I	teneō, tenēre, tenuī
power	imperium, imperiī, n.
praise, I	laudō, laudāre, laudāvī
prepare, I	parō, parāre, parāvī
present	dōnum, dōnī, n.
prize	praemium, praemiī, n.
profit	praemium, praemiī, n.
protect, I	servō, servāre, servāvī
pull, I	trahō, trahere, trāxī
put, put up, I	pōnō, pōnere, posuī
queen	rēgīna, rēgīnae, f.
quiet, I am	taceō, tacēre, tacuī
real	vērus, vēra, vērum
relate, I	nārrō, nārrāre, nārrāvī
report, I	nūntiō, nūntiāre, nūntiāvī
reward	praemium, praemiī, n.
road	via, viae, f.
Roman	Rōmānus, Rōmāna, Rōmānum
rule, I	regō, regere, rēxī
run, I	currō, currere, cucurrī
run away, I	fugiō, fugere, fūgī
sad	miser, misera, miserum
safe	tūtus, tūta, tūtum
sail, I	nāvigō, nāvigāre, nāvigāvī
sailor	nauta, nautae, m.
savage	saevus, saeva, saevum
save, I	servō, servāre, servāvī
say, I	dīcō, dīcere, dīxī
seal	signum, signī, n.
seek, I	petō, petere, petīvī
send, I	mittō, mittere, mīsī
shop	taberna, tabernae, f.
shout, I	clāmō, clāmāre, clāmāvī
sign	signum, signī, n.
silent, I am	taceō, tacēre, tacuī
slave (female)	ancilla, ancillae, f.
slave (male)	servus, servī, m.
sleep, I	dormiō, dormīre, dormīvī
small	parvus, parva, parvum
son	fīlius, fīliī, m.
speak, I	dīcō, dīcere, dīxī
stand, I	stō, stāre, stetī
story	fābula, fābulae, f.
street	via, viae, f.
stupid	stultus, stulta, stultum
suddenly	subitō
supervise, I	cūrō, cūrāre, cūrāvī
sword	gladius, gladiī, m.
take (= capture), I	capiō, capere, cēpī
take (= carry), I	portō, portāre, portāvī
take (= lead), I	dūcō, dūcere, dūxī
tell (= relate), I	nārrō, nārrāre, nārrāvī
tell (= speak), I	dīcō, dīcere, dīxī
temple	templum, templī, n.
terrified	perterritus, perterrita, perterritum
through	per + acc.
to, towards	ad + acc.
true	vērus, vēra, vērum
victorious, I am	vincō, vincere, vīcī
wait for, I	exspectō, exspectāre, exspectāvī
walk, I	ambulō, ambulāre, ambulāvī
wall	mūrus, mūrī, m.
watch, I	spectō, spectāre, spectāvī
water	aqua, aquae, f.
way (= street)	via, viae, f.
weapons	arma, armōrum, n. pl.
weep, I	lacrimō, lacrimāre, lacrimāvī
well	bene
when?	quandō?
why?	cūr?
wide	lātus, lāta, lātum
win, I	vincō, vincere, vīcī
wine	vīnum, vīnī, n.
with	cum + abl.
woman	fēmina, fēminae, f.
wood	silva, silvae, f.
word	verbum, verbī, n.
work, I	labōrō, labōrāre, labōrāvī
wretched	miser, misera, miserum
write, I	scrībō, scrībere, scrīpsī
year	annus, annī, m.
your (singular), yours	tuus, tua, tuum

HOW TO USE THE DICTIONARY

Numbers before words

A number before a word means the word appears in the **Vocabulary for learning** list for that chapter.

For example: 11   **dux**, **ducis**, *m.*   *leader*

means that **dux** appears in the Chapter 11 **Vocabulary for learning** list.

Nouns

The information given is: nominative, genitive, gender.

For example: **gēns**, **gentis**, *f.*   *people, race, family, tribe*
- **gēns** is the nominative form (used for the subject of the sentence);
- **gentis** is the genitive form (meaning 'of the people');
- **gēns** is a feminine word.

m. stands for masculine; *f.* stands for feminine; *n.* stands for neuter.

m.f. is used for a word which can sometimes be masculine, sometimes feminine. For example, the word **familiāris** (*relative*) can be either masculine or feminine, depending on the gender of the relative.

Verbs

The forms given are: 1st person present tense, infinitive, 1st person perfect tense.
You might prefer to think of this as: *I do something, to do something, I did (have done) something*.

For example: **laudō**, **laudāre**, **laudāvī**   *praise, admire*
- **laudō** means *I praise*
- **laudāre** means *to praise*
- **laudāvī** means *I (have) praised*

Adjectives

Most adjectives are given with the following forms: masculine, feminine, neuter (all nominative singular).

For example: **plēnus**, **plēna**, **plēnum**   *full*
                   trīstis, **trīstis**, **trīste**   *sad*

Some third declension adjectives, such as **ferōx** and **vetus**, change their stems. For these adjectives, the forms given are: nominative, genitive.

For example: **vetus**, *gen.* **veteris**   *old*

See pages 157 and 160 for more information on adjectives.

LATIN TO ENGLISH DICTIONARY

A

6	ā, ab + *abl.*	*from, away from*
	abeō, abīre, abiī	*go away, depart*
	abstulī	*see auferō*
11	absum, abesse, āfuī	*am out, am absent, am away*
16	ac	*and*
11	accidō, accidere, accidī	*happen*
10	accipiō, accipere, accēpī	*accept, take in, receive*
	āctor, āctōris, *m.*	*actor*
4	ad + *acc.*	*to, towards; at*
	adiuvō, adiuvāre, adiūvī	*help*
	administrō, administrāre, administrāvī	*manage, administer*
	adōrō, adōrāre, adōrāvī	*worship*
4	adsum, adesse, adfuī	*am here, am present*
9	adveniō, advenīre, advēnī	*arrive*
	aedificō, aedificāre, aedificāvī	*build*
	aeger, aegra, aegrum	*sick, ill*
	aestus, aestūs, *m.*	*heat*
	aeternus, aeterna, aeternum	*everlasting, eternal*
	Āfrica, Āfricae, *f.*	*Africa (Roman province in what is now North Africa)*
	ager, agrī, *m.*	*field*
	agitō, agitāre, agitāvī	*drive, drive on, chase*
	agnōscō, agnōscere, agnōvī	*recognize*
8	agō, agere, ēgī	*do; act; spend (time)*
	grātiās agō	*give thanks*
	age!	*come!*
	agricola, agricolae, *m.*	*farmer*
	āh!	*ah!*
	albus, alba, album	*white; white team*
	Alexander, Alexandrī, *m.*	*Alexander*
	aliquis, aliquid	*someone, something*
10	alius, alia, aliud	*another, other*
	aliī … aliī …	*some … others …*
	alter, altera, alterum	*the other, another, one of two, the second of two*
11	altus, alta, altum	*high, deep*

3	ambulō, ambulāre, ambulāvī	*walk*
	amīca, amīcae, *f.*	*friend (female)*
3	amīcus, amīcī, *m.*	*friend (male)*
	āmīsī	*see āmittō*
	amita, amitae, *f.*	*aunt*
	āmittō, āmittere, āmīsī	*lose*
14	amō, amāre, amāvī	*love, like*
14	amor, amōris, *m.*	*love*
	amphitheātrum, amphitheātrī, *n.*	*amphitheatre*
	amphora, amphorae, *f.*	*amphora, jar*
3	ancilla, ancillae, *f.*	*slave, enslaved person (female)*
	angustus, angusta, angustum	*narrow*
	animal, animālis, *n.*	*animal*
10	annus, annī, *m.*	*year*
	annuus, annua, annuum	*yearly, annual*
	ānser, ānseris, *m.f.*	*goose*
	ante + *acc.*	*before; in front of*
15	anteā	*before*
	Antigonus, Antigonī, *m.*	*Antigonus*
	ānulus, ānulī, *m.*	*ring*
	ānxiē	*anxiously, worriedly*
	ānxius, ānxia, ānxium	*worried, concerned*
	aper, aprī, *m.*	*boar*
	aperiō, aperīre, aperuī	*open*
	apodȳtērium, apodȳtēriī, *n.*	*changing room*
	appāreō, appārēre, appāruī	*appear*
7	appropinquō, appropinquāre, appropinquāvī + *dat.*	*approach, come near to*
	apud + *acc.*	*at the house of; with; among*
5	aqua, aquae, *f.*	*water*
	aquaeductus, aquaeductūs, *m.*	*aqueduct*
	āra, ārae, *f.*	*altar*
	arca, arcae, *f.*	*crate, strongbox*
	arcus, arcūs, *m.*	*arch*
	ardenter	*eagerly*
	ardeō, ardēre, arsī	*burn, am on fire*
	Arelātē, Arelātēs, *f.*	*Arles (town in southern France)*
	Arelātēnsis, Arelātēnsis, Arelātēnse	*of Arles*
	arma, armōrum, *n. pl.*	*arms, weapons*
	artifex, artificis, *m.f.*	*artist*
	ascendō, ascendere, ascendī	*climb*

asinus, asinī, m.	stupid person, fool; donkey
aspectus, aspectūs, m.	view
ātrium, ātriī, n.	reception room, entrance hall
attonitus, attonita, attonitum	shocked, astonished
au!	wow!
Aucissa, Aucissae, f.	Aucissa
audeō, audēre	dare
5 audiō, audīre, audīvī	hear, listen to
16 auferō, auferre, abstulī	steal, take away, carry off
augeō, augēre, auxī	increase
Augustus, Augusta, Augustum	August
aurīga, aurīgae, m.	charioteer
auris, auris, f.	ear
aurum, aurī, n.	gold
aut	or
aut ... aut ...	either ... or ...
autumnus, autumnī, m.	autumn
auxiliāris, auxiliāris, m.	auxiliary soldier
auxilium, auxiliī, n.	help
avis, avis, f.	bird

B

bālō, bālāre, bālāvī	bleat
barba, barbae, f.	beard
basilica, basilicae, f.	hall
Batāvia, Batāviae, f.	Batavia (in Germania Inferior)
bau!	bow!
15 bellum, bellī, n.	war
11 bene	well
benignus, benigna, benignum	kind, generous
8 bibō, bibere, bibī	drink
blandus, blanda, blandum	flattering
Boārius, Boāria, Boārium	Boarium, of cattle
10 bonus, bona, bonum	good
Boudica, Boudicae, f.	Boudica
bracchium, bracchiī, n.	arm
16 brevis, brevis, breve	short, brief
breviter	briefly
Britannī, Britannōrum, m. pl.	Britons
Britannia, Britanniae, f.	Britannia, Britain
Britannicus, Britannica, Britannicum	British

C

C., m.	Gaius
2 cadō, cadere, cecidī	fall
caedēs, caedis, f.	killing, slaughter
12 caelum, caelī, n.	sky, heaven
calcitrō, calcitrāre, calcitrāvī	kick out
calidus, calida, calidum	hot
callidus, callida, callidum	clever
Camulodūnum, Camulodūnī, n.	Camulodunum (Colchester)
canis, canis, m.	dog
Cantaber, Cantabrī, m.	Cantaber
cantō, cantāre, cantāvī	sing
6 capiō, capere, cēpī	take, catch, capture; adopt (a plan)
cōnsilium capiō	make a plan, adopt a plan
Capitōlium, Capitōliī, n.	the Capitoline Hill
captīvus, captīvī, m.	captive, prisoner
12 caput, capitis, n.	head
carcer, carceris, m.	prison
carpō, carpere, carpsī	enjoy, use
cārus, cāra, cārum	expensive; dear
casa, casae, f.	hut, cottage
cāsus, cāsūs, m.	accident
Catia, Catiae, f.	Catia
cautērium, cautēriī, n.	branding iron
cautus, cauta, cautum	careful, cautious
caveō, cavēre, cāvī	beware, look out (for), watch out (for)
cavē! cavēte!	look out! watch out!
cavō, cavāre, cavāvī	hollow out
cecidī	see cadō
celebrō, celebrāre, celebrāvī	celebrate
Celer, Celeris, m.	Celer
celeriter	quickly
celerrimē	very quickly
cella, cellae, f.	room
16 cēlō, cēlāre, cēlāvī	hide
15 cēna, cēnae, f.	dinner, meal
centuriō, centuriōnis, m.	centurion (officer in the army)
cēpī	see capiō
Cerēs, Cereris, f.	Ceres (goddess of agriculture)
certē	certainly, clearly
15 cēterī, cēterae, cētera, pl.	the rest, the others
Chīlō, Chīlōnis, m.	Chilo

chorus, chorī, *m.*	*chorus, choir*
Christiānus, Christiāna, Christiānum	*Christian*
Christus, Christī, *m.*	*Christ*
2 cibus, cibī, *m.*	*food*
cicātrīx, cicātrīcis, *f.*	*scar*
circumspectō, circumspectāre, circumspectāvī	*look around*
Circus, Circī, *m.*	*Circus, Circus Maximus*
9 cīvis, cīvis, *m.f.*	*citizen*
3 clāmō, clāmāre, clāmāvī	*shout*
3 clāmor, clāmōris, *m.*	*noise, shouting, shout*
clāmōsus, clāmōsa, clāmōsum	*noisy, rowdy*
clangor, clangōris, *m.*	*noise*
Claudius, Claudiī, *m.*	*Claudius*
cloāca, cloācae, *f.*	*sewer, drain*
13 coepī	*began*
14 cōgitō, cōgitāre, cōgitāvī	*think, consider*
15 cognōscō, cognōscere, cognōvī	*get to know, find out, learn*
cōgō, cōgere, coēgī	*force, compel*
colōnia, colōniae, *f.*	*colony*
columba, columbae, *f.*	*dove*
15 comes, comitis, *m.*	*comrade, companion, friend*
compressus, compressa, compressum	*constipated*
concipiō, concipere, concēpī	*conceive, become pregnant*
14 cōnficiō, cōnficere, cōnfēcī	*finish*
congelātus, congelāta, congelātum	*frozen*
Conimbrīga, Conimbrīgae, *f.*	*Conimbriga (town in Lusitania)*
coniūrātiō, coniūrātiōnis, *f.*	*plot*
conlāpsus, conlāpsa, conlāpsum	*collapsed*
14 cōnsilium, cōnsiliī, *n.*	*plan, idea, advice*
cōnsilium capiō	*make a plan, adopt a plan*
8 cōnspiciō, cōnspicere, cōnspexī	*catch sight of, notice*
14 cōnstituō, cōnstituere, cōnstituī	*decide*
cōnsul, cōnsulis, *m.*	*consul*
13 cōnsūmō, cōnsūmere, cōnsūmpsī	*consume, eat*
10 contrā + *acc.*	*against*
contrōversia, contrōversiae, *f.*	*argument, dispute*
conveniō, convenīre, convēnī	*come together, gather, meet*
cōpiae, cōpiārum, *f. pl.*	*forces, troops*
Cornēlia, Cornēliae, *f.*	*Cornelia*
12 corpus, corporis, *n.*	*body*
Corsica, Corsicae, *f.*	*Corsica (an island)*
cōtīdiē	*every day*
crās	*tomorrow*
crēdō, crēdere, crēdidī + *dat.*	*believe, trust, have faith in*
crocodīlus, crocodīlī, *m.*	*crocodile*
12 crūdēlis, crūdēlis, crūdēle	*cruel*
cubiculum, cubiculī, *n.*	*bedroom*
cucumis, cucumeris, *m.*	*cucumber*
culīna, culīnae, *f.*	*kitchen*
culter, cultrī, *m.*	*knife*
3 cum + *abl.*	*with*
cunīculus, cunīculī, *m.*	*rabbit*
5 cupiō, cupere, cupīvī	*want, desire*
7 cūr?	*why?*
cūrātor, cūrātōris, *m.*	*manager*
cūria, cūriae, *f.*	*Senate House*
cūrō, cūrāre, cūrāvī	*care about, am bothered about, look after, supervise*
Currāx, Currācis, *m.*	*Currax*
3 currō, currere, cucurrī	*run*
cursus, cursūs, *m.*	*race*
custōdiō, custōdīre, custōdīvī	*guard*
5 custōs, custōdis, *m.f.*	*guard*

D

Darius, Dariī, *m.*	*Darius*
8 dē + *abl.*	*from, down from; about*
10 dea, deae, *f.*	*goddess*
5 dēbeō, dēbēre, dēbuī	*owe; ought, should, must*
dēcidō, dēcidere, dēcidī	*fall down*
decōrus, decōra, decōrum	*proper, right*
dedī	*see dō*
dēfendō, dēfendere, dēfendī	*defend*
10 deinde	*then*
dēlectō, dēlectāre, dēlectāvī	*please, delight*
12 dēleō, dēlēre, dēlēvī	*destroy*
delphīnus, delphīnī, *m.*	*dolphin*

dēmōnstrō, dēmōnstrāre, dēmōnstrāvī	show, point out
dēnārius, dēnāriī, m.	denarius (silver coin)
dēnsus, dēnsa, dēnsum	thick
dēpōnō, dēpōnere, dēposuī	take off, put down
dēscendō, dēscendere, dēscendī	go down, come down
dēsiliō, dēsilīre, dēsiluī	jump, jump down
dēsistō, dēsistere, dēstitī	stop
dēspērō, dēspērāre, dēspērāvī	despair
deus, deī, m.	god
dēvoveō, dēvovēre, dēvōvī	curse
dexter, dextra, dextrum	right
dīcō, dīcere, dīxī	say, speak, tell
diēs, diēī, m.	day
difficilis, difficilis, difficile	difficult
difficultās, difficultātis, f.	difficulty
dīligenter	carefully
dīligentissimē	very carefully, most carefully
dīmittō, dīmittere, dīmīsī	release
dīrus, dīra, dīrum	dreadful
discēdō, discēdere, discessī	depart, leave
diū	for a long time
diūtius	longer, for a longer time
dīxī	see dīcō
dō, dare, dedī	give
doceō, docēre, docuī	teach
dolor, dolōris, m.	pain
domina, dominae, f.	mistress, lady
dominus, dominī, m.	master
domus, domūs, f.	house, home
dōnum, dōnī, n.	gift, present
dormiō, dormīre, dormīvī	sleep
Druidēs, Druidum, m. pl.	Druids
dubiō	see sine dubiō
dubitō, dubitāre, dubitāvī	hesitate, doubt
ducentī, ducentae, ducenta	two hundred
dūcō, dūcere, dūxī	lead, guide, take
in mātrimōnium dūcō	marry
dulcis, dulcis, dulce	sweet
dulcissimus, dulcissima, dulcissimum	very sweet
duo, duae, duo	two
dūrus, dūra, dūrum	hard, harsh
dux, ducis, m.	leader
dūxī	see dūcō

E

ē, ex + abl.	from, out of
ea	they, them, those things
eā	by/with/from her, it
eā nocte	that night
eae	they
eam	her, it
eārum	their, of them
eās	them
ecce!	look! see!
effluō, effluere, effluxī	flow
effugiō, effugere, effūgī	flee, escape
ēgī	see agō
ego, meī	I, me
ēheu!	ah! oh no!
ei!	ai! oh!
eī	they; to/for him, her, it
eīs	to/for/by/with/from them
eius	his, her, its
elephantus, elephantī, m.	elephant
emblēma, emblēmatis, n.	mosaic
emō, emere, ēmī	buy
ēn!	see! look here!
eō, īre, iī	go
eō	by/with/from him, it
eōrum	their, of them
eōs	them
epistula, epistulae, f.	letter
eques, equitis, m.	horseman, pl. = cavalry
equitō, equitāre, equitāvī	ride
equus, equī, m.	horse
erat	(he/she/it) was
erit	(he/she/it) will be
erō	I shall be
errō, errāre, errāvī	make a mistake; wander
ērubēscō, ērubēscere, ērubuī	blush
erunt	(they) will be
es	you (s.) are
est	is, there is, he/she/it is
estis	you (pl.) are
et	and
et ... et ...	both ... and ...
etiam	even, also
eum	him, it

eunt	(they) go
ēvānēscō, ēvānēscere, ēvānuī	disappear
ex, ē + abl.	from, out of
excitō, excitāre, excitāvī	wake someone up
exclāmō, exclāmāre, exclāmāvī	exclaim
exeō, exīre, exiī	come out of
exercitus, exercitūs, m.	army
exspectō, exspectāre, exspectāvī	wait for; expect
exspīrō, exspīrāre, exspīrāvī	die
exstinguō, exstinguere, exstīnxī	put out, extinguish
exstruō, exstruere, exstrūxī	build
exta, extōrum, n. pl.	entrails
extrahō, extrahere, extrāxī	take out, extract

F

faber, fabrī, m.	craftsman
fābula, fābulae, f.	story; play; pl. = nonsense!
faciō, facere, fēcī	do; make
familia, familiae, f.	family, household
familiāris, familiāris, m.f.	relative
fār, farris, n.	grain
Faustus, Faustī, m.	Faustus
fax, facis, f.	torch
febris, febris, f.	fever
fēcī	see faciō
fēlīciter	luckily, happily; good luck!
fēlīx, gen. fēlīcis	lucky, fortunate; happy
fēmina, fēminae, f.	woman
fenestra, fenestrae, f.	window
ferō, ferre, tulī	bring, carry, bear
ferōciter	fiercely
ferōx, gen. ferōcis	fierce, ferocious
ferrārius, ferrāriī, m.	blacksmith
fervor, fervōris, m.	heat
fessus, fessa, fessum	tired
festīnō, festīnāre, festīnāvī	hurry, rush
fēstus, fēsta, fēstum	festival
fībula, fībulae, f.	brooch
fidēlis, fidēlis, fidēle	loyal, faithful; trustworthy
fīlia, fīliae, f.	daughter
fīlius, fīliī, m.	son
fīnis, fīnis, m.	end
firmus, firma, firmum	firm
Flāminius, Flāminia, Flāminium	of Flaminius, Flaminian
flamma, flammae, f.	flame; pl. = fire
flammeum, flammeī, n.	bridal veil
fluitāns, gen. fluitantis	floating
flūmen, flūminis, n.	river
fluō, fluere, flūxī	flow
focus, focī, m.	hearth
fōns, fontis, m.	fountain
fōrma, fōrmae, f.	creature; shape
fornāx, fornācis, f.	furnace
fortasse	perhaps
fortis, fortis, forte	brave
fortiter	bravely
Fortūna, Fortūnae, f.	Fortune (goddess)
forum, forī, n.	forum, market, meeting place
fragor, fragōris, m.	crash, noise
frāter, frātris, m.	brother
frīgidus, frīgida, frīgidum	cold
frōns, frontis	see scaenae frōns
frūctus, frūctūs, m.	fruit
frūmentum, frūmentī, n.	corn, grain
frūstrā	in vain, without success
frūx, frūgis, f.	crop
fuga, fugae, f.	escape
fugiō, fugere, fūgī	run away, flee
fugitīvus, fugitīva, fugitīvum	runaway
fulgeō, fulgēre, fulsī	flash with lightning
fūmōsus, fūmōsa, fūmōsum	smoky
fūmus, fūmī, m.	smoke
fundus, fundī, m.	farm
fūnis, fūnis, m.	rope
fūr, fūris, m.	thief
fūrtim	secretly, like a thief

G

Gabrus, Gabrī, m.	Gabrus
Gāia, Gāiae, f.	Gaia
Gāius, Gāiī, m.	Gaius
Gallia, Galliae, f.	Gaul
Galliō, Galliōnis, m.	Gallio
Gallus, Gallī, m.	a Gaul
gaudeō, gaudēre	am pleased, rejoice
gaudium, gaudiī, n.	joy, pleasure
gēns, gentis, f.	people, race, family, tribe

8 gerō, gerere, gessī	wear (clothes); wage (war)	hūc	here, to this place
		hūc illūc	here and there
gessī	see gerō	hunc	this, this man
Giscō, Giscōnis, *m.*	Gisco		
glaciēs, glaciēī, *f.*	ice	**I**	
3 gladius, gladiī, *m.*	sword		
glis, glīris, *m.*	dormouse	8 iaceō, iacēre, iacuī	lie down
gradus, gradūs, *m.*	step, row	10 iaciō, iacere, iēcī	throw
grātiae, grātiārum, *f. pl.*	thanks	iactō, iactāre, iactāvī	throw
grātiās agō	give thanks	6 iam	now, already
9 gravis, gravis, grave	heavy; serious	12 iānua, iānuae, *f.*	door, doorway
graviter	heavily; seriously	ībat	(he/she/it) was going
grundiō, grundīre, grundīvī	grunt	11 ibi	there
gustō, gustāre, gustāvī	taste	Icēnī, Icēnōrum, *m. pl.*	Iceni
		Īdūs, Īduum, *f. pl.*	Ides (15th day of March, May, July, October, 13th day of other months)
H			
2 habeō, habēre, habuī	have, hold	iēcī	see iaciō
2 habitō, habitāre, habitāvī	live	igitur	so, therefore
hae	these, these women	ignis, ignis, *m.*	fire
haereō, haerēre, haesī	cling	ignōscō, ignōscere, ignōvī	forgive
hahae!	ha ha!	ignōtus, ignōta, ignōtum	unknown
hanc	this, this woman	iit	(he/she/it) went
hās	these, these women	illa	that, that women, she
hasta, hastae, *f.*	spear	illās	those, those women, them
hercle!	oh no! oh dear!		
heri	yesterday	16 ille	that, that man, he
hērōs, hērōis, *m.*	hero	16 ille, illa, illud	that, he, she, it
Hettia, Hettiae, *f.*	Hettia	illam	that, that woman, her
heus!	hey! hey there!	illōs	those, those men, them
hī	these, these men	illūc	there, to that place
hīc	here	hūc illūc	here and there
16 hic, haec, hoc	this, he, she, it	illum	that, that man, him
hiems, hiemis, *f.*	winter	imāgō, imāginis, *f.*	image, picture
hinnītus, hinnītūs, *m.*	neighing	immortālis, immortālis, immortāle	immortal
hippopotamus, hippopotamī, *m.*	hippopotamus	immōtus, immōta, immōtum	motionless
Hispānus, Hispāna, Hispānum	Spanish	9 imperātor, imperātōris, *m.*	emperor; general
historia, historiae, *f.*	history	16 imperium, imperiī, *n.*	power; empire
11 hodiē	today	impleō, implēre, implēvī	fill
7 homō, hominis, *m.*	man, person, human being	īmus	we go
		6 in + *acc.*	into, onto
1 hōra, hōrae, *f.*	hour	1 in + *abl.*	in, on
horreum, horreī, *n.*	barn, granary, warehouse	inānis, inānis, ināne	empty
		incendium, incendiī, *n.*	fire
15 hortus, hortī, *m.*	garden	8 incendō, incendere, incendī	burn, set on fire
hōs	these, these men	incertus, incerta, incertum	uncertain
hospes, hospitis, *m.*	guest	incipiō, incipere, incēpī	begin, start
9 hostis, hostis, *m.*	enemy		

incitō, incitāre, incitāvī	incite, stir up
inclīnō, inclīnāre, inclīnāvī	bend, bow
indicō, indicāre, indicāvī	point out, show
Indus, Indī, *m.*	Indus
inertia, inertiae, *f.*	laziness, inaction
īnfāns, īnfantis, *m.*	baby
īnfēlīx, *gen.* īnfēlīcis	unlucky; unhappy
ingēns, *gen.* ingentis	huge
inquit	says, said
īnsānus, īnsāna, īnsānum	mad, insane
īnspiciō, īnspicere, īnspexī	inspect
īnstitor, īnstitōris, *m.*	stallholder
īnstrūmentum, īnstrūmentī, *n.*	instrument, tool
īnsula, īnsulae, *f.*	block of flats, apartment block; island
intellegō, intellegere, intellēxī	understand, realize
intentē	intently, closely, carefully
inter + *acc.*	among, between
intereā	meanwhile
intolerābilis, intolerābilis, intolerābile	unbearable
intrō, intrāre, intrāvī	come in, enter
inūtilis, inūtilis, inūtile	useless
inveniō, invenīre, invēnī	find
invītō, invītāre, invītāvī	invite
iō!	ho! hurrah!
īra, īrae, *f.*	anger
īrātus, īrāta, īrātum	angry
is, ea, id	he, she, it
īs	you (s.) go
it	(he/she/it) goes
ita	so, in this way
ita vērō	yes, absolutely
itaque	and so, therefore
iter, itineris, *n.*	journey, route, way
iterum	again
ītis	you (pl.) go
iubeō, iubēre, iussī	order
Iūlia, Iūliae, *f.*	Julia
Iūlius, Iūlia, Iūlium	July
iūnior, iūniōris, *m.*	Junior, Younger
iūnior, iūnior, iūnius	younger
Iūnō, Iūnōnis, *f.*	Juno (queen of the gods)
Iuppiter, Iovis, *m.*	Jupiter (king of the gods)
iūstus, iūsta, iūstum	right, proper
iuvenis, iuvenis, *m.f.*	young person
iuvō, iuvāre, iūvī	help, assist

K

Kalendae, Kalendārum, *f. pl.*	Kalends, first day of the month

L

labor, labōris, *m.*	work
labōrō, labōrāre, labōrāvī	work
lacrima, lacrimae, *f.*	tear
lacrimō, lacrimāre, lacrimāvī	cry, weep
Laecānius, Laecānii, *m.*	Laecanius
laena, laenae, *f.*	woollen cloak
laetē	happily, gladly
laetus, laeta, laetum	happy
lambō, lambere, lambī	lick, lap
lāna, lānae, *f.*	wool
Lar, Laris, *m.*	household god, Lar
later, lateris, *m.*	brick
lātrīna, lātrīnae, *f.*	toilet
lātrō, lātrāre, lātrāvī	bark
latrō, latrōnis, *m.*	bandit, robber
laudō, laudāre, laudāvī	praise, admire
lectīca, lectīcae, *f.*	litter (portable couch)
lectus, lectī, *m.*	bed
lēgātus, lēgātī, *m.*	governor; commander
legiō, legiōnis, *f.*	legion
legō, legere, lēgī	read; choose
lentē	slowly
lentus, lenta, lentum	slow
leō, leōnis, *m.*	lion
lepus, leporis, *m.*	hare
Letta, Lettae, *f.*	Letta
libenter	willingly, gladly
liber, librī, *m.*	book
līberī, līberōrum, *m. pl.*	children
līberō, līberāre, līberāvī	free, set free
lībertās, lībertātis, *f.*	freedom
lībertus, lībertī, *m.*	former slave, freedman
Licinius, Licinii, *m.*	Licinius
lignum, lignī, *n.*	log, wood
littera, litterae, *f.*	letter
locus, locī, *m.*	place
Londīnium, Londīniī, *n.*	London
longē	far off

13 longus, longa, longum	long
Luccus, Luccī, m.	Luccus
lūceō, lūcēre, lūxī	shine
lucerna, lucernae, f.	lamp
Lūcīlius, Lūcīliī, m.	Lucilius
Lūcriō, Lūcriōnis, m.	Lucrio
lūdō, lūdere, lūsī	play, am at leisure
lūdus, lūdī, m.	game; pl. = races
lūna, lūnae, f.	moon
Lūsitānia, Lūsitāniae, f.	Lusitania
16 lūx, lūcis, f.	light, daylight
luxuria, luxuriae, f.	luxury

M

Maelō, Maelōnis, m.	Maelo
magister, magistrī, m.	employer
magnificus, magnifica, magnificum	magnificent, wonderful, amazing
2 magnus, magna, magnum	big, large, great
maior, maior, maius	bigger, larger, greater
mālum, mālī, n.	apple
malus, mala, malum	bad, evil
māne	in the morning
5 maneō, manēre, mānsī	remain, stay
Mānius, Māniī, m.	Manius
Manlius, Manliī, m.	Manlius
manus, manūs, f.	hand; group (of people), gang
mappa, mappae, f.	cloth; flag
Marcus, Marcī, m.	Marcus
11 mare, maris, n.	sea
6 marītus, marītī, m.	husband
6 māter, mātris, f.	mother
mātrimōnium, mātrimōniī, n.	marriage
in mātrimōnium dūcō	marry
mātrōna, mātrōnae, f.	lady, married woman
maximē	very much, a lot, very greatly
maximus, maxima, maximum	very big, huge; biggest, greatest
9 medius, media, medium	middle, middle of
melior, melior, melius	better
meminī	remember
mendāx, mendācis, m.f.	liar
mendīcō, mendīcāre, mendīcāvī	beg
mendīcus, mendīcī, m.	beggar
mēnsa, mēnsae, f.	table
mēnsis, mēnsis, m.	month
menta, mentae, f.	mint
mercātor, mercātōris, m.	merchant
mēta, mētae, f.	turning post
metallum, metallī, n.	mine
1 meus, mea, meum	my
7 mīles, mīlitis, m.	soldier
Minerva, Minervae, f.	Minerva (goddess of wisdom and war)
mingō, mingere, mīnxī	urinate
7 minimē	no
ministra, ministrae, f.	employee, assistant
minor, minor, minus	smaller; younger; less
mīrābilis, mīrābilis, mīrābile	strange, wonderful
10 miser, misera, miserum	poor, unfortunate, sad
mīsī	see mittō
12 mittō, mittere, mīsī	send
mōmentum, mōmentī, n.	importance
moneō, monēre, monuī	advise, warn
monēta, monētae, f.	mint, coin factory
14 mōns, montis, m.	mountain
mōnstrum, mōnstrī, n.	monster
morbus, morbī, m.	illness
14 mors, mortis, f.	death
mortuus, mortua, mortuum	dead
moveō, movēre, mōvī	move
8 mox	soon
mūgiō, mūgīre, mūgīvī	moo, bellow
mulceō, mulcēre, mulsī	stroke
multitūdō, multitūdinis, f.	large number, crowd
multō	much, by much
15 multum	much
3 multus, multa, multum	much; pl. = many, a lot of
murmurō, murmurāre, murmurāvī	mutter
13 mūrus, mūrī, m.	wall
mūs, mūris, m.	mouse; rat

N

7 nārrō, nārrāre, nārrāvī	tell, relate
nāsus, nāsī, m.	nose
natō, natāre, natāvī	swim
naufragium, naufragiī, n.	crash, wreck
7 nauta, nautae, m.	sailor
11 nāvigō, nāvigāre, nāvigāvī	sail
11 nāvis, nāvis, f.	ship
-ne	(marks a question)

	nebula, nebulae, *f.*	*mist*
14	nec	*and not, nor, neither*
14	nec ... nec ...	*neither ... nor ...*
	necesse, *n.*	*necessary*
14	necō, necāre, necāvī	*kill*
	neglegenter	*carelessly*
	negōtiātor, negōtiātōris, *m.*	*businessman, dealer, trader*
	negōtium, negōtiī, *n.*	*business*
5	nēmō, nēminis, *m.f.*	*no one, nobody*
	Neptūnus, Neptūnī, *m.*	*Neptune (god of the sea)*
	Nerō, Nerōnis, *m.*	*Nero*
	Nerōniānus, Nerōniāna, Nerōniānum	*of Nero*
14	nesciō, nescīre, nescīvī	*don't know*
8	nihil, *n.*	*nothing*
	nihilōminus	*nevertheless*
	nimium	*too (much)*
	nisi	*unless, except*
	nōbīs	*to/for us*
	noceō, nocēre, nocuī	*harm*
5	nōlō, nōlle, nōluī	*don't want, refuse*
13	nōmen, nōminis, *n.*	*name*
1	nōn	*not*
	nōndum	*not yet*
15	nōnne?	*surely?*
	nōnnūllī, nōnnūllae, nōnnūlla	*some, several*
	nōnus, nōna, nōnum	*ninth*
4	nōs, nostrum	*we, us*
	nōscō, nōscere, nōvī	*get to know*
8	noster, nostra, nostrum	*our*
	notō, notāre, notāvī	*mark, brand*
	nōtus, nōta, nōtum	*known, familiar*
10	novus, nova, novum	*new*
5	nox, noctis, *f.*	*night*
10	nūllus, nūlla, nūllum	*no, not any*
	num?	*surely not?*
	nūmen, nūminis, *n.*	*deity; divine power*
	Numidicus, Numidica, Numidicum	*Numidian*
14	numquam	*never*
7	nunc	*now*
15	nūntiō, nūntiāre, nūntiāvī	*announce, report*
9	nūntius, nūntiī, *m.*	*messenger; message, news*
	nūper	*recently, not long ago*
	nūptiae, nūptiārum, *f. pl.*	*wedding*
	nūptiālis, nūptiālis, nūptiāle	*nuptial, wedding*

O

	ō!	*o!*
	obscūrus, obscūra, obscūrum	*dark*
	obstō, obstāre, obstitī + *dat.*	*am in the way (of), cause an obstruction (to), block*
10	occīdō, occīdere, occīdī	*kill*
	occupātus, occupāta, occupātum	*busy*
	octāvus, octāva, octāvum	*eighth*
	oculus, oculī, *m.*	*eye*
12	offerō, offerre, obtulī	*offer*
	officīna, officīnae, *f.*	*workshop*
	ōh!	*oh! oh dear!*
	ohē!	*hey!*
7	ōlim	*once, some time ago*
	ōmen, ōminis, *n.*	*omen, sign*
3	omnis, omnis, omne	*all, every*
	operārius, operāriī, *m.*	*workman*
	oppidum, oppidī, *n.*	*town*
	opprimō, opprimere, oppressī	*crush, overwhelm*
	oppugnō, oppugnāre, oppugnāvī	*attack*
	optimē	*very well*
	optimus, optima, optimum	*best, very good, excellent*
	opus, operis, *n.*	*work*
	orbis, orbis, *m.*	*globe, sphere*
	orbis terrārum	*world*
16	ōrō, ōrāre, ōrāvī	*beg, beg for*
	ōsculum, ōsculī, *n.*	*kiss*
14	ostendō, ostendere, ostendī	*show*
	Ostia, Ostiae, *f.*	*Ostia*
	Othō, Othōnis, *m.*	*Otho*

P

	paene	*almost, nearly*
	palaestra, palaestrae, *f.*	*exercise ground*
	palma, palmae, *f.*	*palm; victory*
	palūs, palūdis, *f.*	*marsh*
	pānis, pānis, *m.*	*bread*
	pantomīmus, pantomīmī, *m.*	*mime performer*
	parātus, parāta, parātum	*ready*

parcō, parcere, pepercī + dat.	spare, am sparing of
parēns, parentis, m.f.	parent
parō, parāre, parāvī	prepare
pars, partis, f.	part
parvus, parva, parvum	small
pater, patris, m.	father
patrōnus, patrōnī, m.	patron
paucī, paucae, pauca, pl.	few, a few
pauper, gen. pauperis	poor
pauper, pauperis, m.	poor person
pavīmentum, pavīmentī, n.	floor
pāx, pācis, f.	peace
pectus, pectoris, n.	chest, breast
pecūnia, pecūniae, f.	money, sum of money
pellō, pellere, pepulī	drive, push
pēnsiō, pēnsiōnis, f.	payment, rent
pepulī	see pellō
per + acc.	through, along
percutiō, percutere, percussī	strike
pereō, perīre, periī	die, perish
perīculōsus, perīculōsa, perīculōsum	dangerous
perīculum, perīculī, n.	danger
permixtus, permixta, permixtum	mixed
persōna, persōnae, f.	character, part
persuādeō, persuādēre, persuāsī + dat.	persuade
perterritus, perterrita, perterritum	terrified
perveniō, pervenīre, pervēnī	arrive, reach
petō, petere, petīvī	attack; make for; seek; beg, ask for
pff!	pff!
Philētus, Philētī, m.	Philetus
philosophia, philosophiae, f.	philosophy
pīlum, pīlī, n.	javelin
pīrāta, pīrātae, m.	pirate
piscīna, piscīnae, f.	swimming pool
piscis, piscis, m.	fish
pistor, pistōris, m.	baker
pistrīnum, pistrīnī, n.	bakery
placeō, placēre, placuī + dat.	please
plaudō, plaudere, plausī	clap, applaud
plaustrum, plaustrī, n.	wagon, cart
plēnus, plēna, plēnum	full
pluō, pluere, plūvī	rain
plūrimī, plūrimae, plūrima	very many
plūs, plūris, n.	more
pōculum, pōculī, n.	cup
poena, poenae, f.	penalty, punishment
poenās dō	pay the penalty, am punished
pompa, pompae, f.	procession
pōns, pontis, m.	bridge
popīna, popīnae, f.	bar
popīnāria, popīnāriae, f.	barkeeper, bar owner
Poppillus, Poppillī, m.	Poppillus
populus, populī, m.	people
porcus, porcī, m.	pig
porta, portae, f.	gate, grate
portō, portāre, portāvī	carry, bear, take
portus, portūs, m.	harbour
possum, posse, potuī	am able, can
post + acc.	after, behind
posteā	afterwards
postquam	after, when
postrīdiē	on the following day
postulō, postulāre, postulāvī	demand
potuī	see possum
praecipitō, praecipitāre, praecipitāvī	fall
praefectus, praefectī, m.	commander
praemium, praemiī, n.	prize, reward, profit
prasinus, prasina, prasinum	green; green team
precēs, precum, f. pl.	prayers
prīmō	at first
prīmus, prīma, prīmum	first
prīnceps, prīncipis, m.	chief; emperor
prō + abl.	in front of; for
prōcēdō, prōcēdere, prōcessī	go along, advance, proceed
Proclus, Proclī, m.	Proclus
procul	far off
prōcūrātor, prōcūrātōris, m.	procurator (province's finance officer)
proelium, proeliī, n.	battle
prōmittō, prōmittere, prōmīsī	promise
prope + acc.	near
prōtegō, prōtegere, prōtēxī	protect
prōvincia, prōvinciae, f.	province

	proximus, proxima, proximum	nearest; next to
	prūnum, prūnī, n.	plum
	psittacus, psittacī, m.	parrot
	pst!	pst!
4	puella, puellae, f.	girl
7	puer, puerī, m.	boy
	pugiō, pugiōnis, m.	dagger
7	pugnō, pugnāre, pugnāvī	fight
5	pulcher, pulchra, pulchrum	beautiful, handsome
	pulsō, pulsāre, pulsāvī	beat
	pūniō, pūnīre, pūnīvī	punish
15	putō, putāre, putāvī	think
	Pȳramus, Pȳramī, m.	Pyramus

Q

	quadrīga, quadrīgae, f.	chariot
	quae	who, which
2	quaerō, quaerere, quaesīvī	look for, search for
	quālis, quālis, quāle?	what sort of?
10	quam	(1) how ... !
	quam	(2) than
	quam + superlative	(3) as ... as possible
	quam	(4) whom, which
13	quamquam	although
	quandō?	when?
	quantus, quanta, quantum?	how big? how much?
	Quārtilla, Quārtillae, f.	Quartilla
	quārtus, quārta, quārtum	fourth
	quattuor	four
	-que	and
	quem	whom, which
13	quī, quae, quod	who, which
	quid?	what?
	quiētē	quietly
	quiētus, quiēta, quiētum	quiet
	quīntus, quīnta, quīntum	fifth
12	quis? quid?	who? what?
16	quō?	to where?
4	quod	(1) because
	quod	(2) which
13	quōmodo?	how? in what way?
2	quoque	also, too
	quos	whom
	quot?	how many?

R

16	rapiō, rapere, rapuī	seize, grab
	raucus, rauca, raucum	hoarse
	rēctā	directly, straight
	recumbō, recumbere, recubuī	recline, lie down
12	redeō, redīre, rediī	go back, come back, return
	reficiō, reficere, refēcī	fix, mend, repair
16	rēgīna, rēgīnae, f.	queen
	rēgnum, rēgnī, n.	kingdom
	regō, regere, rēxī	rule
	relinquō, relinquere, relīquī	leave, leave behind
	repente	suddenly
	rēpō, rēpere, rēpsī	crawl
7	rēs, reī, f.	story; thing, business, matter, event
16	resistō, resistere, restitī + dat.	resist
	resonō, resonāre, resonāvī	resound
5	respondeō, respondēre, respondī	reply
	retineō, retinēre, retinuī	hold back, restrain
16	reveniō, revenīre, revēnī	come back, return
4	rēx, rēgis, m.	king
	rēxī	see regō
1	rīdeō, rīdēre, rīsī	laugh; smile
	rīma, rīmae, f.	hole, crack
	rīpa, rīpae, f.	bank (of a river)
	rīsī	see rīdeō
6	rogō, rogāre, rogāvī	ask, ask for
12	Rōma, Rōmae, f.	Rome
	Rōmae	in/at Rome
	Rōmānī, Rōmānōrum, m. pl.	Romans
4	Rōmānus, Rōmāna, Rōmānum	Roman
	rotundus, rotunda, rotundum	round, circular
	Rūfīna, Rūfīnae, f.	Rufina
	rūgōsus, rūgōsa, rūgōsum	wrinkly
	ruō, ruere, ruī	rush
	russeus, russea, russeum	red; red team
	rūsticus, rūstica, rūsticum	in the country

S

	Sabīna, Sabīnae, f.	Sabina
	saccus, saccī, m.	sack, bag
10	sacer, sacra, sacrum	sacred, holy

sacerdōs, sacerdōtis, *m.*	priest
sacrificium, sacrificiī, *n.*	sacrifice, offering
7 saepe	often
11 saevus, saeva, saevum	savage, cruel
saliō, salīre, saluī	jump
saltātrīx, saltātrīcis, *f.*	dancer
salūs, salūtis, *f.*	safety
2 salūtō, salūtāre, salūtāvī	greet
salvē! salvēte!	hello! hi!
sanguineus, sanguinea, sanguineum	bloody
9 sanguis, sanguinis, *m.*	blood
sapiēns, *gen.* sapientis	wise
sarcina, sarcinae, *f.*	bag
saxum, saxī, *n.*	rock
scaena, scaenae, *f.*	stage
scaenae frōns	stage building
scapha, scaphae, *f.*	small boat, skiff
scelestus, scelesta, scelestum	wicked
16 sciō, scīre, scīvī	know
scrībō, scrībere, scrīpsī	write
15 sē, suī	himself, herself, itself, themselves
secundus, secunda, secundum	second
sēcūrus, sēcūra, sēcūrum	safe
2 sed	but
6 sedeō, sedēre, sēdī	sit, sit down
sēdō, sēdāre, sēdāvī	settle, calm down
13 semper	always
3 senātor, senātōris, *m.*	senator
Seneca, Senecae, *m.*	Seneca
senectūs, senectūtis, *f.*	old age
8 senex, senis, *m.f.*	old person
16 sentiō, sentīre, sēnsī	feel, notice
Septimus, Septimī, *m.*	Septimus
septimus, septima, septimum	seventh
sepulcrum, sepulcrī, *n.*	tomb
12 servō, servāre, servāvī	save, protect, keep, look after
1 servus, servī, *m.*	slave, enslaved person (male)
sevēriter	severely
16 sī	if
sīc	so, in this way
Sicilia, Siciliae, *f.*	Sicily
sīcut	just as, like
signum, signī, *n.*	sign, signal
silentium, silentiī, *n.*	silence
7 silva, silvae, *f.*	wood, forest
simul	at the same time
simulācrum, simulācrī, *n.*	statue, image
15 simulatque	as soon as
16 sine + *abl.*	without
sine dubiō	without doubt
sīphō, sīphōnis, *m.*	fire engine, pump
Sīrēn, Sīrēnis, *f.*	Siren (mythical creature)
sōl, sōlis, *m.*	sun
soleō, solēre	am accustomed, used
sōlum	only
11 sōlus, sōla, sōlum	alone, only, lonely, on one's own
somnus, somnī, *m.*	sleep
sonor, sonōris, *m.*	shout, sound
sopōrō, sopōrāre, sopōrāvī	drug
sordidus, sordida, sordidum	dirty
soror, sorōris, *f.*	sister
spargō, spargere, sparsī	shower, spray
spectātor, spectātōris, *m.*	spectator
2 spectō, spectāre, spectāvī	look at, watch
spēs, speī, *f.*	hope
spīrō, spīrāre, spīrāvī	breathe
splendidus, splendida, splendidum	splendid, sumptuous
spōnsiō, spōnsiōnis, *f.*	bet
sporta, sportae, *f.*	basket
st!	hey!
9 statim	at once, immediately
statua, statuae, *f.*	statue
stercus, stercoris, *n.*	dung, muck
stetī	see stō
6 stō, stāre, stetī	stand
stola, stolae, *f.*	dress
strēnuē	strenuously, energetically, hard
12 stultus, stulta, stultum	stupid, foolish
10 sub + *acc.* or *abl.*	under, below, beneath
4 subitō	suddenly
Subūra, Subūrae, *f.*	the Subura
Subūrānus, Subūrāna, Subūrānum	from the Subura
Subūrānus, Subūrānī, *m.*	inhabitant of the Subura
subveniō, subvenīre, subvēnī + *dat.*	help

Sūleviae, Sūleviārum, *f. pl.*	Suleviae (Celtic goddesses)
Sūlis, Sūlis, *f.*	Sulis (local Celtic goddess)
sum, esse, fuī	I am, to be, I was
summus, summa, summum	highest, greatest, top (of)
sumus	we are
sunt	are, they are, there are
super + *acc.*	over
superō, superāre, superāvī	overcome, overpower
surgō, surgere, surrēxī	get up, stand up, rise
surrēxī	see surgō
sustulī	see tollō
susurrāns, *gen.* susurrantis	whispering
susurrō, susurrāre, susurrāvī	whisper
suus, sua, suum	her, his, its, their (own)

T

taberna, tabernae, *f.*	shop, inn
tabula, tabulae, *f.*	curse tablet
tabulātum, tabulātī, *n.*	floor, storey
taceō, tacēre, tacuī	am silent, am quiet
tacitē	quietly, silently
tam	so
tamen	however
tandem	at last, finally
tantum	only
tantus, tanta, tantum	so great, such a great, so much
Tarracōnēnsis, Tarracōnēnsis, Tarracōnēnse	of Tarraconensis
taurus, taurī, *m.*	bull
tēctum, tēctī, *n.*	roof
tēgula, tēgulae, *f.*	roof tile
tēlum, tēlī, *n.*	missile, weapon, spear
temperō, temperāre, temperāvī	control, restrain
tempestās, tempestātis, *f.*	storm
templum, templī, *n.*	temple
temptō, temptāre, temptāvī	try
tempus, temporis, *n.*	time
tenebrae, tenebrārum, *f. pl.*	darkness
teneō, tenēre, tenuī	hold, keep, possess
terra, terrae, *f.*	ground, land, country
orbis terrārum	world
terreō, terrēre, terruī	frighten
terribilis, terribilis, terribile	terrible
tertius, tertia, tertium	third
theātrum, theātrī, *n.*	theatre
Thellus, Thellī, *m.*	Thellus
thermae, thermārum, *f. pl.*	baths
Thisba, Thisbae, *f.*	Thisbe
tībīcen, tībīcinis, *m.*	pipe-player
timeō, timēre, timuī	fear, am afraid
Tīrō, Tīrōnis, *m.*	Tiro
tollō, tollere, sustulī	raise, lift up, hold up
tonō, tonāre, tonuī	thunder
torqueō, torquēre, torsī	torture
tōtus, tōta, tōtum	whole
trabs, trabis, *f.*	beam, timber
trādō, trādere, trādidī	hand over
trahō, trahere, trāxī	drag, draw, pull
trāns + *acc.*	across
trānseō, trānsīre, trānsiī	go across
trāxī	see trahō
trēs, trēs, tria	three
tribūnus, tribūnī, *m.*	tribune (officer in the army)
trīclīnium, trīclīniī, *n.*	dining room
Trinobantēs, Trinobantum, *m. pl.*	Trinobantes
trīste	sadly
trīstis, trīstis, trīste	sad
tū, tuī	you (s.)
tuba, tubae, *f.*	trumpet
tulī	see ferō
tum	then
tunica, tunicae, *f.*	tunic
turba, turbae, *f.*	crowd
tūs, tūris, *n.*	frankincense
tūtus, tūta, tūtum	safe
tuus, tua, tuum	your (s.), yours

U

ubi	where? where; when
ubīque	everywhere
ulterior, ulterior, ulterius	further, more distant
umbra, umbrae, *f.*	shade, ghost
ūnā	together
unda, undae, *f.*	wave
unde	from where
ūnus, ūna, ūnum	one
urbs, urbis, *f.*	city
uxor, uxōris, *f.*	wife

V

vae!	woe!
vah!	ha! huh!
valdē	very, very much
valē! valēte!	goodbye! farewell!
validus, valida, validum	strong
vallis, vallis, *f.*	valley
vehementer	loudly, powerfully, forcefully
vēnābulum, vēnābulī, *n.*	hunting spear
vēnātiō, vēnātiōnis, *f.*	hunt
vēndō, vēndere, vēndidī	sell
veniō, venīre, vēnī	come
ventus, ventī, *m.*	wind
verberō, verberāre, verberāvī	hit, beat
verbum, verbī, *n.*	word
vērō	indeed, truly, certainly
ita vērō	yes, absolutely
vertō, vertere, vertī	turn
vērum?	really?
vērum, vērī, *n.*	truth
vesper, vesperī, *m.*	evening
Vesta, Vestae, *f.*	Vesta (goddess of fire and the hearth)
Vestālia, Vestālium, *n. pl.*	Vestalia (festival in honour of Vesta)
Vestālis, Vestālis, Vestāle	Vestal, of Vesta
vester, vestra, vestrum	your (pl.), yours
vestīmenta, vestīmentōrum, *n. pl.*	clothes
veterānus, veterānī, *m.*	veteran, retired soldier
vetus, *gen.* veteris	old
via, viae, *f.*	street, road, way
vīcī	see vincō
victōria, victōriae, *f.*	victory
vīcus, vīcī, *m.*	settlement
videō, vidēre, vīdī	see
vigil, vigilis, *m.*	fireman
vīlla, vīllae, *f.*	country house, house
vīmineus, vīminea, vīmineum	made of wicker
vincō, vincere, vīcī	win, am victorious; conquer
vīnum, vīnī, *n.*	wine
violenter	violently
violentia, violentiae, *f.*	violence
violō, violāre, violāvī	dishonour, violate
vir, virī, *m.*	man
virgō, virginis, *f.*	virgin, girl, young woman
viridis, viridis, viride	green
virtūs, virtūtis, *f.*	courage; virtue
vīs, vim, *f.*	force
vīs	see volō
vīsitō, vīsitāre, vīsitāvī	visit
vīta, vītae, *f.*	life
vītō, vītāre, vītāvī	avoid
vituperō, vituperāre, vituperāvī	criticize, complain about
vīvō, vīvere, vīxī	live, am alive
vīvus, vīva, vīvum	alive, living
vix	scarcely, hardly, with difficulty
vīxī	see vīvō
vōbīs	to/for you (pl.)
vocō, vocāre, vocāvī	call
volitō, volitāre, volitāvī	fly
volō, velle, voluī	want, wish, am willing
vōs, vestrum	you (pl.)
vōtum, vōtī, *n.*	prayer
vōx, vōcis, *f.*	voice; shout
vulnerō, vulnerāre, vulnerāvī	wound, injure
vulnus, vulneris, *n.*	wound
vult	see volō
vultus, vultūs, *m.*	expression; face

ANCIENT AUTHORS

Apicius: (fourth century AD) is the name traditionally given to the author of a collection of recipes, *de Re Coquinaria* (*On the Art of Cooking*). Marcus Gavius Apicius was a gourmet who lived in the early first century AD and wrote about sauces. Seneca says that he claimed to have created a *scientia popīnae* (snack bar cuisine).

Appian: Appianos (late first century AD–AD 160s) was born in Alexandria, in Egypt, and practised as a lawyer in Rome. His history of Rome is written in Greek.

Apuleius: Lucius Apuleius (*C.*AD 155) was born in Africa and lived in Carthage. He was the author of the *Metamorphoses*, also known as *The Golden Ass*, a novel about the adventures of a young man who is turned into an ass. He gave lectures on philosophy and a collection of excerpts from these survives, called *Florida* (*Anthology*).

Augustus: Augustus (63 BC–AD 14) was born Gaius Octavius, and became Gaius Iulius Caesar Octavianus when he was adopted by his great-uncle, Julius Caesar. He was known by the title Augustus after 27 BC when he became Rome's first emperor. The *Res Gestae Divi Augusti* (*Deeds of the Divine Augustus*) is an account of the career of Augustus written in the first person. Augustus left the document with his will, with instructions to the Senate to set up the text as an inscription. It was engraved on a pair of bronze pillars in front of Augustus' tomb in the Campus Martius. The original has not survived, but copies were carved in stone on monuments and temples all over the Roman Empire, and parts of these have survived.

Aulus Gellius: Aulus Gellius (*C.*AD 130–180) lived in Rome and Athens, although his birthplace is unknown. His *Attic Nights* is a collection of essays on a variety of topics, based on his reading of Greek and Roman writers and the lectures and conversations he had heard. The title *Attic Nights* refers to Attica, the district in Greece around Athens, where Gellius was living when he wrote the book.

Cassius Dio (also Dio Cassius): Cassius Dio Cocceianus (*C.*AD 150–235) was born in Bithynia. He had a political career as a consul in Rome and governor of the provinces of Africa and Dalmatia. His history of Rome, written in Greek, covers the period from Aeneas' arrival in Italy to AD 229.

Cato: Marcus Porcius Cato (234–139 BC) was born at Tusculum, a town about 16 miles from Rome. He had a distinguished military and political career, reaching the consulship and the office of censor, despite not being born into a senatorial family. He wrote a book on farming, *de Agri Cultura* (*On Agriculture*). Cato was famous for his strictness and his criticism of contemporary morality. He wanted to return to the old Roman values of frugality and simplicity.

Catullus: Gaius Valerius Catullus (*c.*84–54 BC) was born in Verona, in northern Italy, in a wealthy family. Very little is known about his life. He came to Rome as a young man and spent some time in the province of Bithynia on the staff of the governor. He is best known for his love poems.

Cicero: Marcus Tullius Cicero (106–43 BC) was a politician and lawyer, who was a leading figure in events at the end of the Roman Republic. He was born in a town not far from Rome and came to Rome to study. Although not born into the senatorial class, he reached the highest office of state, the consulship. He was executed on the orders of Mark Antony during the unrest following the assassination of Julius Caesar in 44 BC. His surviving writings include speeches for the law courts, political speeches, philosophical essays, and personal letters to friends and family.

Columella: Lucius Iunius Moderatus Columella (wrote *C.*AD 60–65) was born at Gades (modern Cadiz) in Spain and served in the Roman army in Syria. He wrote a treatise on farming, *de Re Rustica* (*On Farming*).

Diodorus Siculus: Diodorus (wrote *c.*60–30 BC) was a Greek from Sicily who wrote a history of the world centred on Rome, from legendary beginnings to 54 BC. Much of the original forty books survives only in fragments. He wrote in Greek.

Dionysius of Halicarnassus: Dionysius (*c.*60 BC–some time after 7 BC) was a Greek historian from Halicarnassus in Asia Minor (modern Bodrum in Turkey). He lived in Rome for many years from about 30 BC. His history of Rome, *Roman Antiquities*, is written in Greek. It started with Rome's legendary beginnings and went up to 264 BC, the First Punic War. Much of it is lost, and the surviving part finishes in 441 BC.

Frontinus: Sextus Iulius Frontinus (*C.*AD 30–104) had a distinguished career as consul and governor of Britain. After becoming supervisor of the water supply (*cūrātor aquārum*) in Rome in AD 97, he wrote an account of the city's aqueducts and water supply, *On the Waters of Rome*, as a handbook for his successors.

Horace: Quintus Horatius Flaccus (65–8 BC) was born in Apulia, in the south of Italy. He was of humble origins, the son of a freedman who worked as a collector of payments at auctions. His father sent him to Rome and Athens to be educated, and he became one of the most celebrated poets of his day. Maecenas, the friend and adviser of Emperor Augustus, was his patron. His most famous works are the *Odes*, short poems on a variety of subjects, but he also wrote *Epodes*, *Satires*, and *Epistles*.

Julius Caesar: Gaius Iulius Caesar (100–44 BC), the general, politician, and dictator, belonged to an aristocratic Roman family. He was assassinated on the Ides (15th) of March 44 BC, by a group of senators who feared that he intended to put an end to the republican system of government and keep supreme power for himself and his family. Caesar wrote an account of his campaigns in Gaul and Britain (58–52 BC), the *Commentaries* (also known as the *Gallic Wars*). They are written in the third person, as if to give an objective account of events.

Juvenal: Decius Iunius Iuvenalis (early second century AD) was born in a town in Italy, but lived in Rome. He was the author of sixteen *Satires*, long poems criticizing and attacking the vices of his fellow Romans. The *Satires* have a bitter humour and pessimistic attitude, and there is much exaggeration. Nevertheless, Juvenal sheds light on contemporary Roman society and provides lots of detail about everyday life.

Livy: Titus Livius (59 BC–AD 17) was born at Patavium (modern Padua) in north-east Italy. Little is known about his life, but he probably came to Rome as an adult. He wrote *A History of Rome*, starting with its foundation and going up to his own lifetime. Originally there were 142 books, of which about twenty-five have survived.

Martial: Marcus Valerius Martialis (C.AD 40–C.AD 96) was born in Spain, and came to live in Rome in about AD 64. He is best known for his short poems, known as *Epigrams*, which often criticize and mock the faults and vices of his fellow Romans.

Minucius: Marcus Minucius Felix (early third century AD) was a Christian who wrote a defence of Christianity, *Octavius*, in the form of a discussion between two Christian converts, Minucius and Octavius, and Caecilius, a pagan. Minucius defends Christianity against the criticisms of Caecilius, and at the end Caecilius is converted.

Ovid: Publius Ovidius Naso (43 BC–AD 17) was born in a town near Rome and educated in the city. He abandoned a public career to become a poet. Emperor Augustus banished him to Tomi on the Black Sea (in modern Romania). According to Ovid, there were two reasons for his exile, **carmen** (a poem) and **error** (a mistake). The poem was *Ars Amatoria* (*The Art of Love*), advice on how to conduct a love affair, which fell foul of laws introduced by Augustus to improve the morals of contemporary society. The mistake was probably connected to the love affairs of Augustus' granddaughter, Julia. Among his works are love poems such as the *Amores* (*Loves*) and a long epic poem, *The Metamorphoses*, which is a collection of stories from mythology, bound together by the theme of transformation.

Petronius: Petronius Arbiter (died AD 65) was a provincial governor and consul. He then became Emperor Nero's **arbiter ēlegentiae** (arbiter of taste), a play on his name; this meant he advised Nero on what was tasteful or elegant. He was falsely accused of being involved in a plot to kill Nero, and committed suicide. Petronius was the author of the *Satyricon*, a novel about the adventures of three young men travelling in southern Italy. The main episode is the **cēna Trimalchiōnis** (*Trimalchio's Dinner Party*). Trimalchio is a wealthy freedman to whose dinner party the three main characters are invited. Petronius mocks and grotesquely exaggerates the vulgar extravagance and bad taste of Trimalchio, and his ostentatious display of wealth.

Plautus: Titus Maccius Plautus (C.250–184 BC) wrote comedies which were based on Greek originals, adapted for a Roman audience, but set in Greece.

Pliny the Elder: Gaius Plinius Secundus (AD 23/24–79) was born at Comum (modern Como) in northern Italy. He is known as Pliny the Elder to distinguish him from his nephew, known as Pliny the Younger. He had a career in military and government service, serving as procurator in several provinces before his final post as commander of the fleet at Misenum in Italy. He dedicated his spare time to research and writing, and among his many learned works is his *Natural History*, an encyclopaedic collection of facts and stories about a huge variety of subjects. It is a very useful source of information on many aspects of Roman life. In *Suburani* 'Pliny' refers to Pliny the Younger.

Pliny the Younger: Gaius Caecilius Plinius Secundus (AD 61/62–113) was the nephew of Pliny the Elder. He was born at Comum (Como) in northern Italy. He had a successful career as a lawyer, politician, and administrator, and his final post was as governor of the province of Bithynia. His letters to friends, family, and colleagues include an exchange with Emperor Trajan when he was governor of Bithynia. The letters offer a fascinating glimpse into the lives, attitudes, and politics of the society of his time. Pliny wrote with the intention of publishing his letters, and at regular intervals during his lifetime he published collections of them. Although they are real personal letters, many of them resemble short essays on various themes. In *Suburani* 'Pliny' refers to Pliny the Younger.

Plutarch: Ploutarchos (c. AD 46–120) was a Greek biographer, historian, and philosopher. He took the name Lucius Mercius Plutarchus when he became a Roman citizen. Plutarch visited Rome, where he taught and gave lectures, but spent most of his life in his native Greece. Among his many works are biographies of famous Greek and Roman politicians and soldiers, the *Parallel Lives*, so called because they are arranged in pairs of Greek and Roman so that the subjects can be compared. He also wrote biographies of the Roman emperors. His biographies of Galba and Otho survive in full, and there are fragments of his lives of Tiberius and Nero.

Propertius: Sextus Propertius (c. 50 BC–after 16 BC) was born at Assisium (modern Assisi) in central Italy, and educated at Rome. He wrote poems known as *Elegies*, many of them love poems.

Seneca: Lucius Annaeus Seneca (c. 4 BC–AD 65) is sometimes known as Seneca the Younger to distinguish him from his father of the same name, who was also a writer. He was born in Cordoba, in Spain, and came to Rome to be educated. He was Nero's tutor and, when Nero became emperor, Seneca became his political adviser. In AD 65, after he had retired from public life, he was implicated in a conspiracy to overthrow Nero and was forced to commit suicide. Seneca was a philosopher, politician, and dramatist. Among his many writings are several works of moral philosophy which contain interesting details about life in Rome in the first century AD. Some of these are in the form of letters to friends and family, including one to his mother, Helvia.

Servius: Marius Servius Honoratus (early fifth century AD) wrote commentaries on Latin literature.

Strabo: Strabo (64 BC–after AD 24) was a Greek from Pontus who came to Rome in 44 BC to finish his education, then visited the city several times afterwards. His *Geography*, written in Greek, is a description of the main countries in the Roman world, including physical geography, history, and economic development. There is also much incidental detail about customs, animals, and plants.

Suetonius: Gaius Suetonius Tranquillus (born c. 70 AD) was a secretary at the imperial palace. He wrote biographies of Julius Caesar and the first eleven emperors, *Lives of the Caesars*. Although his position gave him access to the state archives, he is not very reliable in his use of sources, and his work relies heavily on uncritical reporting of gossip and anecdote. His other works include lives of teachers of literature and rhetoric, *On the Grammarians* and *On Rhetoricians*; only parts of these have survived.

Tacitus: Publius (or Gaius) Cornelius Tacitus (AD 56/57–after 117) may have been born in Gallia Narbonensis. He had a successful political career in Rome and wrote two major works of history. *Annals* covered the period AD 14–68, from the death of Augustus to the death Nero, and *Histories* continued with the years AD 69–96. Only parts of these works survive. He also wrote a biography of his father-in-law Agricola, the general and governor of Britain. Tacitus used as his sources the writings of earlier historians, official records, and his own experience. Tacitus was a supporter of the republican system of government and a harsh critic of the emperors and the imperial system. He claims to write without prejudice, but his bias is often evident.

Varro: Marcus Terentius Varro (115–27 BC) was born near Rome in Sabine territory. Among his many literary works, only *de Re Rustica* (*On Farming*) survives in complete form. About half of *de Lingua Latina* (*On the Latin Language*) also survives.

Vergil (also Virgil): Publius Vergilius Maro (70–19 BC) was born at Mantua in Cisalpine Gaul and educated at Cremona, Mediolanum (modern Milan), and Rome. Maecenas, the friend and adviser of Emperor Augustus, was his patron, and he became the most celebrated poet of his day. His greatest work is the *Aeneid*, an epic poem which tells the story of the founding of the Roman race by the Trojan hero Aeneas. The poem is a celebration of the origin and growth of the Roman Empire and of the achievements of Augustus. Vergil also wrote the *Eclogues*, pastoral poems about the life of shepherds, and the *Georgics*, a poem about farming.

Vitruvius: Vitruvius Pollio (first century BC), an engineer and architect, wrote *On Architecture*.

TIMELINE

Ruler of Rome	Events in Roman history	Events in the rest of the world
Romulus (753–715 BC)	753 BC Traditional date of the foundation of Rome. According to legend, Romulus was the first ruler of Rome.	776 BC First Olympic Games, in Olympia, Greece.
King Numa Pompilius (715–673 BC)	753-509 BC Rome was ruled by seven legendary kings.	
King Tullus Hostilius (673–642 BC)		660 BC According to legend, Jimmu becomes the first emperor of Japan.
King Ancus Marcius (642–616 BC)		
King Lucius Tarquinius Priscus (616–579 BC)	c.600 BC Construction of the Cloaca Maxima in Rome.	563 BC Buddha, the religious leader, is born.
King Servius Tullius (579–534 BC)		551–479 BC Confucius, Chinese philosopher.
King Lucius Tarquinius Superbus (534–509 BC)	509 BC King Lucius Tarquinius Superbus (Tarquin the Proud) is expelled and the Roman Republic established.	550 BC Foundation of the Achaemenid (First Persian) Empire by Cyrus the Great.
Roman Republic (509–27 BC)		508 BC Democracy is instituted at Athens.
		480 BC Persians, led by Xerxes, invade Greece; Persians are defeated at Battle of Salamis.
	387 BC Gauls capture Rome.	c.460–370 BC Hippocrates, Greek doctor.
	334–264 BC Rome expands to control Italy.	331 BC Alexander the Great founds Alexandria, in Egypt.
	264–241 BC First Punic War, Rome against Carthage.	323 BC Death of Alexander the Great, at Babylon.
	218–201 BC Hannibal crosses Alps, invading Italy; Second Punic War.	c.300 BC Euclid, Greek mathematician.
	202 BC Scipio Africanus defeats Hannibal at Battle of Zama.	c.285–246 BC The Library at Alexandria, in Egypt, is founded.
	149–146 BC Third Punic War; Rome defeats Carthage; Africa becomes a province of the Roman Empire.	261 BC Kalinga War between the Mauryan Empire and the state of Kalinga, in India.
	135–132 BC First Slave War, in Sicily.	221–206 BC King Zheng unifies China as the first emperor of the Qin dynasty.
	104–100 BC Second Slave War, in Sicily.	206 BC–AD 220 Han dynasty in China.
	73–71 BC Third Slave War, in mainland Italy, led by Spartacus.	179 BC The earliest evidence for papermaking, in China.
	67 BC Pompey's campaign against the pirates.	69–30 BC Cleopatra VIII, the last Ptolemaic ruler of Egypt.
	55–54 BC Julius Caesar's two expeditions to Britain.	c.57 BC Three Kingdoms period begins in Korea.
	52 BC Vercingetorix leads Gallic revolt against Rome; Battle of Alesia.	
	44 BC Assassination of Julius Caesar.	
	31 BC Battle of Actium; Octavian (later Augustus) defeats Mark Antony.	30 BC Egypt becomes part of the Roman Empire.
Emperor Augustus (27 BC–AD 14)	27 BC Augustus becomes sole ruler of the Roman Empire: Rome's first emperor.	
	25 BC Baths of Agrippa, in Rome, are completed.	
	19 BC Aqua Virgo completed.	
	9 BC Consecration of the Ara Pacis.	
	2 BC Julia, daughter of Augustus, exiled.	
	AD 14 Pantheon is built on Field of Mars, in Rome.	c.AD 10–70 Hero of Alexandria, inventor of the fire engine.
Emperor Tiberius (AD 14–37)		
	c.AD 30 Crucifixion of Jesus.	
Emperor Gaius (Caligula) (AD 37–41)		
Emperor Claudius (AD 41–54)	AD 43 Emperor Claudius invades Britain.	
	AD 52 Aqua Claudia completed.	
Emperor Nero (AD 54–68)	AD 54 Nero becomes emperor at the age of 16.	
	AD 58–68 Otho governor of Lusitania.	
	AD 60 Boudica's revolt in Britannia; Londinium destroyed by fire.	
	AD 64 Great Fire of Rome.	
	AD 66–73 The Jewish population of Judaea revolts against Roman rule.	c.AD 68 The Dead Sea scrolls are hidden in caves, to save them from the Romans.
Emperors Galba, Otho, Vitellius, and Vespasian (AD 68–69)	AD 69 Year of the Four Emperors.	
	AD 70 Destruction of the Temple in Jerusalem.	

Timeline

Emperor Vespasian (AD 69–79)
Emperor Titus (AD 79–81)
Emperor Domitian (AD 81–96)
Emperor Nerva (AD 96–98)
Emperor Trajan (AD 98–117)
Emperor Hadrian (AD 117–138)

Western Empire (AD 395–476)
Eastern (Byzantine) Empire (AD 395–1453)

AD 73–74 The last of the Jewish rebels are besieged by the Romans in the fortress of Masada.

AD 79 Volcano Vesuvius erupts, destroying Pompeii and nearby towns.
AD 80 The Colosseum is completed in Rome.

AD 100 Londinium replaces Camulodunum as capital of Britannia.

AD 113 Trajan's column, celebrating Roman victory over the Dacians.

AD 122 Emperor Hadrian visits Britannia and orders construction of a wall: Hadrian's Wall.

AD 127 Kanishka becomes king of the Kushan Empire of Afghanistan and northern India.

AD 161–180 Emperor Marcus Aurelius.

AD 166 First recorded Roman envoy arrives in China.

AD 224 The Parthian Empire falls and is succeeded by the Sasanian Empire, in modern Iran.

AD 306–337 Emperor Constantine.
AD 313 All religions, including Christianity, tolerated in the Empire.
AD 324 Byzantium (modern Istanbul) becomes capital of the Empire.
AD 330 Byzantium renamed Constantinople.
AD 380 Christianity becomes the official religion of the Empire.
AD 395 The Roman Empire splits into two empires.
AD 408 Visigoths besiege Rome, the capital of the Western Empire.
AD 410 Visigoths sack Rome.
AD 410 Traditional date for the end of Roman rule in Britain.
AD 455 Vandals sack Rome.
AD 476 Fall of the Western Roman Empire. The Eastern Empire (renamed the Byzantium Empire) survives, with its capital at Constantinople.

c.AD 360–415 Hypatia, female philosopher and mathematician, in Alexandria, in Egypt.

AD 570 The prophet Muhammad is born.
AD 581–618 Sui dynasty in China.
AD 619–907 Tang dynasty in China.
AD 632 Abu Bakr succeeds Muhammad as leader of the Muslim community.

AD 610–641 Byzantine Empire's official language changes to Greek.

AD 674–678 First Arab siege of Constantinople is unsuccessful.

AD 717–718 Second Arab attack on Constantinople, ending in failure.

AD 681 The Bulgarian Empire is established.
AD 750 The Abbasid Caliphate begins its rule in what is now Iraq.
c.AD 780–850 al-Khwarizmi, Persian mathematician.
AD 800 Charlemagne is crowned Holy Roman Emperor.

AD 827–902 Arab conquest of Sicily and parts of southern Italy.
AD 866 Viking army arrives in England.
AD 868 First known printed book, in China.
AD 886 Alfred the Great becomes the first king of England.
AD 904 Gunpowder first used in warfare, in China.

AD 1037 The Great Seljuk Empire is founded in what is now Kazakhstan.
AD 1066 William the Conqueror, Duke of Normandy, invades England and becomes king.

AD 1054 the Christian Church breaks up into two parts, the Western section (Roman Catholic) and the eastern section (Greek Orthodox).
AD 1096–1099 The First Crusade.

c.AD 1150 City of Angkor and temple of Angkor Wat created by the Khmer dynasty in Southeast Asia.
AD 1206 Genghis Khan is elected as Khagan of the Mongols and the Mongol Empire is established.
AD 1215 Magna Carta.
c.AD 1271–1275 Marco Polo travels to China.
c.AD 1299 The Ottoman Empire is founded by Osman I.
c.AD 1325 Aztecs found Tenochtitlan (now Mexico City).
AD 1347 The Black Death ravages Europe for the first time.
AD 1415 Portugal captures Ceuta, in North Africa.
AD 1431 Trial and execution of Joan of Arc.
c.AD 1440 Gutenberg printing press invented.
AD 1485 Henry Tudor becomes King of England.
AD 1452–1519 Leonardo da Vinci.
AD 1492 Christopher Columbus reaches the New World.

AD 1453 The Ottomans capture Constantinople. Fall of the Byzantine Empire.

ACKNOWLEDGEMENTS

Thanks are due to the following for permission to reproduce images:

p.12, Street in Ostia, Alamy, Su concessione del Ministero per i Beni e le Attività Culturali e per il turismo-Parco Archeologico di Ostia Antica; p.13, Street in Ostia, Alamy, Su concessione del Ministero per i Beni e le Attività Culturali e per il turismo-Parco Archeologico di Ostia Antica; p.13, Naples Street, Mstyslav Chernov (commons.wikimedia.org/wiki/File:Streets_of_Naples_(Napoli)._Naples,_Campania,_Italy,_South_Europe-2.jpg), (CC BY-SA 3.0); p.14, Forum of Augustus, Alamy; p.15, Bust of Seneca, 00101888 bpk Berlin / Antikensammlung, SMB / CoDArchLab; p.16, Roman roof tiles, © Corinium Museum, Cirencester; p.18, Oil lamp, The Metropolitan Museum of Art, New York; p.19, Inside the Capitoline Insula, Alamy, Su concessione della Sovrintendenza Capitolina ai Beni Culturali – AFMonAS; p.19, Water fountain in Pompeii, Alamy, Su concessione del Ministero per i Beni e le Attività Culturali e per il turismo-Parco Archeologico di Pompei; p.19, Pot de chambre, n° inv. RHO.2007.6.315, Musée départemental Arles antique © L. Béteille; p.20, Sign from Herculaneum, Alamy, Su concessione del Ministero per i Beni e le Attività Culturali e per il turismo-Parco Archeologico di Ercolano; p.21, Popina in Pompeii, Alamy, Su concessione del Ministero per i Beni e le Attività Culturali e per il turismo-Parco Archeologico di Pompei; p.21, Fresco from a popina in Pompeii, Alamy, Su concessione del Ministero per i Beni e le Attività Culturali e per il turismo-Parco Archeologico di Pompei; p.22, Gold coin of Nero, The Metropolitan Museum of Art, New York; p.26, Via Appia, Alamy; p.26, Museo dell'Ara Pacis, Alamy, © Roma, Sovrintendenze Capitolina ai Beni Culturali; p.26, Aqueduct, Alamy; p.26, Obelisk, Adam Gage (commons.wikimedia.org/wiki/File:SolareObelisk.jpg), Su concessione del Ministero per i Beni e le Attività Culturali e per i Turismo - Soprintendenza Speciale Archeologia Belle Arti e Paesaggio di Roma; p.26, Coin with Arch of Claudius, Classical Numismatic Group, LLC (www.cngcoins.com/); p.27, House of Romulus, Su concessione del Ministero per i beni e le attività culturali e per il turismo–Parco Archeologico del Colosseo; p.28, Cloaca Maxima, Alamy, Su concessione della Sovrintendenza Capitolina ai Beni Culturali – AFMonAS; p.29, Piazza delle Erbe, Mantova, Alamy; p.31, Basilica Aemilia, Alamy; p.32, Foundations of Basilica Julia, Alamy; p.32, Temple of Concordia, Alamy; p.32, Shrine of Vesta, Alamy; p.33, Curia, Alamy; p.34, Coin of Forum Romanum, Alamy; p.35, Cup with hunting dog, © Corinium Museum, Cirencester; p.37, Fragments of Forma Urbis, Roma, Musei Capitolini, Antiquarium © Roma, Sovrintendenze Capitolina ai Beni Culturali; p.38, Altar of Mars and Venus, (commons.wikimedia.org/wiki/File:Altar_Mars_Venus_Massimo.jpg), su concessione del Ministero per i beni e le attività culturali e per il turismo–Museo Nazionale Romano; p.44, Section of the Fasti Praenestini, Alamy, su concessione del Ministero per i beni e le attività culturali e per il turismo–Museo Nazionale Romano; p.45, Relief of a sacrifice, Roma Musei Capitolini, Alamy, © Roma, Sovrintendenze Capitolina ai Beni Culturali; p.47, Mosaïque des jeux du cirque, Collection de Lugdunum, musée & théâtres romains, num. inv. : 2000.0.1209, ©photo : Jean-Michele Deguele, Christian Thioc; p.52, Mosaic of four charioteers, Alamy, su concessione del Ministero per i beni e le attività culturali e per il turismo-Museo Nazionale Romano; p.53, Terracotta plaque with a chariot-racing scene 00034483001 © The Trustees of the British Museum. All rights reserved.; p.54, Drain showing SPQR, Alamy; p.55, Lararium in the House of Vettii, Alamy, Su concessione del Ministero per i beni e le Attività Culturali e per il turismo-Parco Archeologico di Pompei; p.59, Augustus Pontifex Maximus, Alamy, su concessione del Ministero per i beni e le attività culturali e per il turismo-Museo Nazionale Romano; p.63, Maison Carrée, Danichou (commons.wikimedia.org/wiki/File:MaisonCarrée .jpeg); p.65, Rilievo con Enea che sacrifica (frammento dell'Ara Pacis), Galleria delle Statue e delle Pitture degli Uffizi, Inv. Sculture n. 342., Alamy, Su concessione del Ministero per i Beni e le Attività Culturali e per il Turismo; p.65, Temple of Apollo, Alamy, Su concessione del Ministero per i Beni e le Attività Culturali e per il turismo-Parco Archeologico di Pompei; p.66, Relief from Ara Pacis, Roma Museo dell'Ara Pacis, Alamy, © Roma, Sovrintendenze Capitolina ai Beni Culturali; p.67, Relief from Ara Pacis, Roma Museo dell'Ara Pacis, Alamy, © Roma, Sovrintendenze Capitolina ai Beni Culturali; p.68, Statuette of Lar, The Metropolitan Museum of Art, New York; p.68, Votive pregnant female, Science Museum, London. CC BY 4.0; p.69, Lararium, House of the Amorini Dorati, Alamy, Su concessione del Ministero per i Beni e le Attività Culturali e per il turismo-Parco Archeologico di Pompei; p.70, Incarnation of Vishnu as Matsya, © Ann & Bury Peerless Picture Library / Bridgeman Images; p.70, Flood of Earth, etching, Wellcome Collection, London, CC BY 4.0; p.71, Mosaic of sandals, G. Dagli Orti /De Agostini Picture Library / Bridgeman Images; p.72, Public fountain, Alamy, Su concessione del Ministero per i Beni e le Attività Culturali e per il turismo-Parco Archeologico di Pompei; p.77, Statue of a boxer, Alamy, su concessione del Ministero per i beni e le attività culturali e per il turismo-Museo Nazionale Romano; p.79, Bronze strigil, The Metropolitan Museum of Art, New York; p.80, Xylospongium, D. Herdemerten (Hannibal21) (commons.wikimedia.org/wiki/File:Xylospongium, (CC BY 3.0); p.81, The Great Bath, Bath, Alamy; p.81, Public latrine, Alamy, Su concessione del Ministero per i Beni e le Attività Culturali e per il turismo-Parco Archeologico di Pompei; p.82, Lead water pipe, Roman, Science Museum, London. CC BY 4.0; p.83, Aqua Claudia, Chris 73 (commons.wikimedia.org/wiki/File:Aqua_Claudia_01.jpg), (CC BY-SA 3.0); p.84, Wall painting of Fullers, Alamy, su concessione del Ministero per i Beni e le Attività Culturali e per il Turismo-Museo Archeologico Nazionale di Napoli; p.85, Hypocaust, Vieux-la-Romaine, musée et sites archéologiques – Département du Calvados (commons.wikimedia.org/wiki/File:Vieux_la_Romaine_Villa_hypocauste.jpg), (CC BY-SA 3.0); p.86, Brennus and the Romans, Alamy; p.87, Prisoners of war on the Trophy of Augustus, Alamy; p.94, Dougga banquet, Dennis Jarvis, CC BY-SA 2.0; p.97, Coin with head of Otho, Classical Numismatic Group, LLC (www.cngcoins.com/); p.98, Relief of collared slaves, Bridgeman Images; p.99, Slave collar, Terme di Diocleziano, su concessione del Ministero per i beni e le attività culturali e per il turismo-Museo Nazionale Romano; p.102, The "Bull-Leaping Fresco", Alamy, AMH T14 Archaeological Museum of Heraklion-Hellenic Ministry of Culture and Sports-Archaeological Resources Fund; p.102, Minotaur sculpture NAM Γ 1664α, Alamy, The rights on the depicted monument belong to the Hellenic Ministry of Culture and Sports (Law 3028/2002). The monument belongs to the responsibility of the National Archaeological Museum. Hellenic Ministry of Culture and Sports/ Archaeological Resources Fund; p.102, Attic amphora with Theseus, Digital image courtesy of the Getty's Open Content Program; p.108, Iron Age Roundhouse, Pembrokeshire, Wales, Alamy; p.109, Roman Wall, London, Alamy; p.109, Map of London © OpenStreetMap contributors, openstreetmap.org (CC BY-SA); p.110, Iron stamp © Museum of London; p.110, Pegasus intaglio © Museum of London; p.110, Leather shoe © Museum of London; p.110, Glass bead © Andy Chopping/MOLA; p.110, Bloomberg tablet with copper © Andy Chopping/MOLA; p.111, Brooch with dog © Museum of London; p.112, Mosaic from Villa Romana del Casale, Alamy, su concessione del Dipartimento dei Beni Culturali e dell'Indentità Siciliana; p.113, Amphorae, Bodrum, Alamy; p.114, Writing-tablet 00015223001, Vindolanda © The Trustees of the British Museum. All rights reserved.; p.114, Terracotta cup, The Metropolitan Museum of Art, New York; p.116, Soay sheep, Alamy; p.117, Mosaic of man with dogs, Conimbriga, Arquivo DGPC/MMC-MN; p.119, Aerial image of Maiden Castle, Dorset, Alamy; p.123, Wittenham sword, Bridgeman Images; p.125, The Great Torc from Snettisham 00033809001 © The Trustees of the British Museum. All rights reserved.; p.128, Tombstone of Longinus Sdapeze, Alamy, Colchester Museum; p.131, Skull and crown of the 'Deal Warrior' 00032863001 © The Trustees of the British Museum. All rights reserved.; p.133, Hadrian's Wall, Steven Fruitsmaak (commons.wikimedia.org/wiki/File:Hadrian's_Wall_west_of_Housesteads_3.jpg); p.134, Terracotta neck-amphora, The Metropolitan Museum of Art, New York; p.134, Achilles and Penthesilea, 1801, Thorvaldsens Museum, www.thorvaldsensmuseum.dk; p.135, Statue of Boudica, London, Alamy; p.143, Roman legion formation, Neil and Kathy Carey, CC BY-SA 2.0; p.145, Fenwick treasure, Colchester Castle; p.147, Military diploma, The Metropolitan Museum of Art, New York; p.150, Statue of Vercingetorix, France, Alamy; p.154, The Great Bath, Bath, Alamy; p.155, Patera, Bath & North East Somerset Council; p.156, Head of Sulis Minerva, Bath & North East Somerset Council; p.156, The temple of Jupiter in Damascus, Ai@ce (commons.wikimedia.org/wiki/File:The_Jupiter_temple_in_Damascus.jpg), (CC BY 2.0); p.158, Curse tablet with Vilbia, Bath & North East Somerset Council; p.163, Section from Trajan's Column, Alamy; p.163, Section from Trajan's Column, Alamy; p.163, Ivory die, The Metropolitan Museum of Art, New York; p.163, Ivory die, The Metropolitan Museum of Art, New York; p.163, Glass die, The Metropolitan Museum of Art, New York; p.163, Writing-tablet, 00033850001 © The Trustees of the British Museum. All rights reserved.; p.164, Curse tablet in Brittonic, Bath & North East Somerset Council; p.164, Tombstone of Regina, © Tyne & Wear Archives & Museums / Bridgeman Images; p.165, Temple pediment, Bath & North East Somerset Council; p.166, Kylix with Gorgon, The Metropolitan Museum of Art, New York; p.166, Statue of Perseus, The Metropolitan Museum of Art, New York; p.166, Terracotta lekythos, The Metropolitan Museum of Art, New York; p.169, Mosaic of Oceanus, Cordoba, Alamy; p.169, Statue de Neptune, marbre blanc et gris, 3e quart IIe siècle ap. J.-C.-3e quart IIIe siècle ap. J.-C., n° inv. RHO.2007.05.1966, Musée départemental Arles antique © R. Bénali; p.172, Scuba diver, Alamy; p.172, Barge, bois, tissu, poix, métal, Ier s. apr. J.-C., n° inv. RHO.2004.AR3.1, Musée départemental Arles antique © R. Bénali; p.173, Map of the world according to Strabo, Alamy; p.175, Mosaic of sea creatures, Alamy, su concessione del Ministero per i Beni e le Attività Culturali e per il Turismo-Museo Archeologico Nazionale di Napoli; p.176, Mosaic from Villa Romana del Casale, Alamy, su concessione del Dipartimento dei Beni Culturali e dell'Indentità Siciliana; p.181, Section from Lod mosaic, Photo Nicky Davidov, Courtesy of the Israel Antiquities Authority; p.182, Coin of Pompey, cgb (commons.wikimedia.org/wiki/File:Denier_à_l'effigie_de_Pompée.jpg), (CC BY-SA 3.0); p.182, Bust of Pompey, Ny Carlsberg Glyptotek, Copenhagen; p.182, Julius Caesar, The Metropolitan Museum of Art, New York; p.187, Relief of Vulcan, Alamy, su concessione del Ministero per i Beni e le Attività Culturali e per il Turismo-Museo Archeologico Nazionale di Napoli; p.190, Epitaphe d'un Trévère, Collection de Lugdunum, musée & théâtres romains, num.inv. : AD238, ©photo : Jean-Michele Deguele, Christian Thioc; p.191, Terracotta beaker, The Metropolitan Museum of Art, New York; p.191, Glass cup, The Metropolitan Museum of Art, New York; p.191, Glass jug, The Metropolitan Museum of Art, New York; p.191, Glass bowl, The Metropolitan Museum of Art, New York; p.193, Domus Aurea Vestibolo, Altair4 Multimedia Rome, WWW.ALTAIR4.COM; p.196, The Fire of Rome, Hubert Robert, Alamy; p.198, Painting of Prometheus by Constantin Hansen (commons.wikimedia.org/wiki/File:Constantin_Hansen_Prometheus.jpg); p.198, Relief of Prometheus, photo © RMN-Grand Palais (musée du Louvre) / Hervé Lewandowski; p.202, Pont du Gard, Alamy; p.203, El Jem amphitheatre, Alamy; p.203, Maison Carrée, Alamy; p.204, Bakery, Alamy, Su concessione del Ministero per i Beni e le Attività Culturali e per il turismo-Parco Archeologico di Pompei; p.209, Theatre at Orange, Alamy; p.211, Incense burner with comic actor, Digital image courtesy of the Getty's Open Content Program; p.212, Tomb of Eurysaces, Alamy, Su concessione della Sovrintendenza Capitolina ai Beni Culturali – AFMonAS; p.213, Mosaic with theatrical mask, Alamy, su concessione del Ministero per i Beni e le Attività Culturali e per il Turismo-Museo Archeologico Nazionale di Napoli; p.214, Pyramus and Thisbe, The Metropolitan Museum of Art, New York; p.217, Mosaic pattern, Conimbriga, Arquivo DGPC/MMC-MN; p.218, Mosaic of Neptune and Amphitrite, Alamy, Su concessione del Ministero per i Beni e le Attività Culturali e per il turismo-Parco Archeologico di Ercolano; p.218, Mosaic pattern, Conimbriga, Arquivo DGPC/MMC-MN; p.219, Mosaic of labyrinth, Conimbriga, Arquivo DGPC/MMC-MN; p.221, Mosaic 0161324581, Tunisia © The Trustees of the British Museum. All rights reserved.; p.221, Mosaic 01095910001, Sanctuary of Artemis, Ephesus © The Trustees of the British Museum. All rights reserved.; p.221, Mosaic from Fishbourne Roman Palace and Gardens, Chichester, by kind permission of Sussex Archaeological Society; p.221, Mosaic with Triton, Conimbriga, Arquivo DGPC/MMC-MN; p.228, Las Medulas, Alamy; p.228, Rock-cut aqueduct, Karkeixa (commons.wikimedia.org/wiki/File:Canal_romano_de_Llamas.jpg), (CC BY 3.0); p.229, Wooden wheel, Alamy; p.230, Head of Agrippa the Younger, Digital image courtesy of the Getty's Open Content Program; p.235, Conger eel, Alamy; p.235, Snail, Alamy; p.235, Honey bees, Alamy; p.235, Gardens of Getty Villa, Alamy; p.238, Glirarium, MAEC, Museo dell'Accademia Etrusca e della Città di Cortona, Su concessione del Ministero per i beni e attività culturali e il turismo-Soprintendenza Archeologia Belle Arti e Paesaggio per le province di Siena Arezzo e Grosseto; p.238, Dormouse, Alamy; p.240, Serving fork, The Metropolitan Museum of Art, New York; p.240, Glass drinking cup, The Metropolitan Museum of Art, New York; p.241, Wall painting of a dinner party, Pompeii, su concessione del Ministero per i Beni e le Attività Culturali e per il Turismo-Museo Archeologico Nazionale di Napoli; p.242, Table of Roman food, Alamy; p.243, Fresco showing a meal being prepared, Digital image courtesy of the Getty's Open Content Program; p.246, Portrait of Marius, © Staatliche Antikensammlungen und Glyptothek München, Photograph by Renate Kühling.; p.246, Portrait of Sulla, © Staatliche Antikensammlungen und Glyptothek München, Photograph by Renate Kühling.; p.249, Roman brick, Conimbriga, Arquivo DGPC/MMC-MN; p.252, Panel from a sarcophagus, Digital image courtesy of the Getty's Open Content Program; p.253, Glass whorl, The Metropolitan Museum of Art, New York; p.253, Bronze distaff, The Metropolitan Museum of Art, New York; p.253, Roman shears, Science Museum, London. CC BY 4.0; p.256, Gold ring, The Metropolitan Museum of Art, New York; p.257, Bust of Julia, 70143608 bpk Berlin / Antikensammlung, SMB / Johannes Laurentius; p.259, Wall painting of Terentius Neo and wife, Alamy, su concessione del Ministero per i Beni e le Attività Culturali e per il Turismo-Museo Archeologico Nazionale di Napoli; p.259, Grave relief showing a husband and wife 00243129001 © The Trustees of the British Museum. All rights reserved.; p.263, Painting of Arachne (commons.wikimedia.org/wiki/File:René-Antoine_Houasse_-_Minerve_et_Arachne_(Versailles).jpg). We would also like to acknowledge the help of The British School at Rome in securing photo permits.

While every effort has been made to contact copyright-holders of images, the author and publisher would be grateful for information about any illustrations where they have been unable to trace them, and would be glad to make amends in further editions.